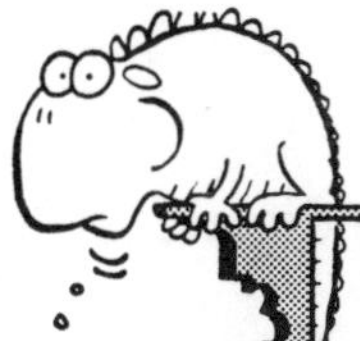

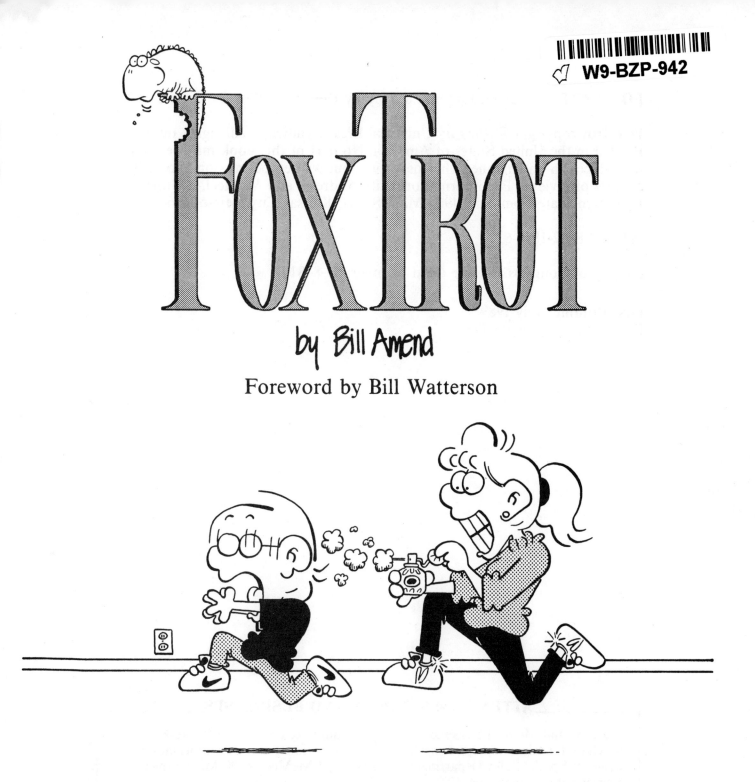

FoxTrot

by Bill Amend

Foreword by Bill Watterson

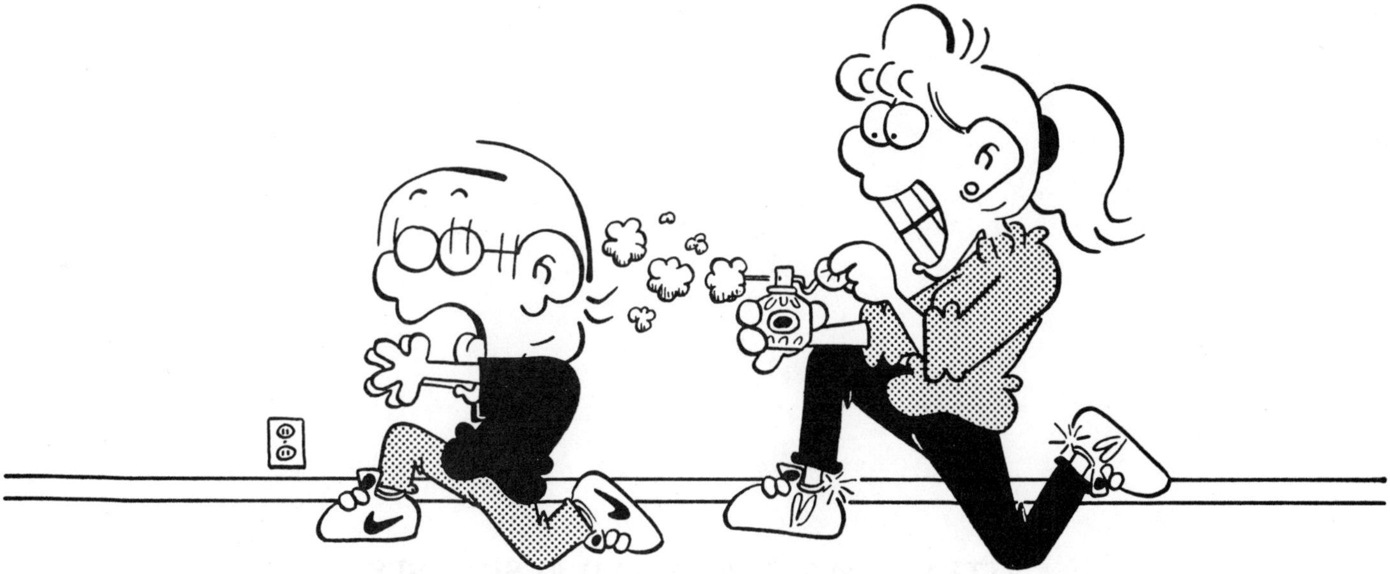

Andrews and McMeel A Universal Press Syndicate Company **Kansas City • New York**

FOX TROT is syndicated internationally by Universal Press Syndicate.

ISBN: 0-8362-1856-6

Library of Congress Catalog Card Number: 89-84810

First Printing, July 1989
Fourth Printing, April 1990

FOREWORD

In far too many comic strips, trendy stereotypes pass for humor, cliches pass for insight, mechanical repetition passes for story, and cute animals designed for merchandising pass for heart and warmth. Fox Trot offers welcome relief from all of this, and not a moment too soon.

It's refreshing to read a comic strip where the characters have real personality. The humor and appeal of Fox Trot derive from the interaction of its characters, not from silly events imposed from without. Each member of the Fox family has a unique identity that goes beyond his or her role in the household, and this gives the world of Fox Trot a veracity other family strips lack. The Fox family has the resonance of honest observation.

Fox Trot particularly captures the Machiavellian nature of adolescents. The balance of power between Peter, 16, Paige, 14, and Jason, 10, is a constantly bartered commodity, and alliances are fragile and short-lived. No collusion will survive an opportunity to get a sibling in trouble, and hesitant parents are goaded with the cry of, "Punish him! Punish him! Ground him! Ground him!" These kids are convincing.

The parents are also authentic, and not just cardboard authority figures propped up to let the kids steal the show, or alternatively, some drippy parental ideal. They disagree and occasionally set bad examples for the kids. Roger and Andy are lively, honest characters. They add another dimension to the strip.

And finally, a word ought to be said about Quincy, Jason's iguana. Amazingly, Quincy does not philosophize or think those cute thoughts that quickly put most comic strip animals into the greeting card business. Instead, Quincy is content to amuse himself with the consumption of mealworms and the havoc they sometimes wreak on his digestive tract. He acts, that is to say, like a real lizard. The strip deserves attention for this bold stroke alone.

In short, all a cartoonist really needs besides pen and paper is two open eyes. Human nature has a way of expressing itself in all people, and the cartoonist who can see this will never run out of ideas. Surprise is the base of all humor, and nothing is more surprising than truth. Fox Trot has the ring of truth to it.

—BILL WATTERSON

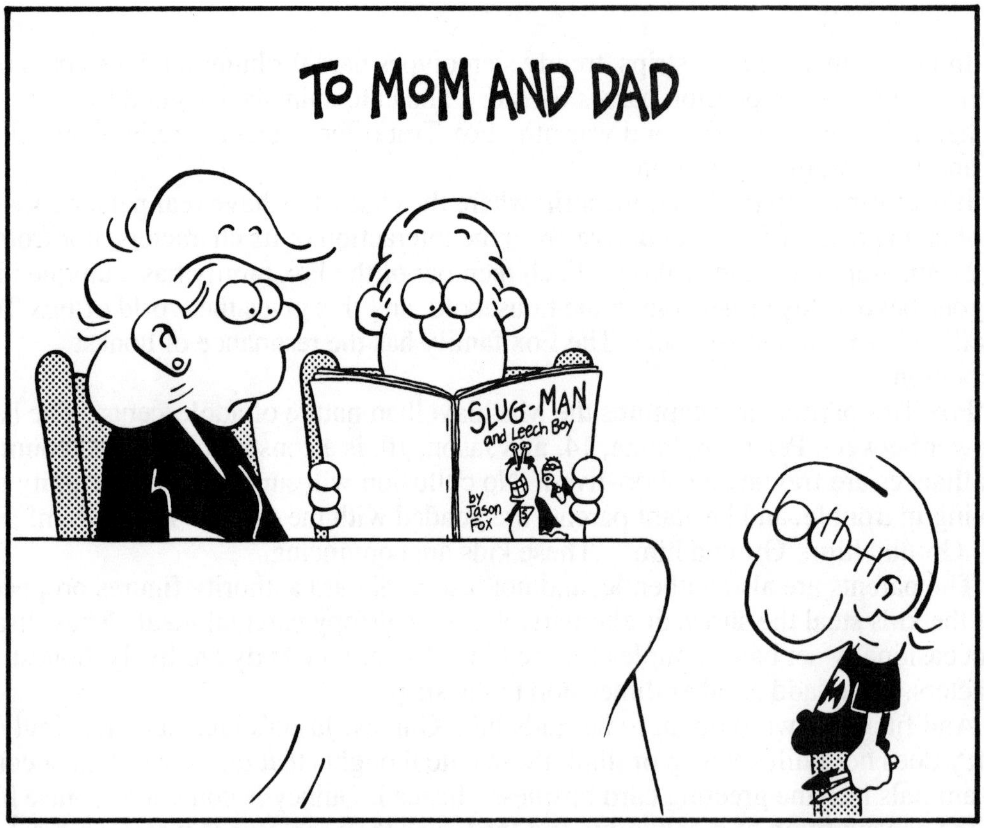
TO MOM AND DAD
SLUG-MAN
and Leech Boy
by Jason Fox

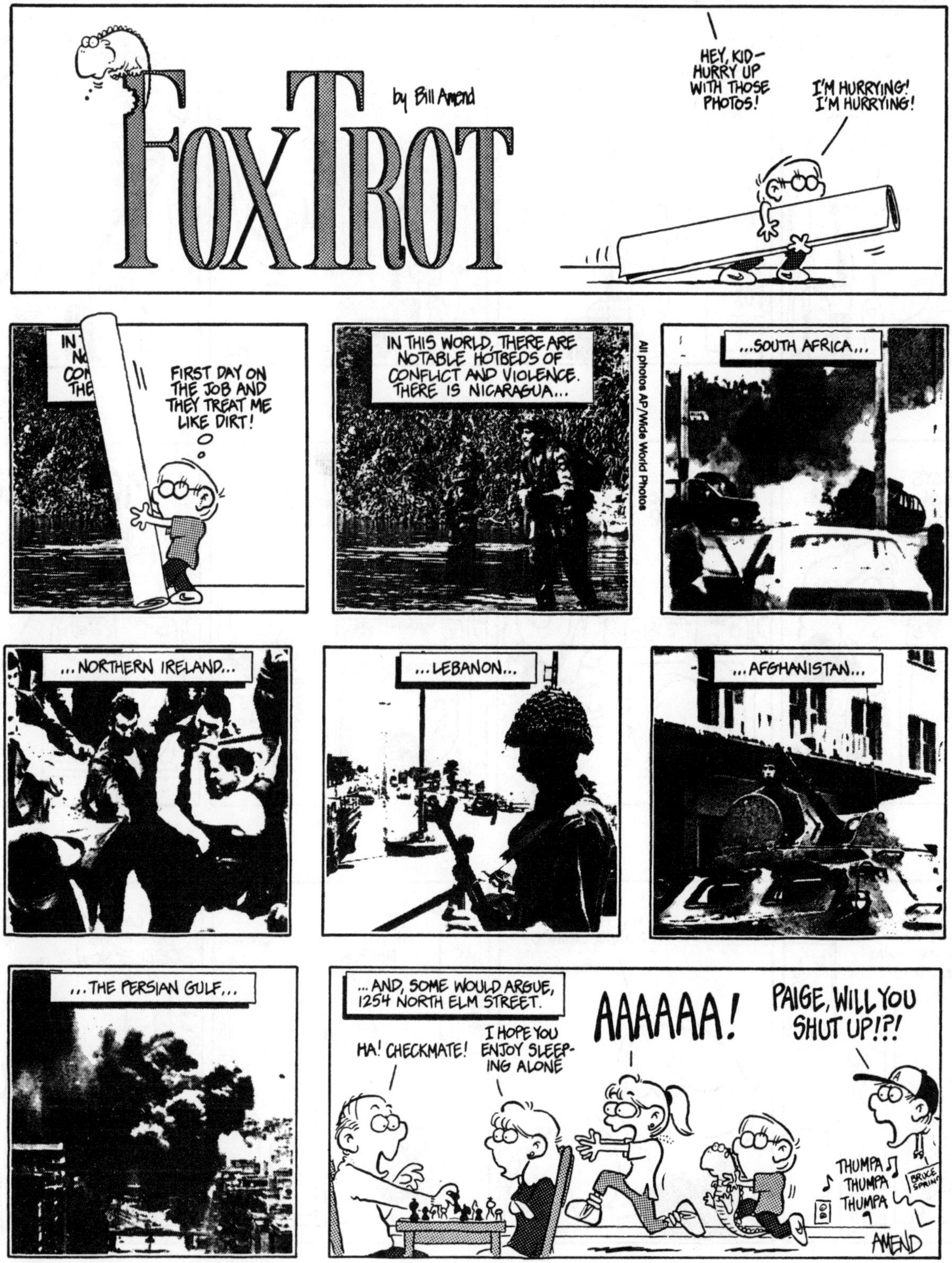
FOXTROT
by Bill Amend
HEY, KID— HURRY UP WITH THOSE PHOTOS!
I'M HURRYING! I'M HURRYING!
FIRST DAY ON THE JOB AND THEY TREAT ME LIKE DIRT!
All photos AP/Wide World Photos
IN THIS WORLD, THERE ARE NOTABLE HOTBEDS OF CONFLICT AND VIOLENCE. THERE IS NICARAGUA...
...SOUTH AFRICA...
...NORTHERN IRELAND...
...LEBANON...
...AFGHANISTAN...
...THE PERSIAN GULF,...
...AND, SOME WOULD ARGUE, 1254 NORTH ELM STREET.
HA! CHECKMATE!
I HOPE YOU ENJOY SLEEPING ALONE
AAAAAA!
PAIGE, WILL YOU SHUT UP!?!
THUMPA THUMPA THUMPA
AMEND

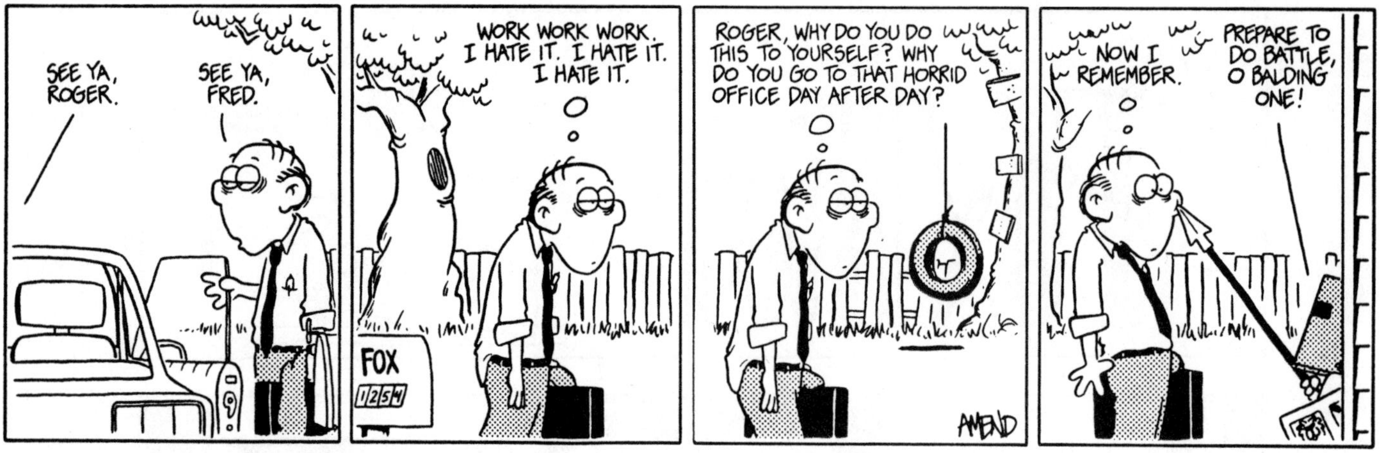
SEE YA, ROGER.
SEE YA, FRED.
WORK WORK WORK. I HATE IT. I HATE IT. I HATE IT.
FOX
1254
ROGER, WHY DO YOU DO THIS TO YOURSELF? WHY DO YOU GO TO THAT HORRID OFFICE DAY AFTER DAY?
AMEND
NOW I REMEMBER.
PREPARE TO DO BATTLE, O BALDING ONE!

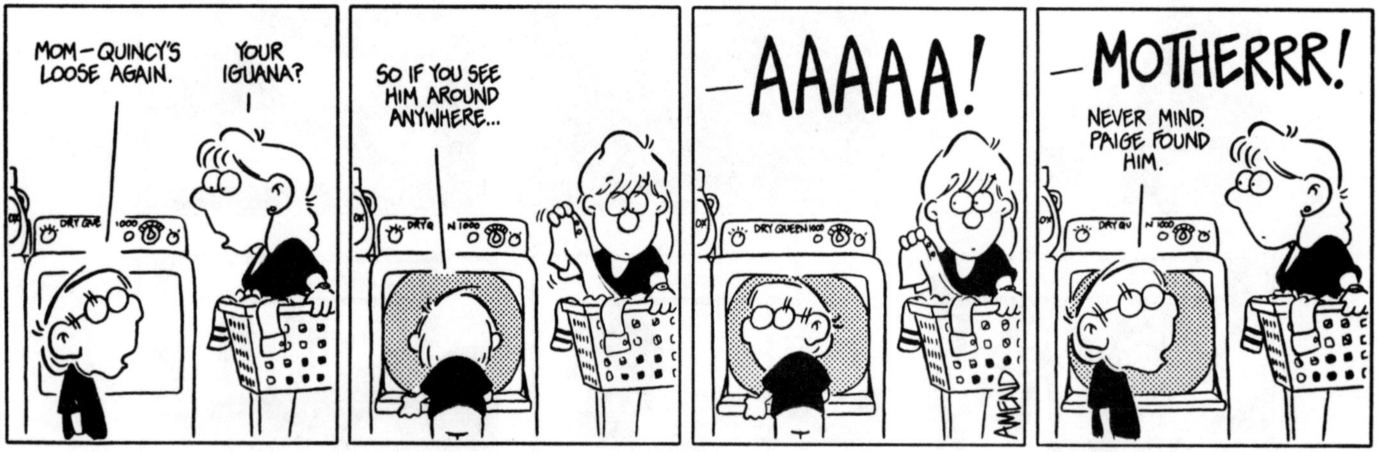
MOM–QUINCY'S LOOSE AGAIN.
YOUR IGUANA?
SO IF YOU SEE HIM AROUND ANYWHERE...
DRY QUEEN 1000
–AAAAA!
AMEND
–MOTHERRR!
NEVER MIND. PAIGE FOUND HIM.

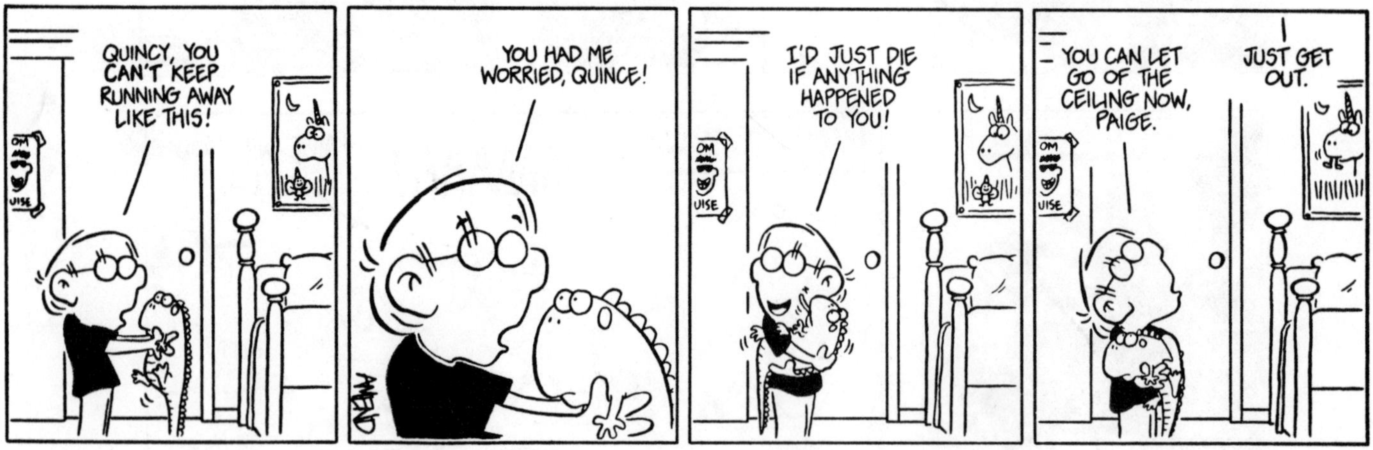
QUINCY, YOU CAN'T KEEP RUNNING AWAY LIKE THIS!
YOU HAD ME WORRIED, QUINCE!
AMEND
I'D JUST DIE IF ANYTHING HAPPENED TO YOU!
YOU CAN LET GO OF THE CEILING NOW, PAIGE.
JUST GET OUT.

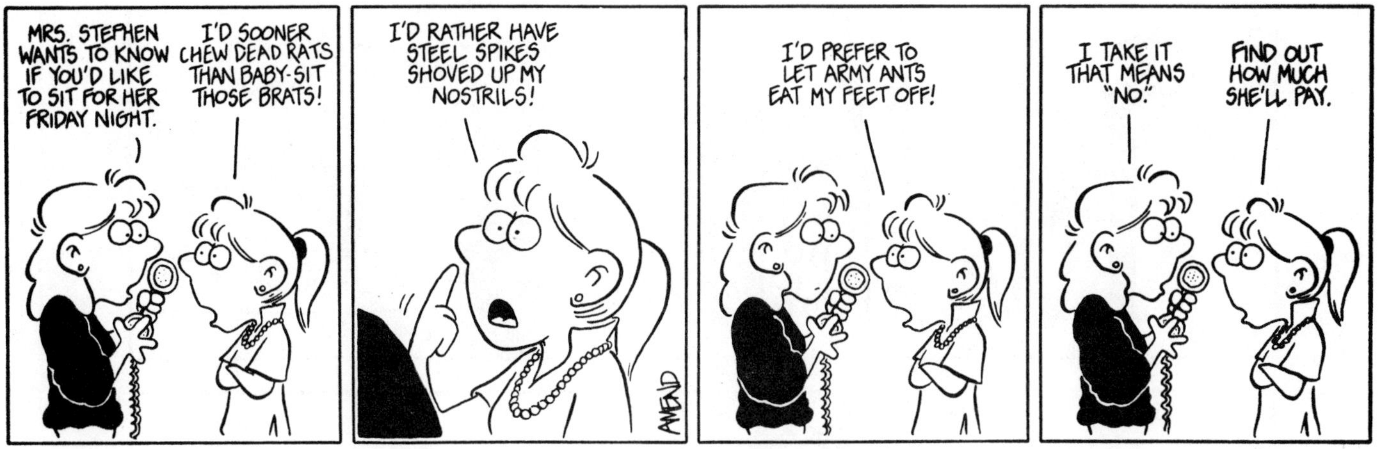
MRS. STEPHEN WANTS TO KNOW IF YOU'D LIKE TO SIT FOR HER FRIDAY NIGHT.
I'D SOONER CHEW DEAD RATS THAN BABY-SIT THOSE BRATS!
I'D RATHER HAVE STEEL SPIKES SHOVED UP MY NOSTRILS!
AMEND
I'D PREFER TO LET ARMY ANTS EAT MY FEET OFF!
I TAKE IT THAT MEANS "NO."
FIND OUT HOW MUCH SHE'LL PAY.

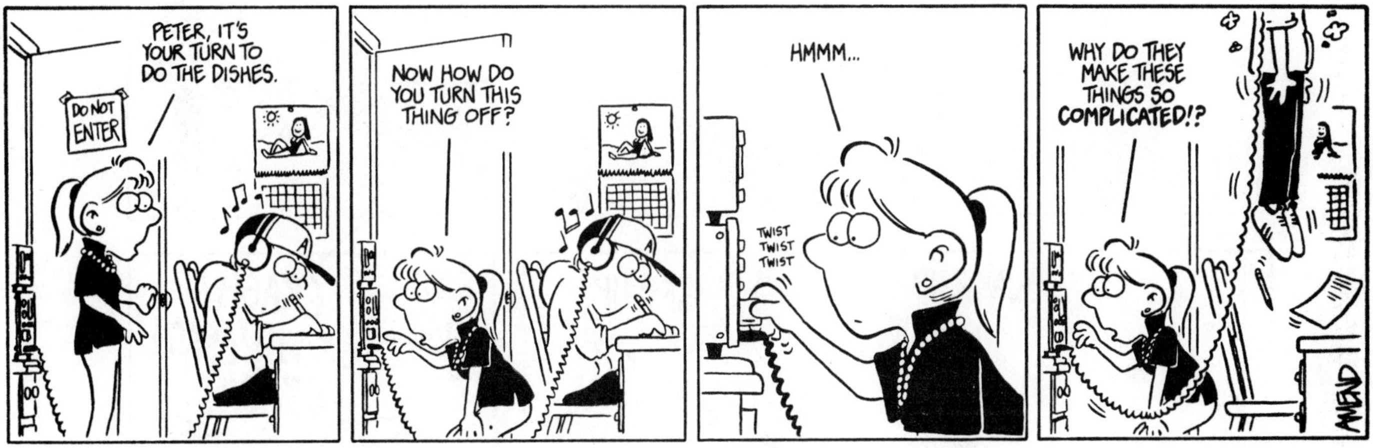
DO NOT ENTER
PETER, IT'S YOUR TURN TO DO THE DISHES.
NOW HOW DO YOU TURN THIS THING OFF?
HMMM...
TWIST TWIST TWIST
WHY DO THEY MAKE THESE THINGS SO COMPLICATED!?
AMEND

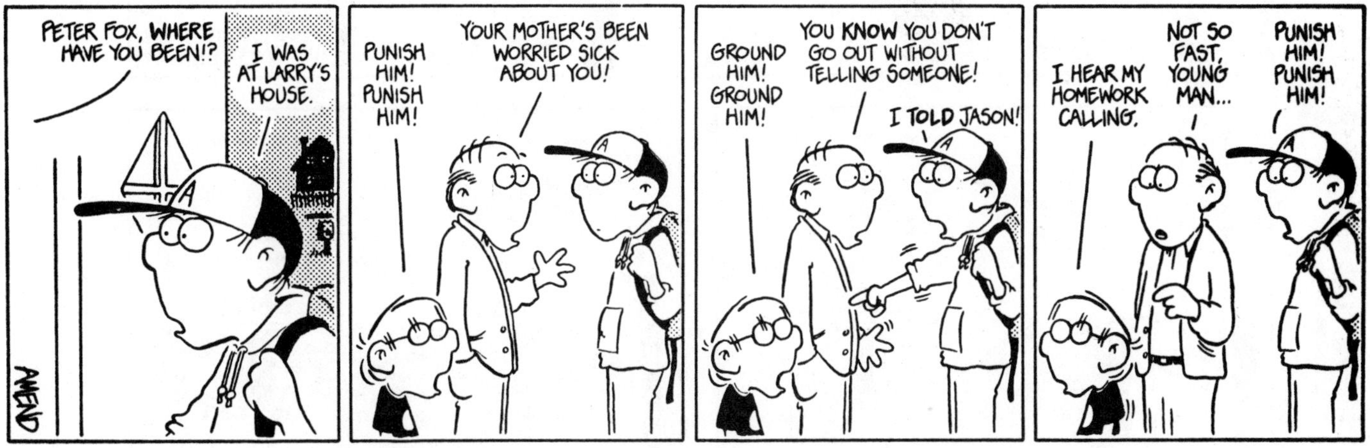
PETER FOX, WHERE HAVE YOU BEEN!?
I WAS AT LARRY'S HOUSE.
AMEND
PUNISH HIM! PUNISH HIM!
YOUR MOTHER'S BEEN WORRIED SICK ABOUT YOU!
GROUND HIM! GROUND HIM!
YOU KNOW YOU DON'T GO OUT WITHOUT TELLING SOMEONE!
I TOLD JASON!
I HEAR MY HOMEWORK CALLING.
NOT SO FAST, YOUNG MAN...
PUNISH HIM! PUNISH HIM!

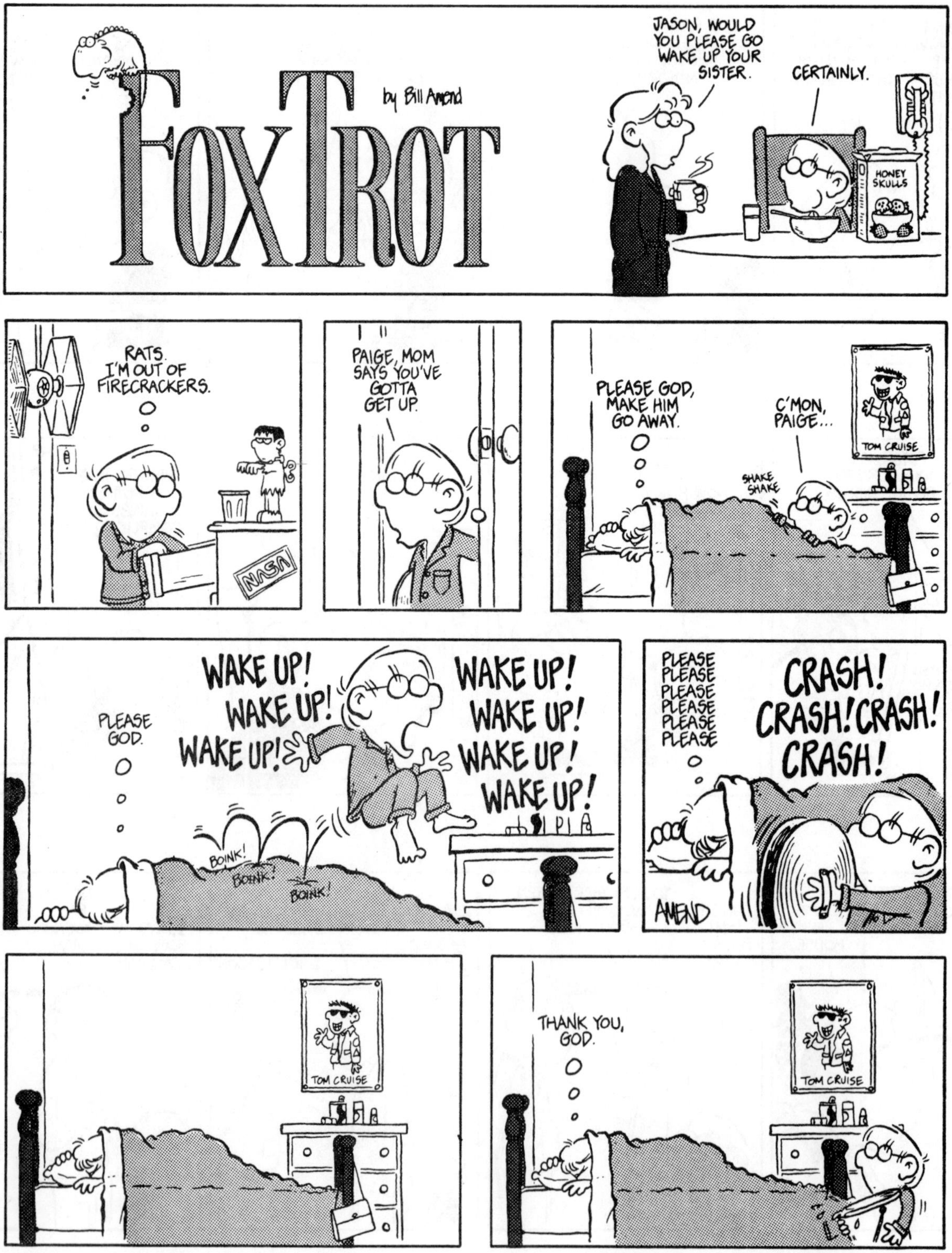
FoxTrot
by Bill Amend
JASON, WOULD YOU PLEASE GO WAKE UP YOUR SISTER.
CERTAINLY.
HONEY SKULLS
RATS. I'M OUT OF FIRECRACKERS.
NASA
PAIGE, MOM SAYS YOU'VE GOTTA GET UP.
PLEASE GOD, MAKE HIM GO AWAY.
C'MON, PAIGE...
SHAKE SHAKE
TOM CRUISE
PLEASE GOD.
WAKE UP! WAKE UP! WAKE UP!
WAKE UP! WAKE UP! WAKE UP! WAKE UP!
BOINK! BOINK! BOINK!
PLEASE PLEASE PLEASE PLEASE PLEASE PLEASE
CRASH! CRASH! CRASH! CRASH!
AMEND
TOM CRUISE
THANK YOU, GOD.
TOM CRUISE

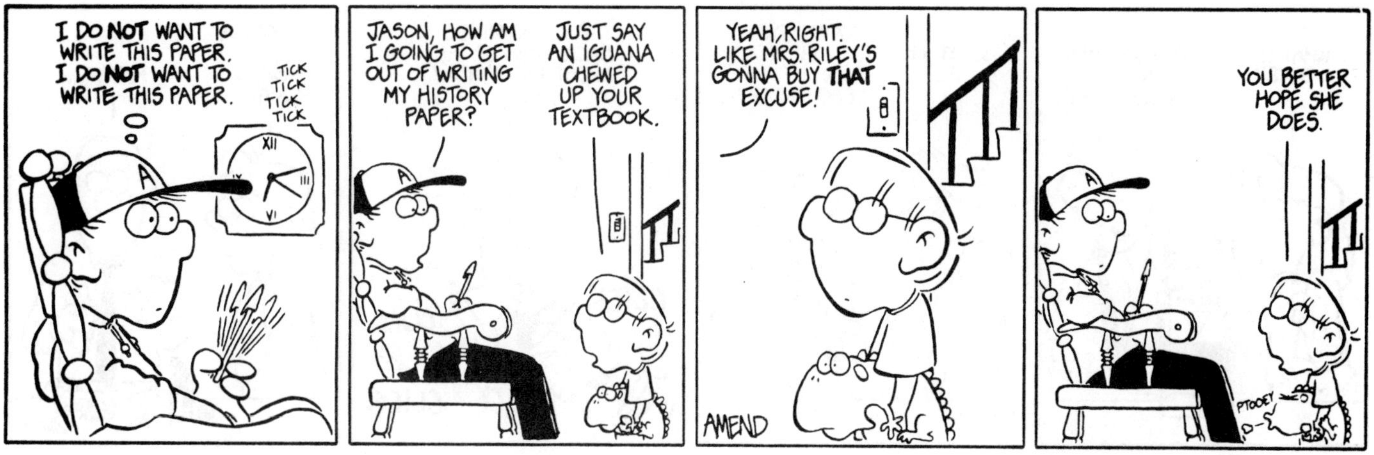
I DO **NOT** WANT TO WRITE THIS PAPER. I DO **NOT** WANT TO WRITE THIS PAPER.
TICK TICK TICK TICK
XII
IX
III
VI
JASON, HOW AM I GOING TO GET OUT OF WRITING MY HISTORY PAPER?
JUST SAY AN IGUANA CHEWED UP YOUR TEXTBOOK.
YEAH, RIGHT. LIKE MRS. RILEY'S GONNA BUY **THAT** EXCUSE!
AMEND
YOU BETTER HOPE SHE DOES.
PTOOEY

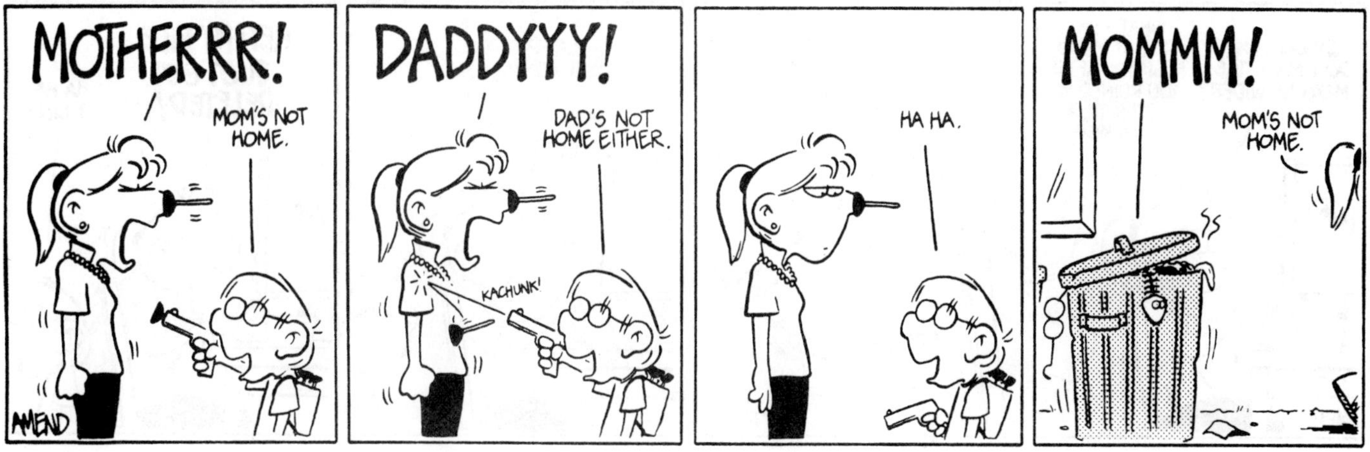
MOTHERRR!
MOM'S NOT HOME.
AMEND
DADDYYY!
DAD'S NOT HOME EITHER.
KACHUNK!
HA HA.
MOMMM!
MOM'S NOT HOME.

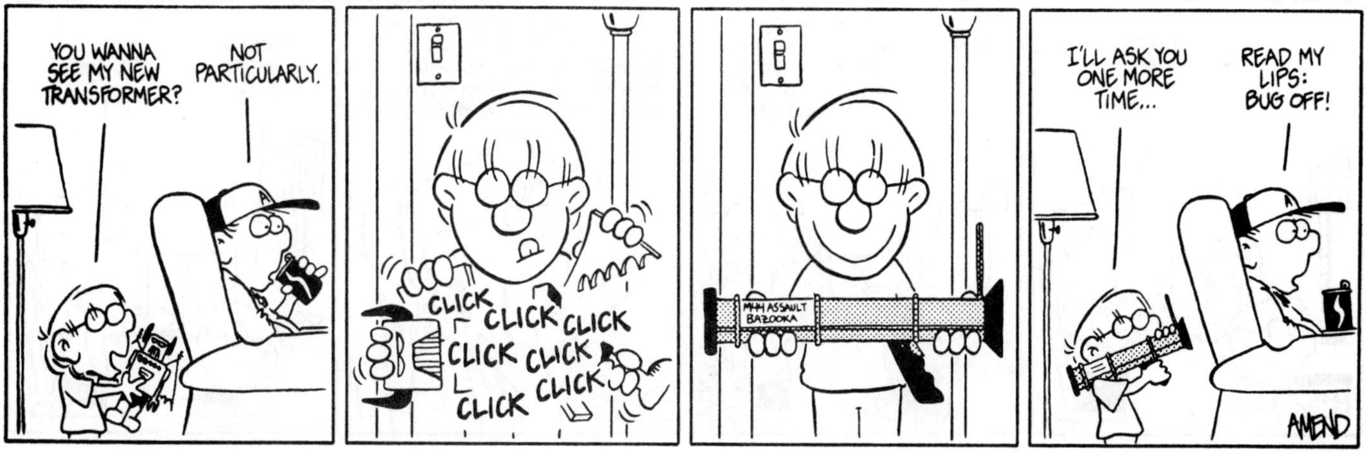
YOU WANNA SEE MY NEW TRANSFORMER?
NOT PARTICULARLY.
CLICK CLICK CLICK CLICK CLICK CLICK CLICK
M-44 ASSAULT BAZOOKA
I'LL ASK YOU ONE MORE TIME...
READ MY LIPS: BUG OFF!
AMEND

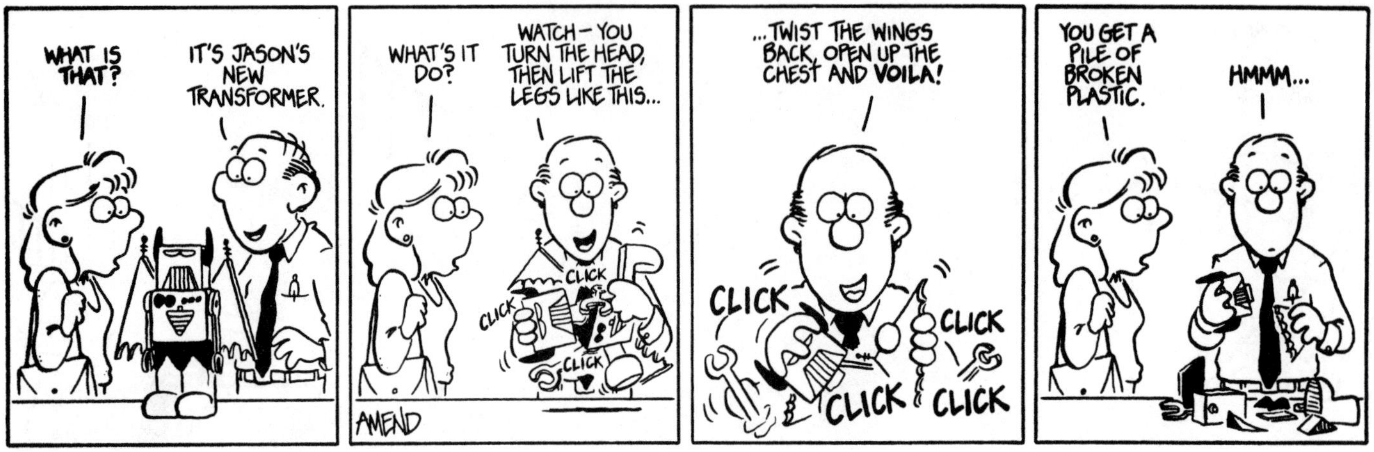

WHAT IS THAT?
IT'S JASON'S NEW TRANSFORMER.
WHAT'S IT DO?
WATCH—YOU TURN THE HEAD, THEN LIFT THE LEGS LIKE THIS...
CLICK CLICK CLICK CLICK
AMEND
...TWIST THE WINGS BACK, OPEN UP THE CHEST AND VOILA!
CLICK CLICK CLICK CLICK
YOU GET A PILE OF BROKEN PLASTIC.
HMMM...

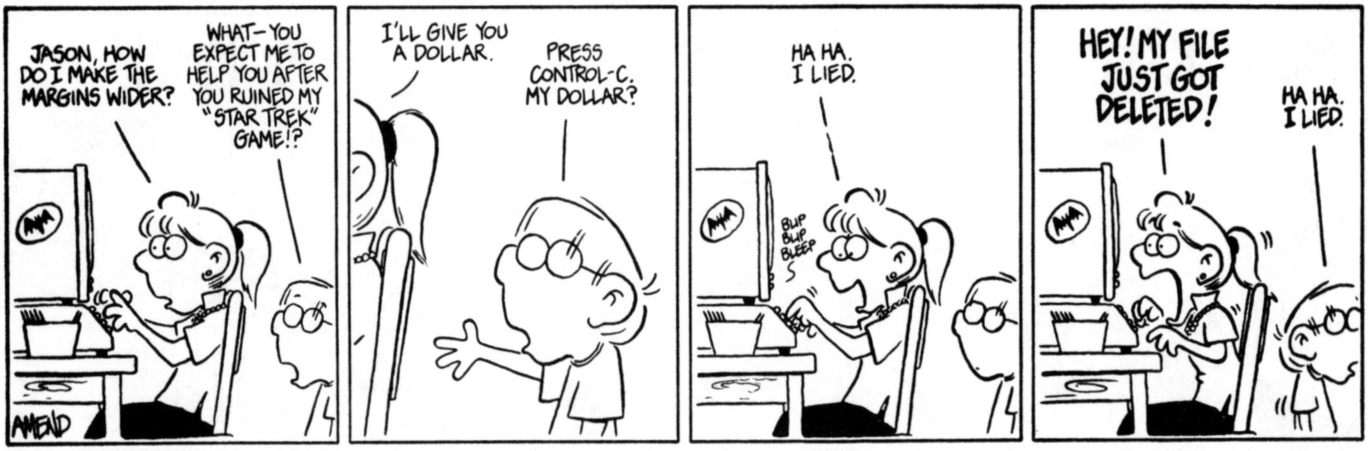

JASON, HOW DO I MAKE THE MARGINS WIDER?
WHAT—YOU EXPECT ME TO HELP YOU AFTER YOU RUINED MY "STAR TREK" GAME!?
AMEND
I'LL GIVE YOU A DOLLAR.
PRESS CONTROL-C. MY DOLLAR?
HA HA. I LIED.
BLIP BLIP BLEEP
HEY! MY FILE JUST GOT DELETED!
HA HA. I LIED.

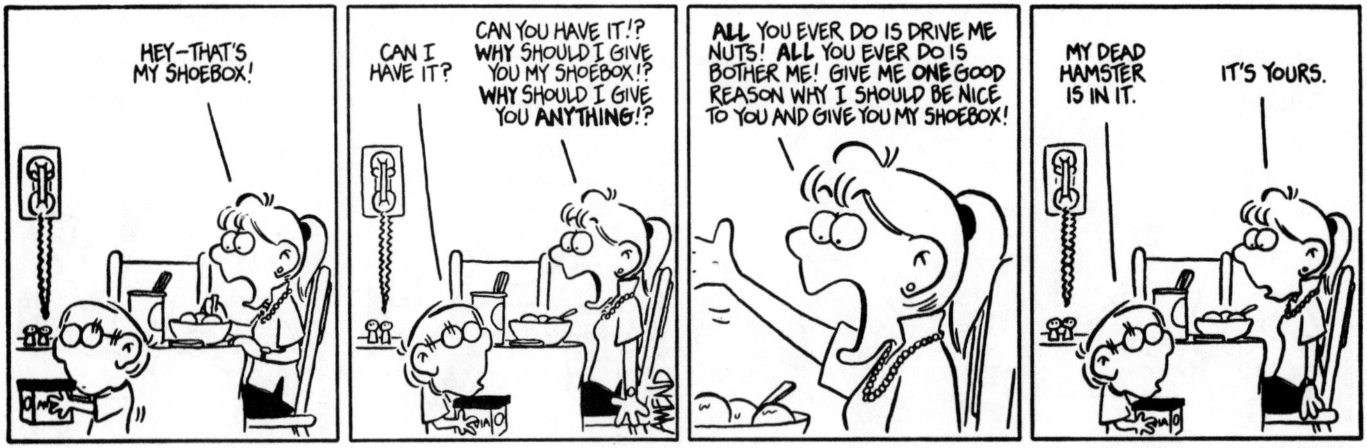

HEY—THAT'S MY SHOEBOX!
CAN I HAVE IT?
CAN YOU HAVE IT!? WHY SHOULD I GIVE YOU MY SHOEBOX!? WHY SHOULD I GIVE YOU ANYTHING!?
AMEND
ALL YOU EVER DO IS DRIVE ME NUTS! ALL YOU EVER DO IS BOTHER ME! GIVE ME ONE GOOD REASON WHY I SHOULD BE NICE TO YOU AND GIVE YOU MY SHOEBOX!
MY DEAD HAMSTER IS IN IT.
IT'S YOURS.

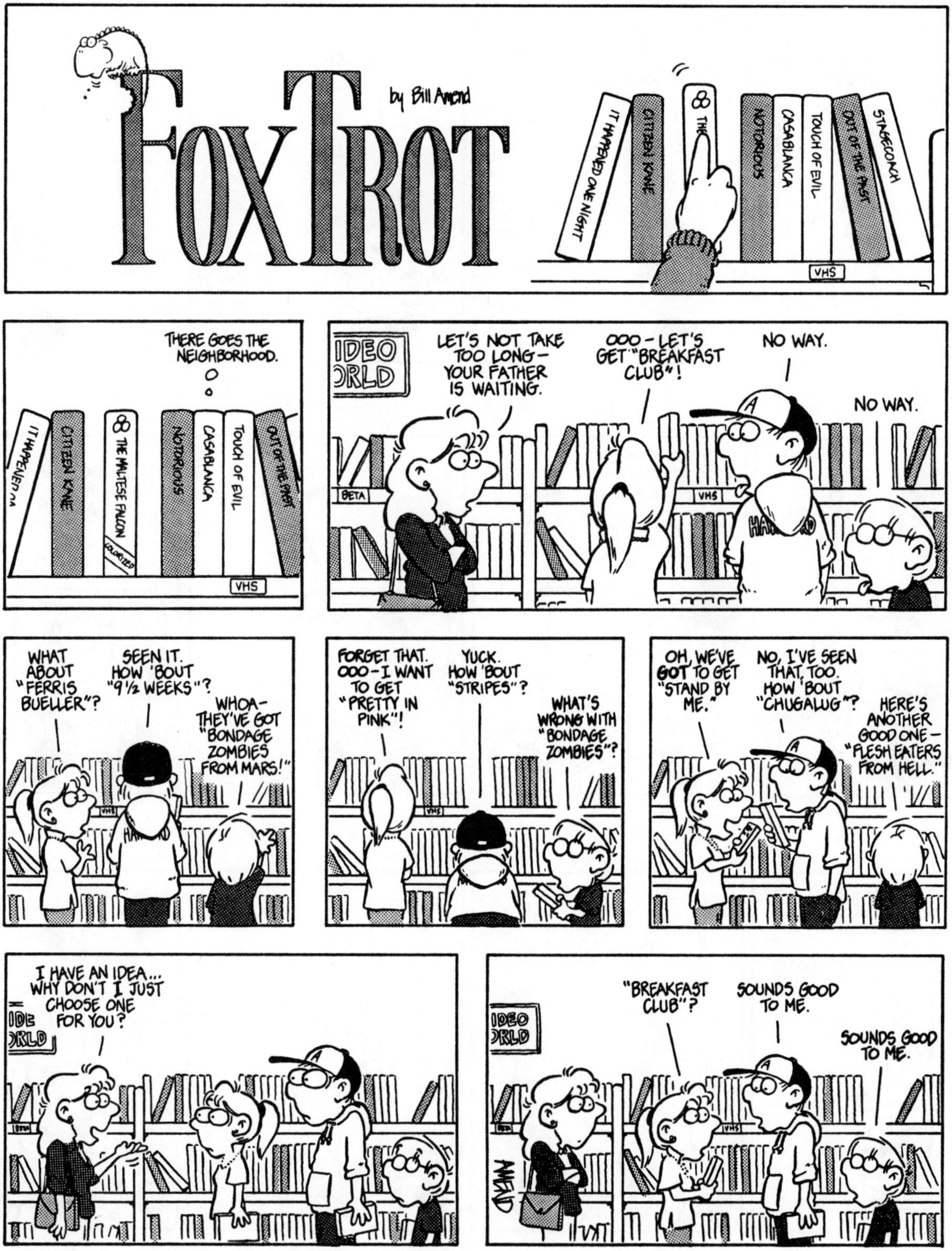
FoxTrot
by Bill Amend
IT HAPPENED ONE NIGHT
CITIZEN KANE
THE
NOTORIOUS
CASABLANCA
TOUCH OF EVIL
OUT OF THE PAST
STAGECOACH
VHS
THERE GOES THE NEIGHBORHOOD.
THE MALTESE FALCON
COLORIZED
LET'S NOT TAKE TOO LONG – YOUR FATHER IS WAITING.
OOO – LET'S GET "BREAKFAST CLUB"!
NO WAY.
NO WAY.
WHAT ABOUT "FERRIS BUELLER"?
SEEN IT. HOW 'BOUT "9½ WEEKS"?
WHOA – THEY'VE GOT "BONDAGE ZOMBIES FROM MARS!"
FORGET THAT. OOO – I WANT TO GET "PRETTY IN PINK"!
YUCK. HOW 'BOUT "STRIPES"?
WHAT'S WRONG WITH "BONDAGE ZOMBIES"?
OH, WE'VE GOT TO GET "STAND BY ME."
NO, I'VE SEEN THAT, TOO. HOW 'BOUT "CHUGALUG"?
HERE'S ANOTHER GOOD ONE – "FLESH EATERS FROM HELL."
I HAVE AN IDEA... WHY DON'T I JUST CHOOSE ONE FOR YOU?
"BREAKFAST CLUB"?
SOUNDS GOOD TO ME.
SOUNDS GOOD TO ME.
AMEND

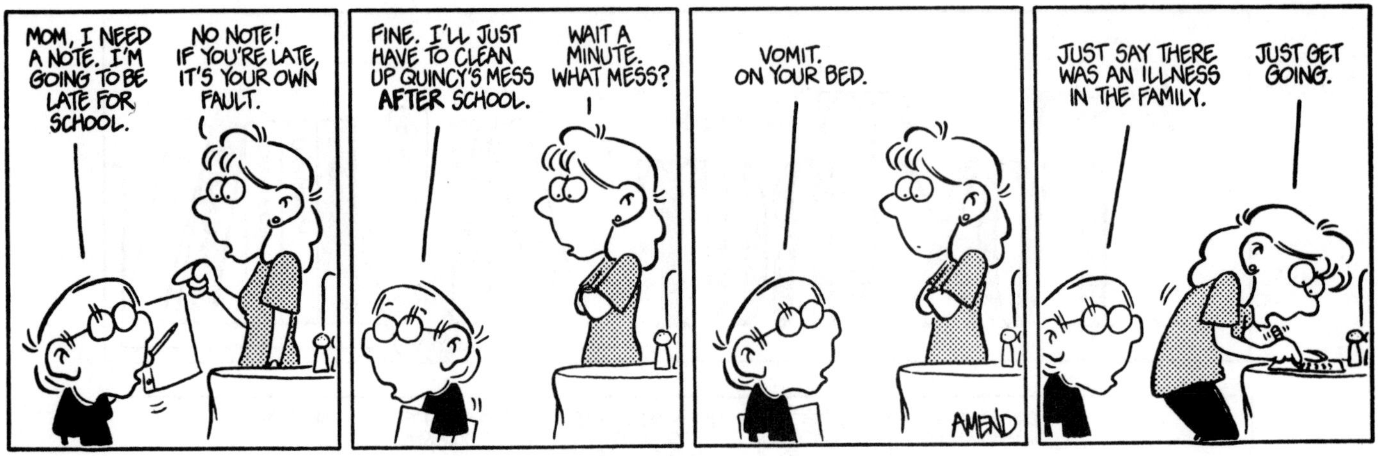
MOM, I NEED A NOTE. I'M GOING TO BE LATE FOR SCHOOL.
NO NOTE! IF YOU'RE LATE, IT'S YOUR OWN FAULT.
FINE. I'LL JUST HAVE TO CLEAN UP QUINCY'S MESS AFTER SCHOOL.
WAIT A MINUTE. WHAT MESS?
VOMIT. ON YOUR BED.
AMEND
JUST SAY THERE WAS AN ILLNESS IN THE FAMILY.
JUST GET GOING.

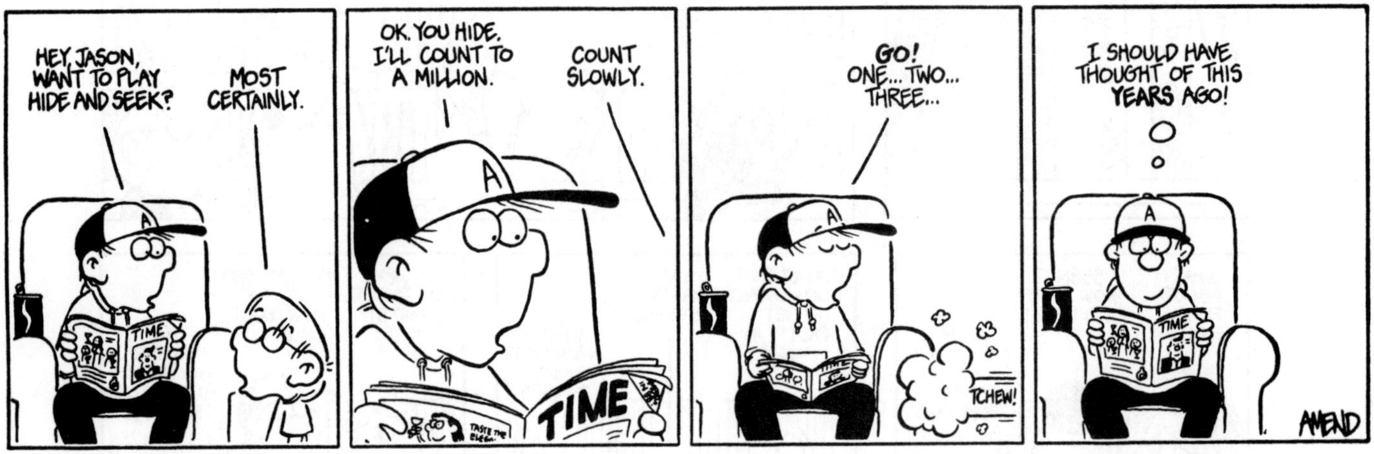
HEY, JASON, WANT TO PLAY HIDE AND SEEK?
MOST CERTAINLY.
TIME
OK. YOU HIDE. I'LL COUNT TO A MILLION.
COUNT SLOWLY.
TIME
GO! ONE... TWO... THREE...
TCHEW!
I SHOULD HAVE THOUGHT OF THIS YEARS AGO!
TIME
AMEND

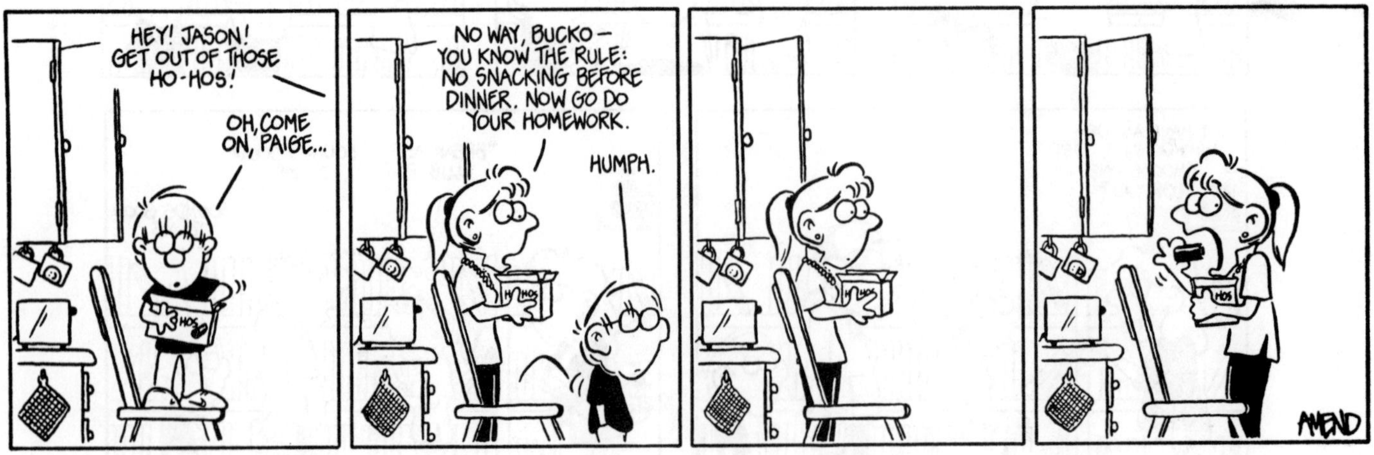
HEY! JASON! GET OUT OF THOSE HO-HOS!
OH, COME ON, PAIGE...
NO WAY, BUCKO – YOU KNOW THE RULE: NO SNACKING BEFORE DINNER. NOW GO DO YOUR HOMEWORK.
HUMPH.
AMEND

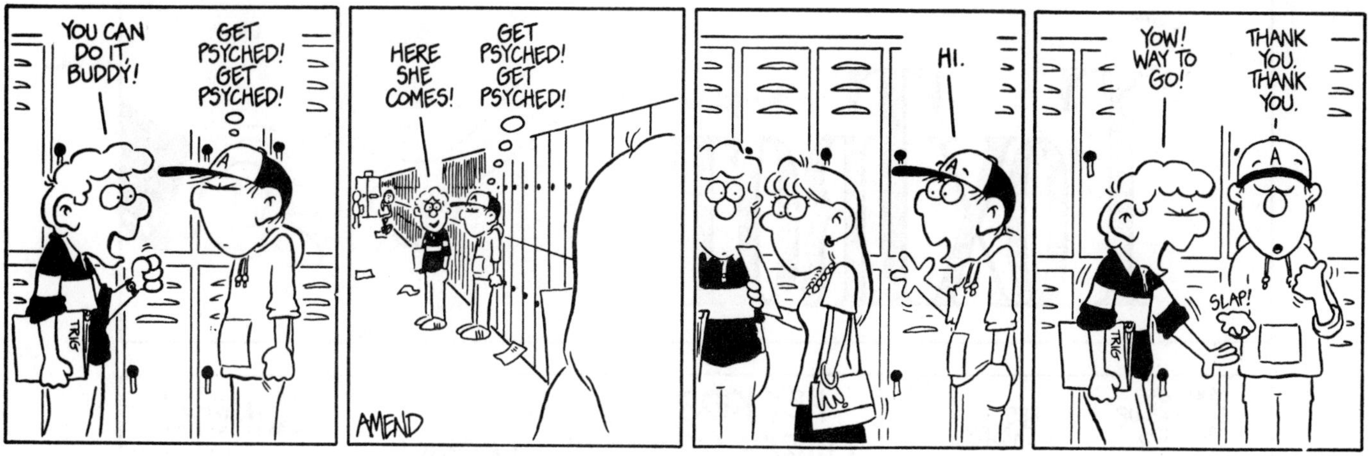
YOU CAN DO IT, BUDDY!
GET PSYCHED! GET PSYCHED!
HERE SHE COMES!
GET PSYCHED! GET PSYCHED!
AMEND
HI.
YOW! WAY TO GO!
THANK YOU. THANK YOU.
SLAP!
TRIG

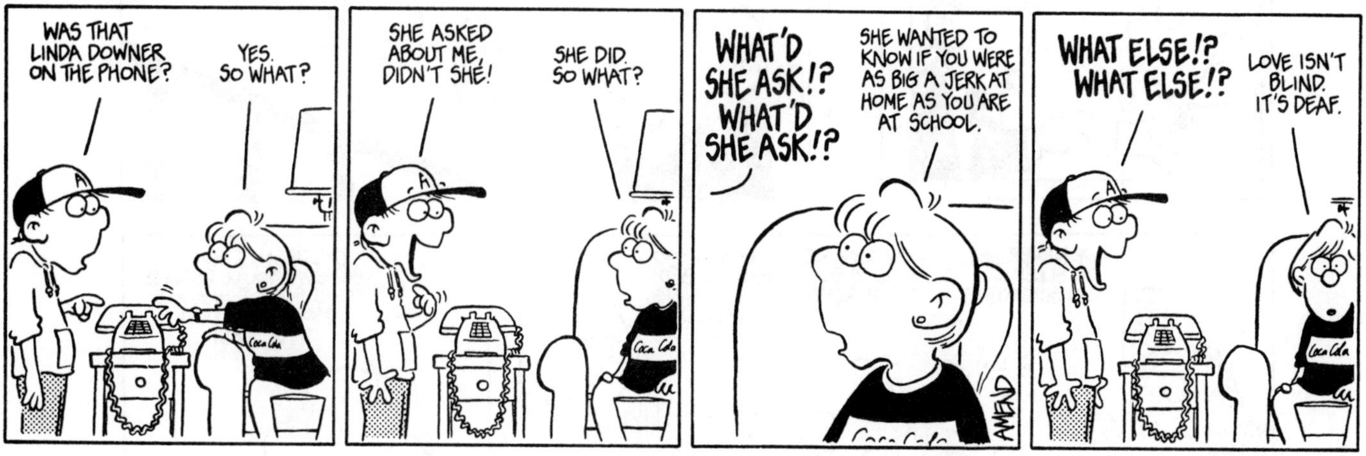
WAS THAT LINDA DOWNER ON THE PHONE?
YES. SO WHAT?
SHE ASKED ABOUT ME, DIDN'T SHE!
SHE DID. SO WHAT?
WHAT'D SHE ASK!? WHAT'D SHE ASK!?
SHE WANTED TO KNOW IF YOU WERE AS BIG A JERK AT HOME AS YOU ARE AT SCHOOL.
AMEND
WHAT ELSE!? WHAT ELSE!?
LOVE ISN'T BLIND. IT'S DEAF.

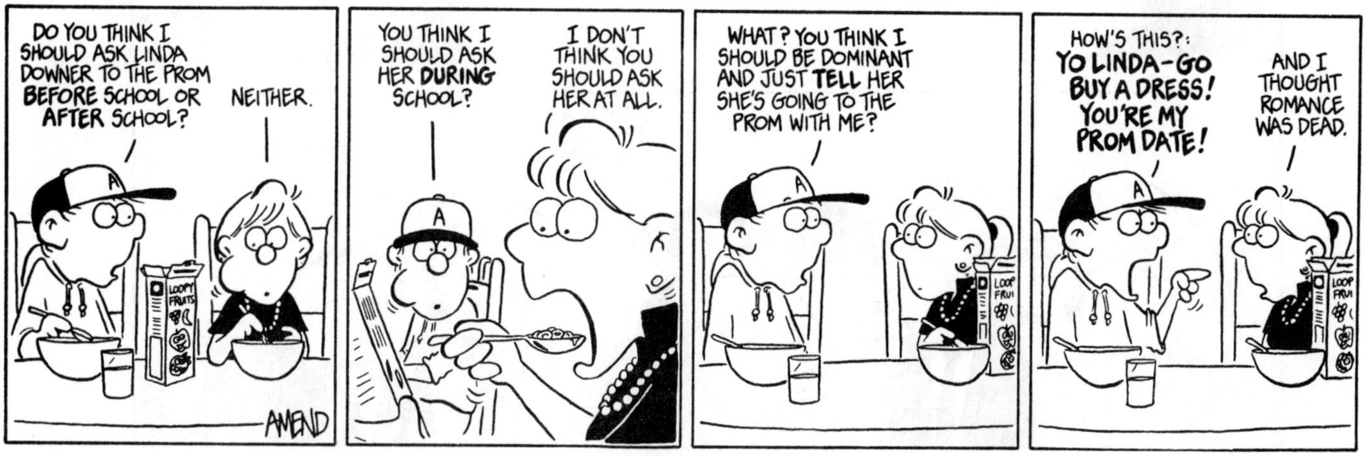
DO YOU THINK I SHOULD ASK LINDA DOWNER TO THE PROM BEFORE SCHOOL OR AFTER SCHOOL?
NEITHER.
AMEND
YOU THINK I SHOULD ASK HER DURING SCHOOL?
I DON'T THINK YOU SHOULD ASK HER AT ALL.
WHAT? YOU THINK I SHOULD BE DOMINANT AND JUST TELL HER SHE'S GOING TO THE PROM WITH ME?
HOW'S THIS?: YO LINDA-GO BUY A DRESS! YOU'RE MY PROM DATE!
AND I THOUGHT ROMANCE WAS DEAD.

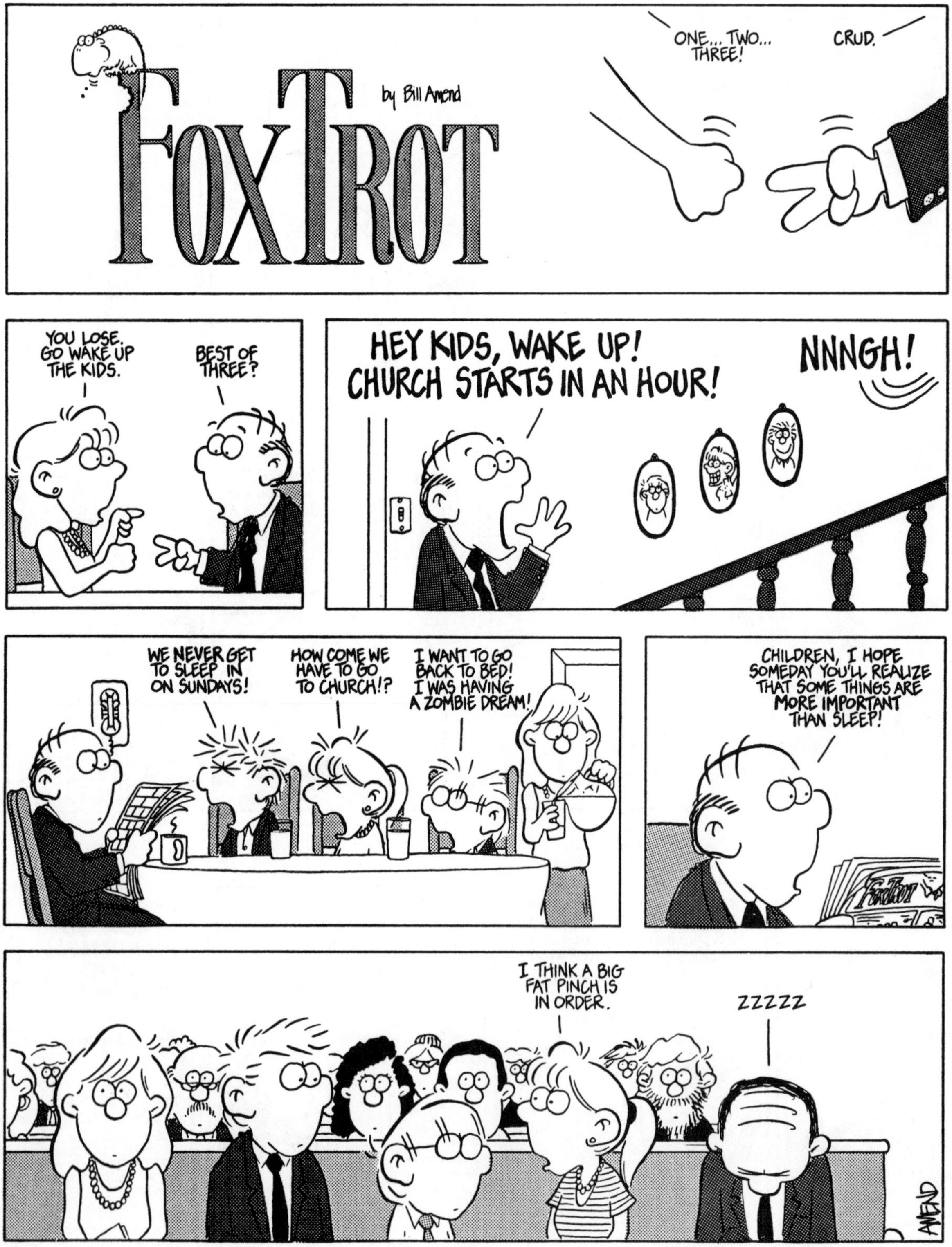
FoxTrot
by Bill Amend
ONE... TWO... THREE!
CRUD.
YOU LOSE. GO WAKE UP THE KIDS.
BEST OF THREE?
HEY KIDS, WAKE UP! CHURCH STARTS IN AN HOUR!
NNNGH!
WE NEVER GET TO SLEEP IN ON SUNDAYS!
HOW COME WE HAVE TO GO TO CHURCH!?
I WANT TO GO BACK TO BED! I WAS HAVING A ZOMBIE DREAM!
CHILDREN, I HOPE SOMEDAY YOU'LL REALIZE THAT SOME THINGS ARE MORE IMPORTANT THAN SLEEP!
I THINK A BIG FAT PINCH IS IN ORDER.
ZZZZZ
AMEND

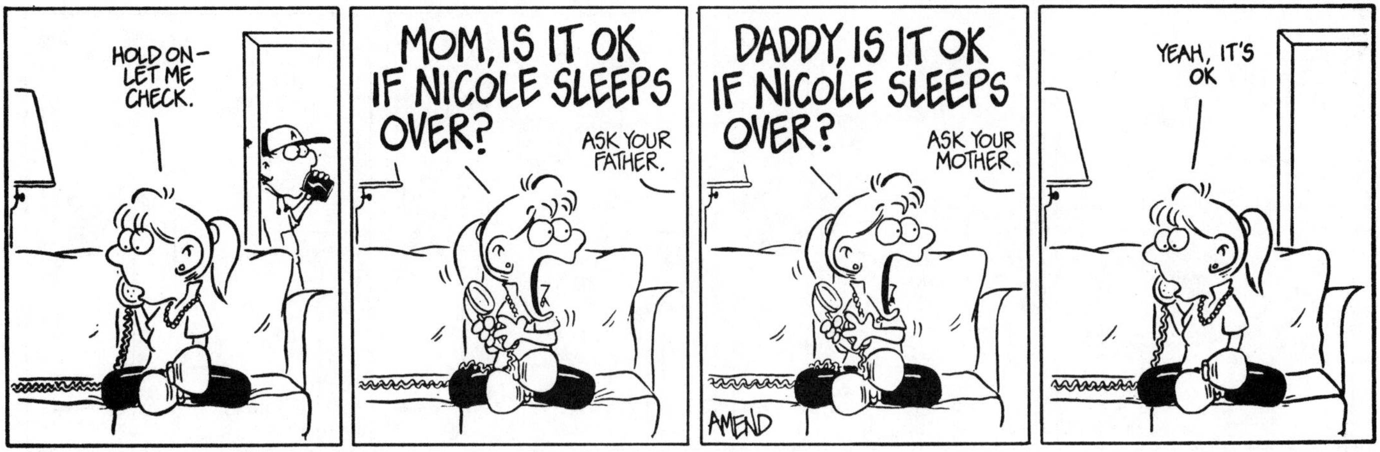
HOLD ON- LET ME CHECK.
MOM, IS IT OK IF NICOLE SLEEPS OVER?
ASK YOUR FATHER.
DADDY, IS IT OK IF NICOLE SLEEPS OVER?
ASK YOUR MOTHER.
YEAH, IT'S OK

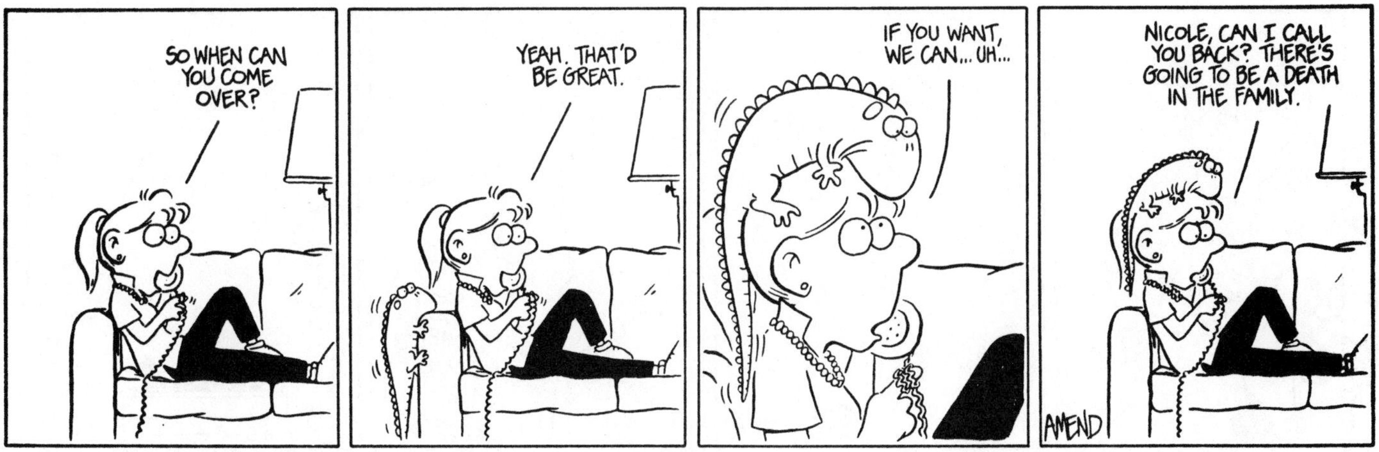
SO WHEN CAN YOU COME OVER?
YEAH. THAT'D BE GREAT.
IF YOU WANT, WE CAN... UH...
NICOLE, CAN I CALL YOU BACK? THERE'S GOING TO BE A DEATH IN THE FAMILY.

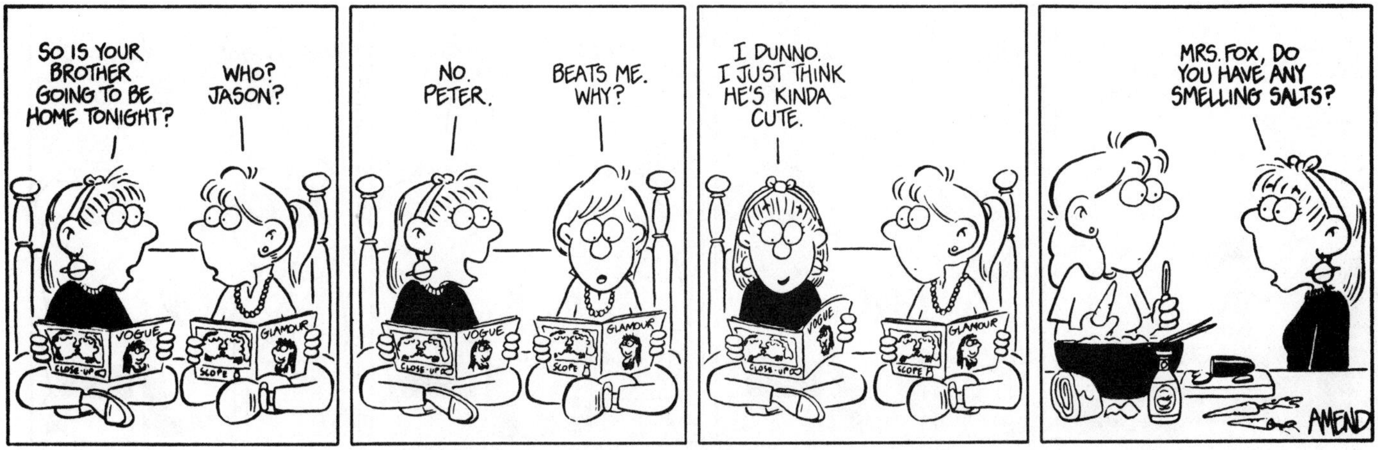
SO IS YOUR BROTHER GOING TO BE HOME TONIGHT?
WHO? JASON?
NO. PETER.
BEATS ME. WHY?
I DUNNO. I JUST THINK HE'S KINDA CUTE.
MRS. FOX, DO YOU HAVE ANY SMELLING SALTS?

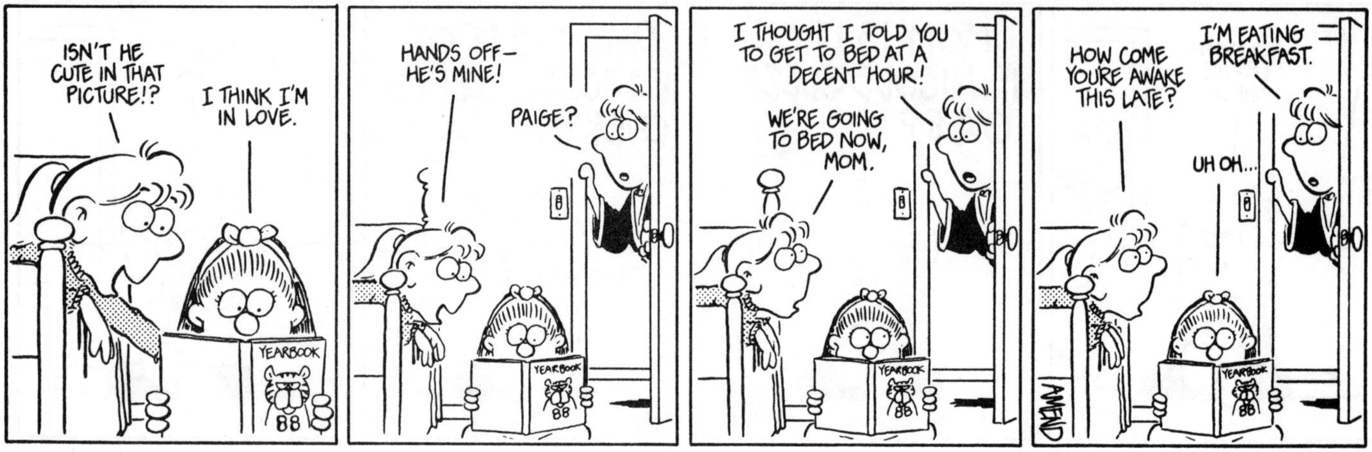
ISN'T HE CUTE IN THAT PICTURE!?
I THINK I'M IN LOVE.
YEARBOOK
HANDS OFF– HE'S MINE!
PAIGE?
I THOUGHT I TOLD YOU TO GET TO BED AT A DECENT HOUR!
WE'RE GOING TO BED NOW, MOM.
HOW COME YOU'RE AWAKE THIS LATE?
I'M EATING BREAKFAST.
UH OH...
AMEND

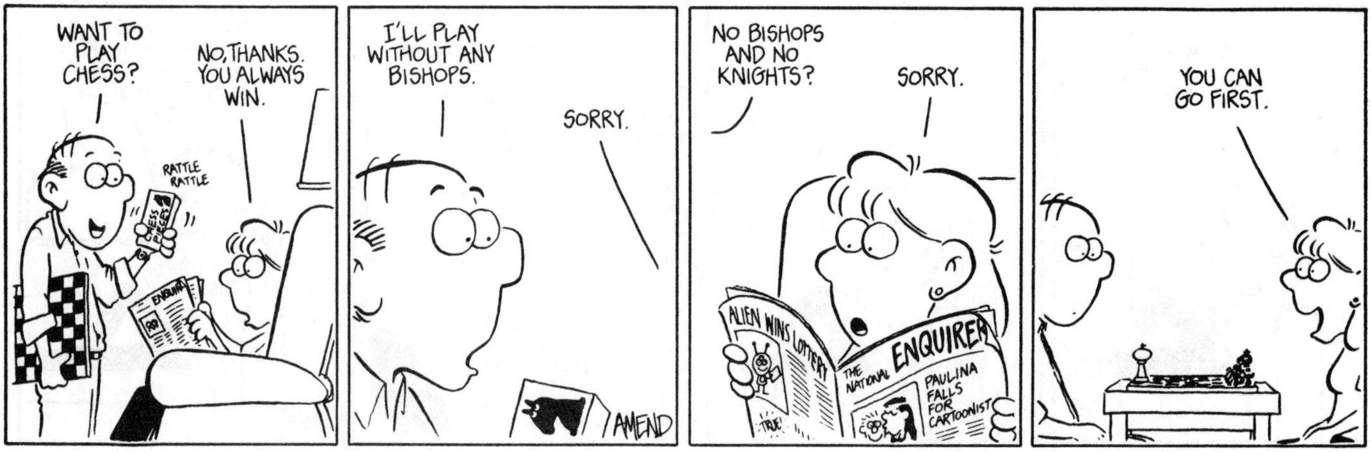
WANT TO PLAY CHESS?
NO, THANKS. YOU ALWAYS WIN.
RATTLE RATTLE
I'LL PLAY WITHOUT ANY BISHOPS.
SORRY.
AMEND
NO BISHOPS AND NO KNIGHTS?
SORRY.
ALIEN WINS LOTTERY
THE NATIONAL ENQUIRER
PAULINA FALLS FOR CARTOONIST
TRUE!
YOU CAN GO FIRST.

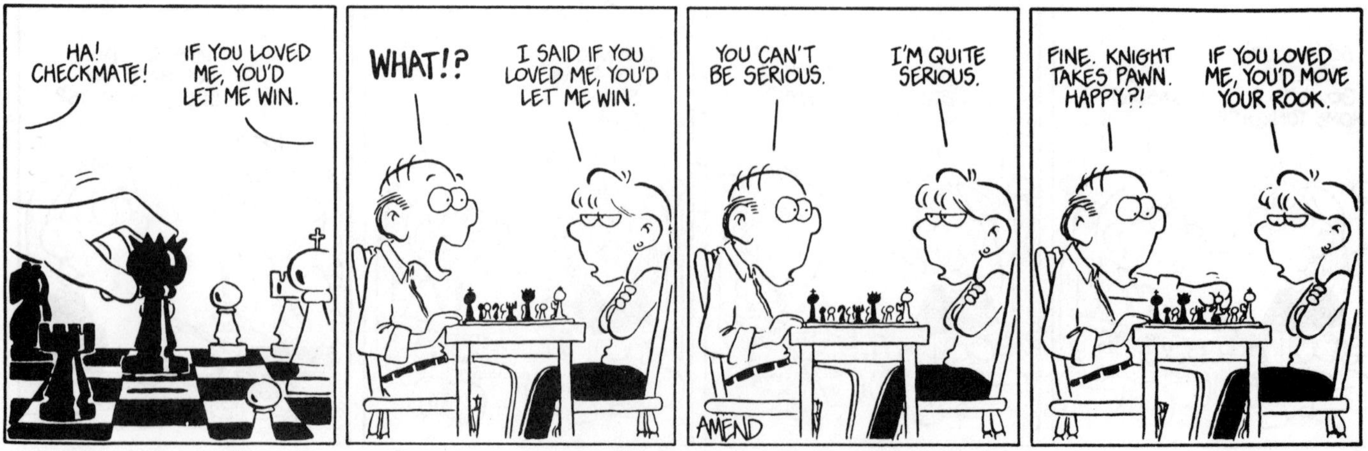
HA! CHECKMATE!
IF YOU LOVED ME, YOU'D LET ME WIN.
WHAT!?
I SAID IF YOU LOVED ME, YOU'D LET ME WIN.
YOU CAN'T BE SERIOUS.
I'M QUITE SERIOUS.
AMEND
FINE. KNIGHT TAKES PAWN. HAPPY?!
IF YOU LOVED ME, YOU'D MOVE YOUR ROOK.

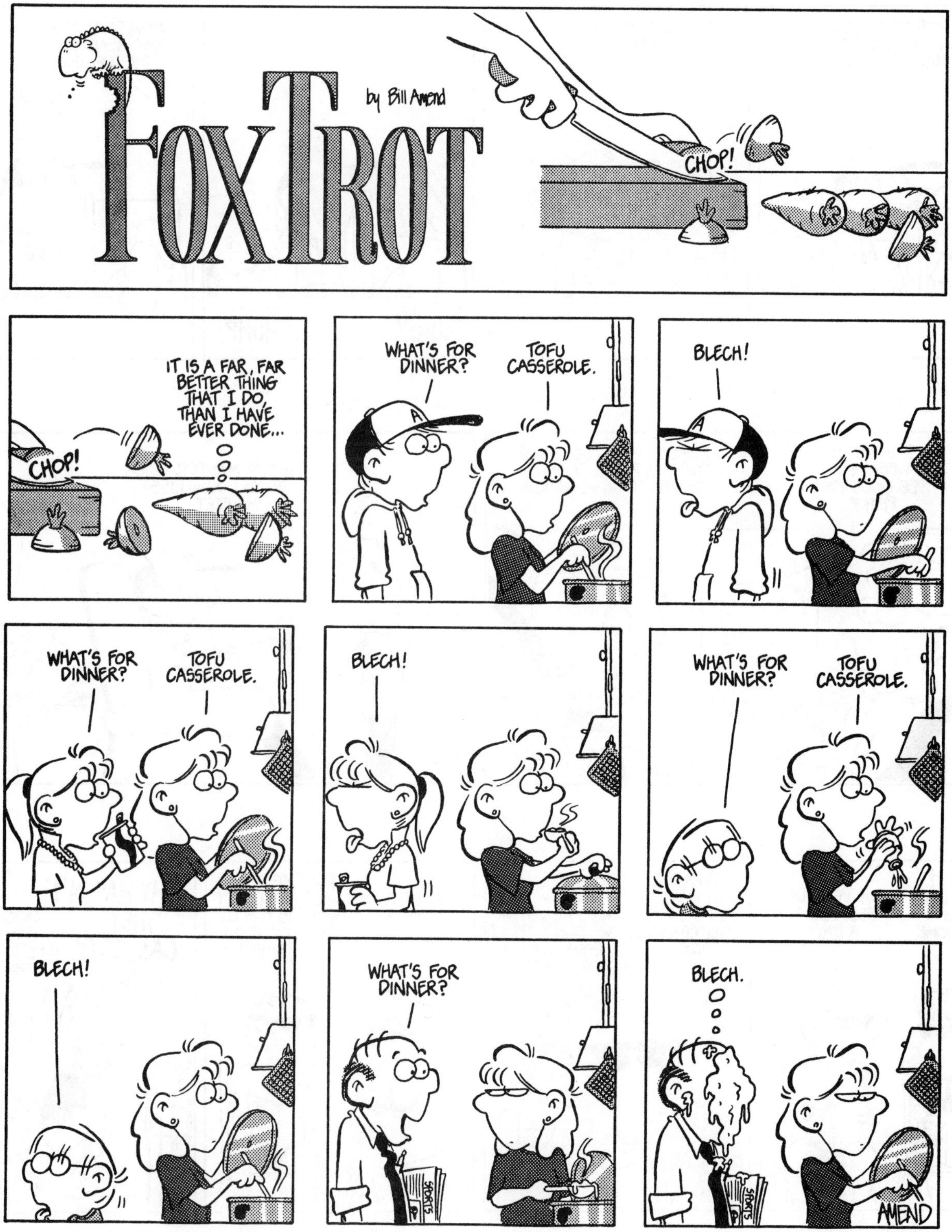
FOXTROT
by Bill Amend
CHOP!
CHOP!
IT IS A FAR, FAR BETTER THING THAT I DO, THAN I HAVE EVER DONE...
WHAT'S FOR DINNER?
TOFU CASSEROLE.
BLECH!
WHAT'S FOR DINNER?
TOFU CASSEROLE.
BLECH!
WHAT'S FOR DINNER?
TOFU CASSEROLE.
BLECH!
WHAT'S FOR DINNER?
BLECH.
AMEND

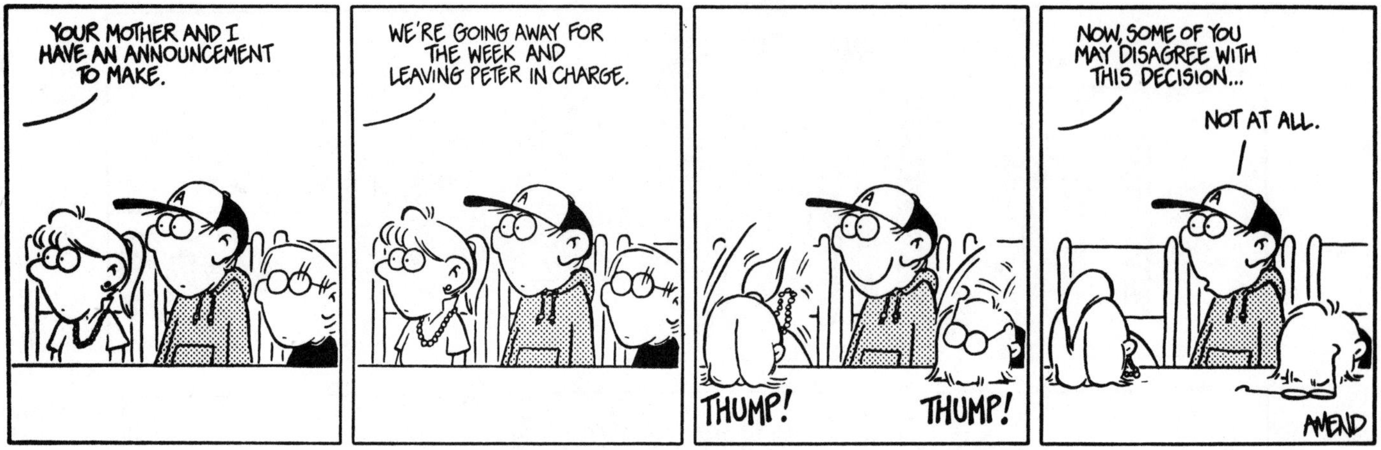
YOUR MOTHER AND I HAVE AN ANNOUNCEMENT TO MAKE.
WE'RE GOING AWAY FOR THE WEEK AND LEAVING PETER IN CHARGE.
THUMP!
THUMP!
NOW, SOME OF YOU MAY DISAGREE WITH THIS DECISION...
NOT AT ALL.
AMEND

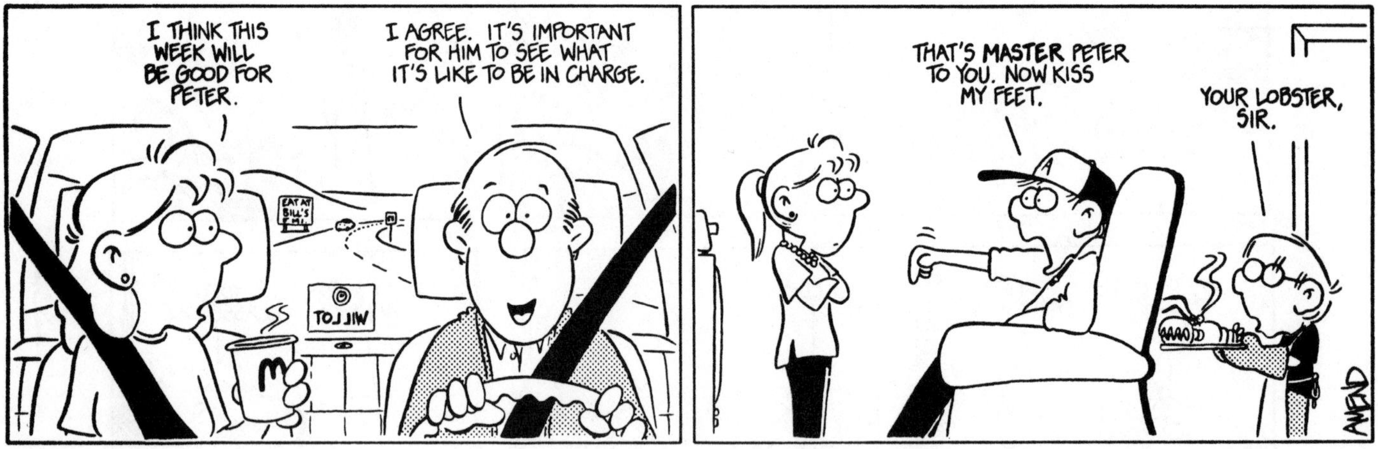
I THINK THIS WEEK WILL BE GOOD FOR PETER.
I AGREE. IT'S IMPORTANT FOR HIM TO SEE WHAT IT'S LIKE TO BE IN CHARGE.
THAT'S MASTER PETER TO YOU. NOW KISS MY FEET.
YOUR LOBSTER, SIR.
AMEND

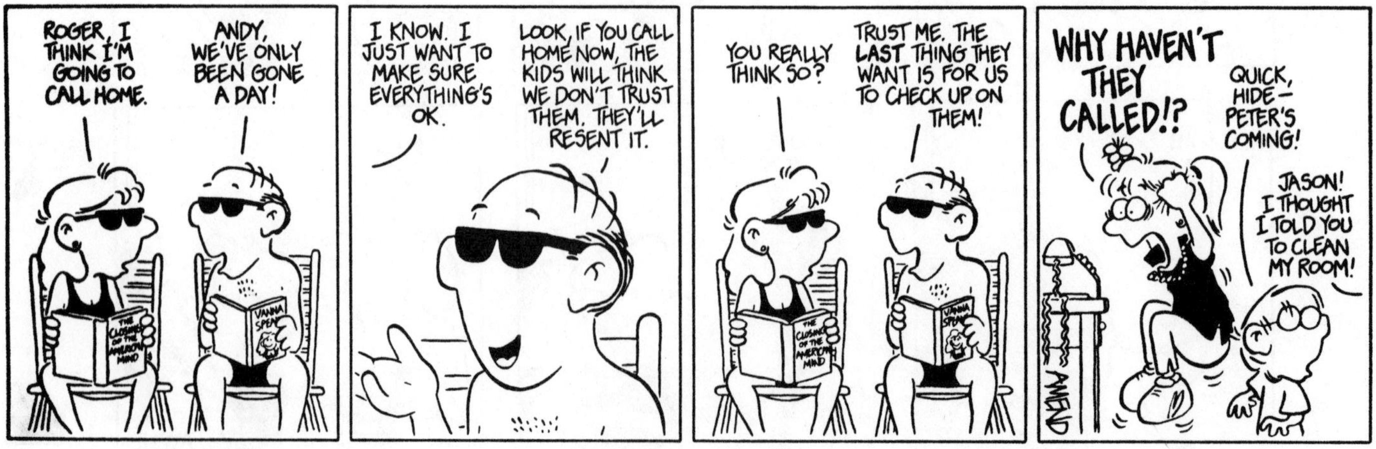
ROGER, I THINK I'M GOING TO CALL HOME.
ANDY, WE'VE ONLY BEEN GONE A DAY!
I KNOW. I JUST WANT TO MAKE SURE EVERYTHING'S OK.
LOOK, IF YOU CALL HOME NOW, THE KIDS WILL THINK WE DON'T TRUST THEM. THEY'LL RESENT IT.
YOU REALLY THINK SO?
TRUST ME. THE LAST THING THEY WANT IS FOR US TO CHECK UP ON THEM!
WHY HAVEN'T THEY CALLED!?
QUICK, HIDE— PETER'S COMING!
JASON! I THOUGHT I TOLD YOU TO CLEAN MY ROOM!
AMEND

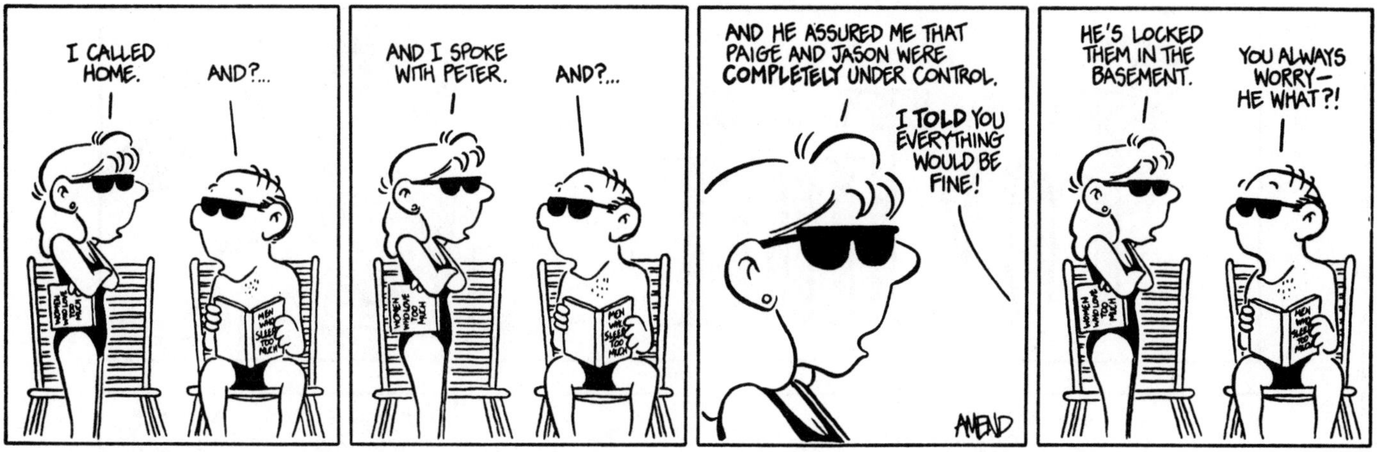
I CALLED HOME.
AND?...
AND I SPOKE WITH PETER.
AND?...
AND HE ASSURED ME THAT PAIGE AND JASON WERE **COMPLETELY** UNDER CONTROL.
I **TOLD** YOU EVERYTHING WOULD BE FINE!
AMEND
HE'S LOCKED THEM IN THE BASEMENT.
YOU ALWAYS WORRY— HE WHAT?!

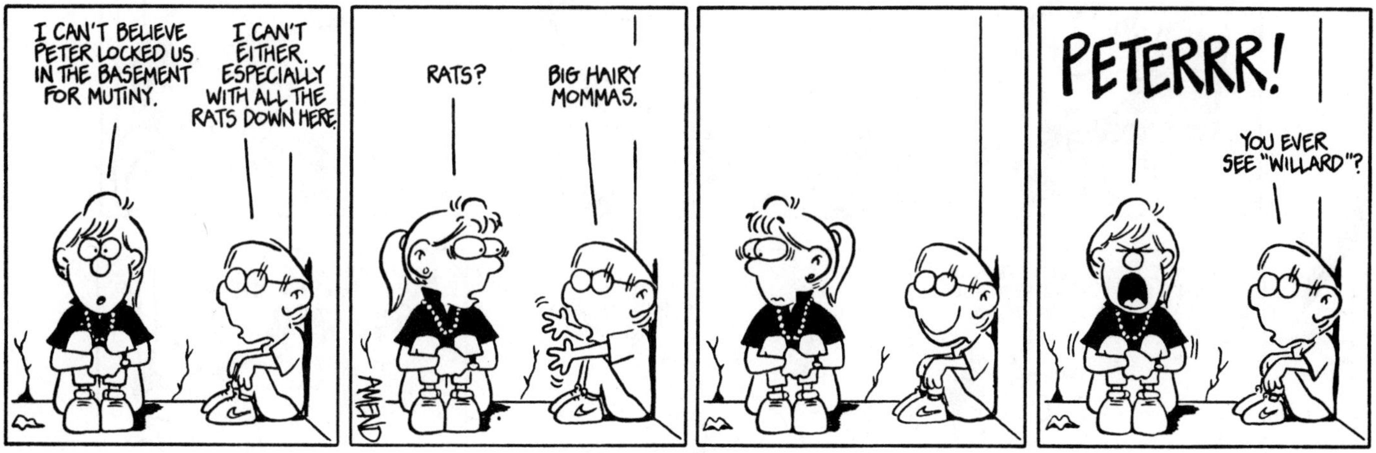
I CAN'T BELIEVE PETER LOCKED US IN THE BASEMENT FOR MUTINY.
I CAN'T EITHER. ESPECIALLY WITH ALL THE RATS DOWN HERE.
RATS?
BIG HAIRY MOMMAS.
AMEND
PETERRR!
YOU EVER SEE "WILLARD"?

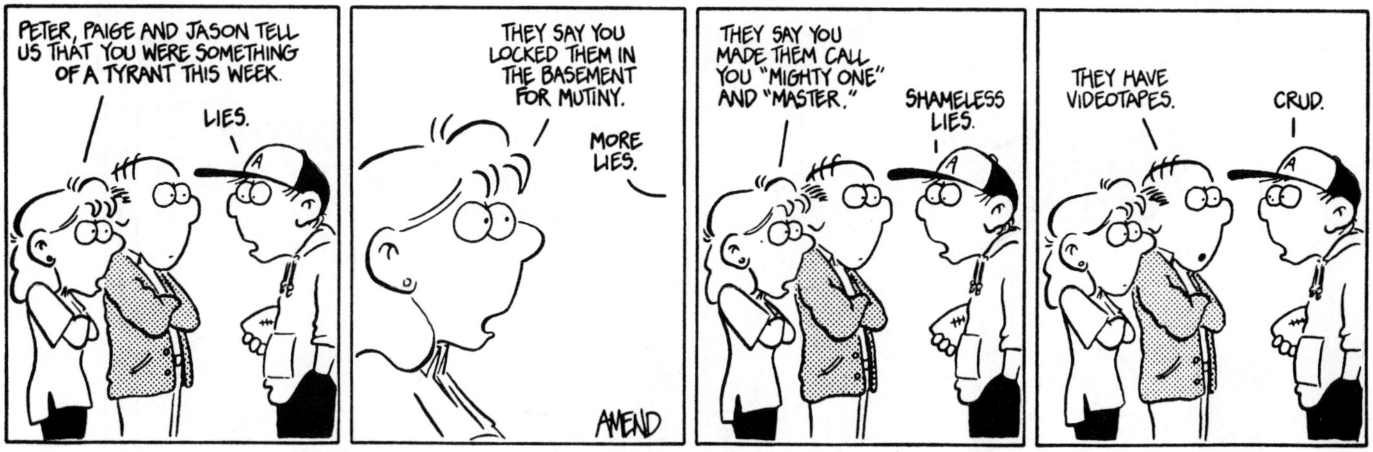
PETER, PAIGE AND JASON TELL US THAT YOU WERE SOMETHING OF A TYRANT THIS WEEK.
LIES.
THEY SAY YOU LOCKED THEM IN THE BASEMENT FOR MUTINY.
MORE LIES.
AMEND
THEY SAY YOU MADE THEM CALL YOU "MIGHTY ONE" AND "MASTER."
SHAMELESS LIES.
THEY HAVE VIDEOTAPES.
CRUD.

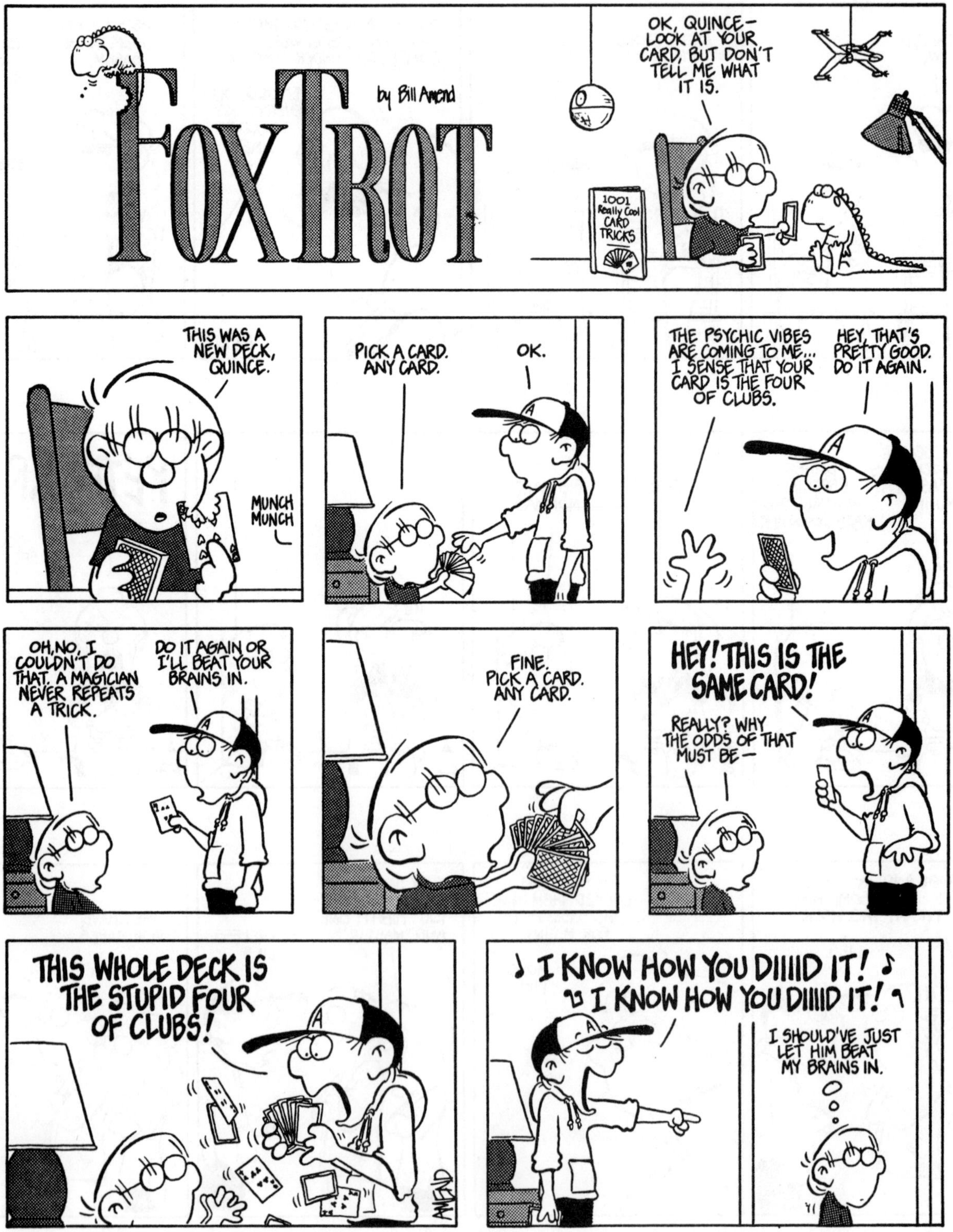
FoxTrot
by Bill Amend
OK, QUINCE— LOOK AT YOUR CARD, BUT DON'T TELL ME WHAT IT IS.
1001 Really Cool CARD TRICKS
THIS WAS A NEW DECK, QUINCE.
MUNCH MUNCH
PICK A CARD. ANY CARD.
OK.
THE PSYCHIC VIBES ARE COMING TO ME... I SENSE THAT YOUR CARD IS THE FOUR OF CLUBS.
HEY, THAT'S PRETTY GOOD. DO IT AGAIN.
OH, NO, I COULDN'T DO THAT. A MAGICIAN NEVER REPEATS A TRICK.
DO IT AGAIN OR I'LL BEAT YOUR BRAINS IN.
FINE. PICK A CARD. ANY CARD.
HEY! THIS IS THE SAME CARD!
REALLY? WHY THE ODDS OF THAT MUST BE—
THIS WHOLE DECK IS THE STUPID FOUR OF CLUBS!
AMEND
♪ I KNOW HOW YOU DIIIID IT! ♪
♫ I KNOW HOW YOU DIIIID IT! ♪
I SHOULD'VE JUST LET HIM BEAT MY BRAINS IN.

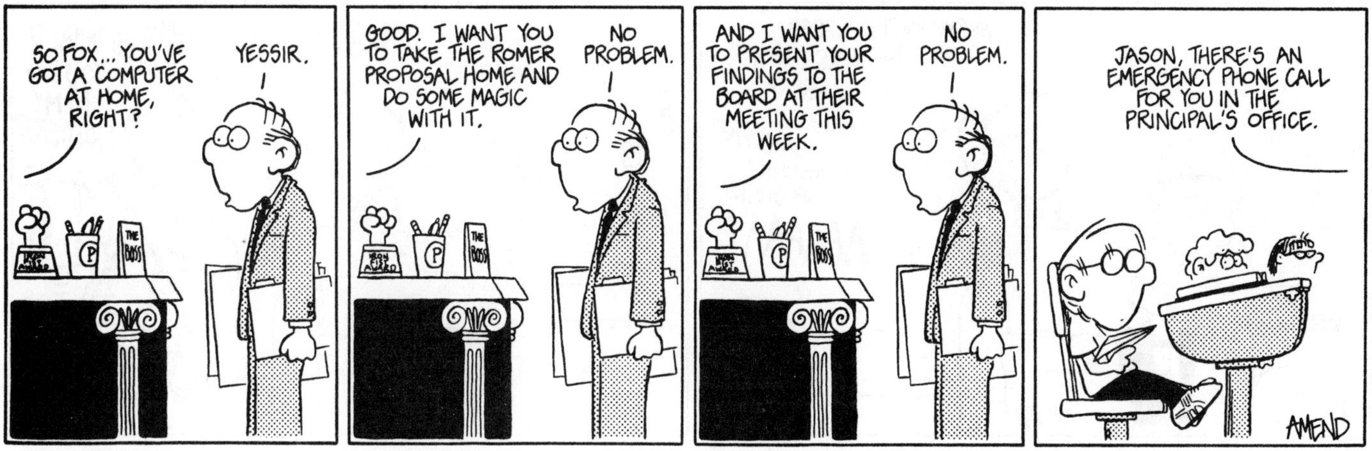
SO FOX... YOU'VE GOT A COMPUTER AT HOME, RIGHT?
YESSIR.
GOOD. I WANT YOU TO TAKE THE ROMER PROPOSAL HOME AND DO SOME MAGIC WITH IT.
NO PROBLEM.
AND I WANT YOU TO PRESENT YOUR FINDINGS TO THE BOARD AT THEIR MEETING THIS WEEK.
NO PROBLEM.
JASON, THERE'S AN EMERGENCY PHONE CALL FOR YOU IN THE PRINCIPAL'S OFFICE.
AMEND

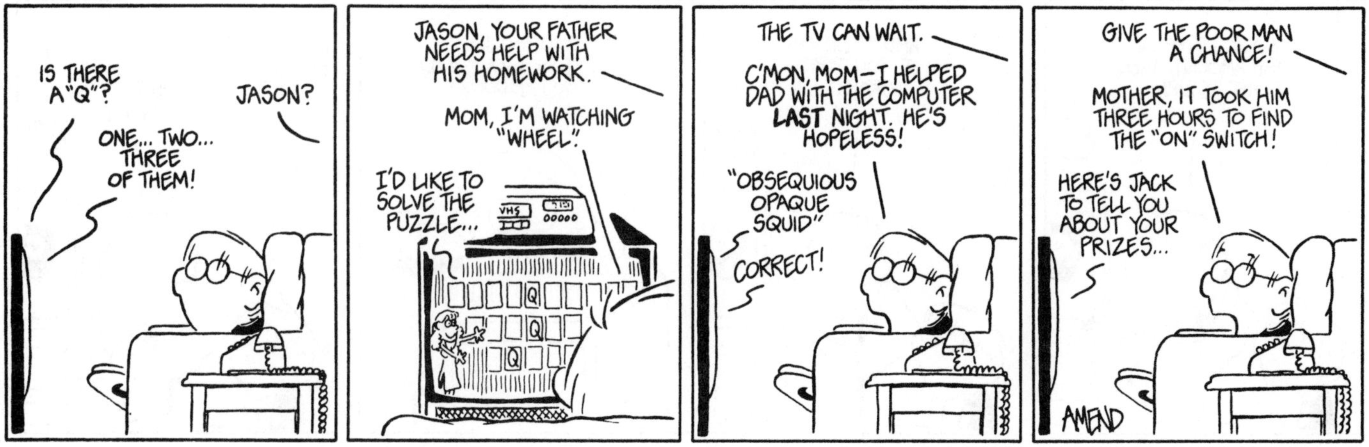
IS THERE A "Q"?
ONE... TWO... THREE OF THEM!
JASON?
JASON, YOUR FATHER NEEDS HELP WITH HIS HOMEWORK.
MOM, I'M WATCHING "WHEEL."
I'D LIKE TO SOLVE THE PUZZLE...
THE TV CAN WAIT.
C'MON, MOM—I HELPED DAD WITH THE COMPUTER LAST NIGHT. HE'S HOPELESS!
"OBSEQUIOUS OPAQUE SQUID"
CORRECT!
GIVE THE POOR MAN A CHANCE!
MOTHER, IT TOOK HIM THREE HOURS TO FIND THE "ON" SWITCH!
HERE'S JACK TO TELL YOU ABOUT YOUR PRIZES...
AMEND

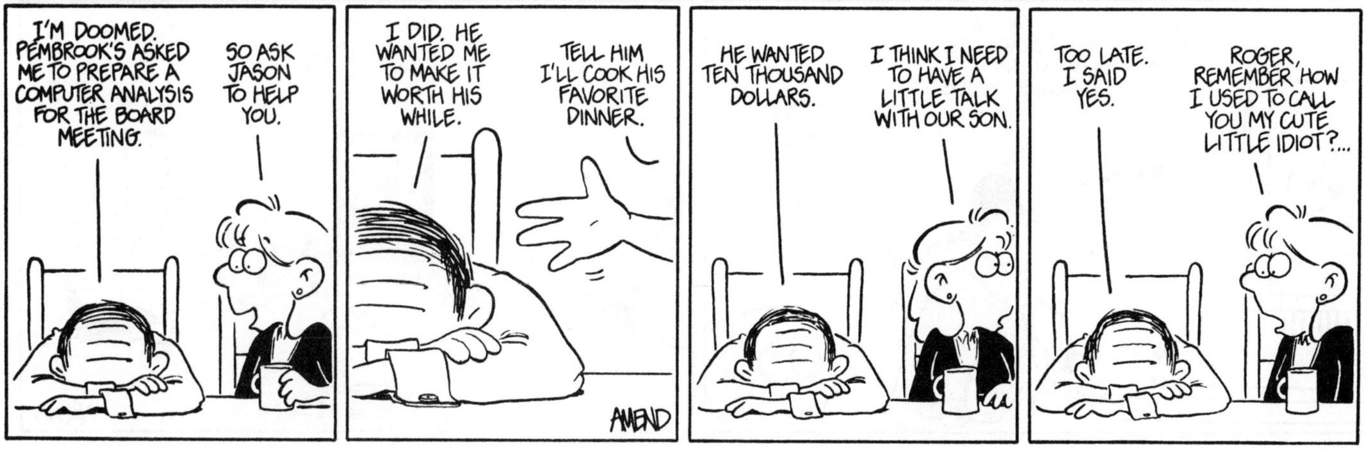
I'M DOOMED. PEMBROOK'S ASKED ME TO PREPARE A COMPUTER ANALYSIS FOR THE BOARD MEETING.
SO ASK JASON TO HELP YOU.
I DID. HE WANTED ME TO MAKE IT WORTH HIS WHILE.
TELL HIM I'LL COOK HIS FAVORITE DINNER.
HE WANTED TEN THOUSAND DOLLARS.
I THINK I NEED TO HAVE A LITTLE TALK WITH OUR SON.
TOO LATE. I SAID YES.
ROGER, REMEMBER HOW I USED TO CALL YOU MY CUTE LITTLE IDIOT?...
AMEND

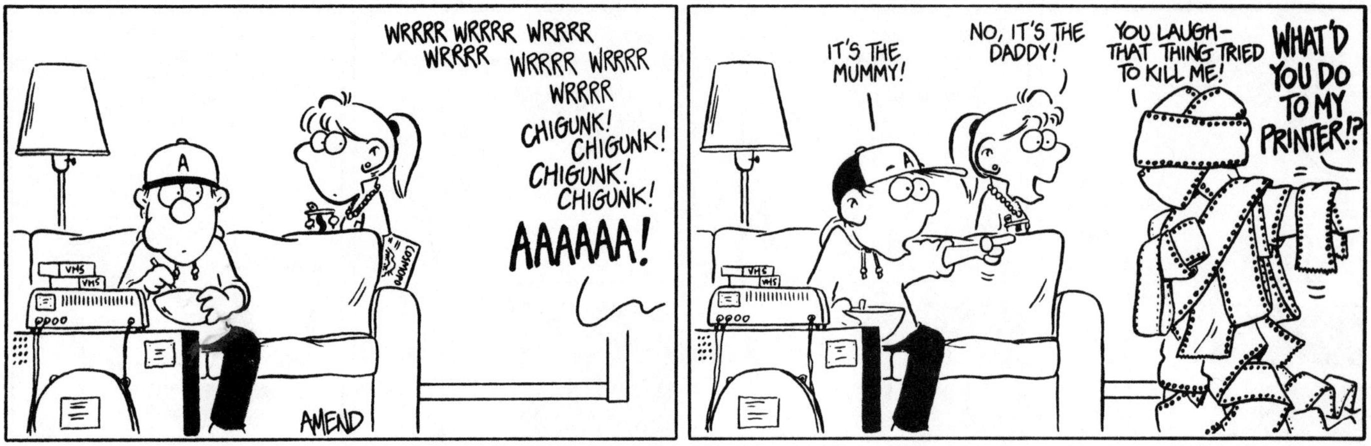
WRRRR WRRRR WRRRR
WRRRR WRRRR WRRRR
WRRRR
CHIGUNK! CHIGUNK!
CHIGUNK! CHIGUNK!
AAAAAA!
AMEND
IT'S THE MUMMY!
NO, IT'S THE DADDY!
YOU LAUGH– THAT THING TRIED TO KILL ME!
WHAT'D YOU DO TO MY PRINTER!?

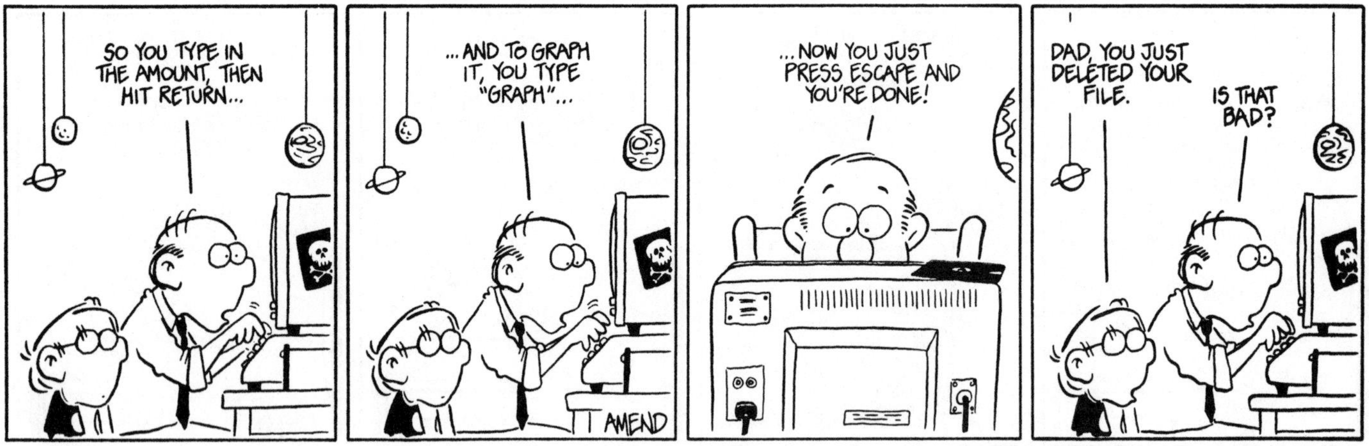
SO YOU TYPE IN THE AMOUNT, THEN HIT RETURN...
...AND TO GRAPH IT, YOU TYPE "GRAPH"...
AMEND
...NOW YOU JUST PRESS ESCAPE AND YOU'RE DONE!
DAD, YOU JUST DELETED YOUR FILE.
IS THAT BAD?

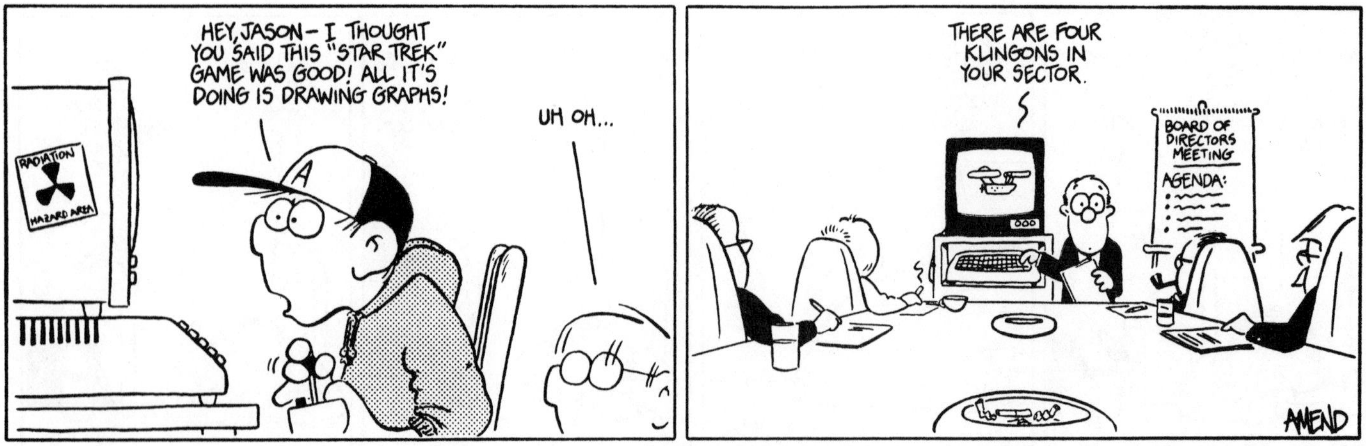
RADIATION
HAZARD AREA
HEY, JASON– I THOUGHT YOU SAID THIS "STAR TREK" GAME WAS GOOD! ALL IT'S DOING IS DRAWING GRAPHS!
UH OH...
THERE ARE FOUR KLINGONS IN YOUR SECTOR.
BOARD OF DIRECTORS MEETING
AGENDA:
AMEND

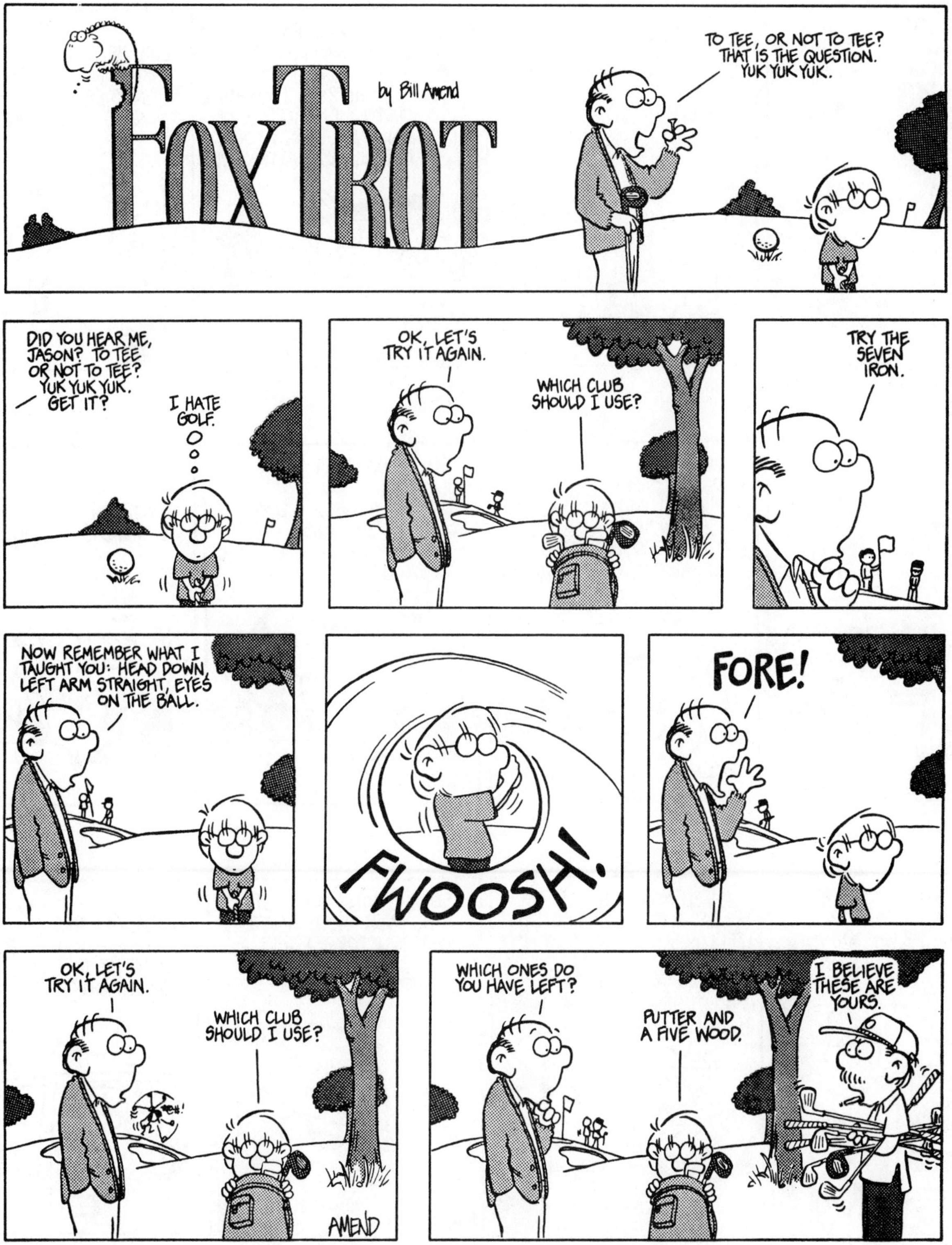
FoxTrot
by Bill Amend
TO TEE, OR NOT TO TEE? THAT IS THE QUESTION. YUK YUK YUK.
DID YOU HEAR ME, JASON? TO TEE OR NOT TO TEE? YUK YUK YUK. GET IT?
I HATE GOLF.
OK, LET'S TRY IT AGAIN.
WHICH CLUB SHOULD I USE?
TRY THE SEVEN IRON.
NOW REMEMBER WHAT I TAUGHT YOU: HEAD DOWN, LEFT ARM STRAIGHT, EYES ON THE BALL.
FWOOSH!
FORE!
OK, LET'S TRY IT AGAIN.
WHICH CLUB SHOULD I USE?
AMEND
WHICH ONES DO YOU HAVE LEFT?
PUTTER AND A FIVE WOOD.
I BELIEVE THESE ARE YOURS.

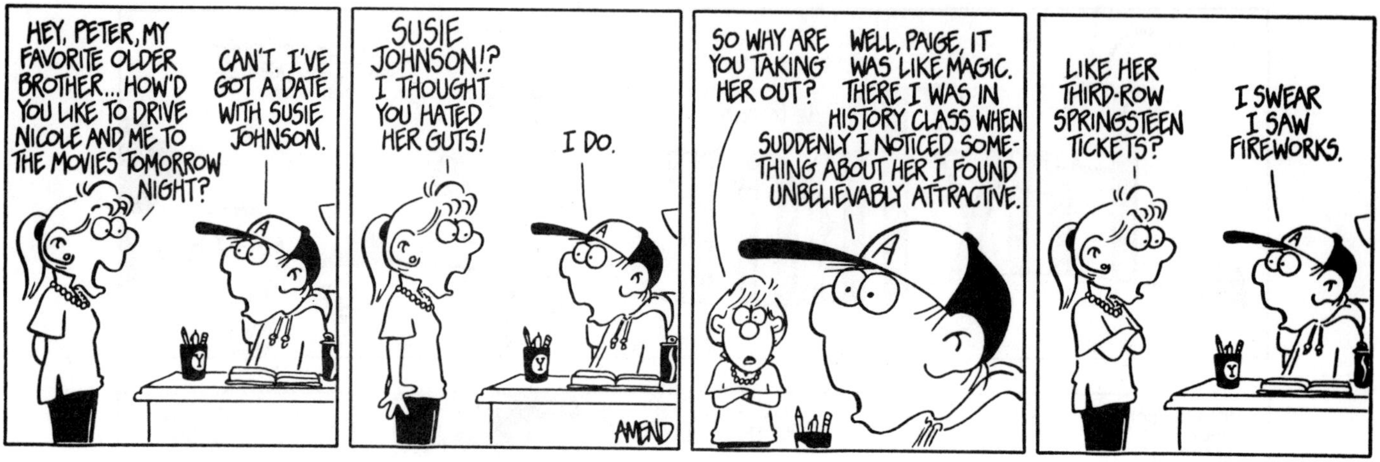
HEY, PETER, MY FAVORITE OLDER BROTHER... HOW'D YOU LIKE TO DRIVE NICOLE AND ME TO THE MOVIES TOMORROW NIGHT?
CAN'T. I'VE GOT A DATE WITH SUSIE JOHNSON.
SUSIE JOHNSON!? I THOUGHT YOU HATED HER GUTS!
I DO.
AMEND
SO WHY ARE YOU TAKING HER OUT?
WELL, PAIGE, IT WAS LIKE MAGIC. THERE I WAS IN HISTORY CLASS WHEN SUDDENLY I NOTICED SOMETHING ABOUT HER I FOUND UNBELIEVABLY ATTRACTIVE.
LIKE HER THIRD-ROW SPRINGSTEEN TICKETS?
I SWEAR I SAW FIREWORKS.

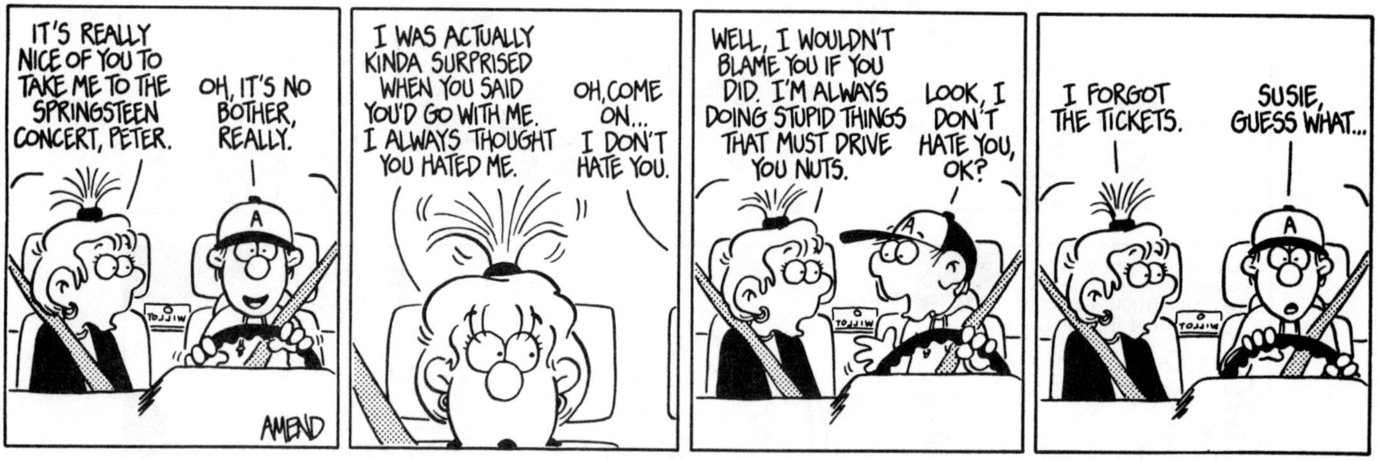
IT'S REALLY NICE OF YOU TO TAKE ME TO THE SPRINGSTEEN CONCERT, PETER.
OH, IT'S NO BOTHER, REALLY.
AMEND
I WAS ACTUALLY KINDA SURPRISED WHEN YOU SAID YOU'D GO WITH ME. I ALWAYS THOUGHT YOU HATED ME.
OH, COME ON... I DON'T HATE YOU.
WELL, I WOULDN'T BLAME YOU IF YOU DID. I'M ALWAYS DOING STUPID THINGS THAT MUST DRIVE YOU NUTS.
LOOK, I DON'T HATE YOU, OK?
SUSIE, GUESS WHAT...
I FORGOT THE TICKETS.

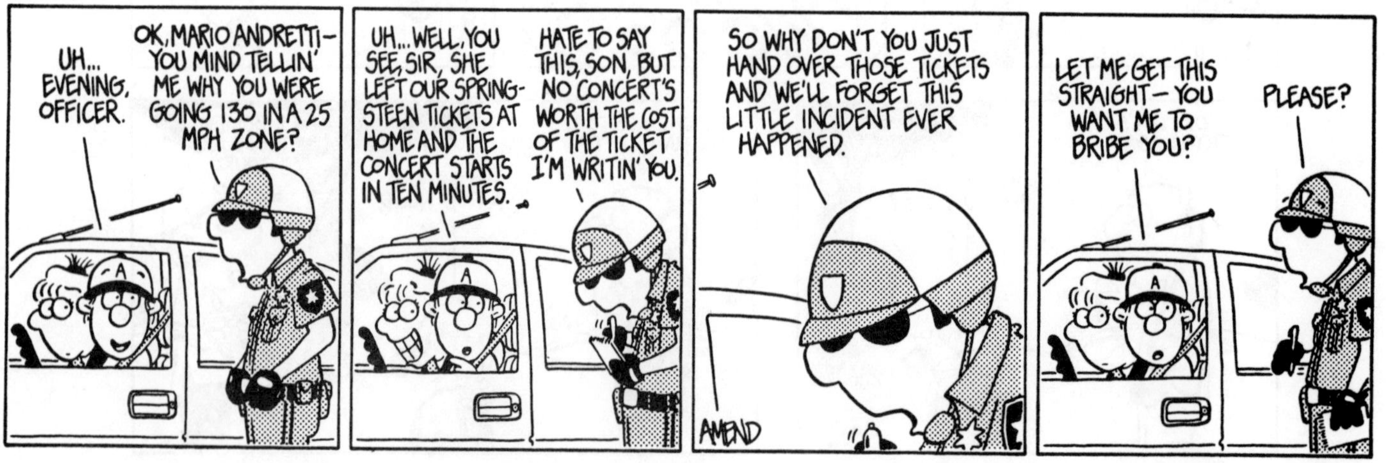
UH... EVENING, OFFICER.
OK, MARIO ANDRETTI— YOU MIND TELLIN' ME WHY YOU WERE GOING 130 IN A 25 MPH ZONE?
UH... WELL, YOU SEE, SIR, SHE LEFT OUR SPRINGSTEEN TICKETS AT HOME AND THE CONCERT STARTS IN TEN MINUTES.
HATE TO SAY THIS, SON, BUT NO CONCERT'S WORTH THE COST OF THE TICKET I'M WRITIN' YOU.
SO WHY DON'T YOU JUST HAND OVER THOSE TICKETS AND WE'LL FORGET THIS LITTLE INCIDENT EVER HAPPENED.
AMEND
LET ME GET THIS STRAIGHT— YOU WANT ME TO BRIBE YOU?
PLEASE?

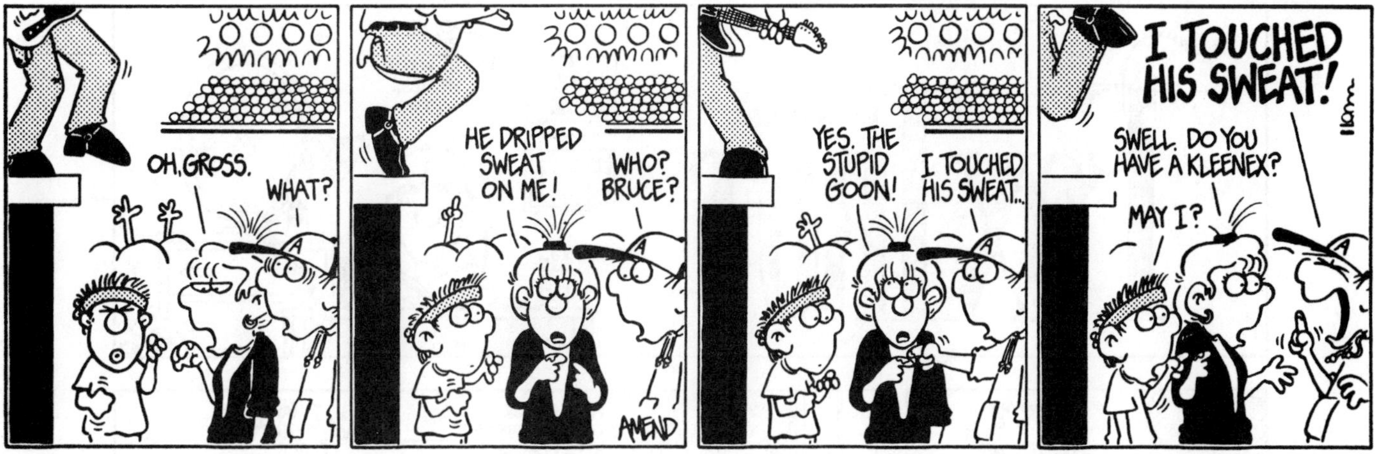
OH, GROSS.
WHAT?
HE DRIPPED SWEAT ON ME!
WHO? BRUCE?
YES. THE STUPID GOON!
I TOUCHED HIS SWEAT...
I TOUCHED HIS SWEAT!
SWELL. DO YOU HAVE A KLEENEX?
MAY I?

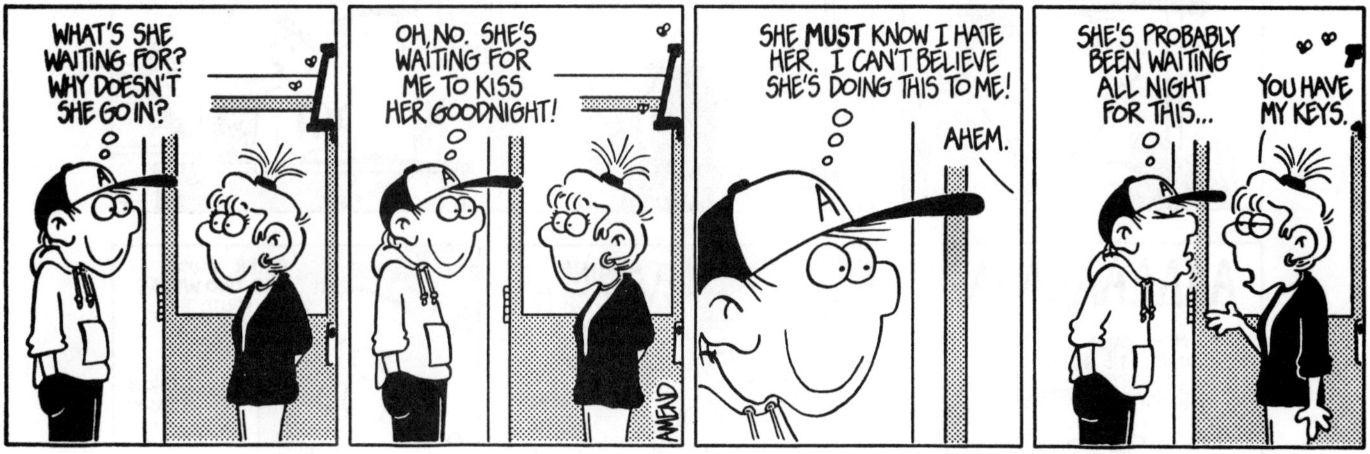
WHAT'S SHE WAITING FOR? WHY DOESN'T SHE GO IN?
OH, NO. SHE'S WAITING FOR ME TO KISS HER GOODNIGHT!
SHE MUST KNOW I HATE HER. I CAN'T BELIEVE SHE'S DOING THIS TO ME!
AHEM.
SHE'S PROBABLY BEEN WAITING ALL NIGHT FOR THIS...
YOU HAVE MY KEYS.

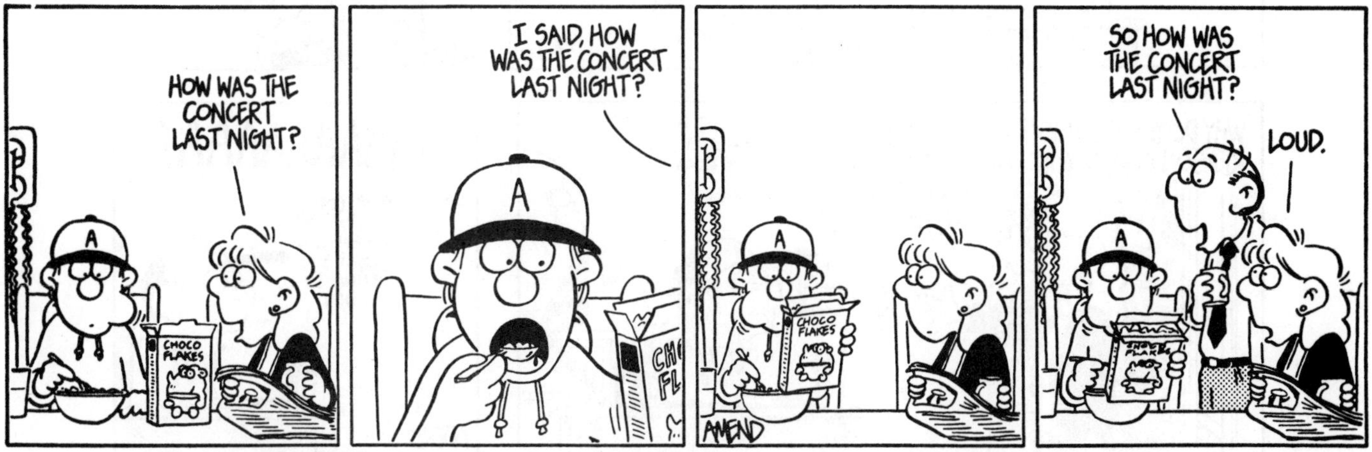
HOW WAS THE CONCERT LAST NIGHT?
I SAID, HOW WAS THE CONCERT LAST NIGHT?
SO HOW WAS THE CONCERT LAST NIGHT?
LOUD.

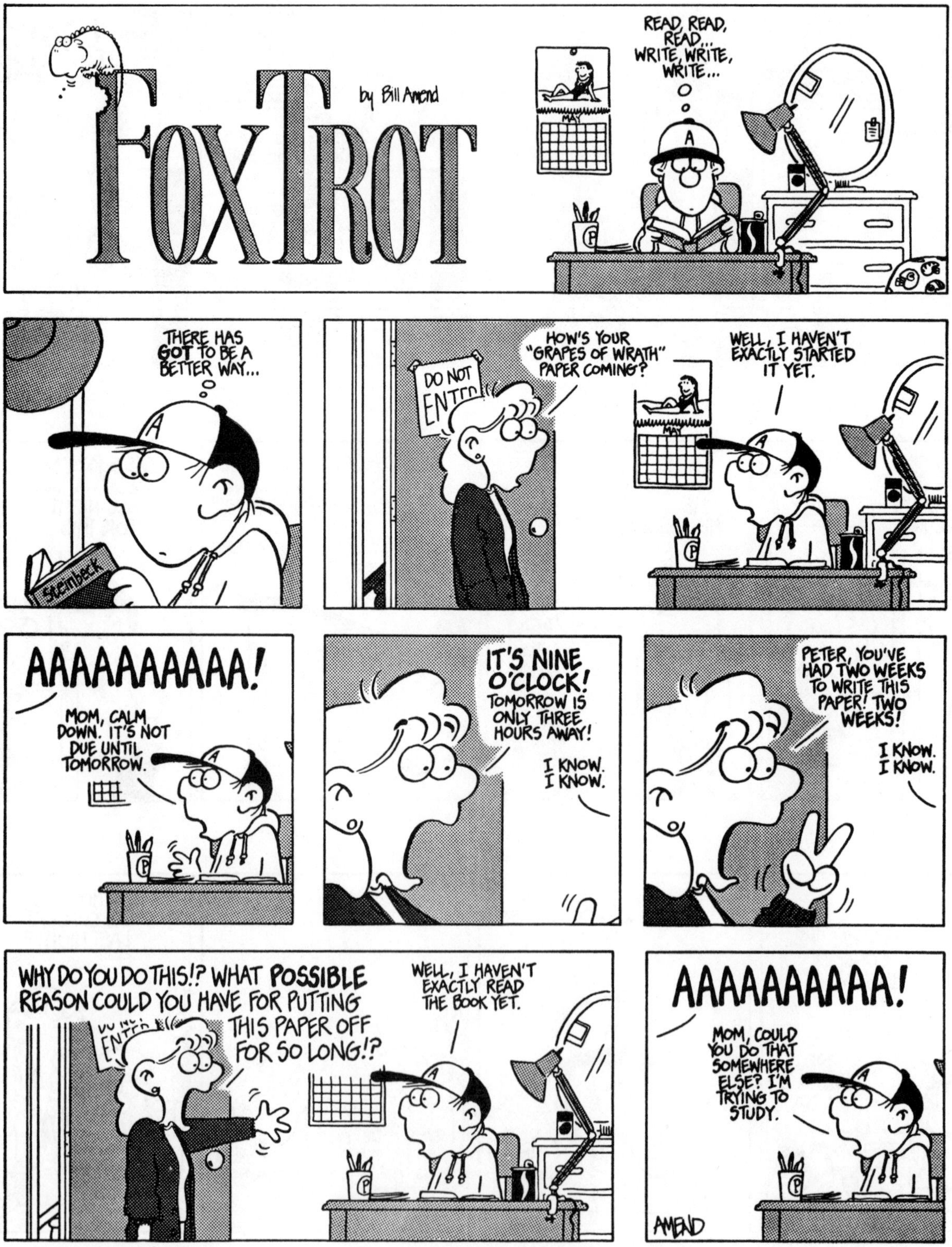
FoxTrot
by Bill Amend
READ, READ, READ... WRITE, WRITE, WRITE...
MAY
THERE HAS GOT TO BE A BETTER WAY...
Steinbeck
DO NOT ENTER
HOW'S YOUR "GRAPES OF WRATH" PAPER COMING?
WELL, I HAVEN'T EXACTLY STARTED IT YET.
MAY
AAAAAAAAAA!
MOM, CALM DOWN. IT'S NOT DUE UNTIL TOMORROW.
IT'S NINE O'CLOCK! TOMORROW IS ONLY THREE HOURS AWAY!
I KNOW. I KNOW.
PETER, YOU'VE HAD TWO WEEKS TO WRITE THIS PAPER! TWO WEEKS!
I KNOW. I KNOW.
WHY DO YOU DO THIS!? WHAT POSSIBLE REASON COULD YOU HAVE FOR PUTTING THIS PAPER OFF FOR SO LONG!?
WELL, I HAVEN'T EXACTLY READ THE BOOK YET.
AAAAAAAAAA!
MOM, COULD YOU DO THAT SOMEWHERE ELSE? I'M TRYING TO STUDY.
AMEND

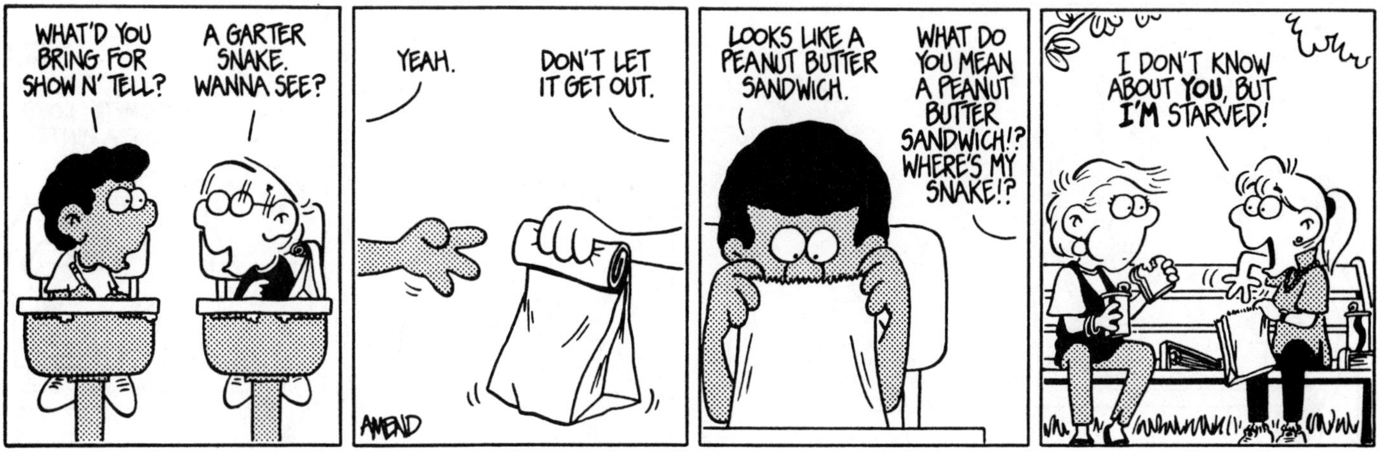
WHAT'D YOU BRING FOR SHOW N' TELL?
A GARTER SNAKE. WANNA SEE?
YEAH.
DON'T LET IT GET OUT.
AMEND
LOOKS LIKE A PEANUT BUTTER SANDWICH.
WHAT DO YOU MEAN A PEANUT BUTTER SANDWICH!? WHERE'S MY SNAKE!?
I DON'T KNOW ABOUT YOU, BUT I'M STARVED!

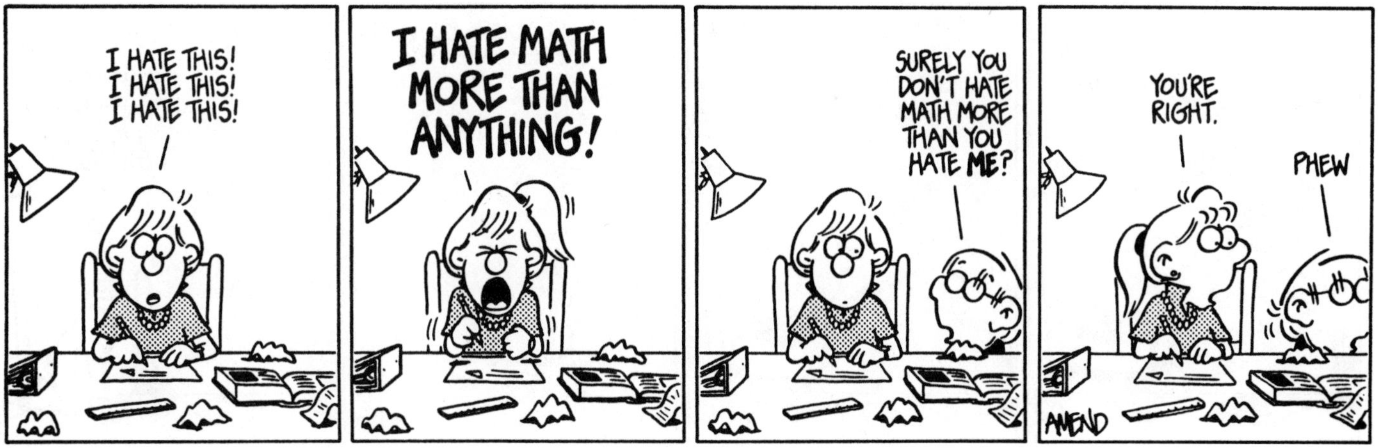
I HATE THIS! I HATE THIS! I HATE THIS!
I HATE MATH MORE THAN ANYTHING!
SURELY YOU DON'T HATE MATH MORE THAN YOU HATE ME?
YOU'RE RIGHT.
PHEW
AMEND

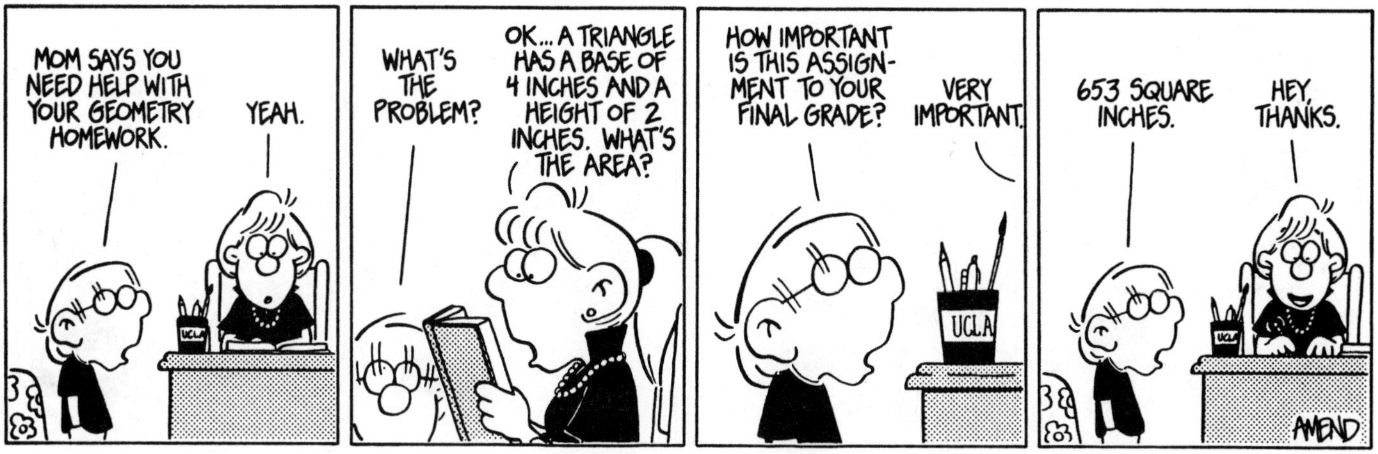
MOM SAYS YOU NEED HELP WITH YOUR GEOMETRY HOMEWORK.
YEAH.
WHAT'S THE PROBLEM?
OK... A TRIANGLE HAS A BASE OF 4 INCHES AND A HEIGHT OF 2 INCHES. WHAT'S THE AREA?
HOW IMPORTANT IS THIS ASSIGNMENT TO YOUR FINAL GRADE?
VERY IMPORTANT.
UCLA
653 SQUARE INCHES.
HEY, THANKS.
AMEND

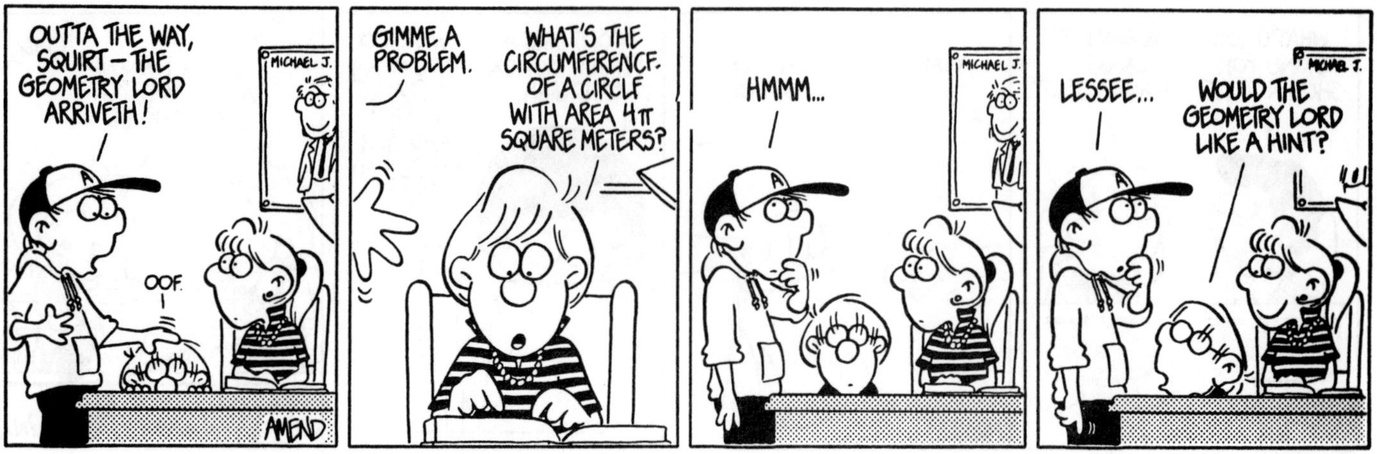
OUTTA THE WAY, SQUIRT — THE GEOMETRY LORD ARRIVETH!
MICHAEL J.
OOF.
AMEND
GIMME A PROBLEM.
WHAT'S THE CIRCUMFERENCE OF A CIRCLE WITH AREA 4π SQUARE METERS?
HMMM...
LESSEE...
WOULD THE GEOMETRY LORD LIKE A HINT?

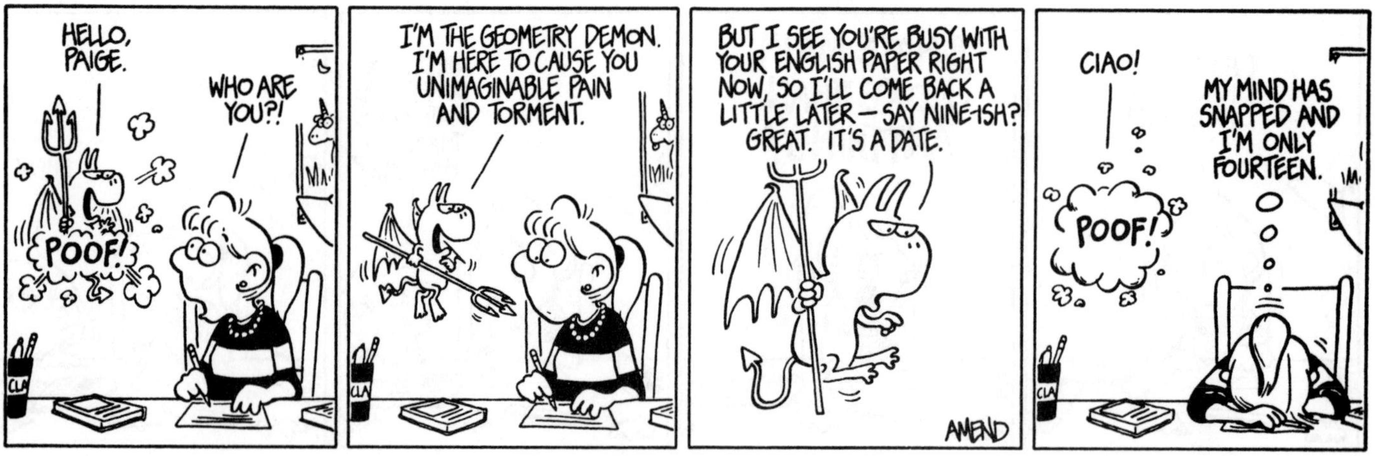
HELLO, PAIGE.
WHO ARE YOU?!
POOF!
I'M THE GEOMETRY DEMON. I'M HERE TO CAUSE YOU UNIMAGINABLE PAIN AND TORMENT.
BUT I SEE YOU'RE BUSY WITH YOUR ENGLISH PAPER RIGHT NOW, SO I'LL COME BACK A LITTLE LATER — SAY NINE-ISH? GREAT. IT'S A DATE.
AMEND
CIAO!
POOF!
MY MIND HAS SNAPPED AND I'M ONLY FOURTEEN.

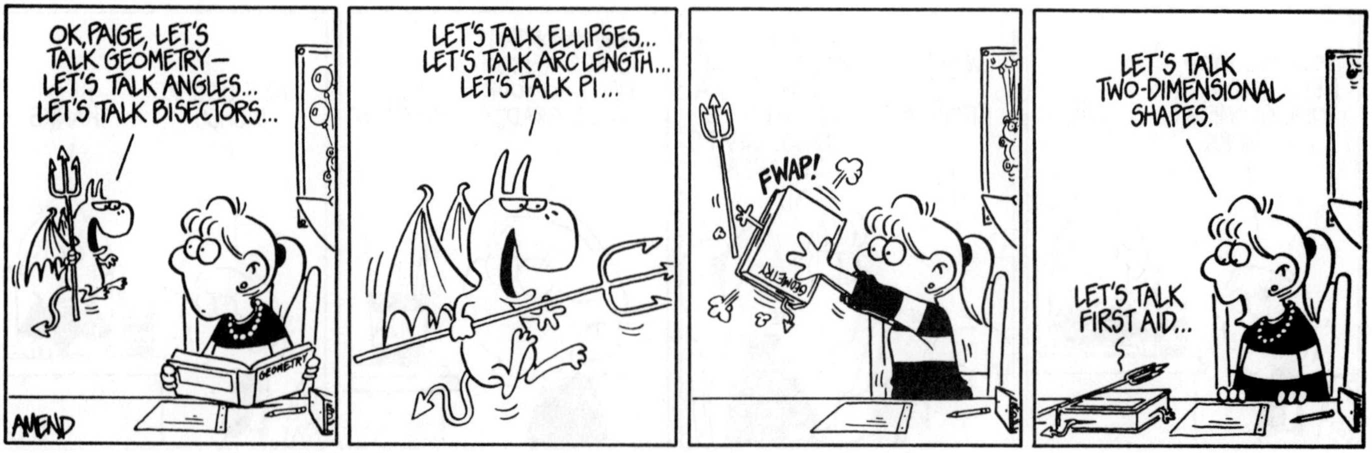
OK, PAIGE, LET'S TALK GEOMETRY — LET'S TALK ANGLES... LET'S TALK BISECTORS...
GEOMETRY
AMEND
LET'S TALK ELLIPSES... LET'S TALK ARC LENGTH... LET'S TALK PI...
FWAP!
GEOMETRY
LET'S TALK TWO-DIMENSIONAL SHAPES.
LET'S TALK FIRST AID...

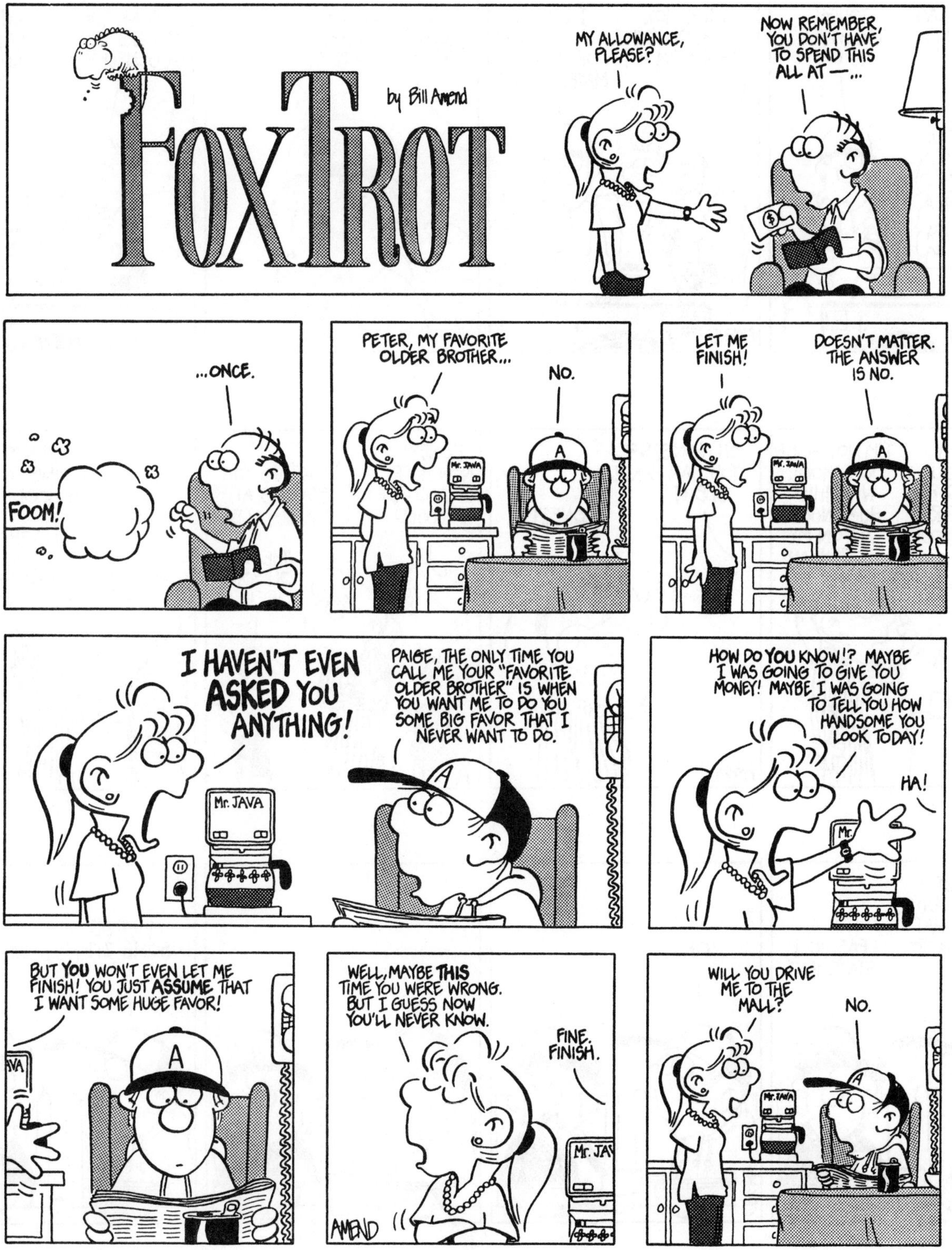
FoxTrot
by Bill Amend
MY ALLOWANCE, PLEASE?
NOW REMEMBER, YOU DON'T HAVE TO SPEND THIS ALL AT —...
FOOM!
...ONCE.
PETER, MY FAVORITE OLDER BROTHER...
NO.
Mr. JAVA
LET ME FINISH!
DOESN'T MATTER. THE ANSWER IS NO.
I HAVEN'T EVEN ASKED YOU ANYTHING!
PAIGE, THE ONLY TIME YOU CALL ME YOUR "FAVORITE OLDER BROTHER" IS WHEN YOU WANT ME TO DO YOU SOME BIG FAVOR THAT I NEVER WANT TO DO.
HOW DO YOU KNOW!? MAYBE I WAS GOING TO GIVE YOU MONEY! MAYBE I WAS GOING TO TELL YOU HOW HANDSOME YOU LOOK TODAY!
HA!
BUT YOU WON'T EVEN LET ME FINISH! YOU JUST ASSUME THAT I WANT SOME HUGE FAVOR!
WELL, MAYBE THIS TIME YOU WERE WRONG. BUT I GUESS NOW YOU'LL NEVER KNOW.
FINE. FINISH.
AMEND
WILL YOU DRIVE ME TO THE MALL?
NO.

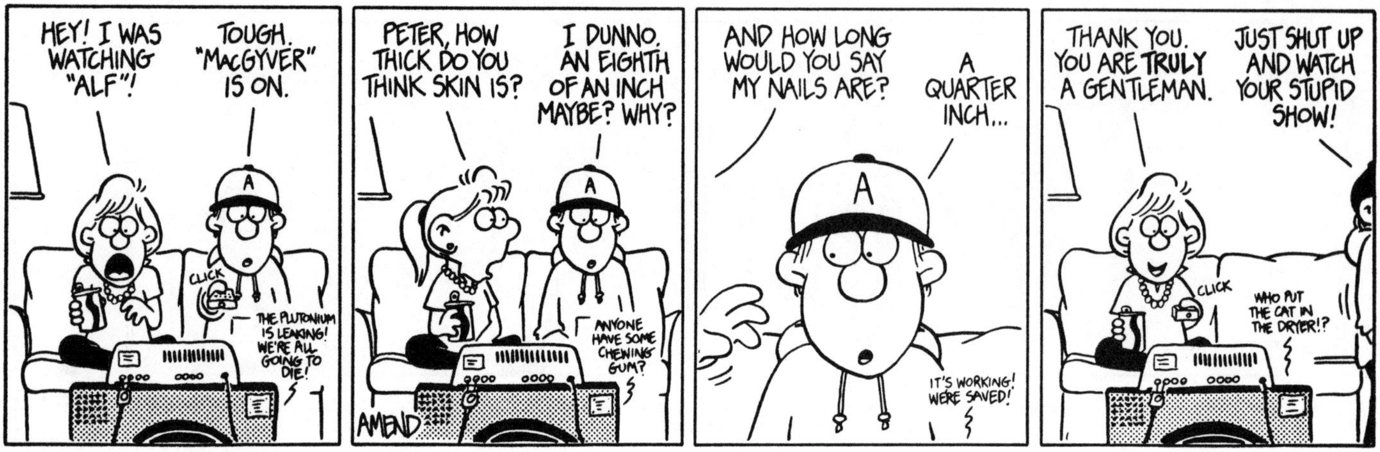
HEY! I WAS WATCHING "ALF"!
TOUGH. "MACGYVER" IS ON.
CLICK
THE PLUTONIUM IS LEAKING! WE'RE ALL GOING TO DIE!
PETER, HOW THICK DO YOU THINK SKIN IS?
I DUNNO. AN EIGHTH OF AN INCH MAYBE? WHY?
ANYONE HAVE SOME CHEWING GUM?
AMEND
AND HOW LONG WOULD YOU SAY MY NAILS ARE?
A QUARTER INCH...
IT'S WORKING! WE'RE SAVED!
THANK YOU. YOU ARE TRULY A GENTLEMAN.
JUST SHUT UP AND WATCH YOUR STUPID SHOW!
CLICK
WHO PUT THE CAT IN THE DRYER!?

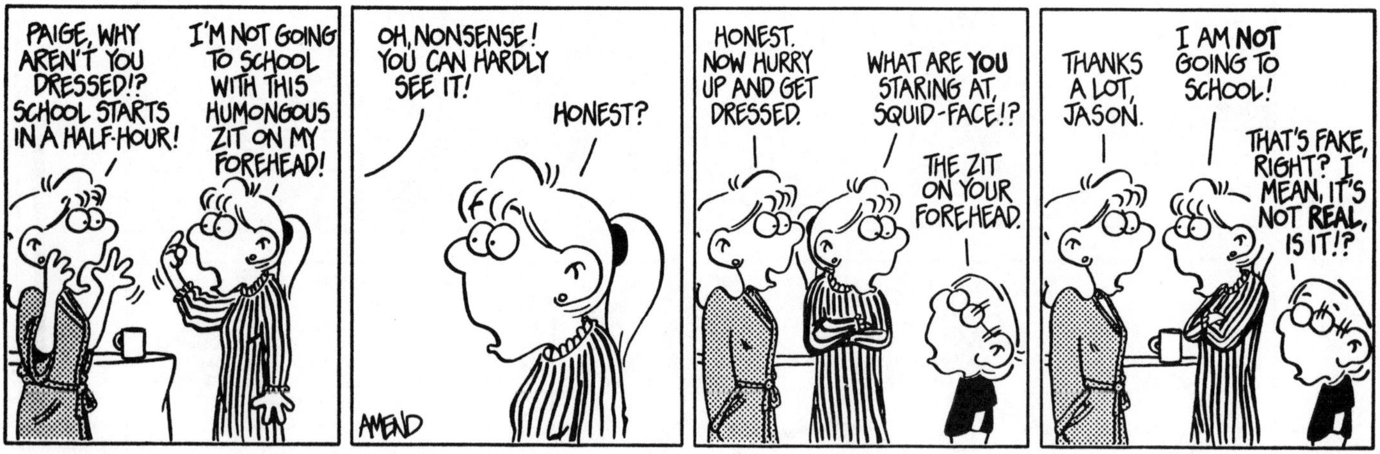
PAIGE, WHY AREN'T YOU DRESSED!? SCHOOL STARTS IN A HALF-HOUR!
I'M NOT GOING TO SCHOOL WITH THIS HUMONGOUS ZIT ON MY FOREHEAD!
OH, NONSENSE! YOU CAN HARDLY SEE IT!
HONEST?
AMEND
HONEST. NOW HURRY UP AND GET DRESSED.
WHAT ARE YOU STARING AT, SQUID-FACE!?
THE ZIT ON YOUR FOREHEAD.
THANKS A LOT, JASON.
I AM NOT GOING TO SCHOOL!
THAT'S FAKE, RIGHT? I MEAN, IT'S NOT REAL, IS IT!?

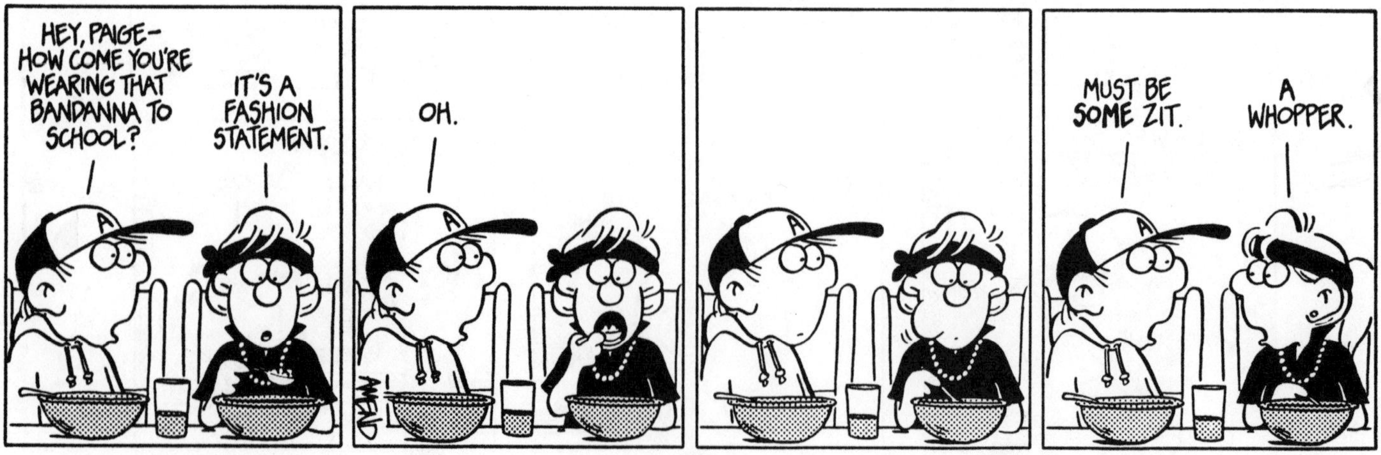
HEY, PAIGE- HOW COME YOU'RE WEARING THAT BANDANNA TO SCHOOL?
IT'S A FASHION STATEMENT.
OH.
AMEND
MUST BE SOME ZIT.
A WHOPPER.

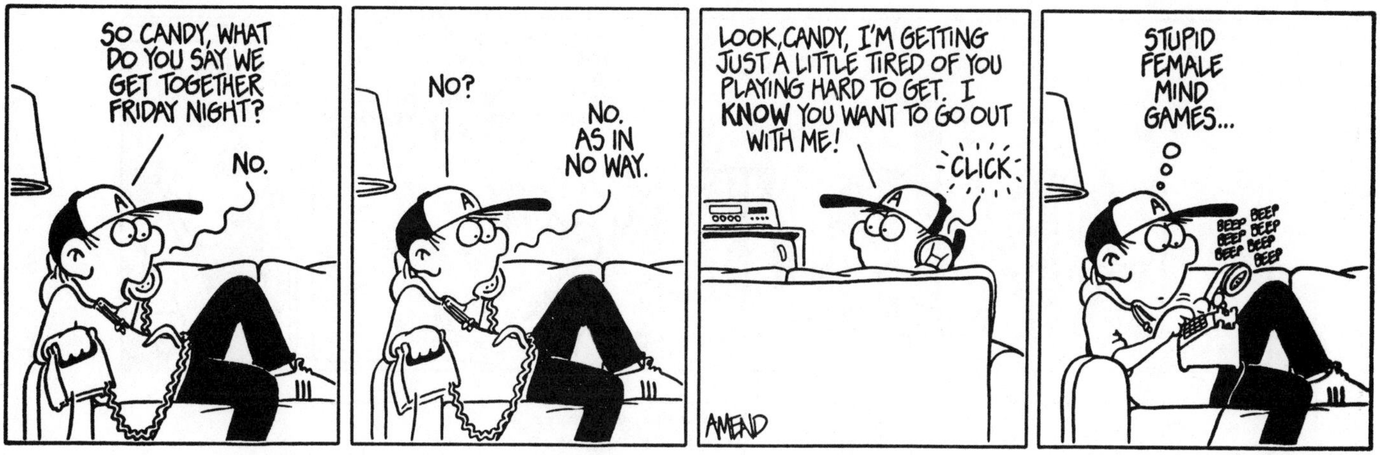
SO CANDY, WHAT DO YOU SAY WE GET TOGETHER FRIDAY NIGHT?
NO.
NO?
NO. AS IN NO WAY.
LOOK, CANDY, I'M GETTING JUST A LITTLE TIRED OF YOU PLAYING HARD TO GET. I **KNOW** YOU WANT TO GO OUT WITH ME!
CLICK
AMEND
STUPID FEMALE MIND GAMES...
BEEP BEEP BEEP BEEP BEEP BEEP BEEP BEEP

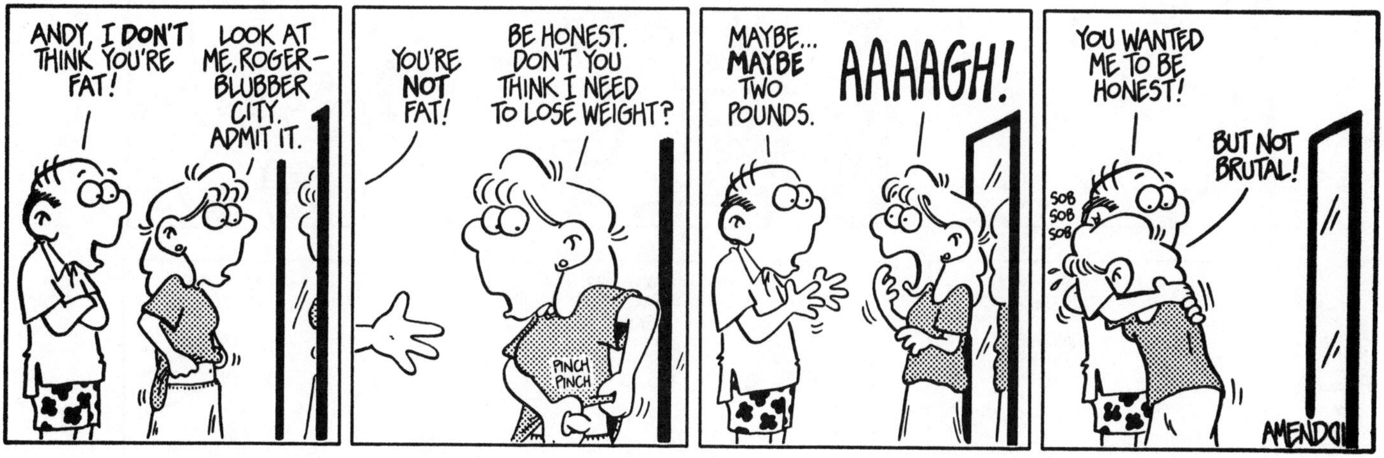
ANDY, I **DON'T** THINK YOU'RE FAT!
LOOK AT ME, ROGER— BLUBBER CITY. ADMIT IT.
YOU'RE **NOT** FAT!
BE HONEST. DON'T YOU THINK I NEED TO LOSE WEIGHT?
PINCH PINCH
MAYBE... **MAYBE** TWO POUNDS.
AAAAGH!
YOU WANTED ME TO BE HONEST!
SOB SOB SOB
BUT NOT BRUTAL!
AMEND

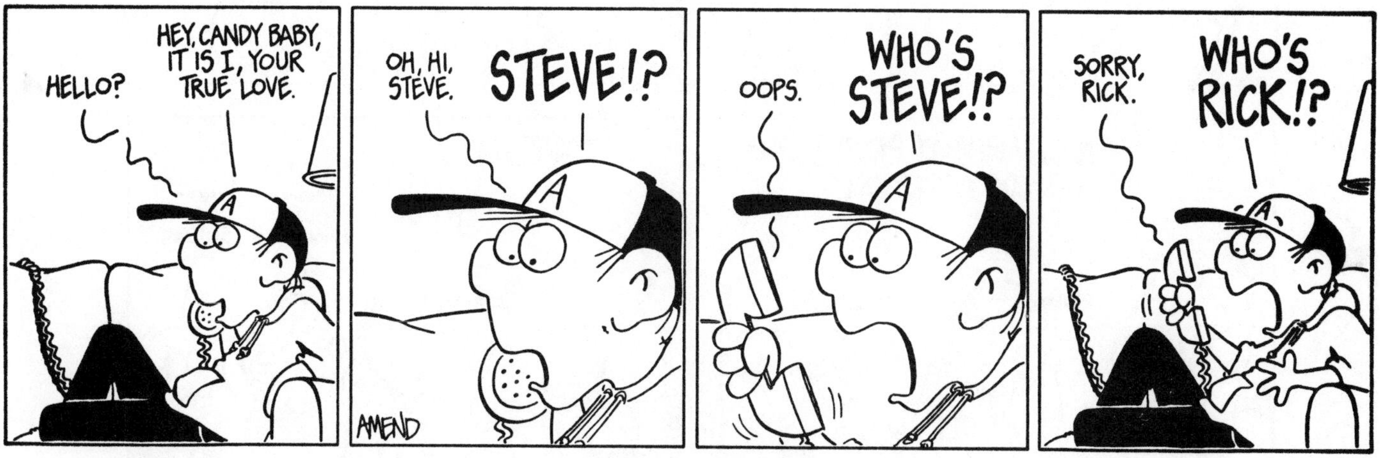
HELLO?
HEY, CANDY BABY, IT IS I, YOUR TRUE LOVE.
OH, HI, STEVE.
STEVE!?
AMEND
OOPS.
WHO'S STEVE!?
SORRY, RICK.
WHO'S RICK!?

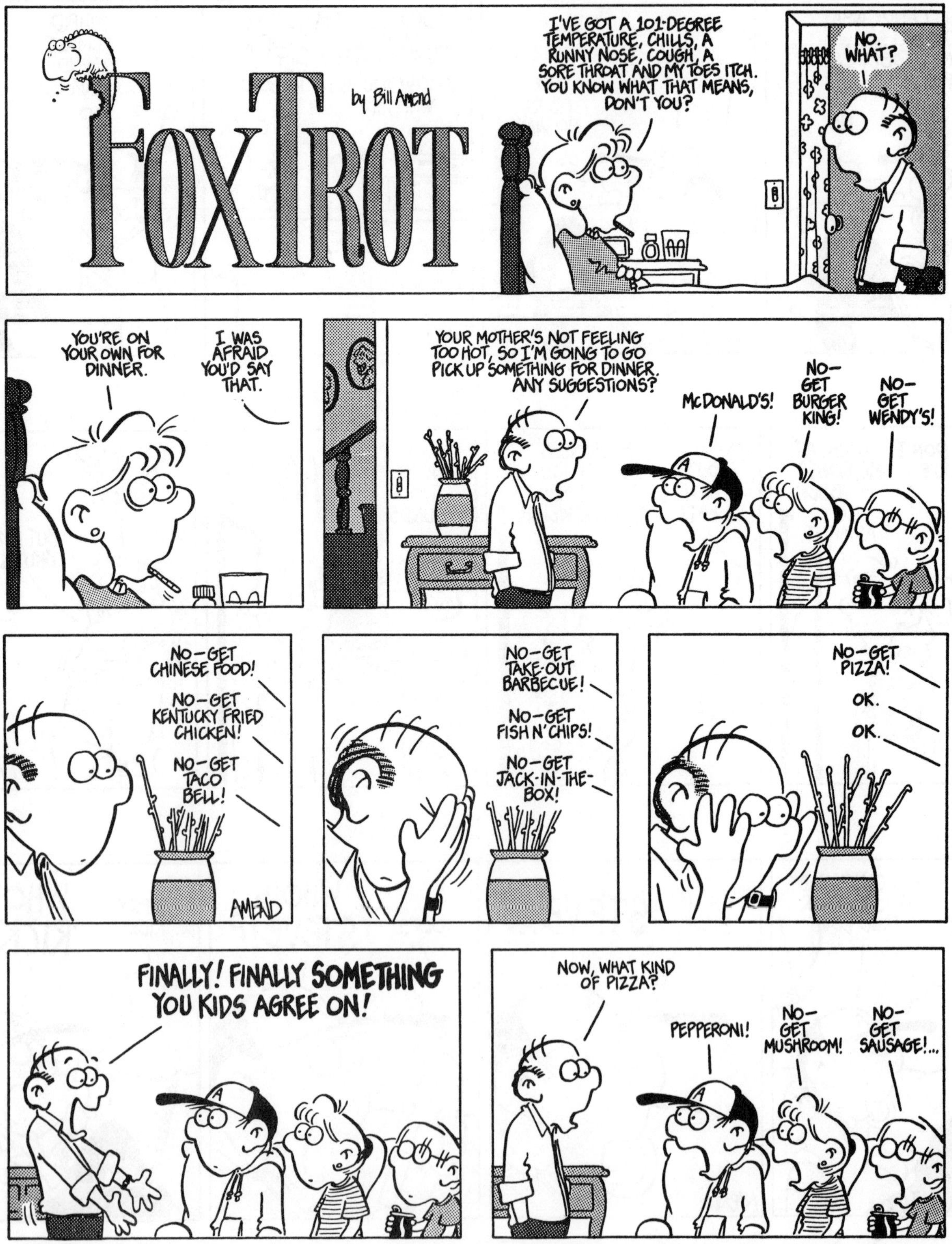

FoxTrot
by Bill Amend
I'VE GOT A 101-DEGREE TEMPERATURE, CHILLS, A RUNNY NOSE, COUGH, A SORE THROAT AND MY TOES ITCH. YOU KNOW WHAT THAT MEANS, DON'T YOU?
NO. WHAT?
YOU'RE ON YOUR OWN FOR DINNER.
I WAS AFRAID YOU'D SAY THAT.
YOUR MOTHER'S NOT FEELING TOO HOT, SO I'M GOING TO GO PICK UP SOMETHING FOR DINNER. ANY SUGGESTIONS?
McDONALD'S!
NO-GET BURGER KING!
NO-GET WENDY'S!
NO-GET CHINESE FOOD!
NO-GET KENTUCKY FRIED CHICKEN!
NO-GET TACO BELL!
AMEND
NO-GET TAKE-OUT BARBECUE!
NO-GET FISH N' CHIPS!
NO-GET JACK-IN-THE-BOX!
NO-GET PIZZA!
OK.
OK.
FINALLY! FINALLY SOMETHING YOU KIDS AGREE ON!
NOW, WHAT KIND OF PIZZA?
PEPPERONI!
NO-GET MUSHROOM!
NO-GET SAUSAGE!...

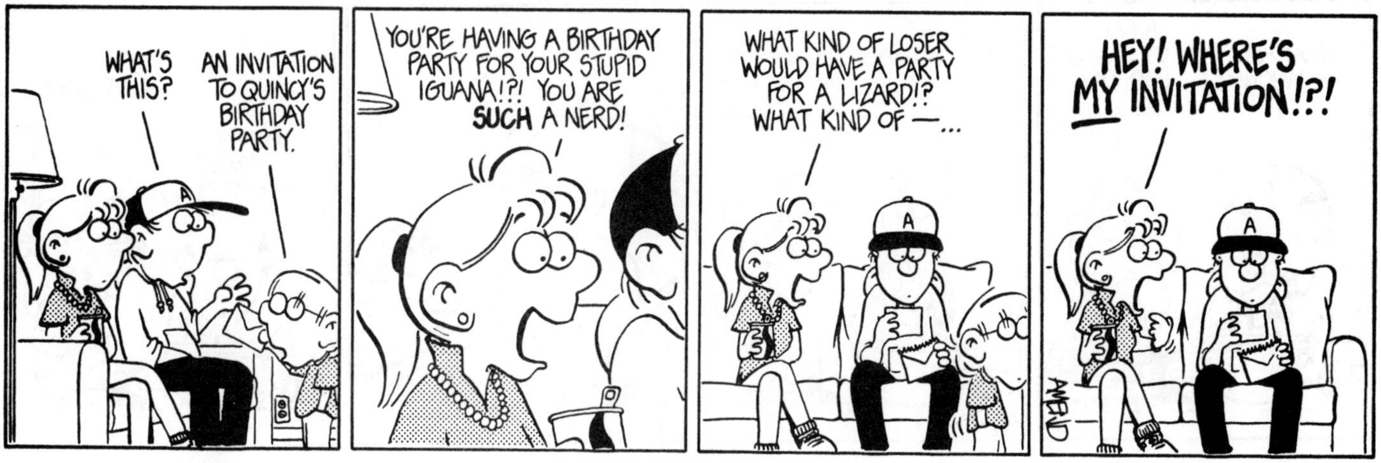
WHAT'S THIS?
AN INVITATION TO QUINCY'S BIRTHDAY PARTY.
YOU'RE HAVING A BIRTHDAY PARTY FOR YOUR STUPID IGUANA!?! YOU ARE **SUCH** A NERD!
WHAT KIND OF LOSER WOULD HAVE A PARTY FOR A LIZARD!? WHAT KIND OF —...
HEY! WHERE'S MY INVITATION!?!
AMEND

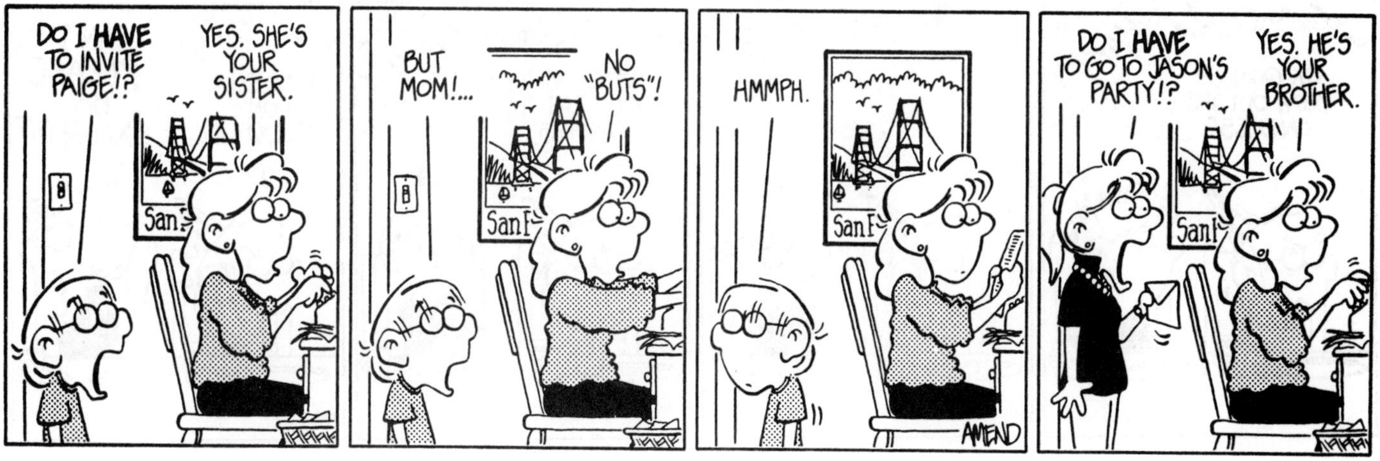
DO I **HAVE** TO INVITE PAIGE!?
YES. SHE'S YOUR SISTER.
San
BUT MOM!...
NO "BUTS"!
HMMPH.
AMEND
DO I **HAVE** TO GO TO JASON'S PARTY!?
YES. HE'S YOUR BROTHER.

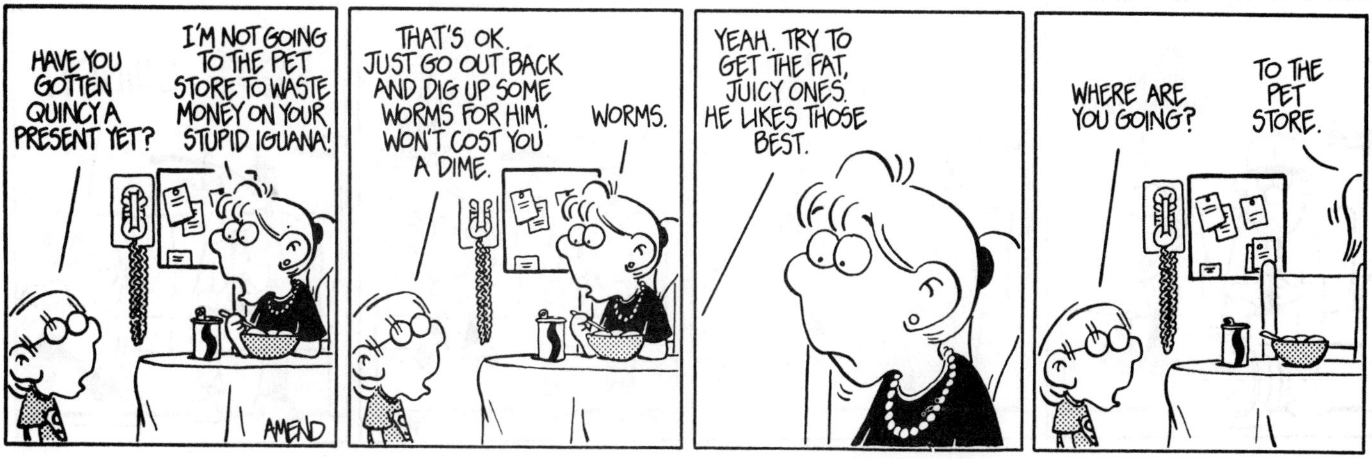
HAVE YOU GOTTEN QUINCY A PRESENT YET?
I'M NOT GOING TO THE PET STORE TO WASTE MONEY ON YOUR STUPID IGUANA!
AMEND
THAT'S OK. JUST GO OUT BACK AND DIG UP SOME WORMS FOR HIM. WON'T COST YOU A DIME.
WORMS.
YEAH. TRY TO GET THE FAT, JUICY ONES. HE LIKES THOSE BEST.
WHERE ARE YOU GOING?
TO THE PET STORE.

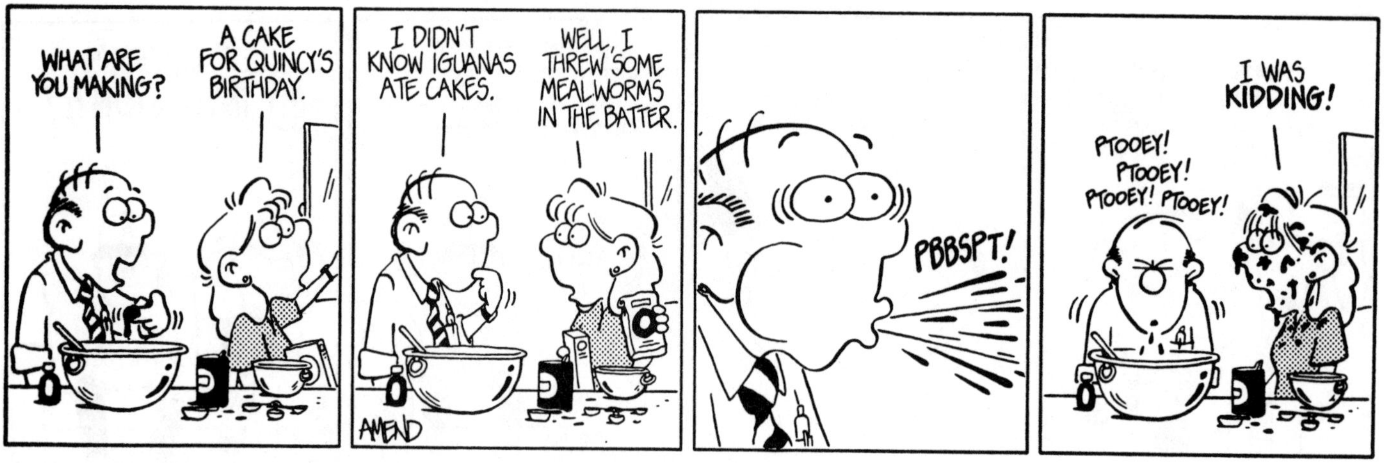
WHAT ARE YOU MAKING?
A CAKE FOR QUINCY'S BIRTHDAY.
I DIDN'T KNOW IGUANAS ATE CAKES.
WELL, I THREW SOME MEALWORMS IN THE BATTER.
AMEND
PBBSPT!
PTOOEY! PTOOEY! PTOOEY! PTOOEY!
I WAS KIDDING!

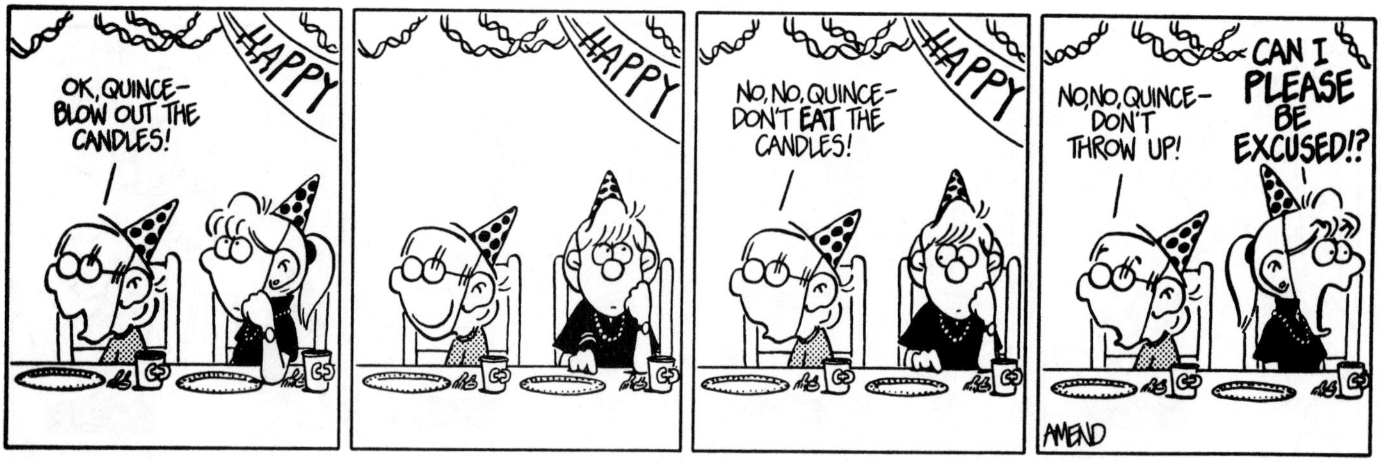
HAPPY
OK, QUINCE– BLOW OUT THE CANDLES!
HAPPY
HAPPY
NO, NO, QUINCE– DON'T EAT THE CANDLES!
NO, NO, QUINCE– DON'T THROW UP!
CAN I PLEASE BE EXCUSED!?
AMEND

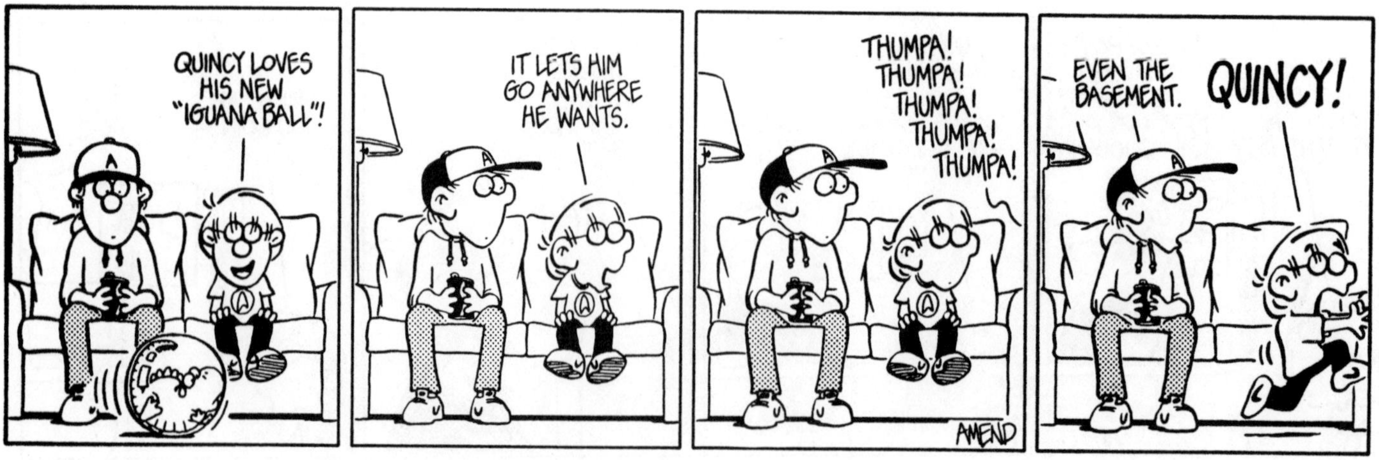
QUINCY LOVES HIS NEW "IGUANA BALL"!
IT LETS HIM GO ANYWHERE HE WANTS.
THUMPA! THUMPA! THUMPA! THUMPA! THUMPA!
AMEND
EVEN THE BASEMENT.
QUINCY!

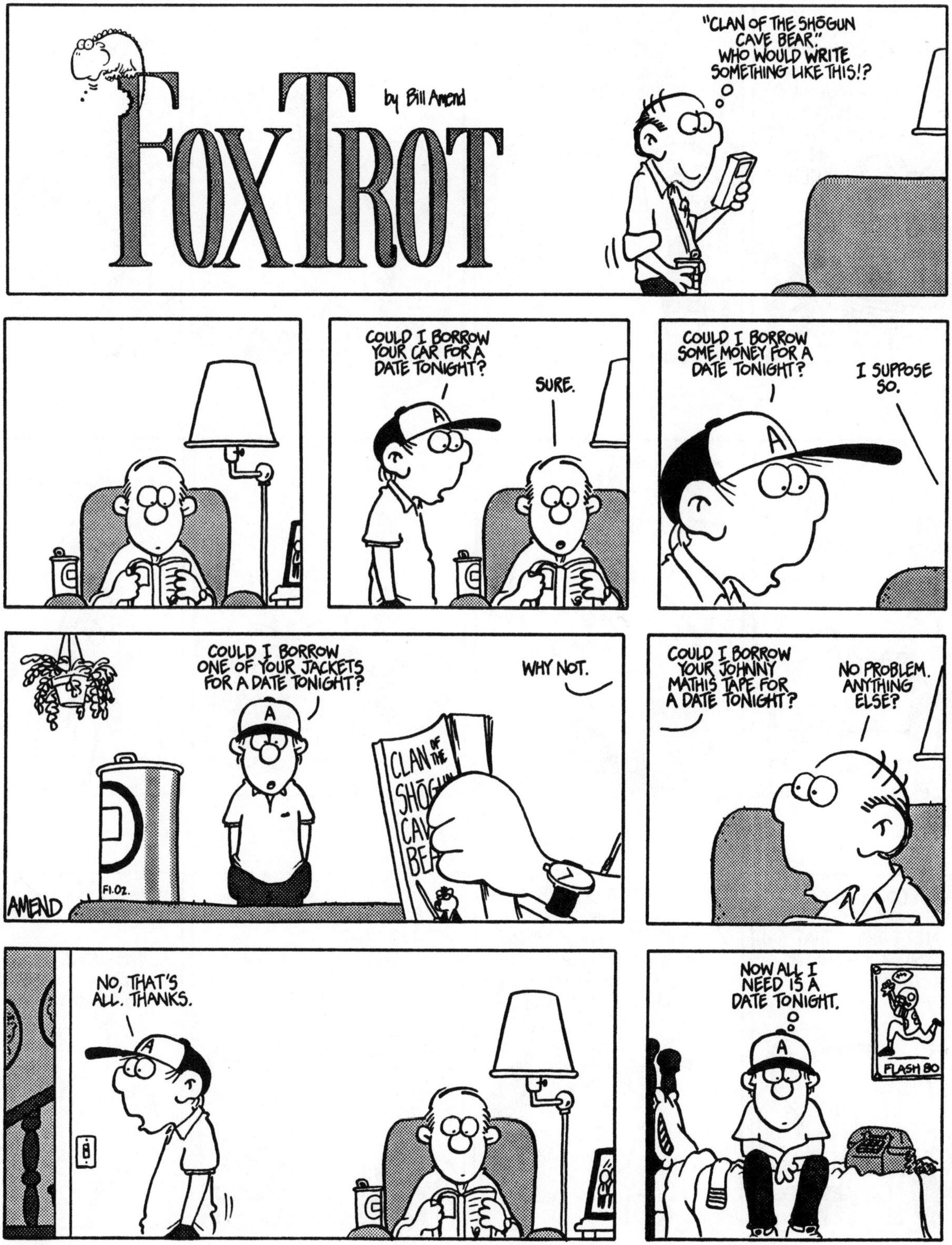
FoxTrot
by Bill Amend
"CLAN OF THE SHŌGUN CAVE BEAR." WHO WOULD WRITE SOMETHING LIKE THIS!?
COULD I BORROW YOUR CAR FOR A DATE TONIGHT?
SURE.
COULD I BORROW SOME MONEY FOR A DATE TONIGHT?
I SUPPOSE SO.
COULD I BORROW ONE OF YOUR JACKETS FOR A DATE TONIGHT?
WHY NOT.
CLAN OF THE SHŌGUN CAVE BEAR
AMEND
COULD I BORROW YOUR JOHNNY MATHIS TAPE FOR A DATE TONIGHT?
NO PROBLEM. ANYTHING ELSE?
NO, THAT'S ALL. THANKS.
NOW ALL I NEED IS A DATE TONIGHT.
FLASH 80

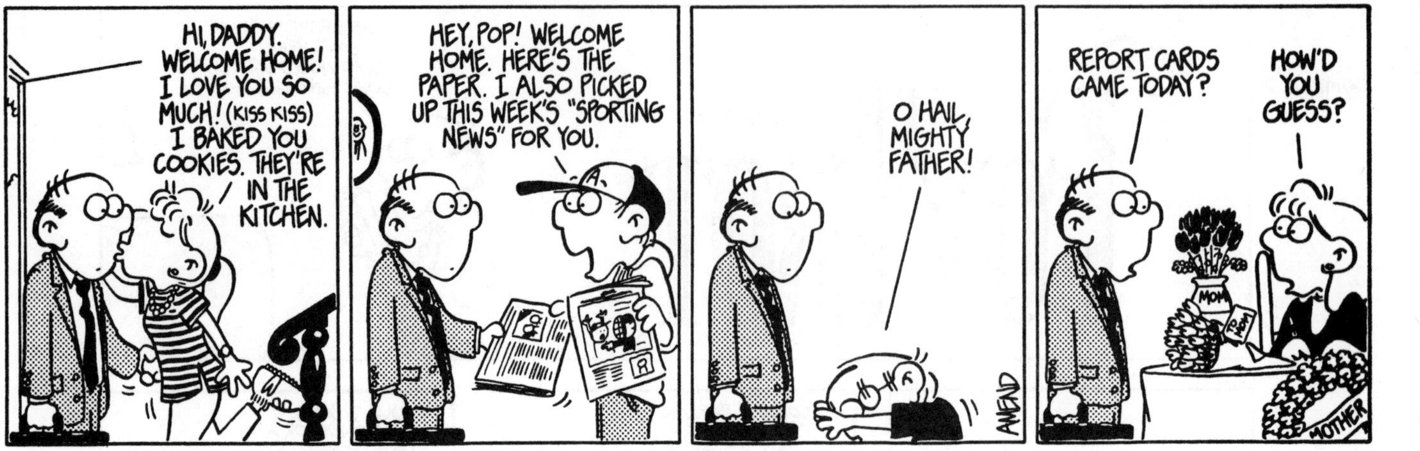
HI, DADDY. WELCOME HOME! I LOVE YOU SO MUCH! (KISS KISS) I BAKED YOU COOKIES. THEY'RE IN THE KITCHEN.
HEY, POP! WELCOME HOME. HERE'S THE PAPER. I ALSO PICKED UP THIS WEEK'S "SPORTING NEWS" FOR YOU.
O HAIL, MIGHTY FATHER!
AMEND
REPORT CARDS CAME TODAY?
HOW'D YOU GUESS?
MOM
MOTHER

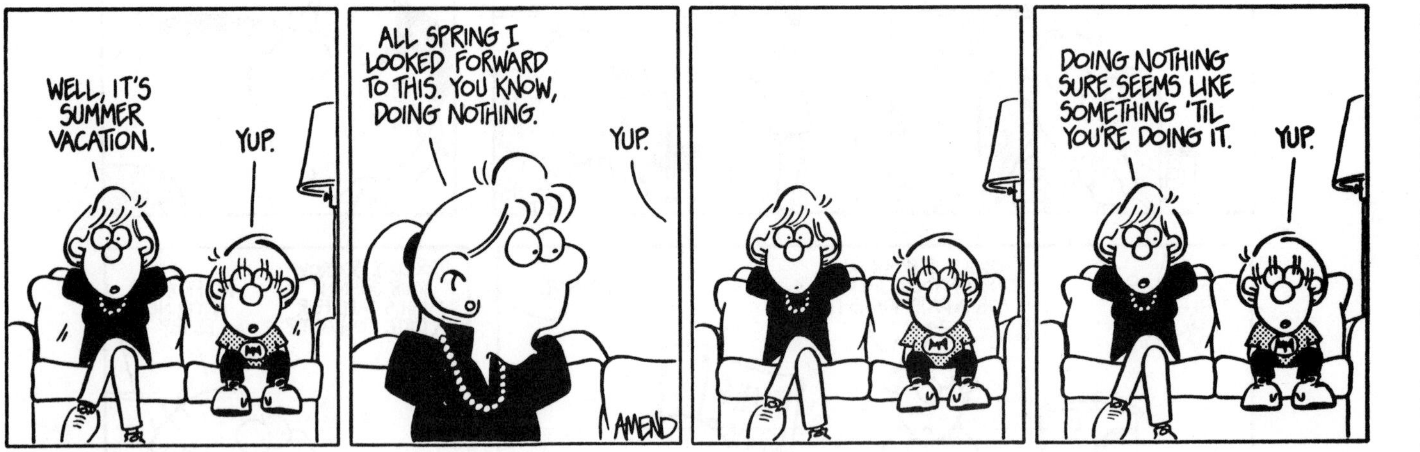
WELL, IT'S SUMMER VACATION.
YUP.
ALL SPRING I LOOKED FORWARD TO THIS. YOU KNOW, DOING NOTHING.
YUP.
AMEND
DOING NOTHING SURE SEEMS LIKE SOMETHING 'TIL YOU'RE DOING IT.
YUP.

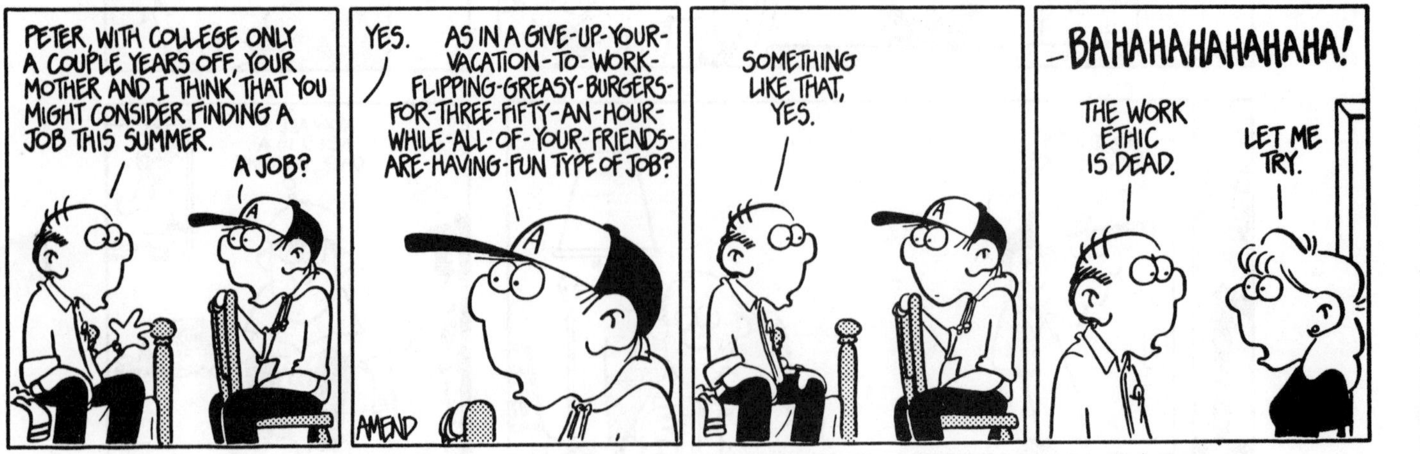
PETER, WITH COLLEGE ONLY A COUPLE YEARS OFF, YOUR MOTHER AND I THINK THAT YOU MIGHT CONSIDER FINDING A JOB THIS SUMMER.
A JOB?
YES.
AS IN A GIVE-UP-YOUR-VACATION-TO-WORK-FLIPPING-GREASY-BURGERS-FOR-THREE-FIFTY-AN-HOUR-WHILE-ALL-OF-YOUR-FRIENDS-ARE-HAVING-FUN TYPE OF JOB?
AMEND
SOMETHING LIKE THAT, YES.
BAHAHAHAHAHAHA!
THE WORK ETHIC IS DEAD.
LET ME TRY.

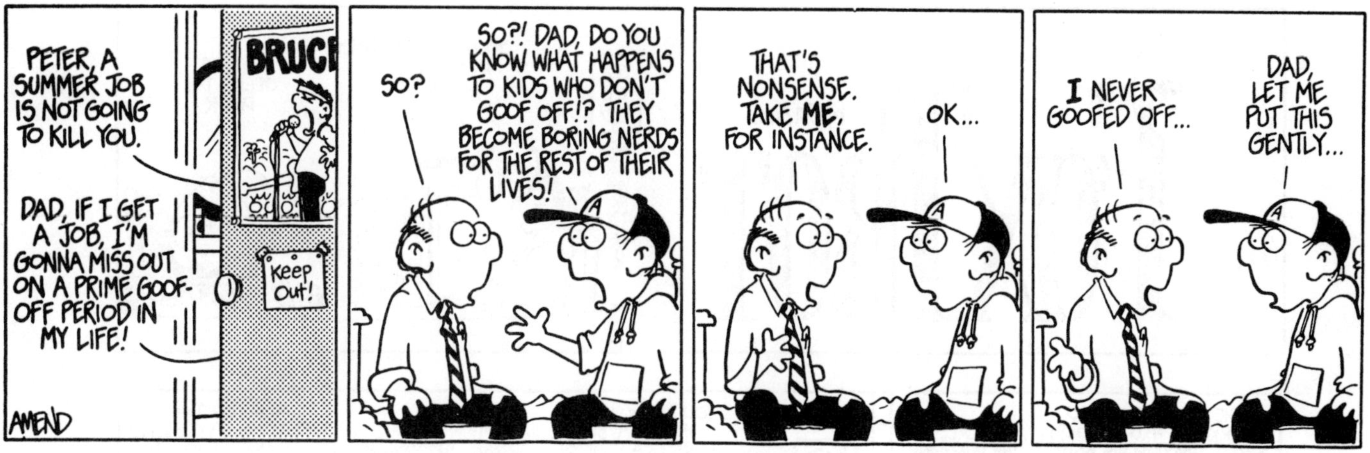
PETER, A SUMMER JOB IS NOT GOING TO KILL YOU.
DAD, IF I GET A JOB, I'M GONNA MISS OUT ON A PRIME GOOF-OFF PERIOD IN MY LIFE!
Keep Out!
AMEND
SO?
SO?! DAD, DO YOU KNOW WHAT HAPPENS TO KIDS WHO DON'T GOOF OFF!? THEY BECOME BORING NERDS FOR THE REST OF THEIR LIVES!
THAT'S NONSENSE. TAKE **ME**, FOR INSTANCE.
OK...
I NEVER GOOFED OFF...
DAD, LET ME PUT THIS GENTLY...

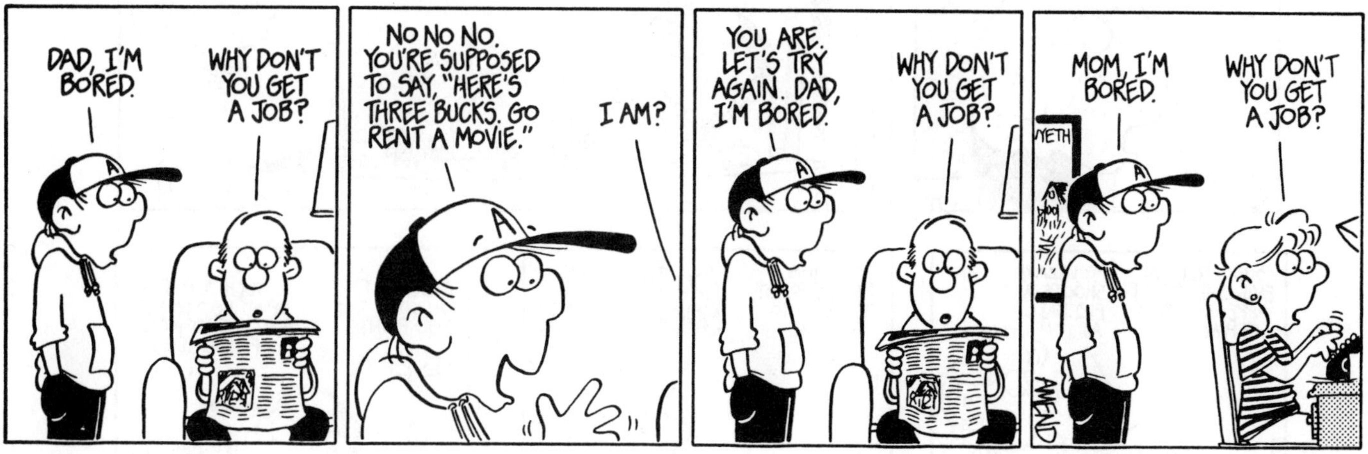
DAD, I'M BORED.
WHY DON'T YOU GET A JOB?
NO NO NO. YOU'RE SUPPOSED TO SAY, "HERE'S THREE BUCKS. GO RENT A MOVIE."
I AM?
YOU ARE. LET'S TRY AGAIN. DAD, I'M BORED.
WHY DON'T YOU GET A JOB?
MOM, I'M BORED.
WHY DON'T YOU GET A JOB?
AMEND

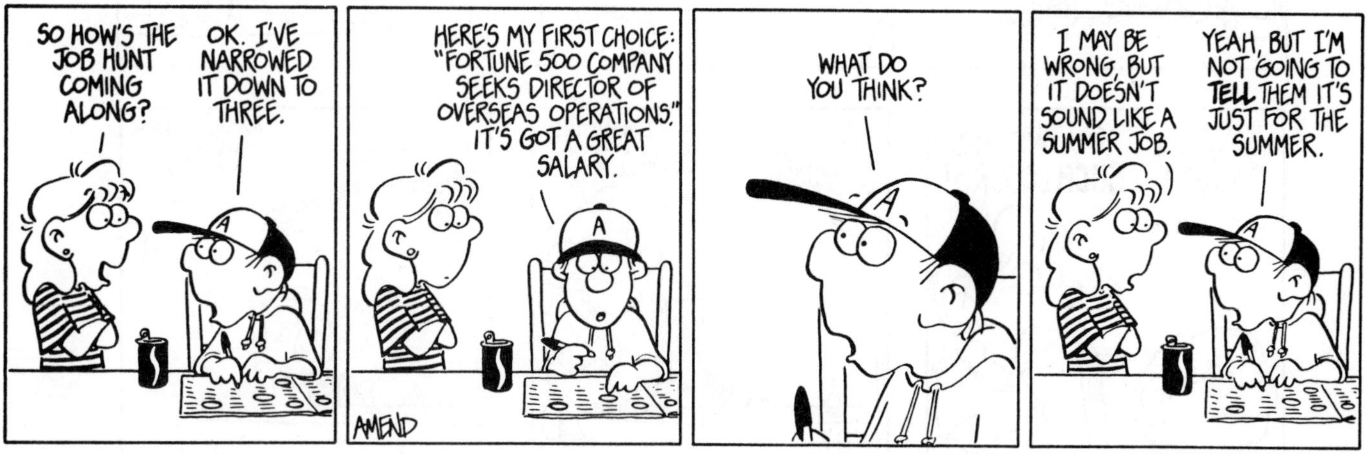
SO HOW'S THE JOB HUNT COMING ALONG?
OK. I'VE NARROWED IT DOWN TO THREE.
HERE'S MY FIRST CHOICE: "FORTUNE 500 COMPANY SEEKS DIRECTOR OF OVERSEAS OPERATIONS." IT'S GOT A GREAT SALARY.
AMEND
WHAT DO YOU THINK?
I MAY BE WRONG, BUT IT DOESN'T SOUND LIKE A SUMMER JOB.
YEAH, BUT I'M NOT GOING TO **TELL** THEM IT'S JUST FOR THE SUMMER.

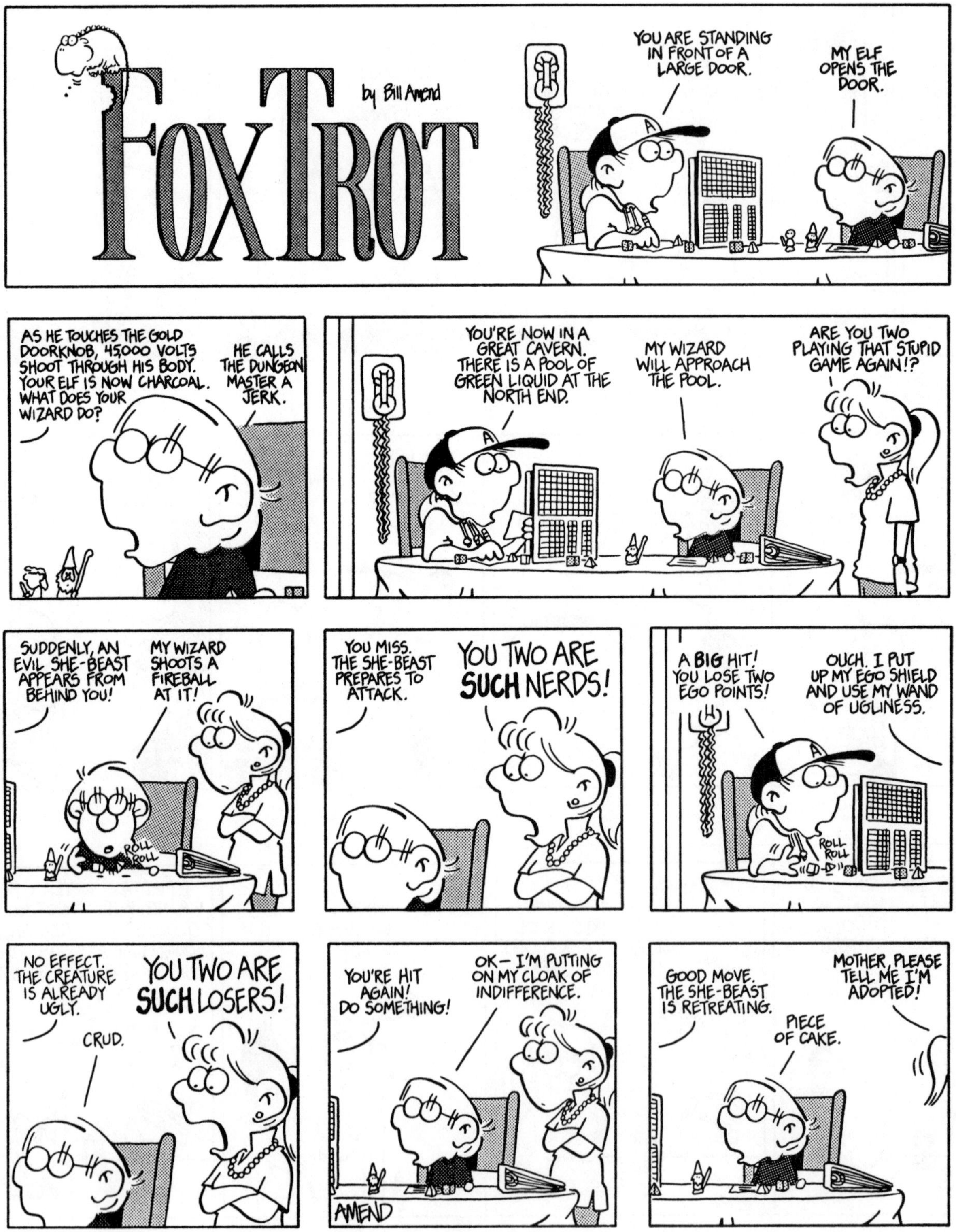
FOXTROT
by Bill Amend
YOU ARE STANDING IN FRONT OF A LARGE DOOR.
MY ELF OPENS THE DOOR.
AS HE TOUCHES THE GOLD DOORKNOB, 45,000 VOLTS SHOOT THROUGH HIS BODY. YOUR ELF IS NOW CHARCOAL. WHAT DOES YOUR WIZARD DO?
HE CALLS THE DUNGEON MASTER A JERK.
YOU'RE NOW IN A GREAT CAVERN. THERE IS A POOL OF GREEN LIQUID AT THE NORTH END.
MY WIZARD WILL APPROACH THE POOL.
ARE YOU TWO PLAYING THAT STUPID GAME AGAIN!?
SUDDENLY, AN EVIL SHE-BEAST APPEARS FROM BEHIND YOU!
MY WIZARD SHOOTS A FIREBALL AT IT!
ROLL ROLL
YOU MISS. THE SHE-BEAST PREPARES TO ATTACK.
YOU TWO ARE SUCH NERDS!
A BIG HIT! YOU LOSE TWO EGO POINTS!
OUCH. I PUT UP MY EGO SHIELD AND USE MY WAND OF UGLINESS.
ROLL ROLL
NO EFFECT. THE CREATURE IS ALREADY UGLY.
CRUD.
YOU TWO ARE SUCH LOSERS!
YOU'RE HIT AGAIN! DO SOMETHING!
OK— I'M PUTTING ON MY CLOAK OF INDIFFERENCE.
AMEND
GOOD MOVE. THE SHE-BEAST IS RETREATING.
PIECE OF CAKE.
MOTHER, PLEASE TELL ME I'M ADOPTED!

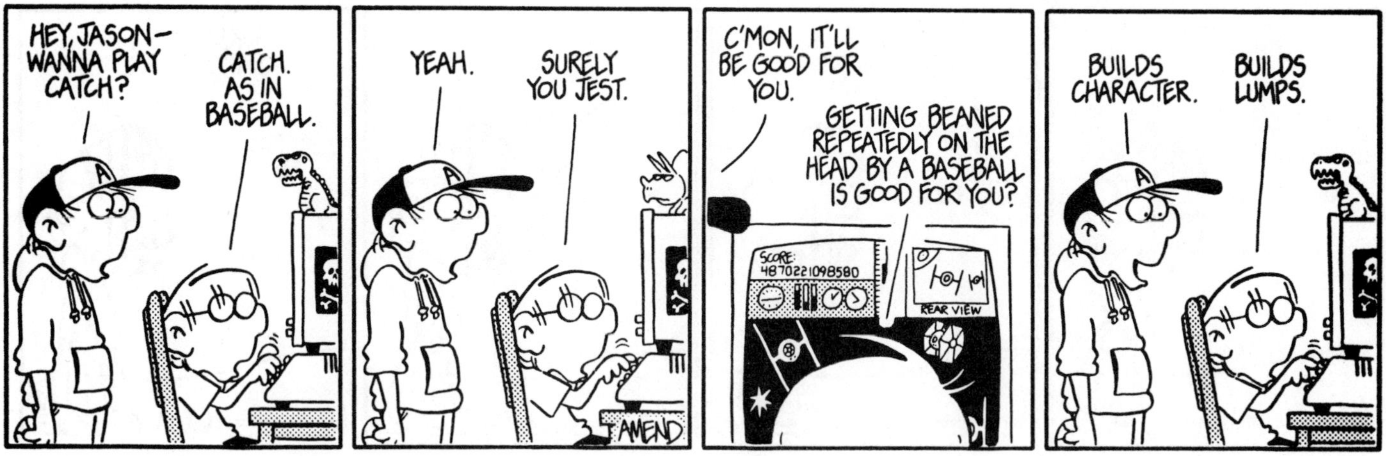
HEY, JASON—WANNA PLAY CATCH?
CATCH. AS IN BASEBALL.
YEAH.
SURELY YOU JEST.
AMEND
C'MON, IT'LL BE GOOD FOR YOU.
GETTING BEANED REPEATEDLY ON THE HEAD BY A BASEBALL IS GOOD FOR YOU?
SCORE: 4870221098580
REAR VIEW
BUILDS CHARACTER.
BUILDS LUMPS.

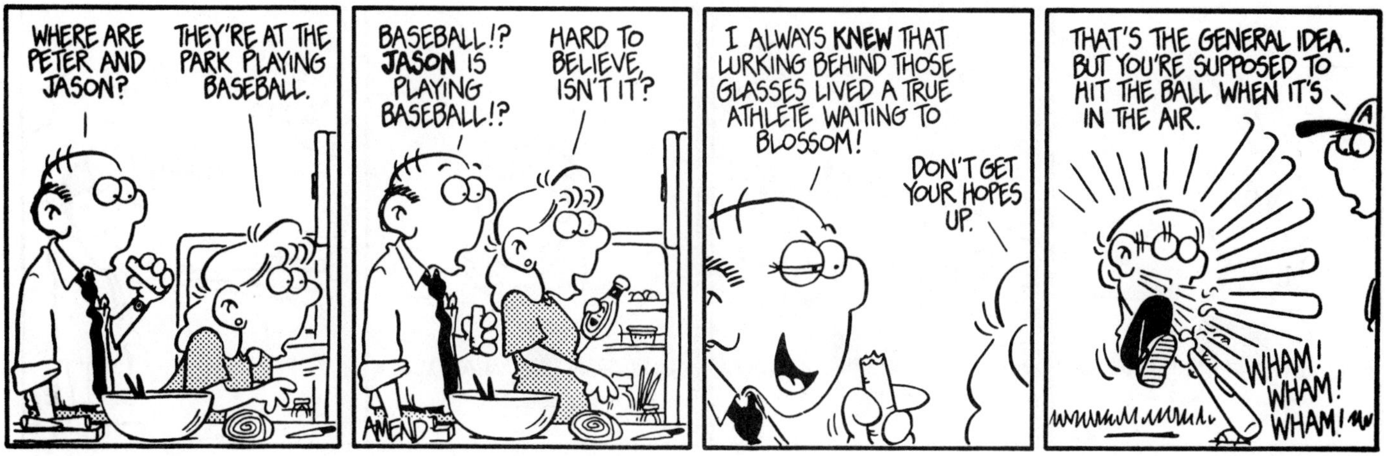
WHERE ARE PETER AND JASON?
THEY'RE AT THE PARK PLAYING BASEBALL.
BASEBALL!? **JASON** IS PLAYING BASEBALL!?
HARD TO BELIEVE, ISN'T IT?
AMEND
I ALWAYS **KNEW** THAT LURKING BEHIND THOSE GLASSES LIVED A TRUE ATHLETE WAITING TO BLOSSOM!
DON'T GET YOUR HOPES UP.
THAT'S THE GENERAL IDEA. BUT YOU'RE SUPPOSED TO HIT THE BALL WHEN IT'S IN THE AIR.
WHAM! WHAM! WHAM!

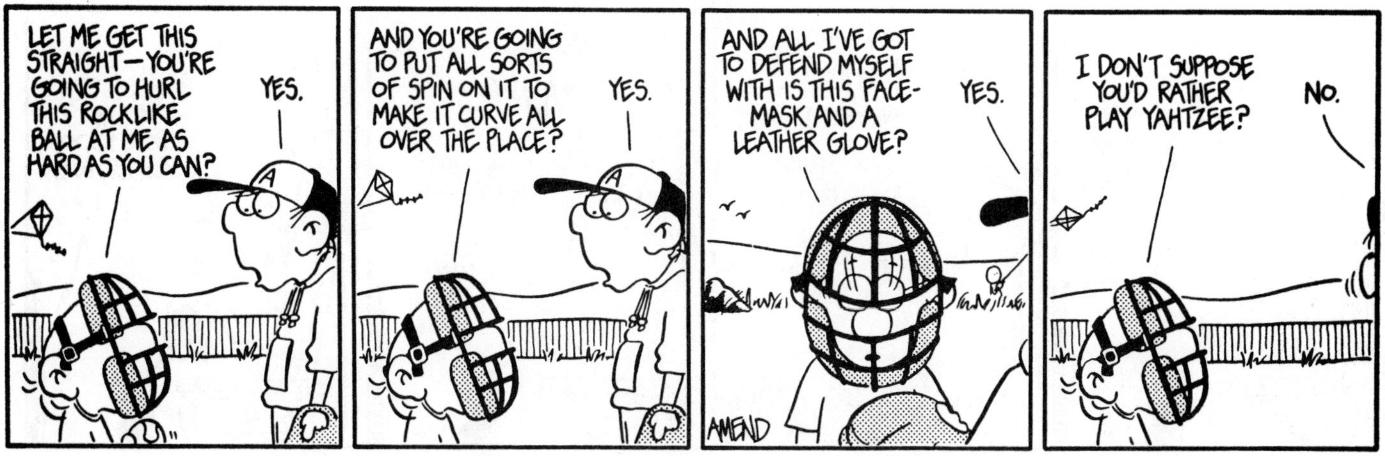
LET ME GET THIS STRAIGHT—YOU'RE GOING TO HURL THIS ROCKLIKE BALL AT ME AS HARD AS YOU CAN?
YES.
AND YOU'RE GOING TO PUT ALL SORTS OF SPIN ON IT TO MAKE IT CURVE ALL OVER THE PLACE?
YES.
AND ALL I'VE GOT TO DEFEND MYSELF WITH IS THIS FACE-MASK AND A LEATHER GLOVE?
YES.
AMEND
I DON'T SUPPOSE YOU'D RATHER PLAY YAHTZEE?
NO.

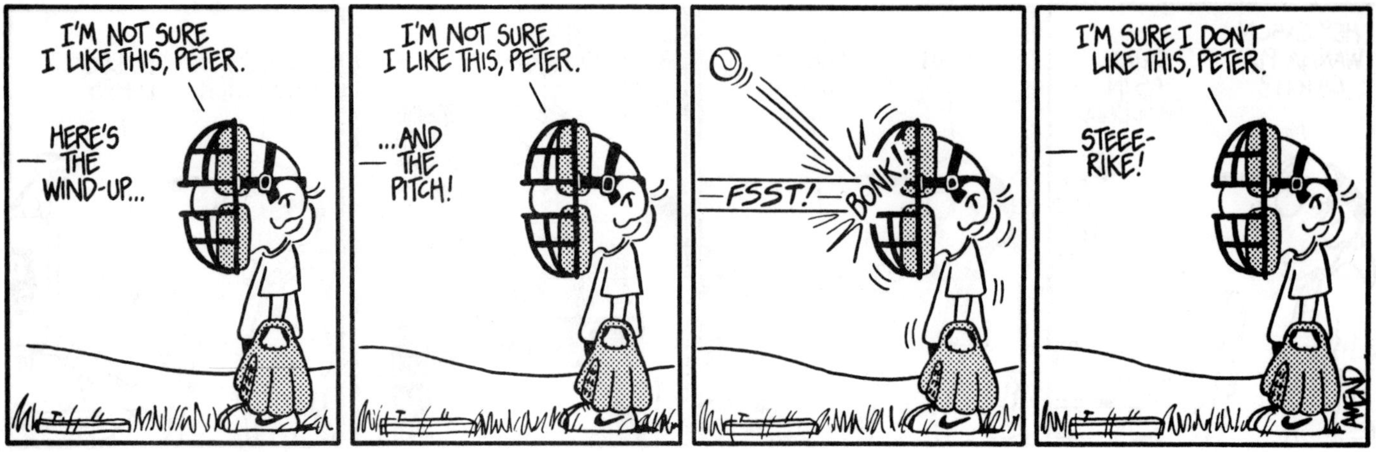
I'M NOT SURE I LIKE THIS, PETER.
HERE'S THE WIND-UP...
I'M NOT SURE I LIKE THIS, PETER.
...AND THE PITCH!
FSST!
BONK!
I'M SURE I DON'T LIKE THIS, PETER.
STEEE-RIKE!
AMEND

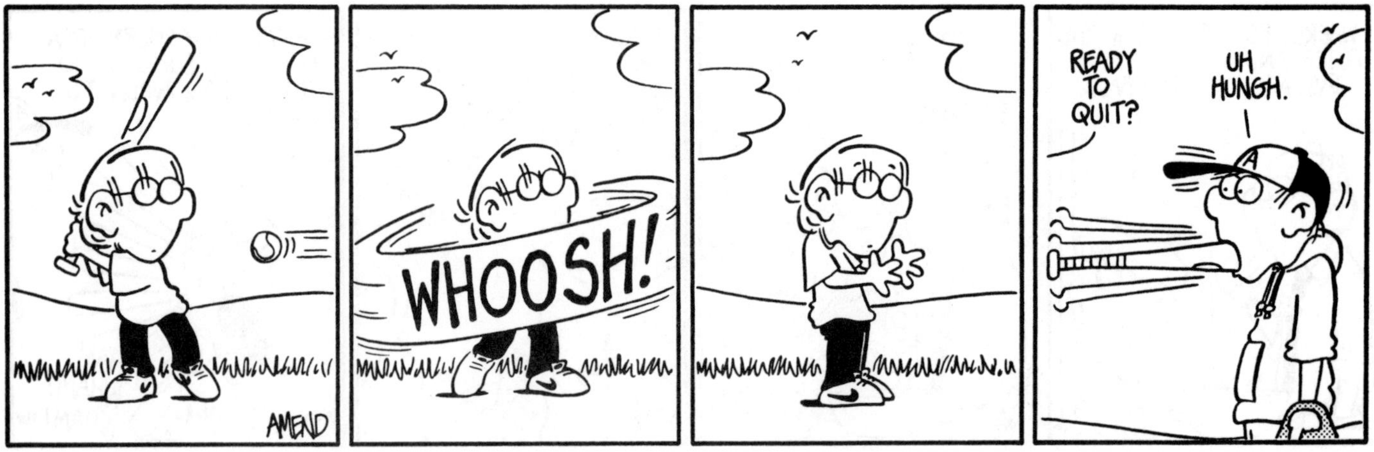
AMEND
WHOOSH!
READY TO QUIT?
UH HUNGH.

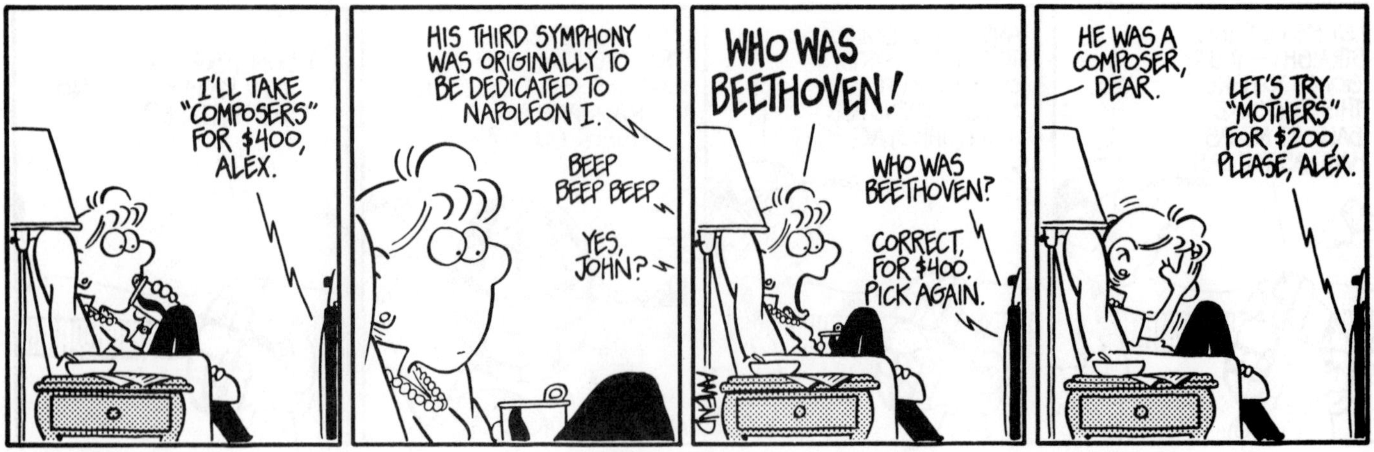
I'LL TAKE "COMPOSERS" FOR $400, ALEX.
HIS THIRD SYMPHONY WAS ORIGINALLY TO BE DEDICATED TO NAPOLEON I.
BEEP BEEP BEEP
YES, JOHN?
WHO WAS BEETHOVEN!
WHO WAS BEETHOVEN?
CORRECT, FOR $400. PICK AGAIN.
AMEND
HE WAS A COMPOSER, DEAR.
LET'S TRY "MOTHERS" FOR $200, PLEASE, ALEX.

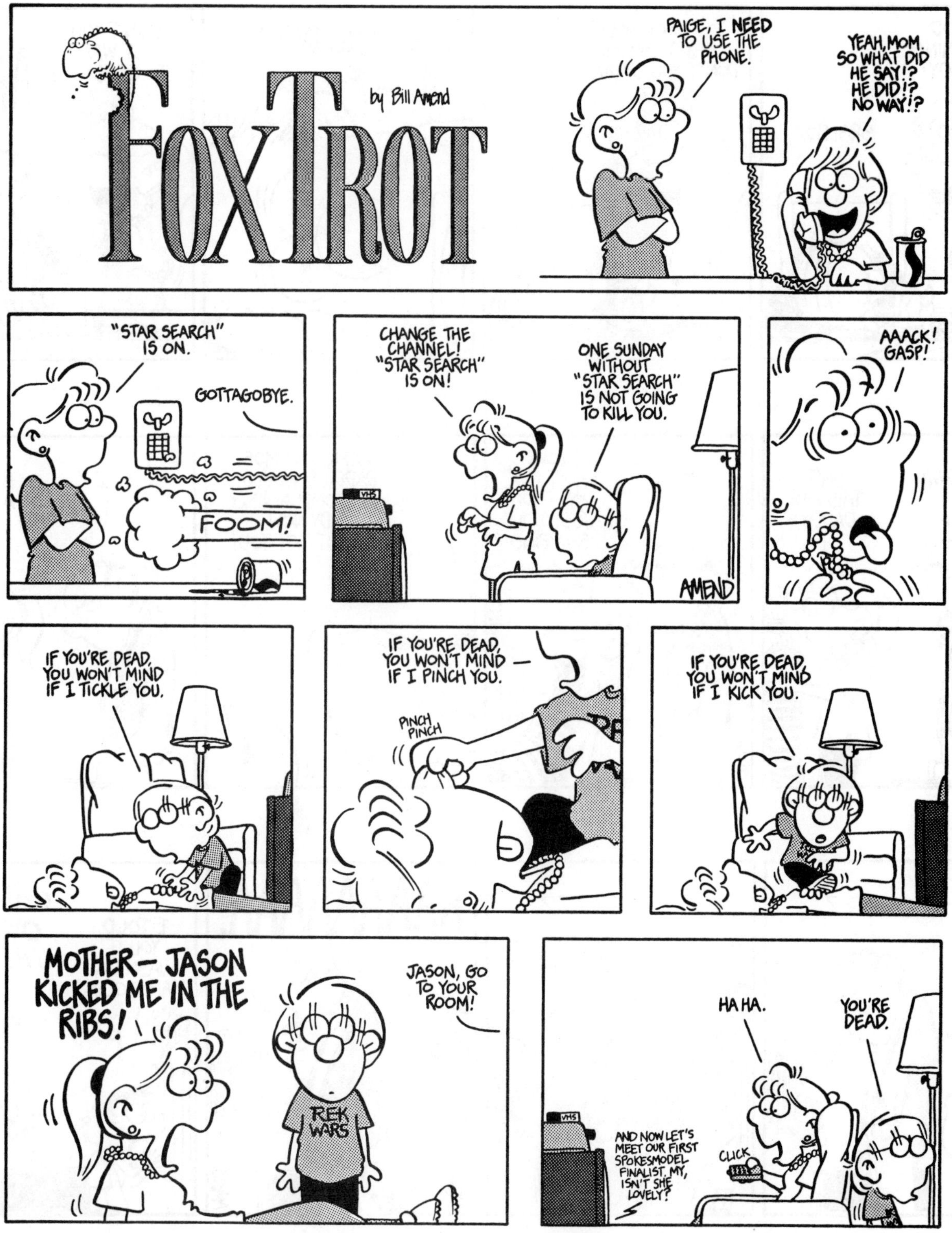
FoxTrot
by Bill Amend
PAIGE, I NEED TO USE THE PHONE.
YEAH, MOM. SO WHAT DID HE SAY!? HE DID!? NO WAY!?
"STAR SEARCH" IS ON.
GOTTAGOBYE.
FOOM!
CHANGE THE CHANNEL! "STAR SEARCH" IS ON!
ONE SUNDAY WITHOUT "STAR SEARCH" IS NOT GOING TO KILL YOU.
AMEND
AAACK! GASP!
IF YOU'RE DEAD, YOU WON'T MIND IF I TICKLE YOU.
IF YOU'RE DEAD, YOU WON'T MIND IF I PINCH YOU.
PINCH PINCH
IF YOU'RE DEAD YOU WON'T MIND IF I KICK YOU.
MOTHER– JASON KICKED ME IN THE RIBS!
JASON, GO TO YOUR ROOM!
REK WARS
HA HA.
YOU'RE DEAD.
AND NOW LET'S MEET OUR FIRST SPOKESMODEL FINALIST. MY, ISN'T SHE LOVELY?
CLICK

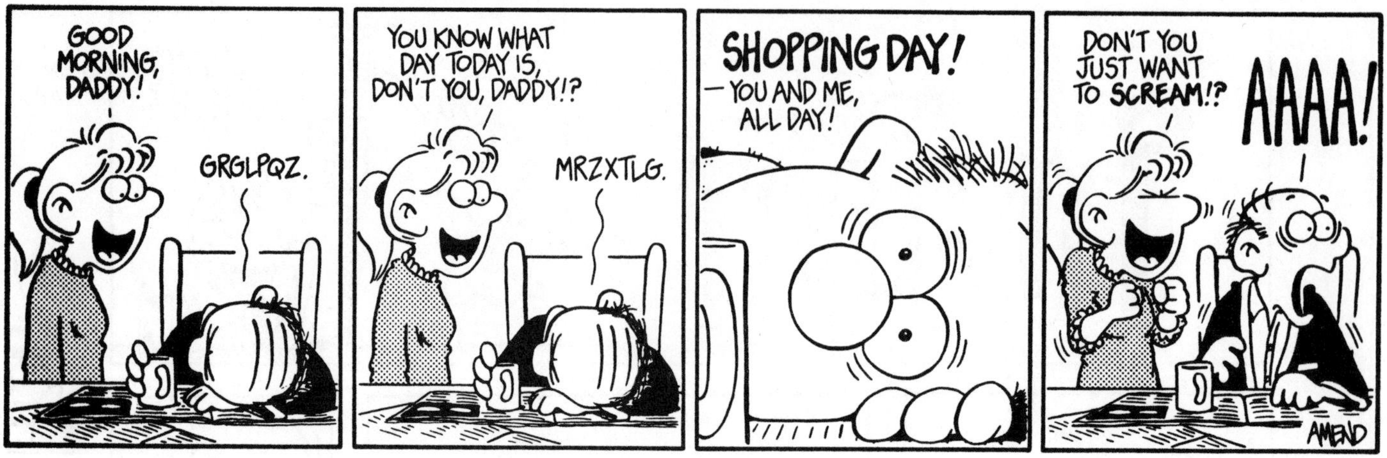
GOOD MORNING, DADDY!
GRGLPQZ.
YOU KNOW WHAT DAY TODAY IS, DON'T YOU, DADDY!?
MRZXTLG.
SHOPPING DAY!
— YOU AND ME, ALL DAY!
DON'T YOU JUST WANT TO SCREAM!?
AAAA!
AMEND

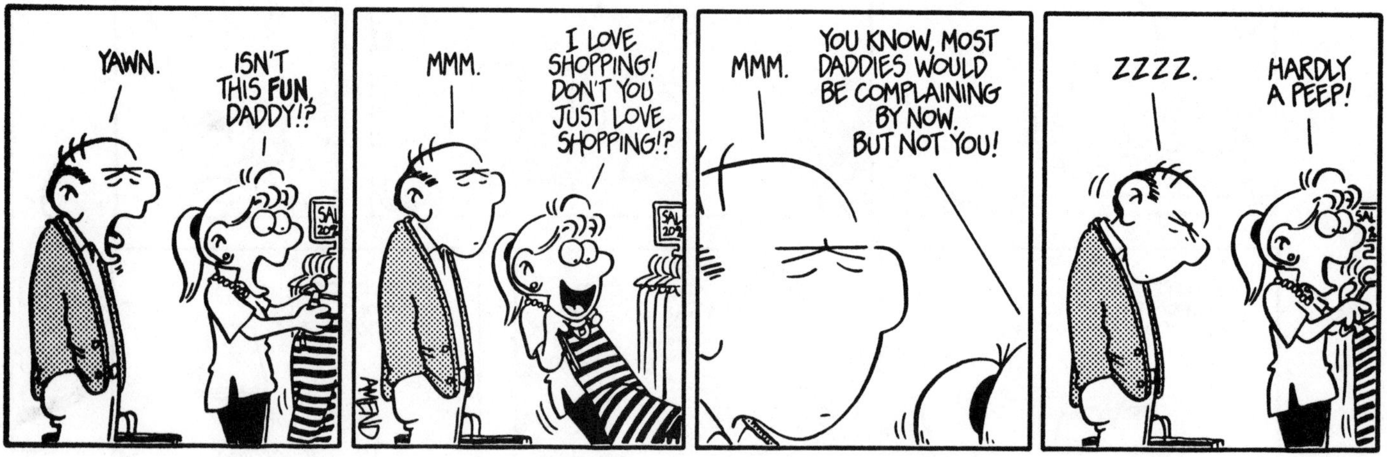
YAWN.
ISN'T THIS FUN, DADDY!?
MMM.
I LOVE SHOPPING! DON'T YOU JUST LOVE SHOPPING!?
AMEND
MMM.
YOU KNOW, MOST DADDIES WOULD BE COMPLAINING BY NOW. BUT NOT YOU!
ZZZZ.
HARDLY A PEEP!

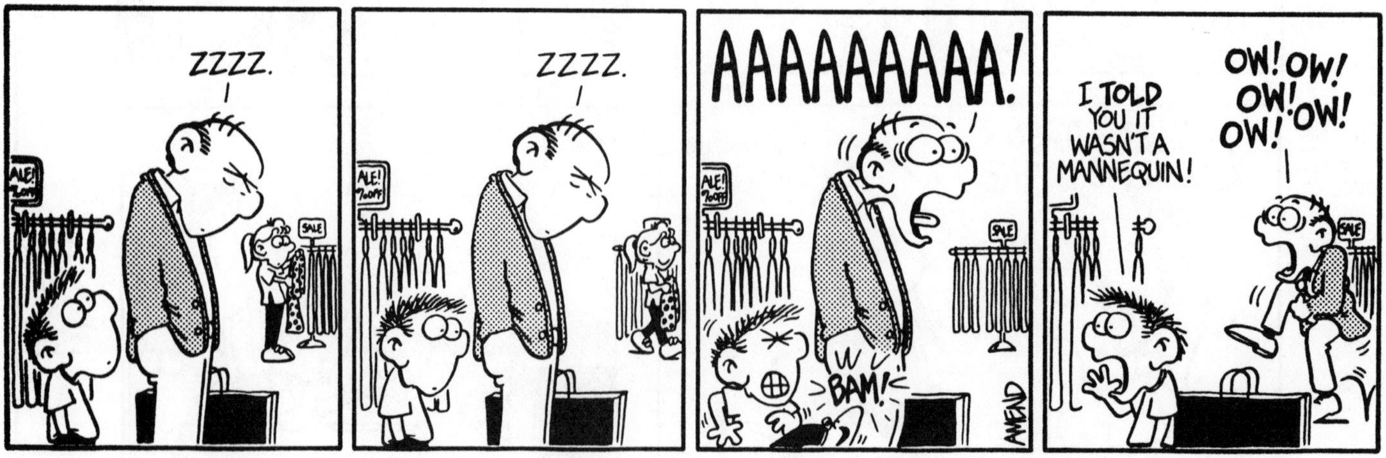
ZZZZ.
ZZZZ.
AAAAAAAAA!
BAM!
AMEND
I TOLD YOU IT WASN'T A MANNEQUIN!
OW! OW! OW! OW! OW!

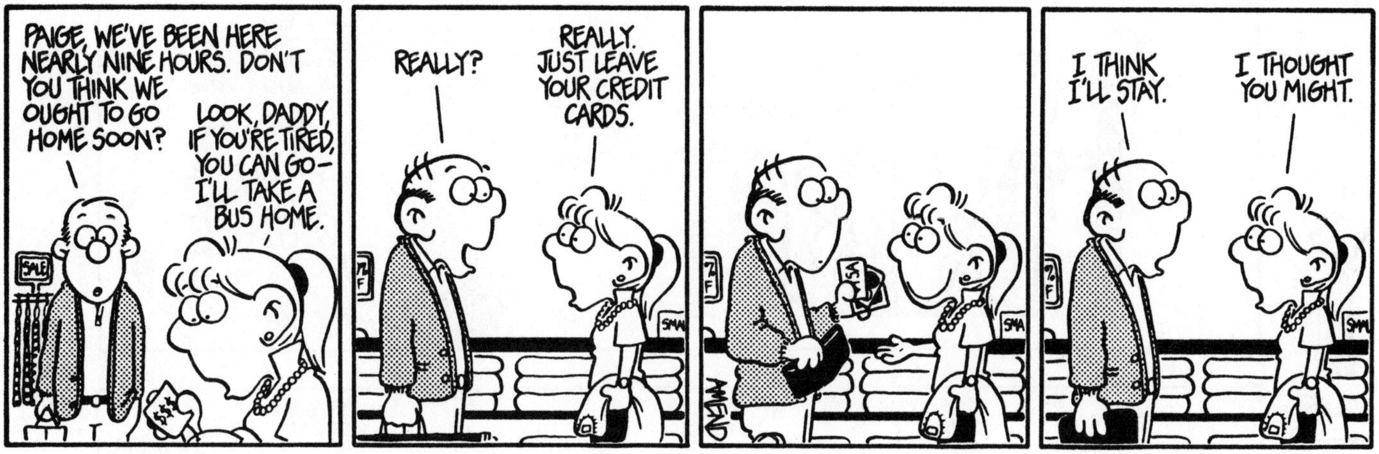
PAIGE, WE'VE BEEN HERE NEARLY NINE HOURS. DON'T YOU THINK WE OUGHT TO GO HOME SOON?
LOOK, DADDY, IF YOU'RE TIRED, YOU CAN GO– I'LL TAKE A BUS HOME.
SALE
REALLY?
REALLY. JUST LEAVE YOUR CREDIT CARDS.
I THINK I'LL STAY.
I THOUGHT YOU MIGHT.
AMEND

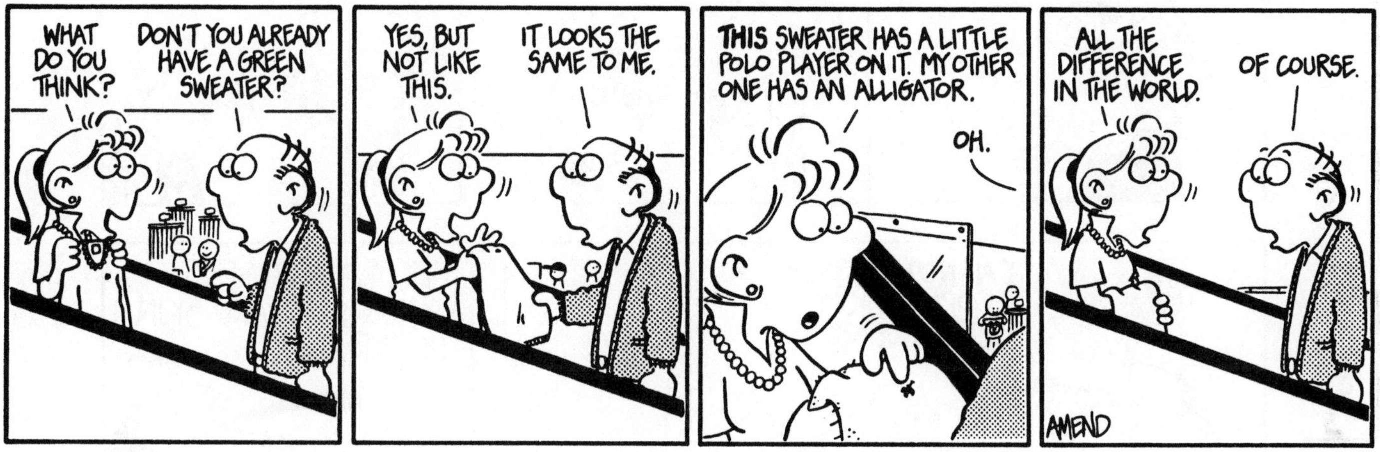
WHAT DO YOU THINK?
DON'T YOU ALREADY HAVE A GREEN SWEATER?
YES, BUT NOT LIKE THIS.
IT LOOKS THE SAME TO ME.
THIS SWEATER HAS A LITTLE POLO PLAYER ON IT. MY OTHER ONE HAS AN ALLIGATOR.
OH.
ALL THE DIFFERENCE IN THE WORLD.
OF COURSE.
AMEND

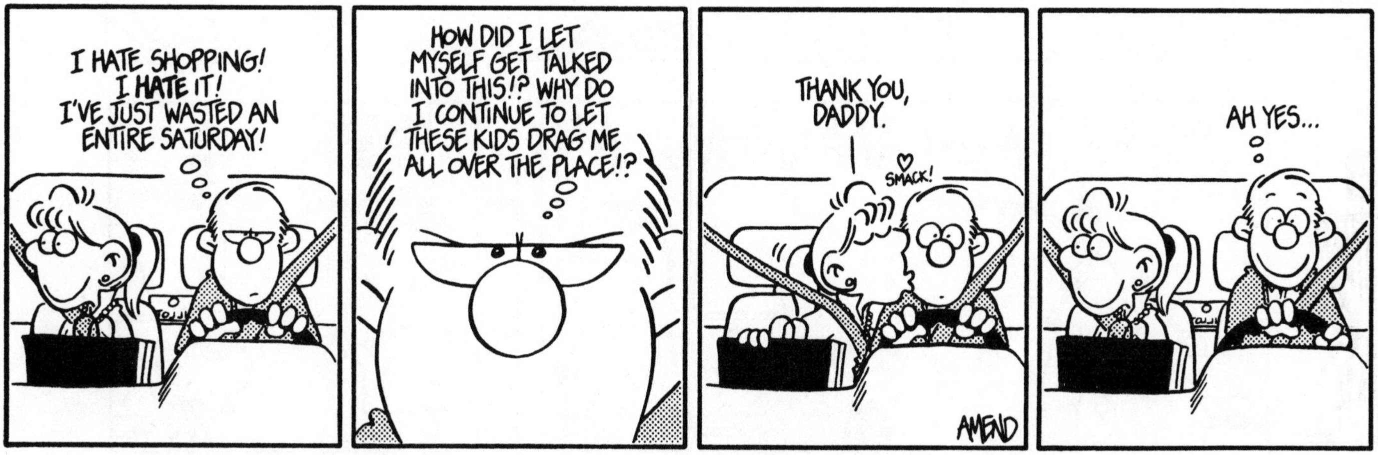
I HATE SHOPPING! I HATE IT! I'VE JUST WASTED AN ENTIRE SATURDAY!
HOW DID I LET MYSELF GET TALKED INTO THIS!? WHY DO I CONTINUE TO LET THESE KIDS DRAG ME ALL OVER THE PLACE!?
THANK YOU, DADDY.
SMACK!
AMEND
AH YES...

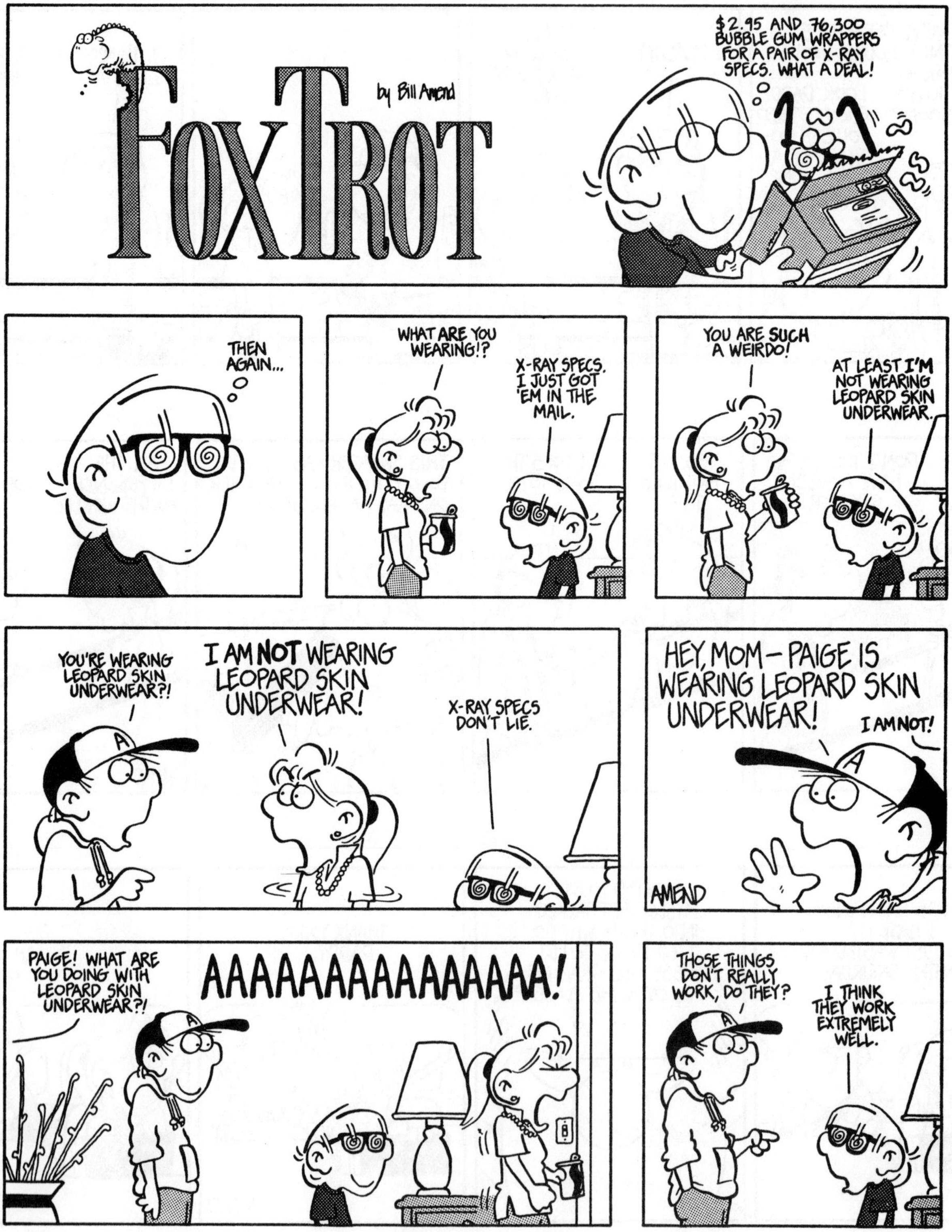
FoxTrot
by Bill Amend
$2.95 AND 76,300 BUBBLE GUM WRAPPERS FOR A PAIR OF X-RAY SPECS. WHAT A DEAL!
THEN AGAIN...
WHAT ARE YOU WEARING!?
X-RAY SPECS. I JUST GOT 'EM IN THE MAIL.
YOU ARE SUCH A WEIRDO!
AT LEAST I'M NOT WEARING LEOPARD SKIN UNDERWEAR.
YOU'RE WEARING LEOPARD SKIN UNDERWEAR?!
I AM NOT WEARING LEOPARD SKIN UNDERWEAR!
X-RAY SPECS DON'T LIE.
HEY, MOM—PAIGE IS WEARING LEOPARD SKIN UNDERWEAR!
I AM NOT!
AMEND
PAIGE! WHAT ARE YOU DOING WITH LEOPARD SKIN UNDERWEAR?!
AAAAAAAAAAAAAAA!
THOSE THINGS DON'T REALLY WORK, DO THEY?
I THINK THEY WORK EXTREMELY WELL.

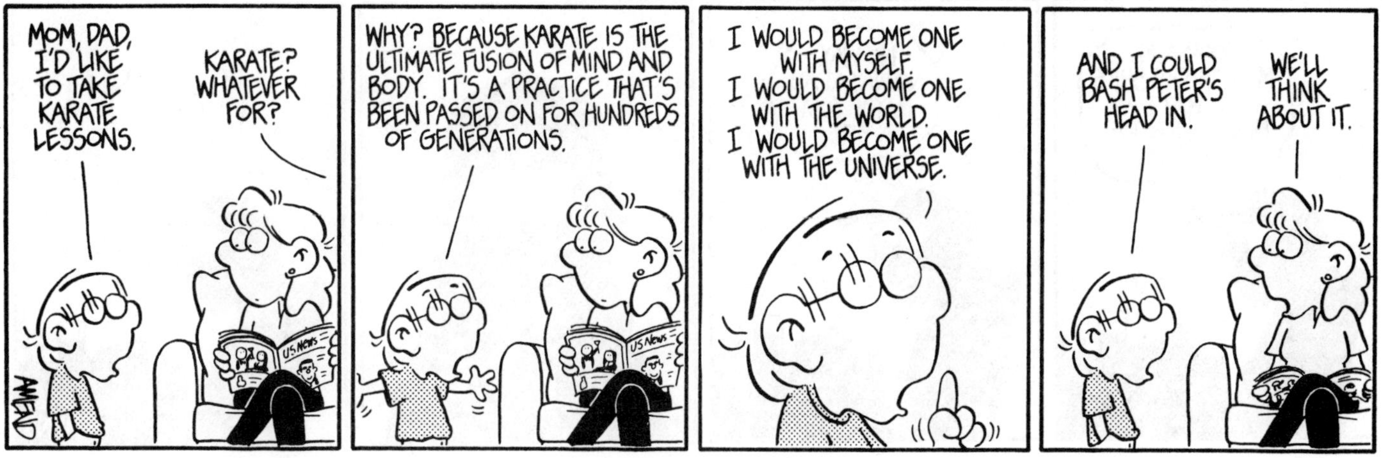

MOM, DAD, I'D LIKE TO TAKE KARATE LESSONS.
KARATE? WHATEVER FOR?
WHY? BECAUSE KARATE IS THE ULTIMATE FUSION OF MIND AND BODY. IT'S A PRACTICE THAT'S BEEN PASSED ON FOR HUNDREDS OF GENERATIONS.
I WOULD BECOME ONE WITH MYSELF. I WOULD BECOME ONE WITH THE WORLD. I WOULD BECOME ONE WITH THE UNIVERSE.
AND I COULD BASH PETER'S HEAD IN.
WE'LL THINK ABOUT IT.
AMEND

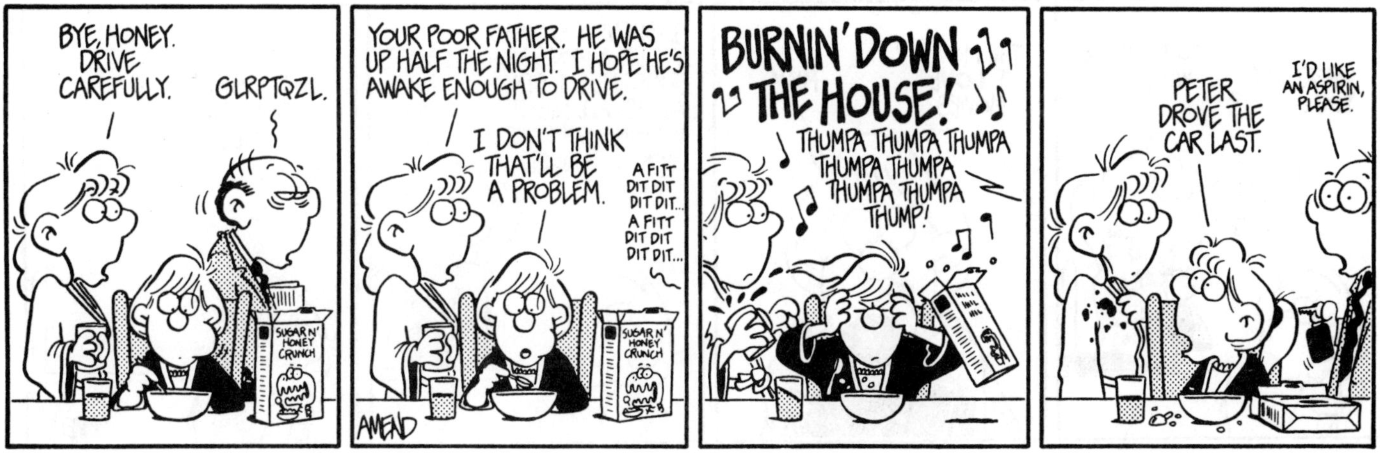

BYE, HONEY. DRIVE CAREFULLY.
GLRPTQZL.
SUGAR N' HONEY CRUNCH
YOUR POOR FATHER. HE WAS UP HALF THE NIGHT. I HOPE HE'S AWAKE ENOUGH TO DRIVE.
I DON'T THINK THAT'LL BE A PROBLEM.
A FITT DIT DIT DIT DIT... A FITT DIT DIT DIT DIT...
BURNIN' DOWN THE HOUSE!
THUMPA THUMPA THUMPA THUMPA THUMPA THUMPA THUMPA THUMP!
PETER DROVE THE CAR LAST.
I'D LIKE AN ASPIRIN, PLEASE.
AMEND

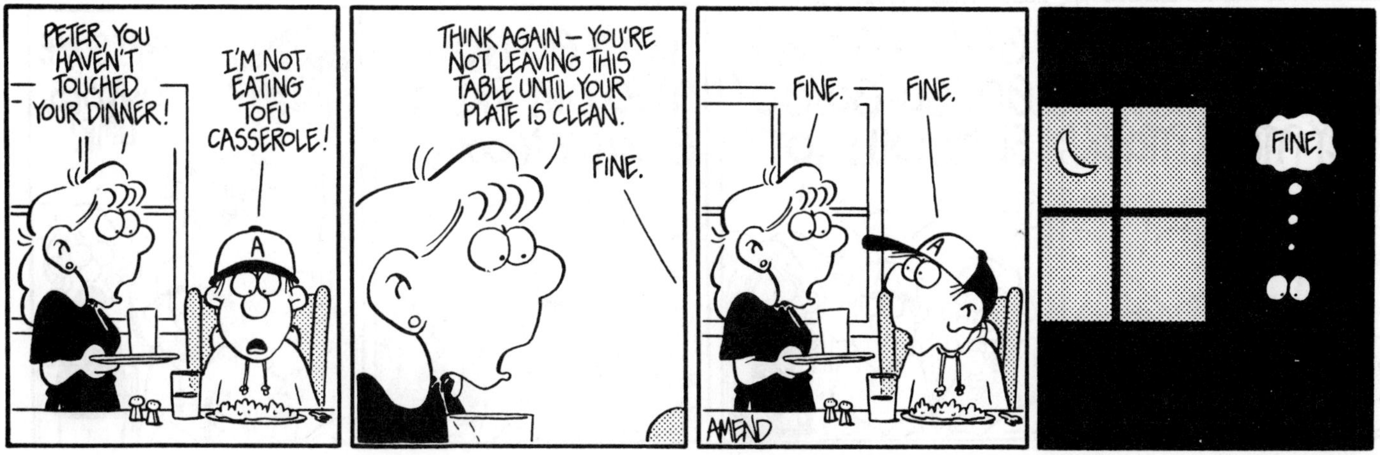

PETER, YOU HAVEN'T TOUCHED YOUR DINNER!
I'M NOT EATING TOFU CASSEROLE!
THINK AGAIN — YOU'RE NOT LEAVING THIS TABLE UNTIL YOUR PLATE IS CLEAN.
FINE.
FINE.
FINE.
FINE.
AMEND

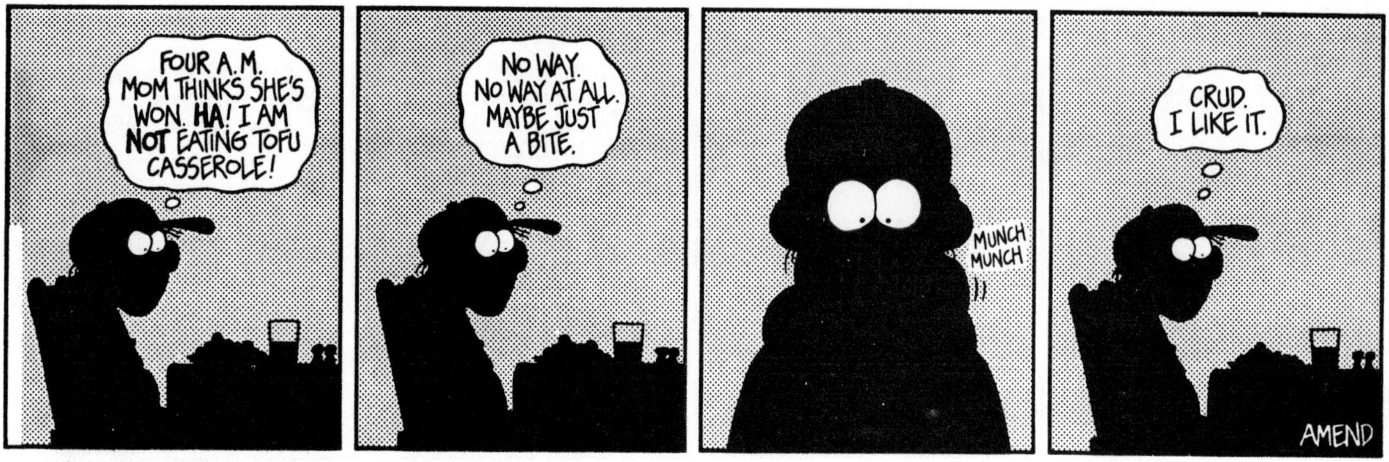
FOUR A.M. MOM THINKS SHE'S WON. HA! I AM NOT EATING TOFU CASSEROLE!
NO WAY. NO WAY AT ALL. MAYBE JUST A BITE.
MUNCH MUNCH
CRUD. I LIKE IT.
AMEND

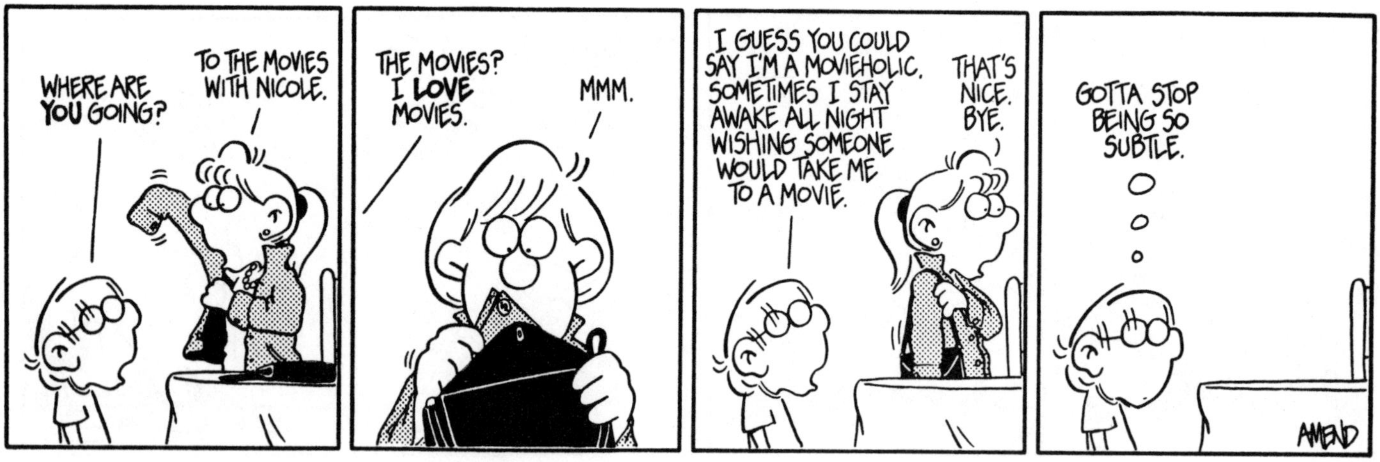
WHERE ARE YOU GOING?
TO THE MOVIES WITH NICOLE.
THE MOVIES? I LOVE MOVIES.
MMM.
I GUESS YOU COULD SAY I'M A MOVIEHOLIC. SOMETIMES I STAY AWAKE ALL NIGHT WISHING SOMEONE WOULD TAKE ME TO A MOVIE.
THAT'S NICE. BYE.
GOTTA STOP BEING SO SUBTLE.
AMEND

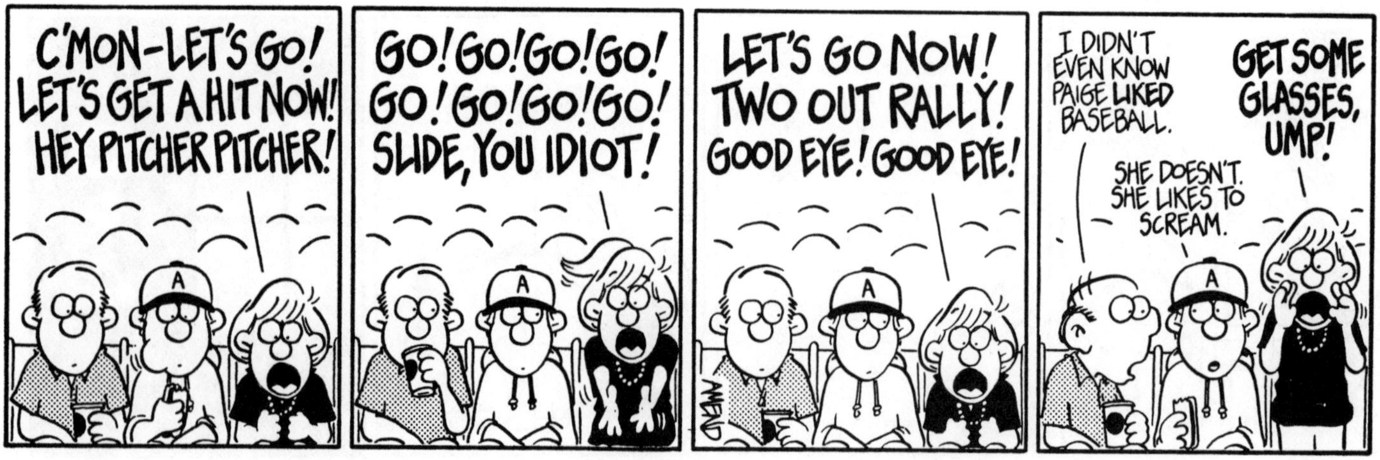
C'MON-LET'S GO! LET'S GET A HIT NOW! HEY PITCHER PITCHER!
GO! GO! GO! GO! GO! GO! GO! GO! SLIDE, YOU IDIOT!
AMEND
LET'S GO NOW! TWO OUT RALLY! GOOD EYE! GOOD EYE!
I DIDN'T EVEN KNOW PAIGE LIKED BASEBALL.
SHE DOESN'T. SHE LIKES TO SCREAM.
GET SOME GLASSES, UMP!

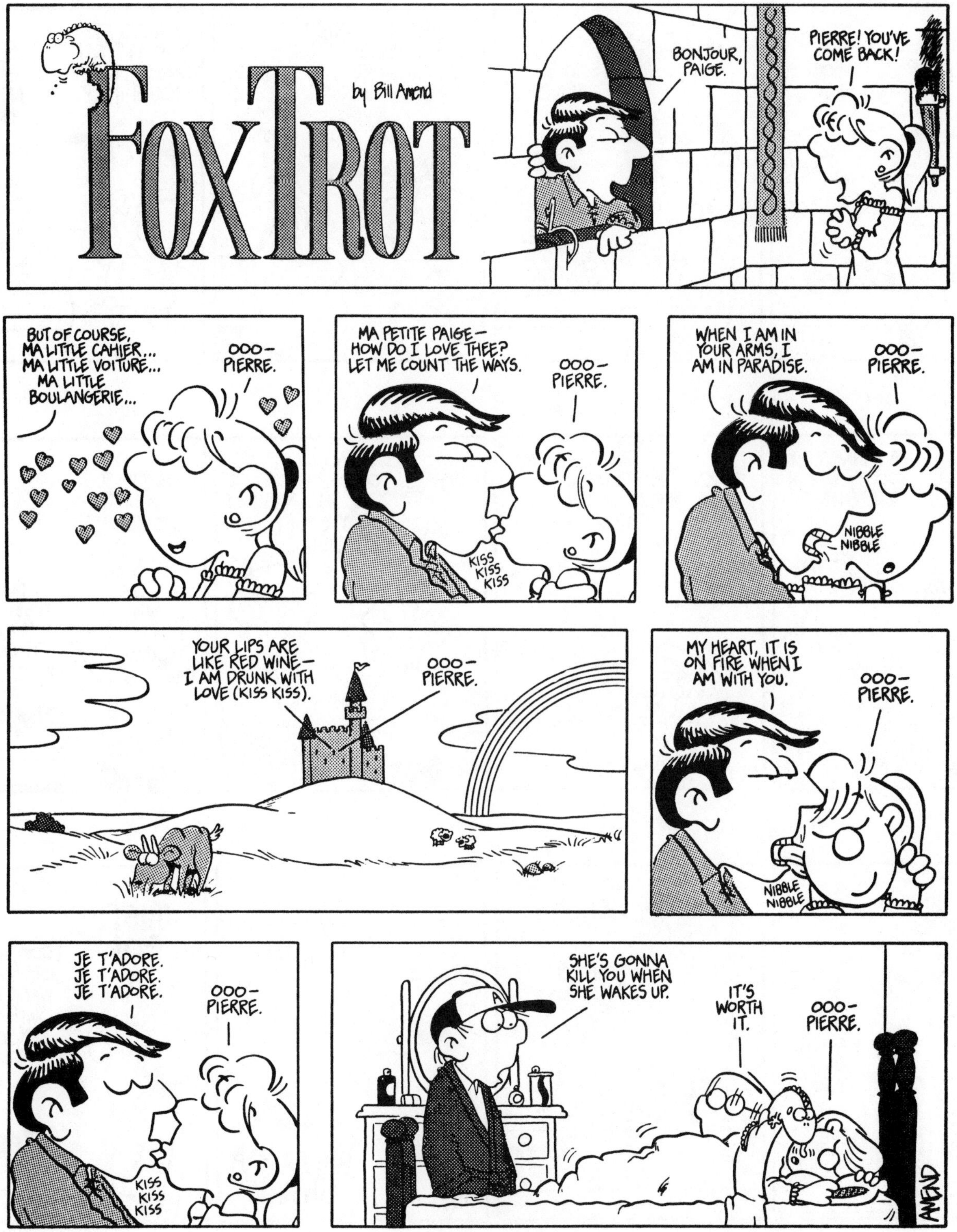
FoxTrot
by Bill Amend
BONJOUR, PAIGE.
PIERRE! YOU'VE COME BACK!
BUT OF COURSE, MA LITTLE CAHIER... MA LITTLE VOITURE... MA LITTLE BOULANGERIE...
OOO-PIERRE.
MA PETITE PAIGE-HOW DO I LOVE THEE? LET ME COUNT THE WAYS.
OOO-PIERRE.
KISS KISS KISS
WHEN I AM IN YOUR ARMS, I AM IN PARADISE.
OOO-PIERRE.
NIBBLE NIBBLE
YOUR LIPS ARE LIKE RED WINE-I AM DRUNK WITH LOVE (KISS KISS).
OOO-PIERRE.
MY HEART, IT IS ON FIRE WHEN I AM WITH YOU.
OOO-PIERRE.
NIBBLE NIBBLE
JE T'ADORE. JE T'ADORE. JE T'ADORE.
OOO-PIERRE.
KISS KISS KISS
SHE'S GONNA KILL YOU WHEN SHE WAKES UP.
IT'S WORTH IT.
OOO-PIERRE.
AMEND

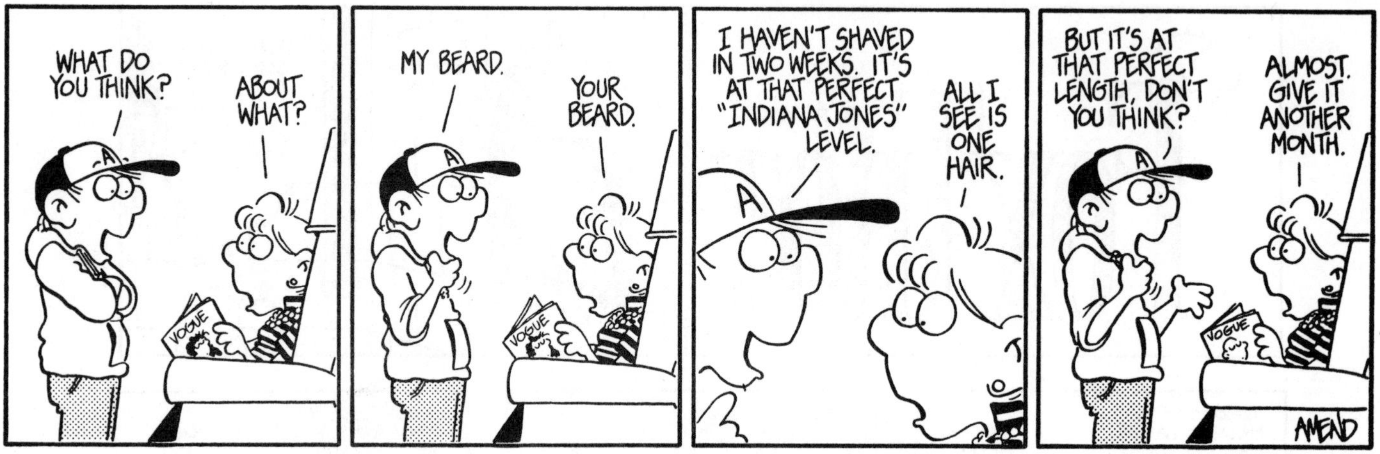
WHAT DO YOU THINK?
ABOUT WHAT?
MY BEARD.
YOUR BEARD.
I HAVEN'T SHAVED IN TWO WEEKS. IT'S AT THAT PERFECT "INDIANA JONES" LEVEL.
ALL I SEE IS ONE HAIR.
BUT IT'S AT THAT PERFECT LENGTH, DON'T YOU THINK?
ALMOST. GIVE IT ANOTHER MONTH.
AMEND

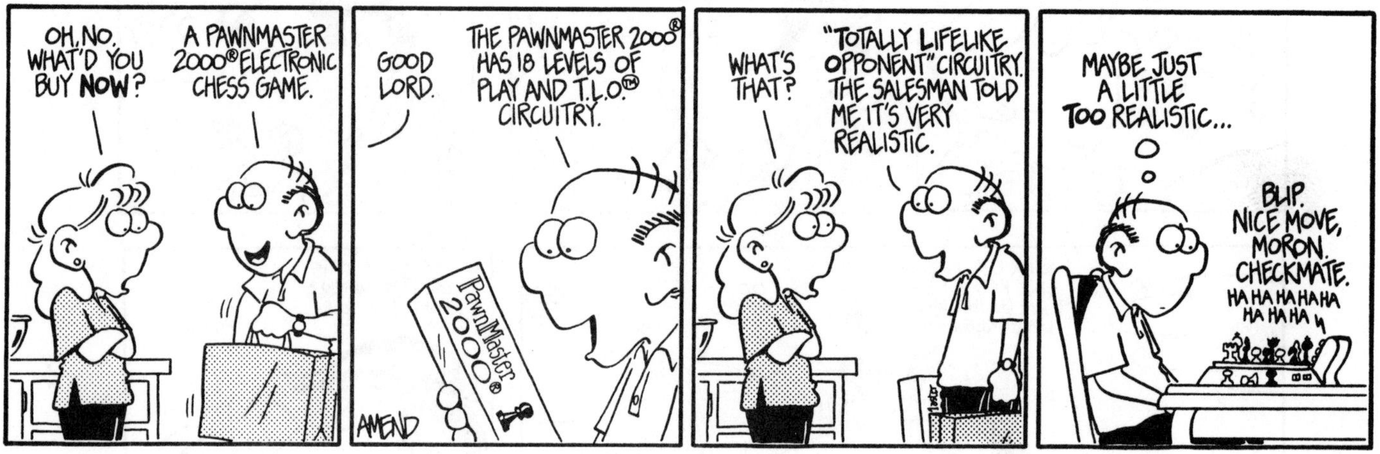
OH, NO. WHAT'D YOU BUY NOW?
A PAWNMASTER 2000® ELECTRONIC CHESS GAME.
GOOD LORD.
THE PAWNMASTER 2000® HAS 18 LEVELS OF PLAY AND T.L.O.™ CIRCUITRY.
PawnMaster 2000®
AMEND
WHAT'S THAT?
"TOTALLY LIFELIKE OPPONENT" CIRCUITRY. THE SALESMAN TOLD ME IT'S VERY REALISTIC.
MAYBE JUST A LITTLE TOO REALISTIC...
BLIP. NICE MOVE, MORON. CHECKMATE.
HA HA HA HA HA HA HA HA HA

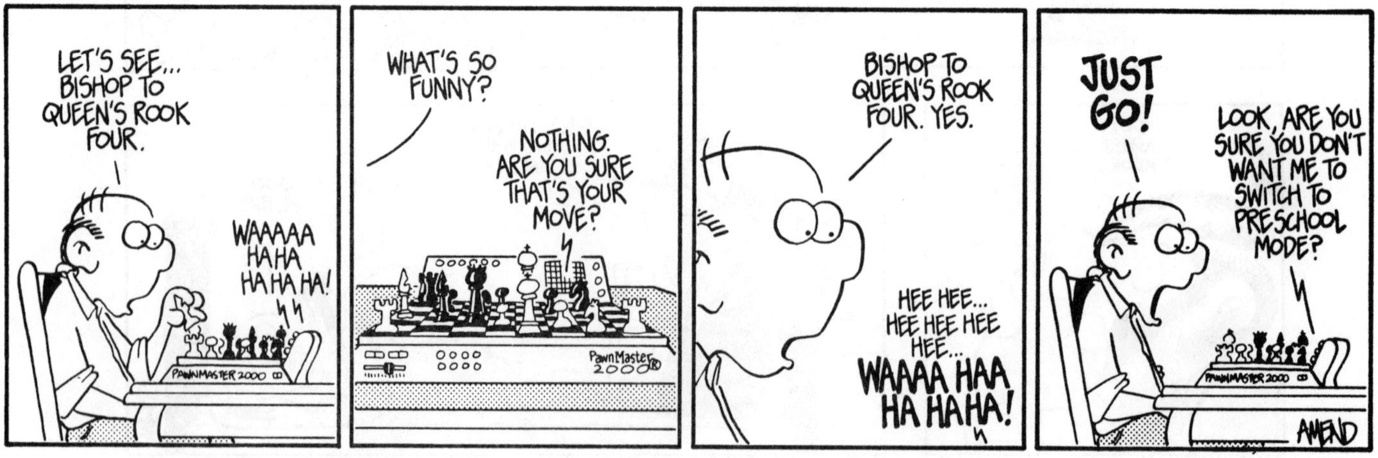
LET'S SEE... BISHOP TO QUEEN'S ROOK FOUR.
WAAAAA HA HA HA HA HA!
PAWNMASTER 2000
WHAT'S SO FUNNY?
NOTHING. ARE YOU SURE THAT'S YOUR MOVE?
PawnMaster 2000®
BISHOP TO QUEEN'S ROOK FOUR. YES.
HEE HEE... HEE HEE HEE HEE...
WAAAA HAA HA HA HA!
JUST GO!
LOOK, ARE YOU SURE YOU DON'T WANT ME TO SWITCH TO PRESCHOOL MODE?
PAWNMASTER 2000
AMEND

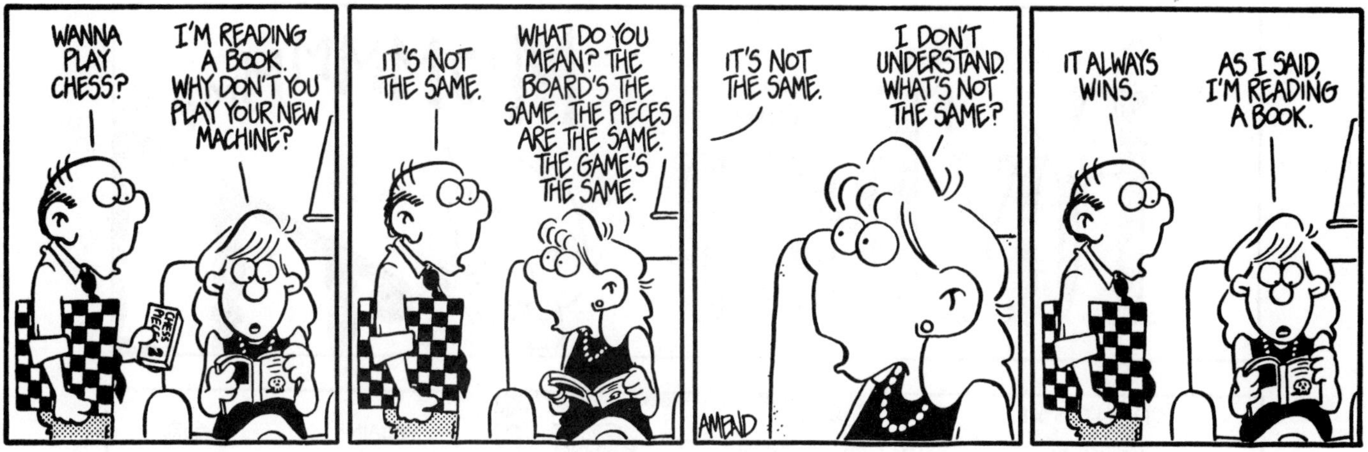
WANNA PLAY CHESS?
I'M READING A BOOK. WHY DON'T YOU PLAY YOUR NEW MACHINE?
IT'S NOT THE SAME.
WHAT DO YOU MEAN? THE BOARD'S THE SAME. THE PIECES ARE THE SAME. THE GAME'S THE SAME.
IT'S NOT THE SAME.
I DON'T UNDERSTAND. WHAT'S NOT THE SAME?
AMEND
IT ALWAYS WINS.
AS I SAID, I'M READING A BOOK.

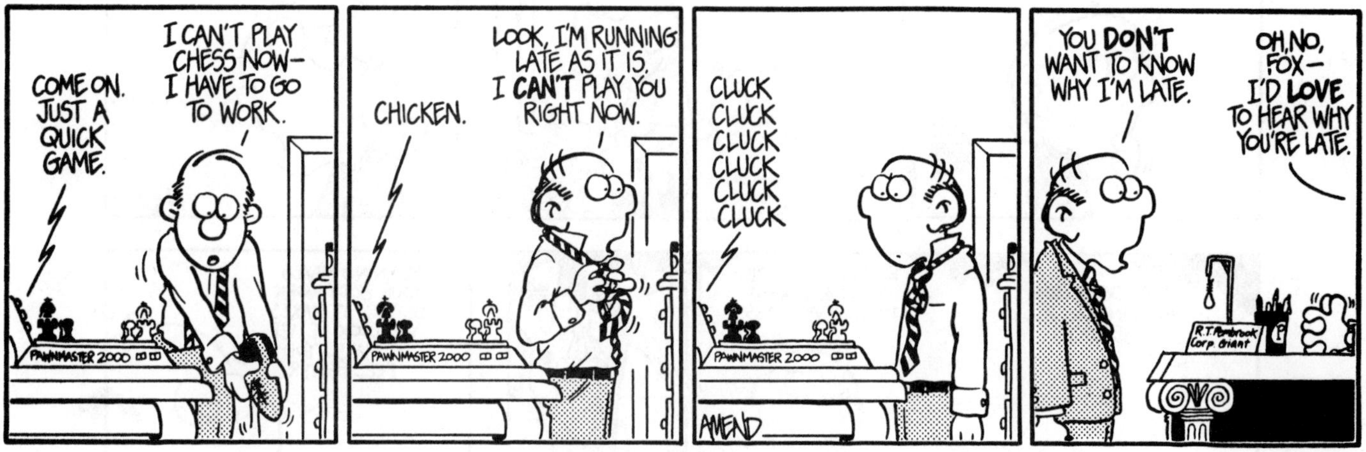
COME ON. JUST A QUICK GAME.
I CAN'T PLAY CHESS NOW— I HAVE TO GO TO WORK.
PAWNMASTER 2000
CHICKEN.
LOOK, I'M RUNNING LATE AS IT IS. I **CAN'T** PLAY YOU RIGHT NOW.
PAWNMASTER 2000
CLUCK CLUCK CLUCK CLUCK CLUCK CLUCK
PAWNMASTER 2000
AMEND
YOU **DON'T** WANT TO KNOW WHY I'M LATE.
OH, NO, FOX— I'D **LOVE** TO HEAR WHY YOU'RE LATE.

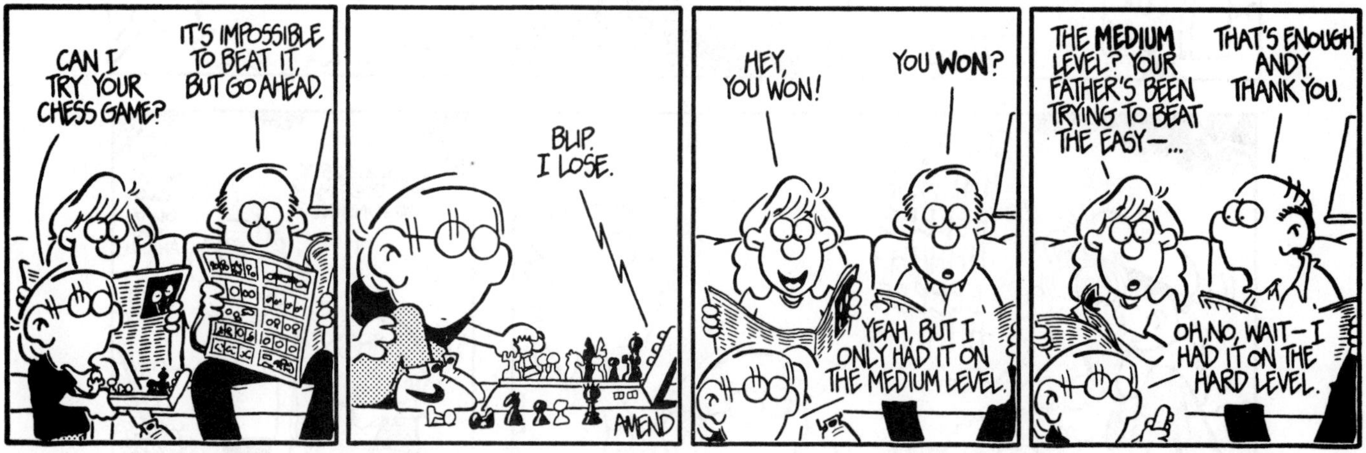
CAN I TRY YOUR CHESS GAME?
IT'S IMPOSSIBLE TO BEAT IT, BUT GO AHEAD.
BLIP. I LOSE.
AMEND
HEY, YOU WON!
YOU **WON**?
YEAH, BUT I ONLY HAD IT ON THE MEDIUM LEVEL.
THE **MEDIUM** LEVEL? YOUR FATHER'S BEEN TRYING TO BEAT THE EASY—...
THAT'S ENOUGH, ANDY. THANK YOU.
OH, NO, WAIT— I HAD IT ON THE HARD LEVEL.

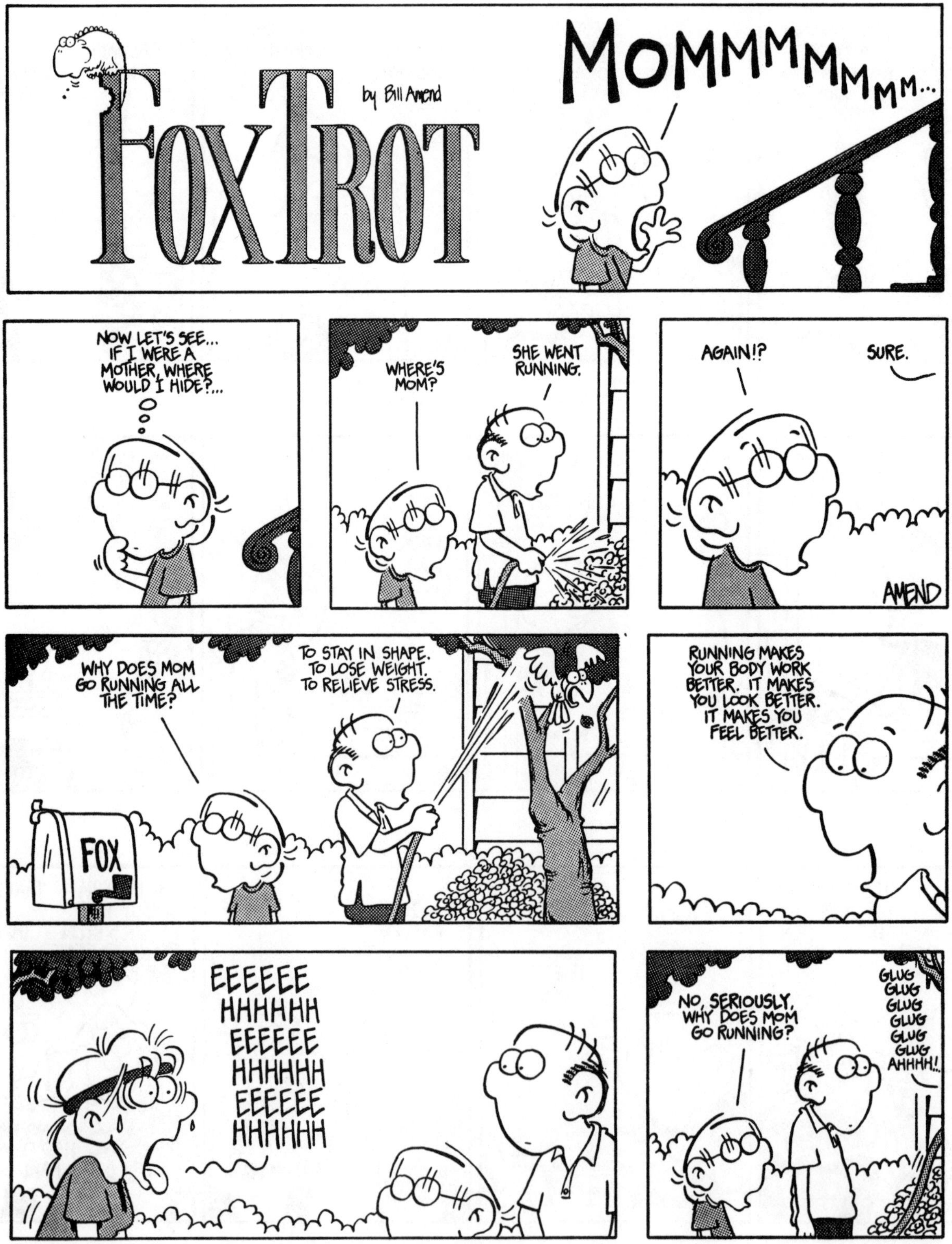
FoxTrot
by Bill Amend
MOMMMMMMMM...
NOW LET'S SEE... IF I WERE A MOTHER, WHERE WOULD I HIDE?...
WHERE'S MOM?
SHE WENT RUNNING.
AGAIN!?
SURE.
AMEND
WHY DOES MOM GO RUNNING ALL THE TIME?
TO STAY IN SHAPE. TO LOSE WEIGHT. TO RELIEVE STRESS.
FOX
RUNNING MAKES YOUR BODY WORK BETTER. IT MAKES YOU LOOK BETTER. IT MAKES YOU FEEL BETTER.
EEEEEE HHHHHH EEEEEE HHHHHH EEEEEE HHHHHH
NO, SERIOUSLY, WHY DOES MOM GO RUNNING?
GLUG GLUG GLUG GLUG GLUG GLUG AHHHH!

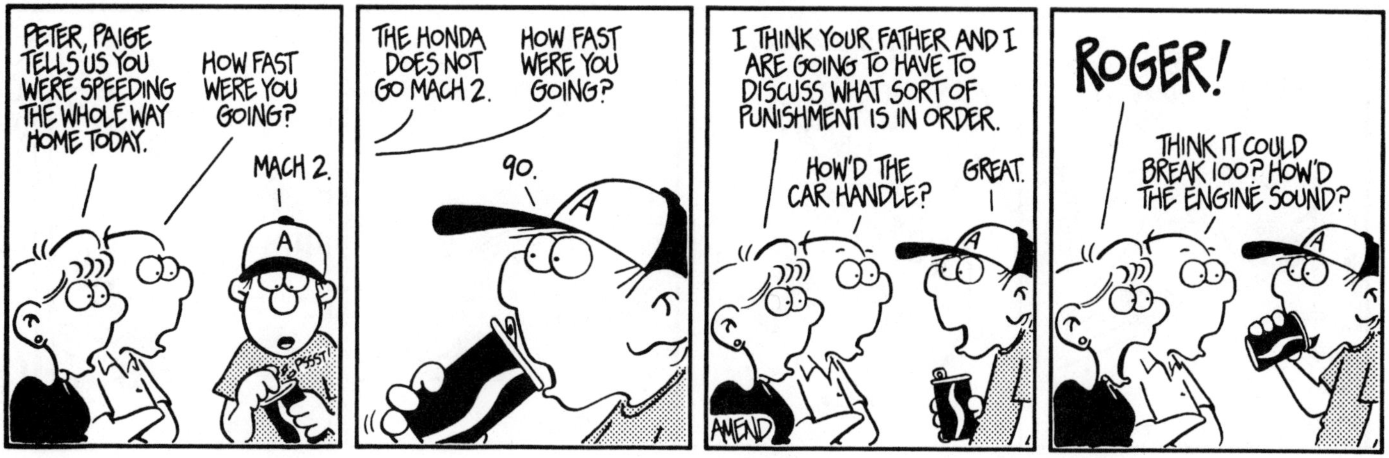
PETER, PAIGE TELLS US YOU WERE SPEEDING THE WHOLE WAY HOME TODAY.
HOW FAST WERE YOU GOING?
MACH 2.
PSSST!
THE HONDA DOES NOT GO MACH 2.
HOW FAST WERE YOU GOING?
90.
I THINK YOUR FATHER AND I ARE GOING TO HAVE TO DISCUSS WHAT SORT OF PUNISHMENT IS IN ORDER.
HOW'D THE CAR HANDLE?
GREAT.
AMEND
ROGER!
THINK IT COULD BREAK 100? HOW'D THE ENGINE SOUND?

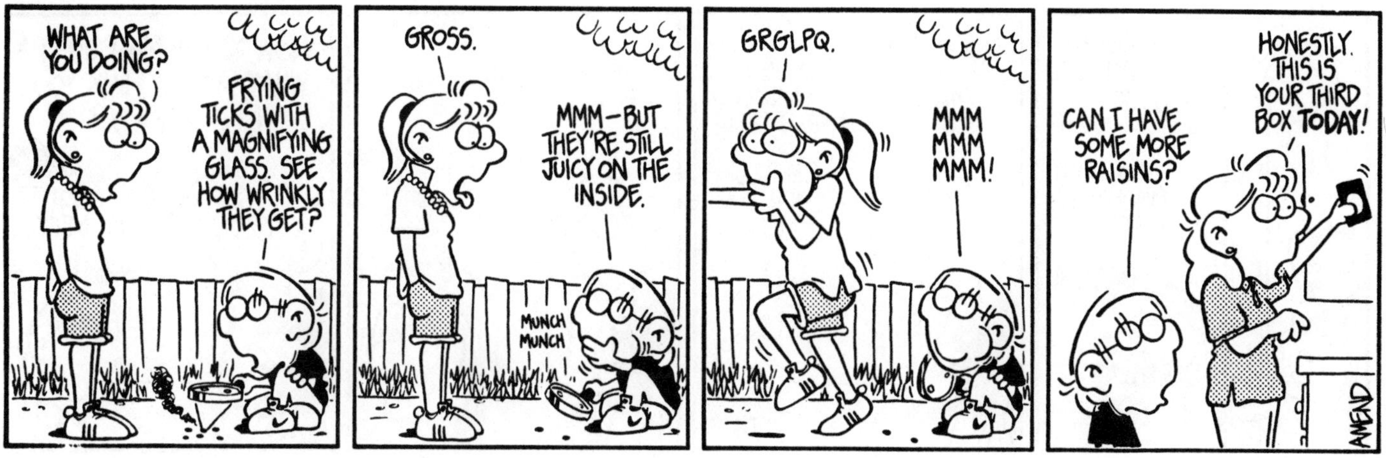
WHAT ARE YOU DOING?
FRYING TICKS WITH A MAGNIFYING GLASS. SEE HOW WRINKLY THEY GET?
GROSS.
MMM—BUT THEY'RE STILL JUICY ON THE INSIDE.
MUNCH MUNCH
GRGLPQ.
MMM MMM MMM!
CAN I HAVE SOME MORE RAISINS?
HONESTLY. THIS IS YOUR THIRD BOX TODAY!
AMEND

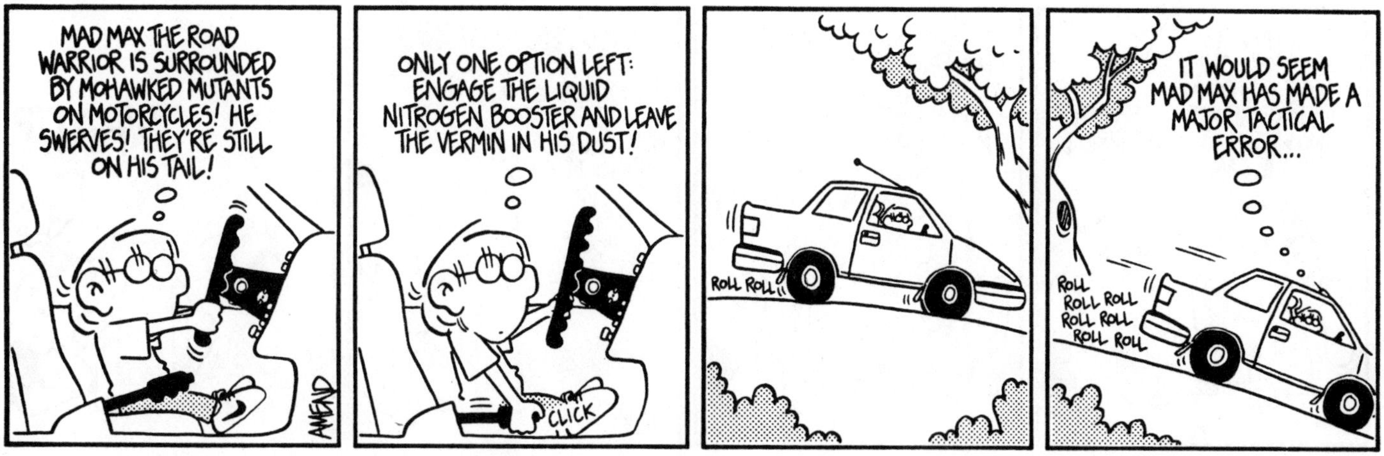
MAD MAX THE ROAD WARRIOR IS SURROUNDED BY MOHAWKED MUTANTS ON MOTORCYCLES! HE SWERVES! THEY'RE STILL ON HIS TAIL!
AMEND
ONLY ONE OPTION LEFT: ENGAGE THE LIQUID NITROGEN BOOSTER AND LEAVE THE VERMIN IN HIS DUST!
CLICK
ROLL ROLL
IT WOULD SEEM MAD MAX HAS MADE A MAJOR TACTICAL ERROR...
ROLL ROLL ROLL ROLL ROLL ROLL ROLL

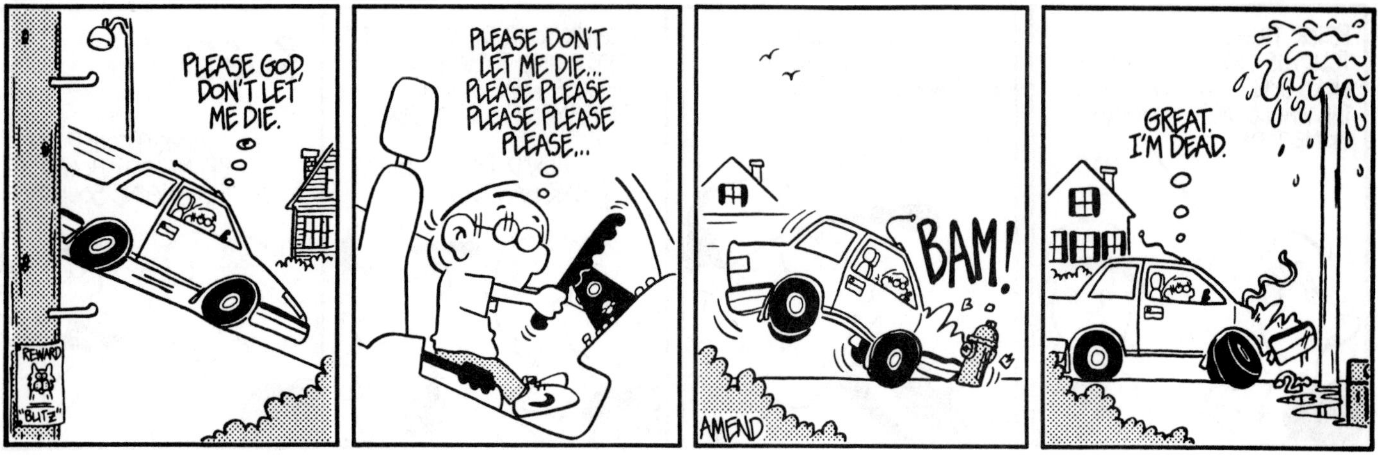
PLEASE GOD DON'T LET ME DIE.
REWARD
"BLITZ"
PLEASE DON'T LET ME DIE... PLEASE PLEASE PLEASE PLEASE PLEASE...
BAM!
AMEND
GREAT. I'M DEAD.

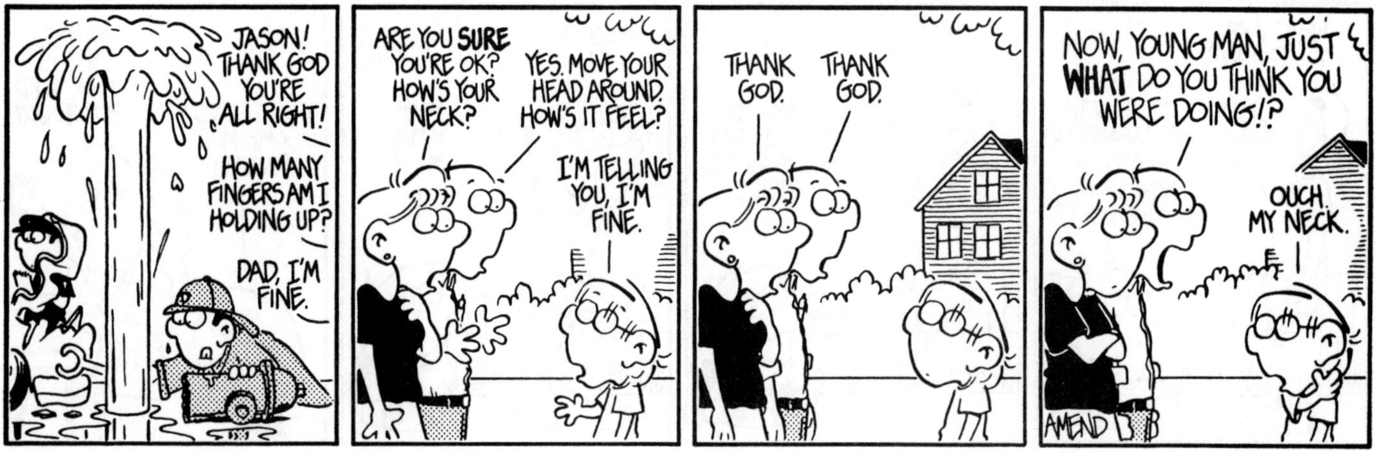
JASON! THANK GOD YOU'RE ALL RIGHT!
HOW MANY FINGERS AM I HOLDING UP?
DAD, I'M FINE.
ARE YOU **SURE** YOU'RE OK? HOW'S YOUR NECK?
YES. MOVE YOUR HEAD AROUND. HOW'S IT FEEL?
I'M TELLING YOU, I'M FINE.
THANK GOD.
THANK GOD.
NOW, YOUNG MAN, JUST **WHAT** DO YOU THINK YOU WERE DOING!?
OUCH. MY NECK.
AMEND

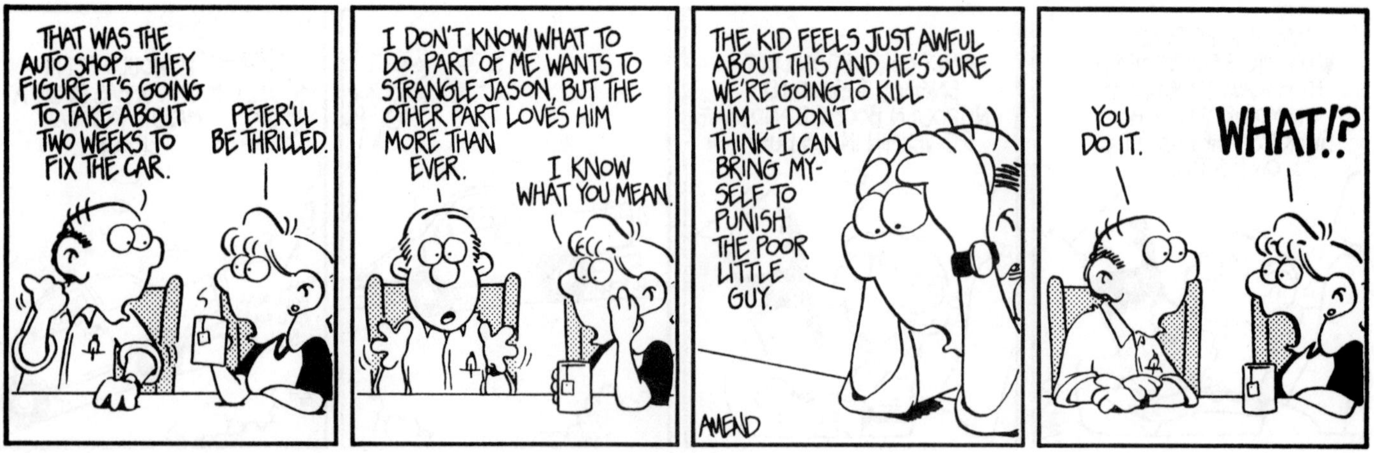
THAT WAS THE AUTO SHOP—THEY FIGURE IT'S GOING TO TAKE ABOUT TWO WEEKS TO FIX THE CAR.
PETER'LL BE THRILLED.
I DON'T KNOW WHAT TO DO. PART OF ME WANTS TO STRANGLE JASON, BUT THE OTHER PART LOVES HIM MORE THAN EVER.
I KNOW WHAT YOU MEAN.
THE KID FEELS JUST AWFUL ABOUT THIS AND HE'S SURE WE'RE GOING TO KILL HIM. I DON'T THINK I CAN BRING MYSELF TO PUNISH THE POOR LITTLE GUY.
AMEND
YOU DO IT.
WHAT!?

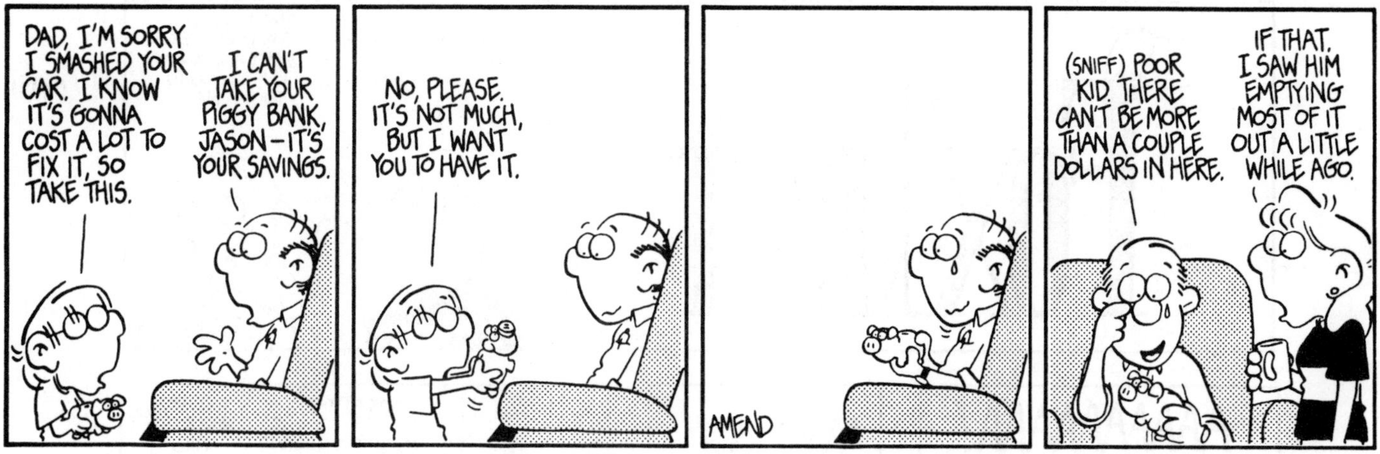
DAD, I'M SORRY I SMASHED YOUR CAR. I KNOW IT'S GONNA COST A LOT TO FIX IT, SO TAKE THIS.
I CAN'T TAKE YOUR PIGGY BANK, JASON – IT'S YOUR SAVINGS.
NO, PLEASE. IT'S NOT MUCH, BUT I WANT YOU TO HAVE IT.
AMEND
(SNIFF) POOR KID. THERE CAN'T BE MORE THAN A COUPLE DOLLARS IN HERE.
IF THAT. I SAW HIM EMPTYING MOST OF IT OUT A LITTLE WHILE AGO.

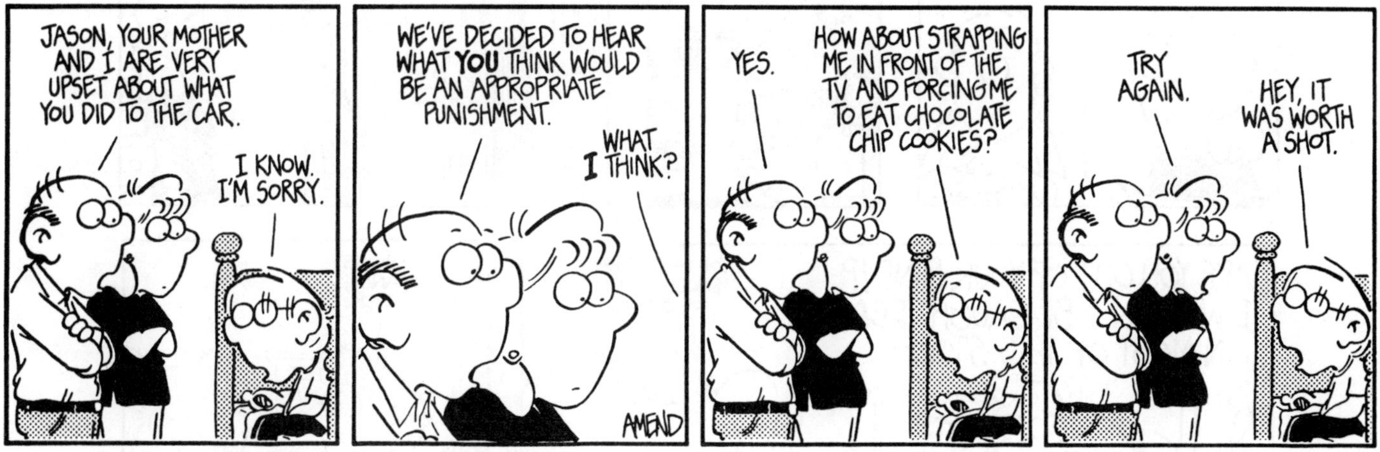
JASON, YOUR MOTHER AND I ARE VERY UPSET ABOUT WHAT YOU DID TO THE CAR.
I KNOW. I'M SORRY.
WE'VE DECIDED TO HEAR WHAT **YOU** THINK WOULD BE AN APPROPRIATE PUNISHMENT.
WHAT **I** THINK?
AMEND
YES.
HOW ABOUT STRAPPING ME IN FRONT OF THE TV AND FORCING ME TO EAT CHOCOLATE CHIP COOKIES?
TRY AGAIN.
HEY, IT WAS WORTH A SHOT.

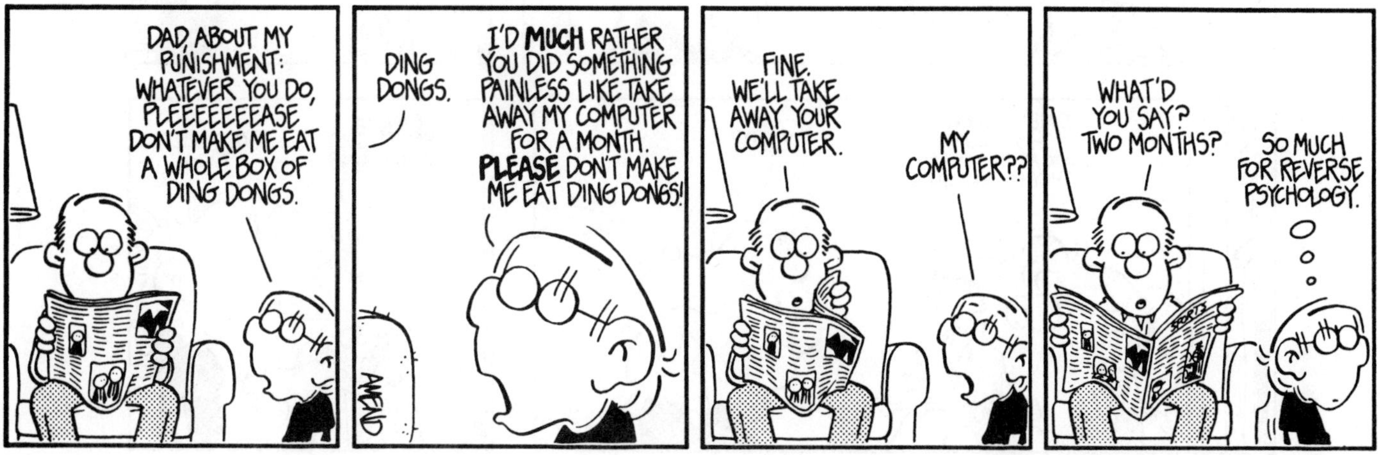
DAD, ABOUT MY PUNISHMENT: WHATEVER YOU DO, PLEEEEEEEASE DON'T MAKE ME EAT A WHOLE BOX OF DING DONGS.
DING DONGS.
I'D **MUCH** RATHER YOU DID SOMETHING PAINLESS LIKE TAKE AWAY MY COMPUTER FOR A MONTH. **PLEASE** DON'T MAKE ME EAT DING DONGS!
AMEND
FINE. WE'LL TAKE AWAY YOUR COMPUTER.
MY COMPUTER??
WHAT'D YOU SAY? TWO MONTHS?
SO MUCH FOR REVERSE PSYCHOLOGY.

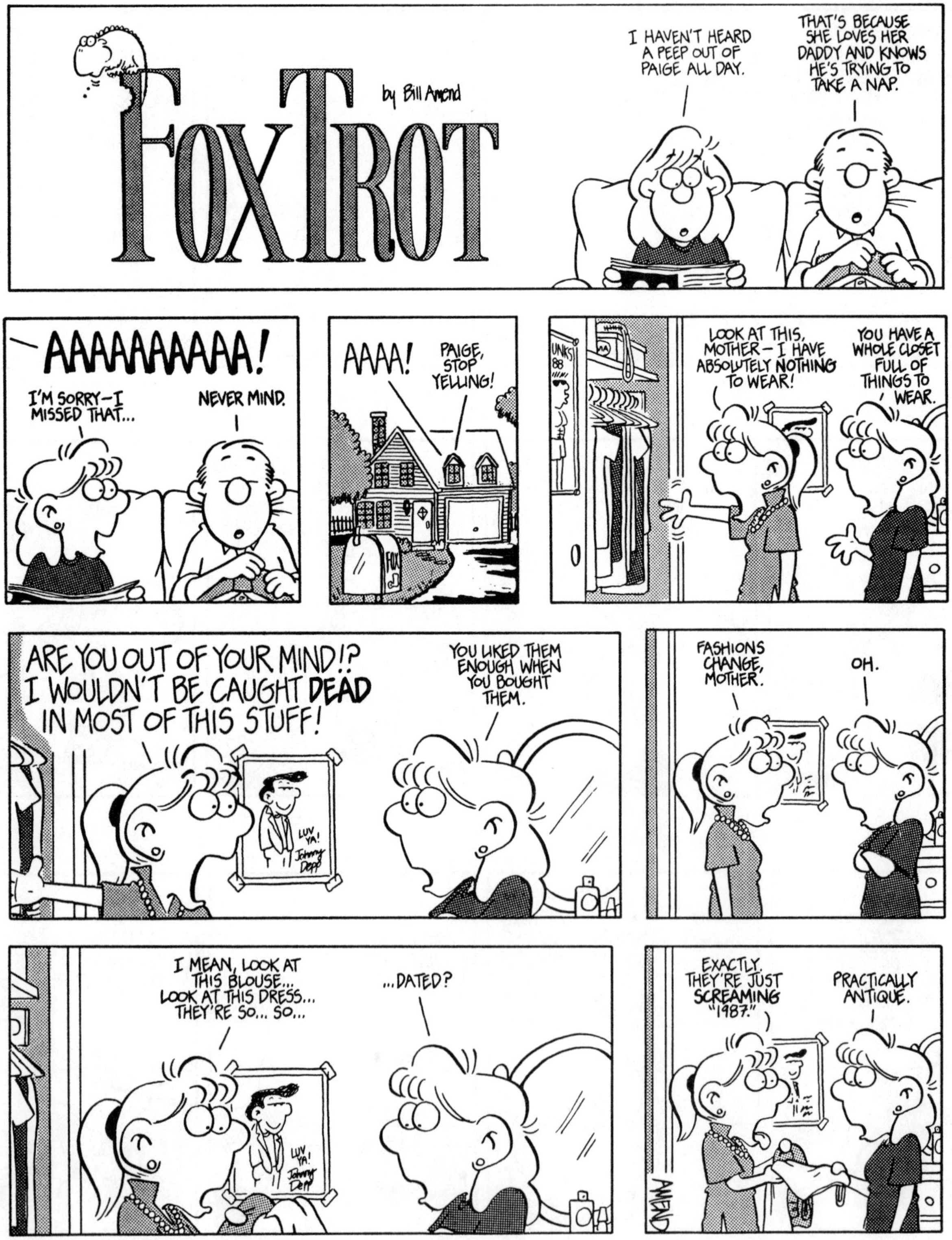
FoxTrot
by Bill Amend
I HAVEN'T HEARD A PEEP OUT OF PAIGE ALL DAY.
THAT'S BECAUSE SHE LOVES HER DADDY AND KNOWS HE'S TRYING TO TAKE A NAP.
AAAAAAAAAA!
I'M SORRY—I MISSED THAT...
NEVER MIND.
AAAA!
PAIGE, STOP YELLING!
FOX
LOOK AT THIS, MOTHER—I HAVE ABSOLUTELY NOTHING TO WEAR!
YOU HAVE A WHOLE CLOSET FULL OF THINGS TO WEAR.
ARE YOU OUT OF YOUR MIND!? I WOULDN'T BE CAUGHT DEAD IN MOST OF THIS STUFF!
LUV YA! Johnny Depp
YOU LIKED THEM ENOUGH WHEN YOU BOUGHT THEM.
FASHIONS CHANGE, MOTHER.
OH.
I MEAN, LOOK AT THIS BLOUSE... LOOK AT THIS DRESS... THEY'RE SO... SO...
...DATED?
LUV YA! Johnny Depp
EXACTLY. THEY'RE JUST SCREAMING "1987."
PRACTICALLY ANTIQUE.
AMEND

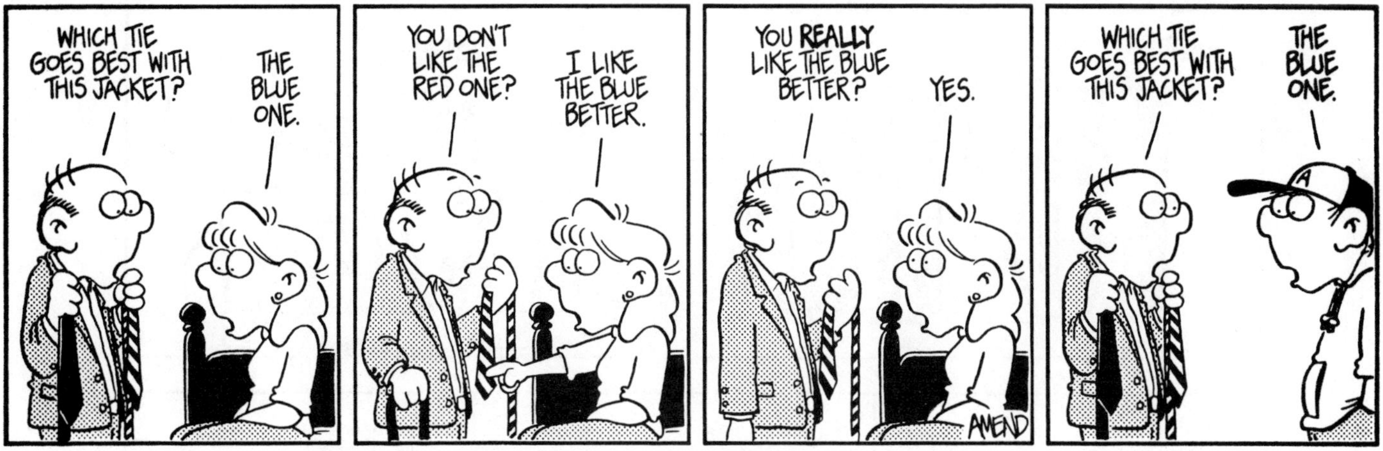
WHICH TIE GOES BEST WITH THIS JACKET?
THE BLUE ONE.
YOU DON'T LIKE THE RED ONE?
I LIKE THE BLUE BETTER.
YOU REALLY LIKE THE BLUE BETTER?
YES.
AMEND
WHICH TIE GOES BEST WITH THIS JACKET?
THE BLUE ONE.

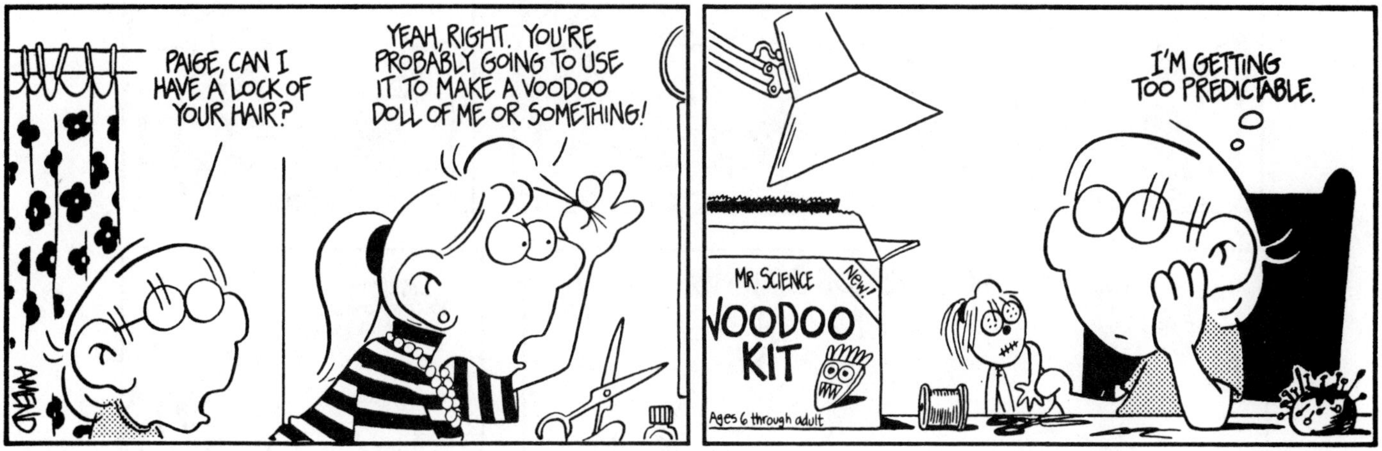
PAIGE, CAN I HAVE A LOCK OF YOUR HAIR?
AMEND
YEAH, RIGHT. YOU'RE PROBABLY GOING TO USE IT TO MAKE A VOODOO DOLL OF ME OR SOMETHING!
I'M GETTING TOO PREDICTABLE.
MR. SCIENCE
New!
VOODOO KIT
Ages 6 through adult

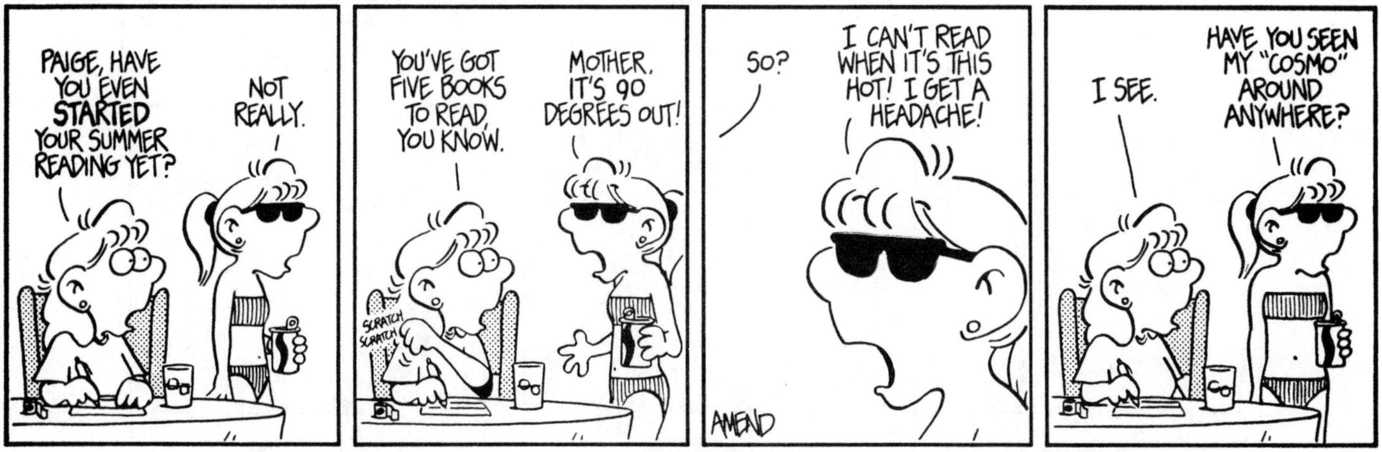
PAIGE, HAVE YOU EVEN STARTED YOUR SUMMER READING YET?
NOT REALLY.
YOU'VE GOT FIVE BOOKS TO READ, YOU KNOW.
MOTHER, IT'S 90 DEGREES OUT!
SCRATCH SCRATCH
SO?
I CAN'T READ WHEN IT'S THIS HOT! I GET A HEADACHE!
AMEND
I SEE.
HAVE YOU SEEN MY "COSMO" AROUND ANYWHERE?

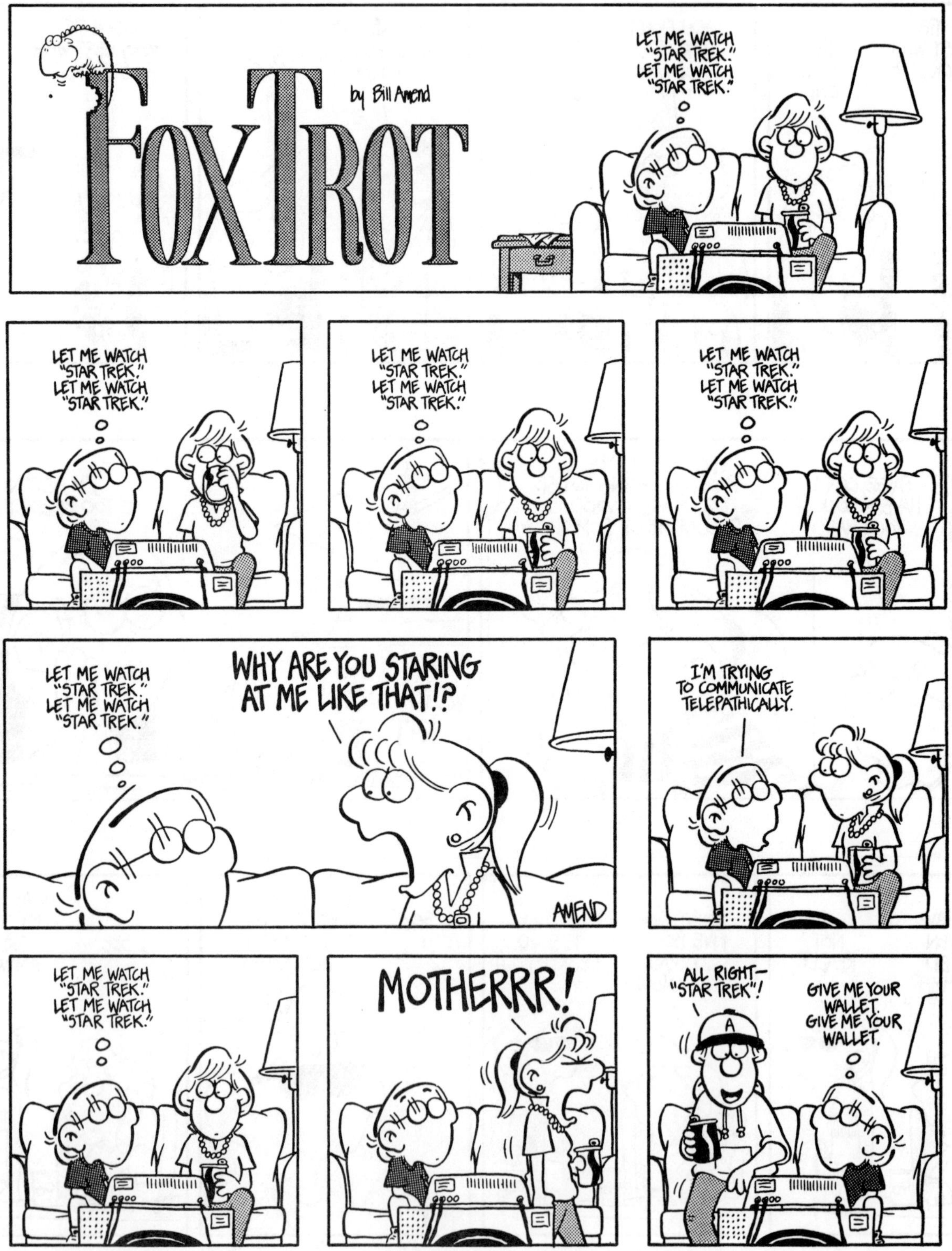
FoxTrot
by Bill Amend
LET ME WATCH "STAR TREK." LET ME WATCH "STAR TREK."
LET ME WATCH "STAR TREK." LET ME WATCH "STAR TREK."
LET ME WATCH "STAR TREK." LET ME WATCH "STAR TREK."
LET ME WATCH "STAR TREK." LET ME WATCH "STAR TREK."
LET ME WATCH "STAR TREK." LET ME WATCH "STAR TREK."
WHY ARE YOU STARING AT ME LIKE THAT!?
AMEND
I'M TRYING TO COMMUNICATE TELEPATHICALLY.
LET ME WATCH "STAR TREK." LET ME WATCH "STAR TREK."
MOTHERRR!
ALL RIGHT— "STAR TREK"!
A
GIVE ME YOUR WALLET. GIVE ME YOUR WALLET.

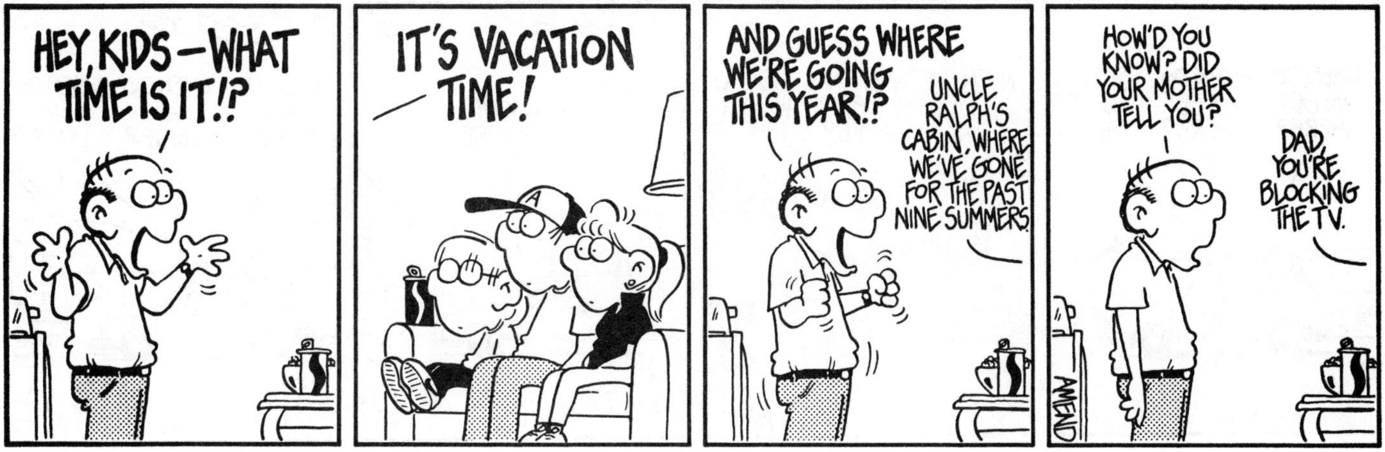
HEY, KIDS—WHAT TIME IS IT!?
IT'S VACATION TIME!
AND GUESS WHERE WE'RE GOING THIS YEAR!?
UNCLE RALPH'S CABIN, WHERE WE'VE GONE FOR THE PAST NINE SUMMERS.
HOW'D YOU KNOW? DID YOUR MOTHER TELL YOU?
DAD, YOU'RE BLOCKING THE T.V.
AMEND

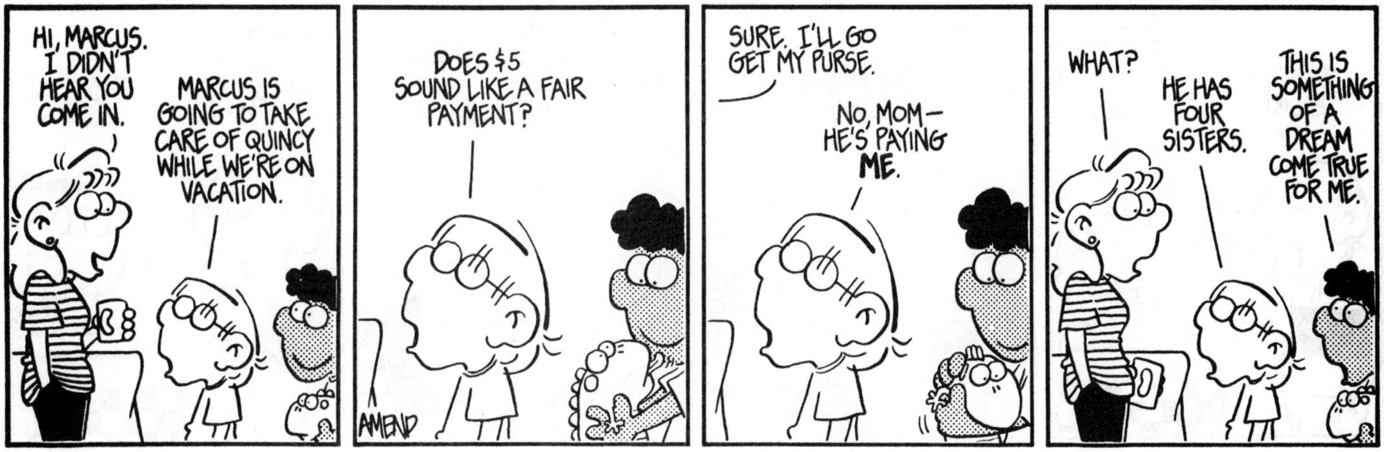
HI, MARCUS. I DIDN'T HEAR YOU COME IN.
MARCUS IS GOING TO TAKE CARE OF QUINCY WHILE WE'RE ON VACATION.
DOES $5 SOUND LIKE A FAIR PAYMENT?
AMEND
SURE. I'LL GO GET MY PURSE.
NO, MOM—HE'S PAYING **ME**.
WHAT?
HE HAS FOUR SISTERS.
THIS IS SOMETHING OF A DREAM COME TRUE FOR ME.

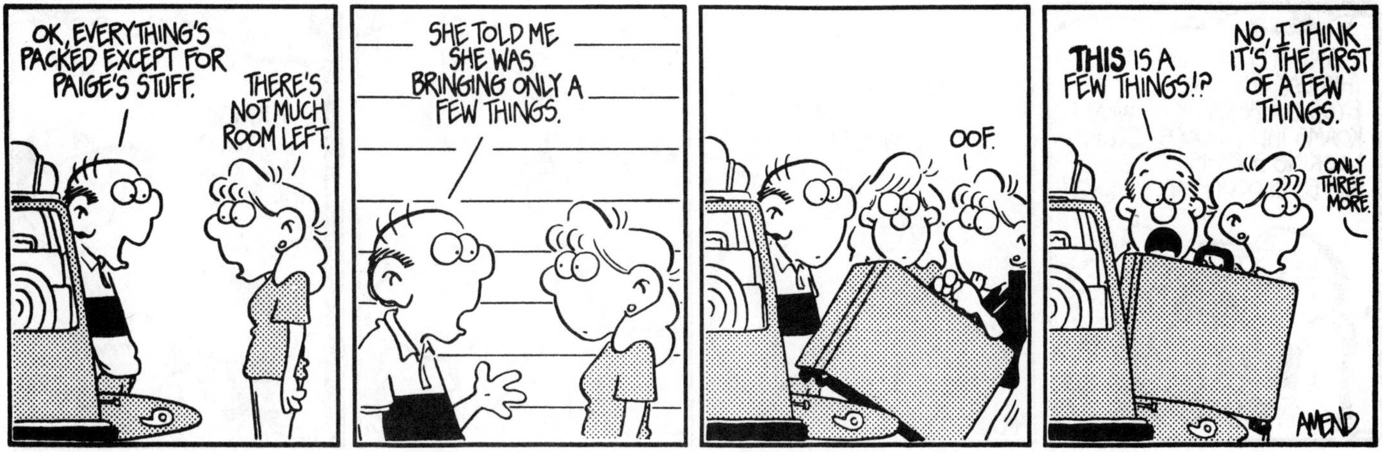
OK, EVERYTHING'S PACKED EXCEPT FOR PAIGE'S STUFF.
THERE'S NOT MUCH ROOM LEFT.
SHE TOLD ME SHE WAS BRINGING ONLY A FEW THINGS.
OOF.
THIS IS A FEW THINGS!?
NO, I THINK IT'S THE FIRST OF A FEW THINGS.
ONLY THREE MORE.
AMEND

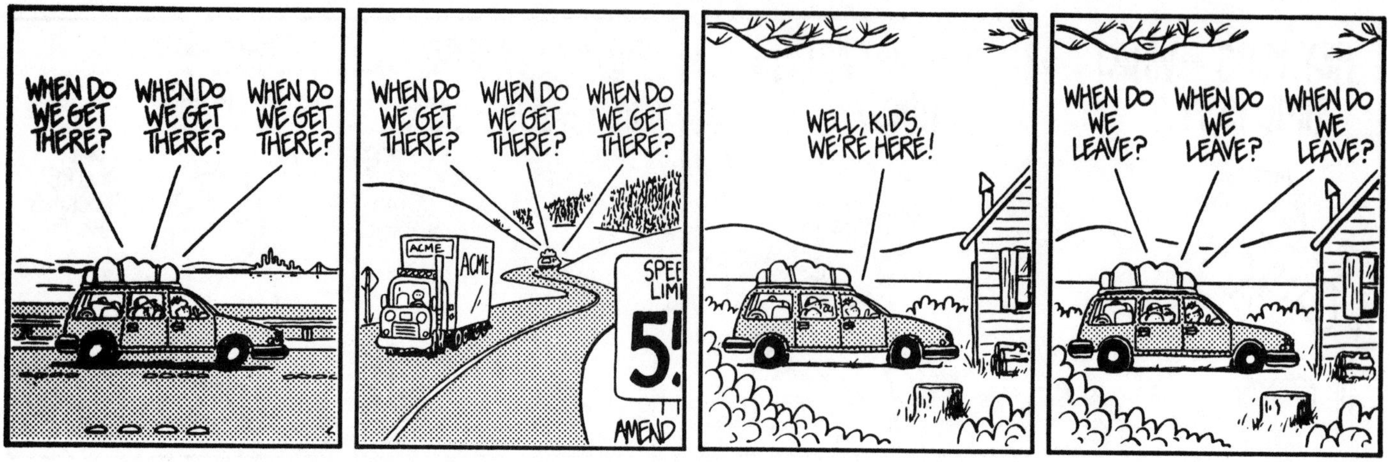
WHEN DO WE GET THERE?
WHEN DO WE GET THERE?
WHEN DO WE GET THERE?
WHEN DO WE GET THERE?
WHEN DO WE GET THERE?
WHEN DO WE GET THERE?
ACME
ACME
AMEND
WELL, KIDS, WE'RE HERE!
WHEN DO WE LEAVE?
WHEN DO WE LEAVE?
WHEN DO WE LEAVE?

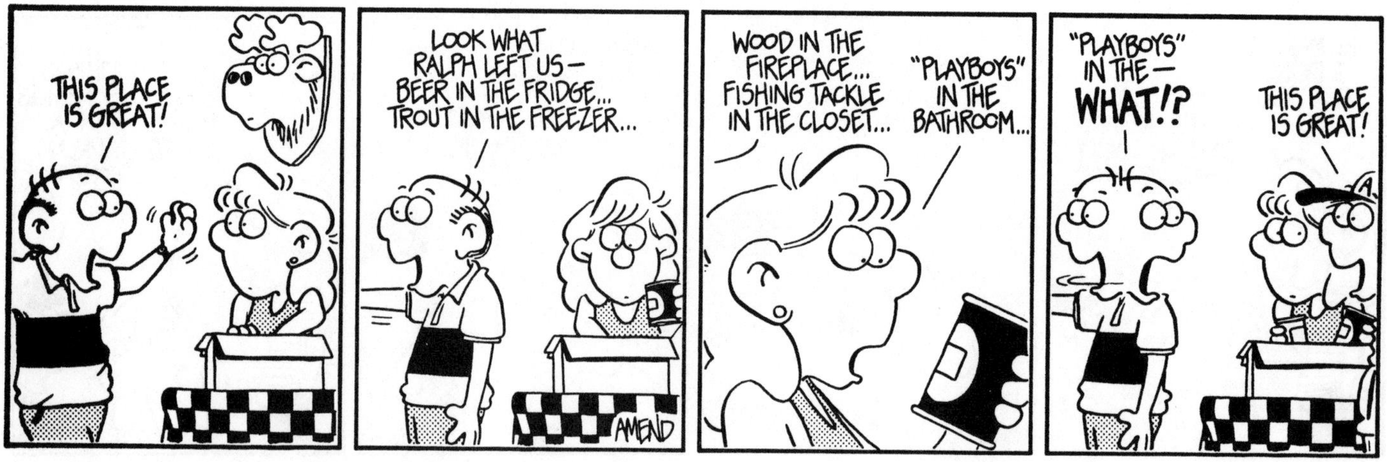
THIS PLACE IS GREAT!
LOOK WHAT RALPH LEFT US— BEER IN THE FRIDGE... TROUT IN THE FREEZER...
AMEND
WOOD IN THE FIREPLACE... FISHING TACKLE IN THE CLOSET...
"PLAYBOYS" IN THE BATHROOM...
"PLAYBOYS" IN THE— WHAT!?
THIS PLACE IS GREAT!

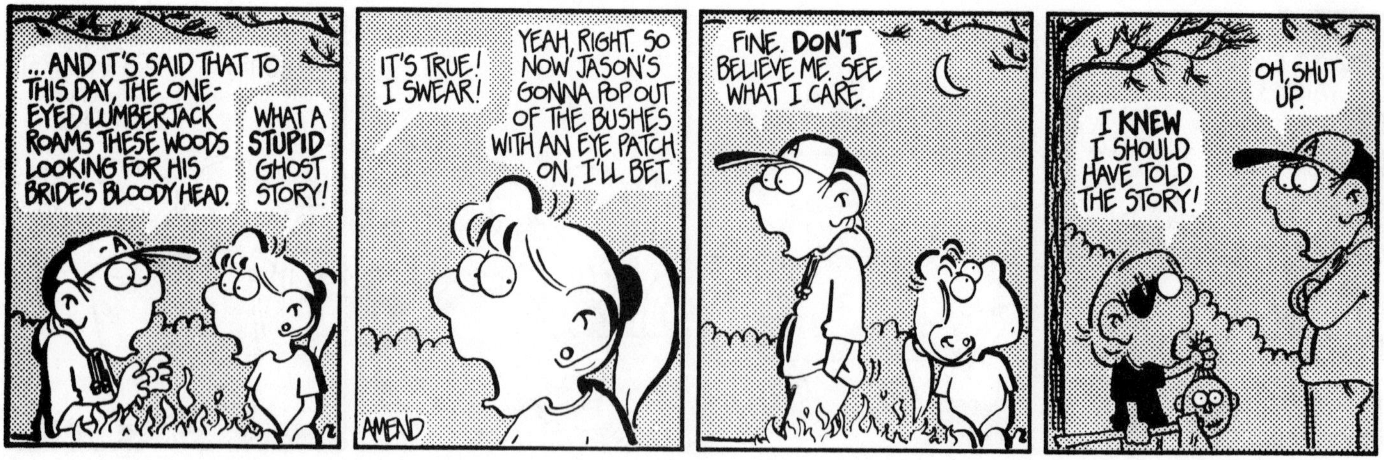
...AND IT'S SAID THAT TO THIS DAY, THE ONE-EYED LUMBERJACK ROAMS THESE WOODS LOOKING FOR HIS BRIDE'S BLOODY HEAD.
WHAT A STUPID GHOST STORY!
IT'S TRUE! I SWEAR!
YEAH, RIGHT. SO NOW JASON'S GONNA POP OUT OF THE BUSHES WITH AN EYE PATCH ON, I'LL BET.
AMEND
FINE. DON'T BELIEVE ME. SEE WHAT I CARE.
OH, SHUT UP.
I KNEW I SHOULD HAVE TOLD THE STORY!

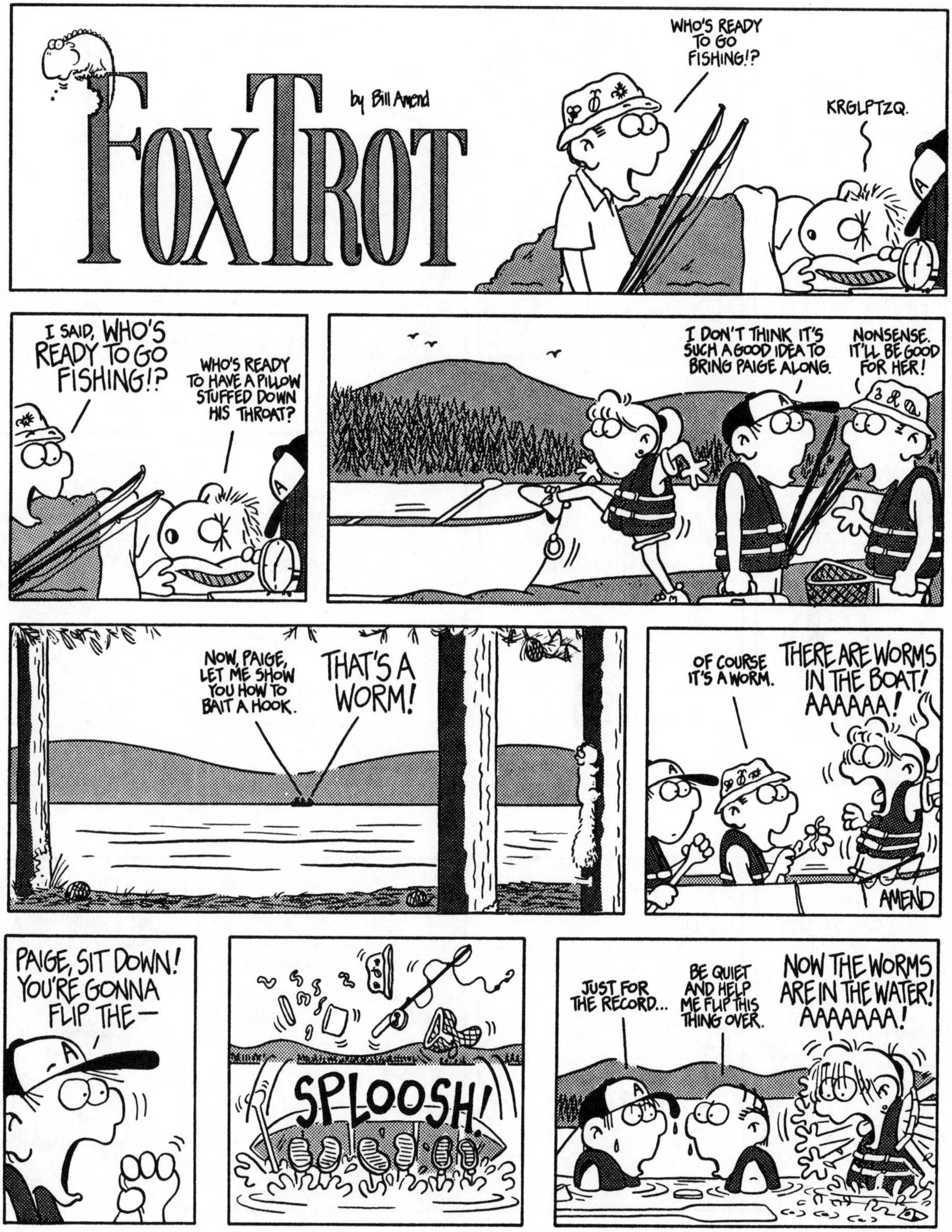
FoxTrot
by Bill Amend
WHO'S READY TO GO FISHING!?
KRGLPTZQ.
I SAID, WHO'S READY TO GO FISHING!?
WHO'S READY TO HAVE A PILLOW STUFFED DOWN HIS THROAT?
I DON'T THINK IT'S SUCH A GOOD IDEA TO BRING PAIGE ALONG.
NONSENSE. IT'LL BE GOOD FOR HER!
NOW, PAIGE, LET ME SHOW YOU HOW TO BAIT A HOOK.
THAT'S A WORM!
OF COURSE IT'S A WORM.
THERE ARE WORMS IN THE BOAT! AAAAAA!
AMEND
PAIGE, SIT DOWN! YOU'RE GONNA FLIP THE—
SPLOOSH!
JUST FOR THE RECORD...
BE QUIET AND HELP ME FLIP THIS THING OVER.
NOW THE WORMS ARE IN THE WATER! AAAAAAA!

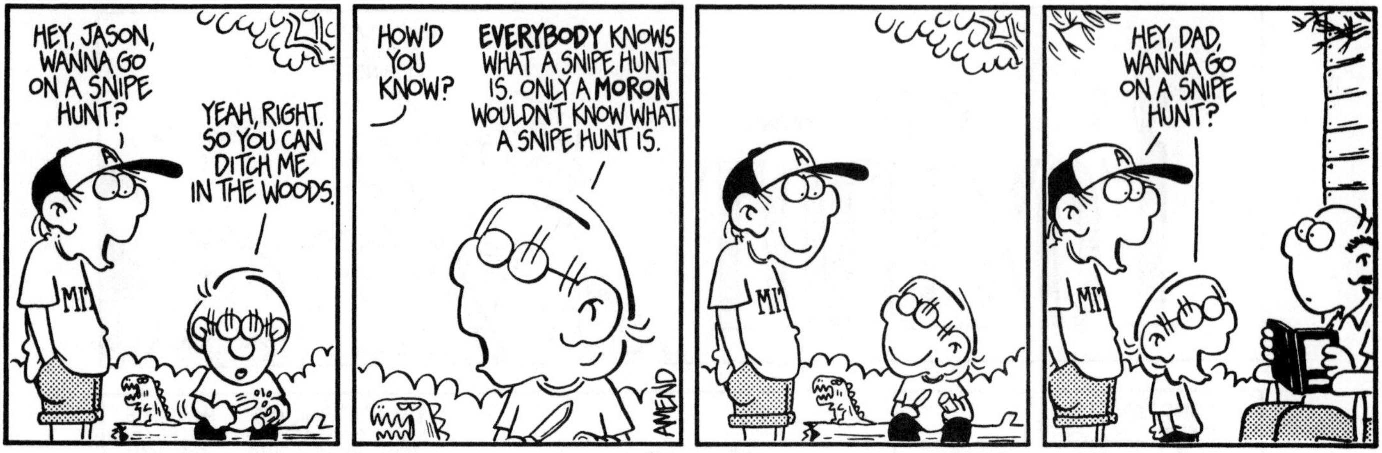
HEY, JASON, WANNA GO ON A SNIPE HUNT?
YEAH, RIGHT. SO YOU CAN DITCH ME IN THE WOODS.
HOW'D YOU KNOW?
EVERYBODY KNOWS WHAT A SNIPE HUNT IS. ONLY A MORON WOULDN'T KNOW WHAT A SNIPE HUNT IS.
AMEND
HEY, DAD, WANNA GO ON A SNIPE HUNT?

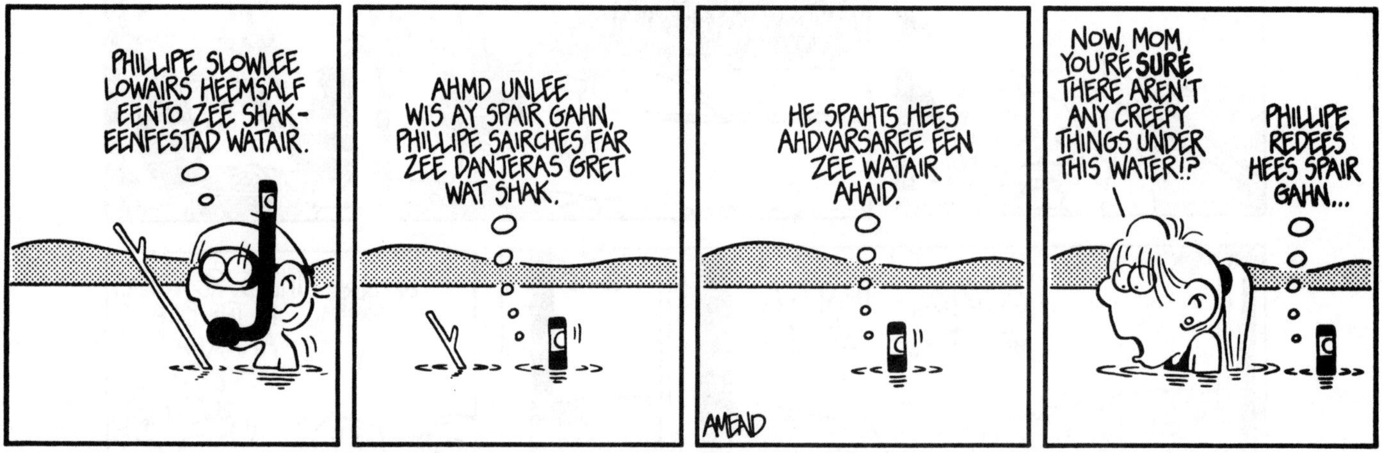
PHILLIPE SLOWLEE LOWAIRS HEEMSALF EENTO ZEE SHAK-EENFESTAD WATAIR.
AHMD UNLEE WIS AY SPAIR GAHN, PHILLIPE SAIRCHES FAR ZEE DANJERAS GRET WAT SHAK.
HE SPAHTS HEES AHDVARSAREE EEN ZEE WATAIR AHAID.
AMEND
NOW, MOM, YOU'RE SURE THERE AREN'T ANY CREEPY THINGS UNDER THIS WATER!?
PHILLIPE REDEES HEES SPAIR GAHN...

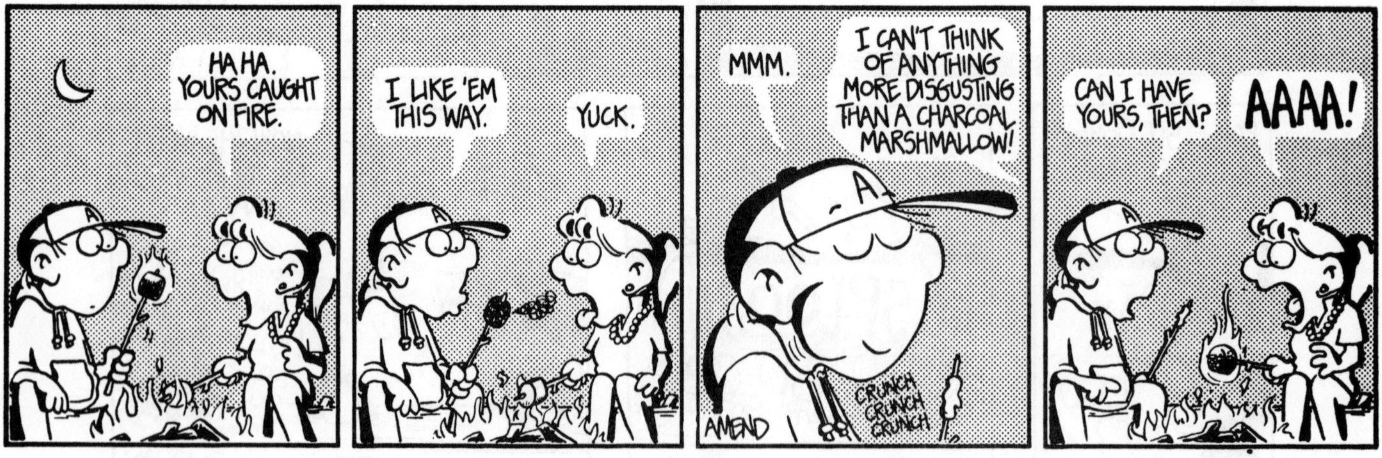
HA HA. YOURS CAUGHT ON FIRE.
I LIKE 'EM THIS WAY.
YUCK.
MMM.
I CAN'T THINK OF ANYTHING MORE DISGUSTING THAN A CHARCOAL MARSHMALLOW!
AMEND
CRUNCH CRUNCH CRUNCH
CAN I HAVE YOURS, THEN?
AAAA!

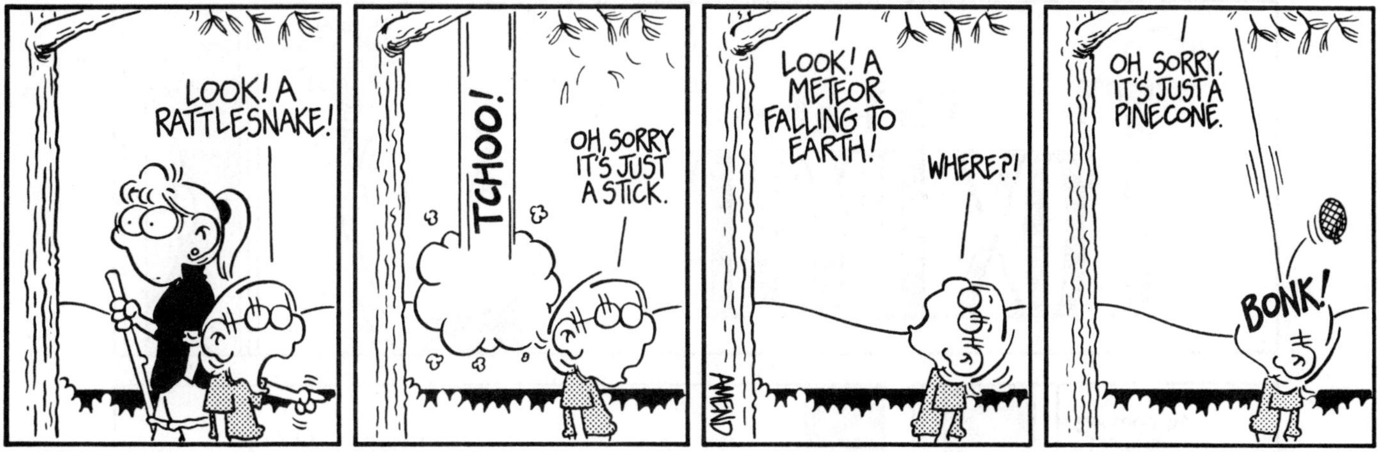
LOOK! A RATTLESNAKE!
TCHOO!
OH, SORRY IT'S JUST A STICK.
LOOK! A METEOR FALLING TO EARTH!
WHERE?!
AMEND
OH, SORRY. IT'S JUST A PINECONE.
BONK!

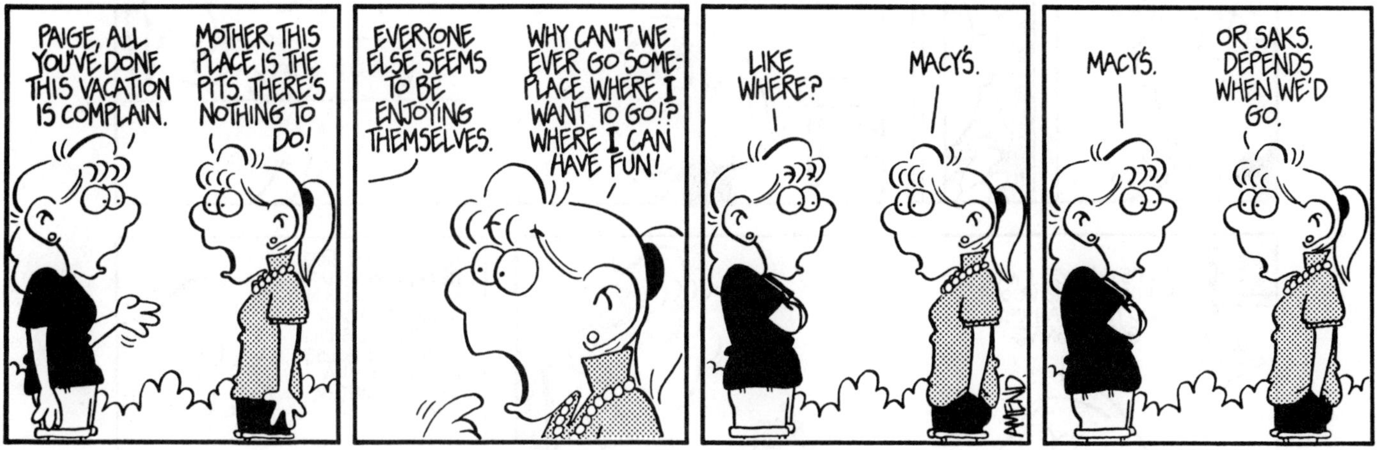
PAIGE, ALL YOU'VE DONE THIS VACATION IS COMPLAIN.
MOTHER, THIS PLACE IS THE PITS. THERE'S NOTHING TO DO!
EVERYONE ELSE SEEMS TO BE ENJOYING THEMSELVES.
WHY CAN'T WE EVER GO SOMEPLACE WHERE I WANT TO GO!? WHERE I CAN HAVE FUN!
LIKE WHERE?
MACY'S.
AMEND
MACY'S.
OR SAKS. DEPENDS WHEN WE'D GO.

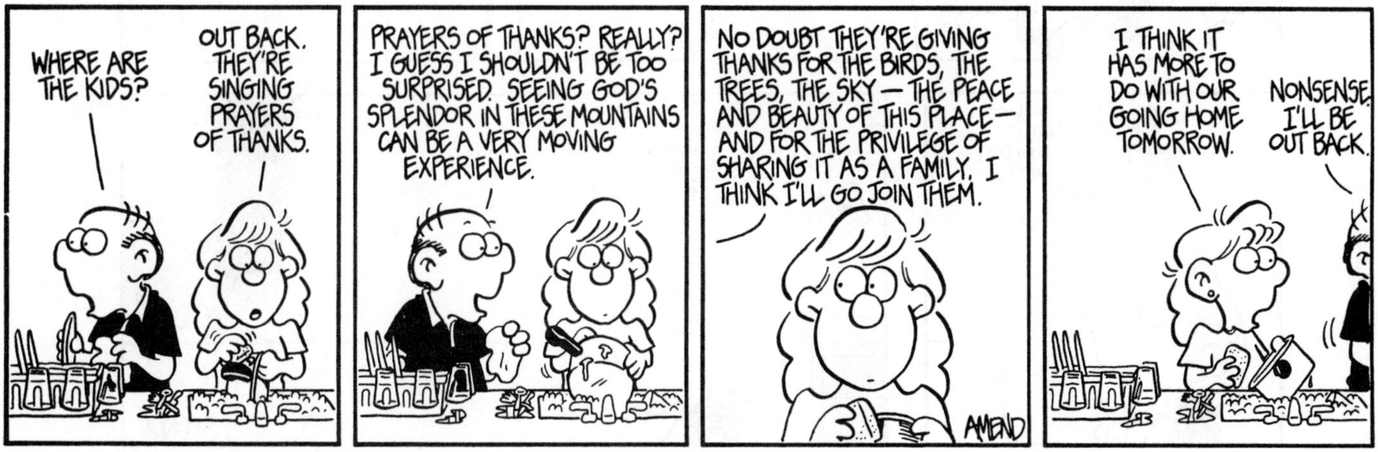
WHERE ARE THE KIDS?
OUT BACK. THEY'RE SINGING PRAYERS OF THANKS.
PRAYERS OF THANKS? REALLY? I GUESS I SHOULDN'T BE TOO SURPRISED. SEEING GOD'S SPLENDOR IN THESE MOUNTAINS CAN BE A VERY MOVING EXPERIENCE.
NO DOUBT THEY'RE GIVING THANKS FOR THE BIRDS, THE TREES, THE SKY — THE PEACE AND BEAUTY OF THIS PLACE — AND FOR THE PRIVILEGE OF SHARING IT AS A FAMILY. I THINK I'LL GO JOIN THEM.
AMEND
I THINK IT HAS MORE TO DO WITH OUR GOING HOME TOMORROW.
NONSENSE. I'LL BE OUT BACK.

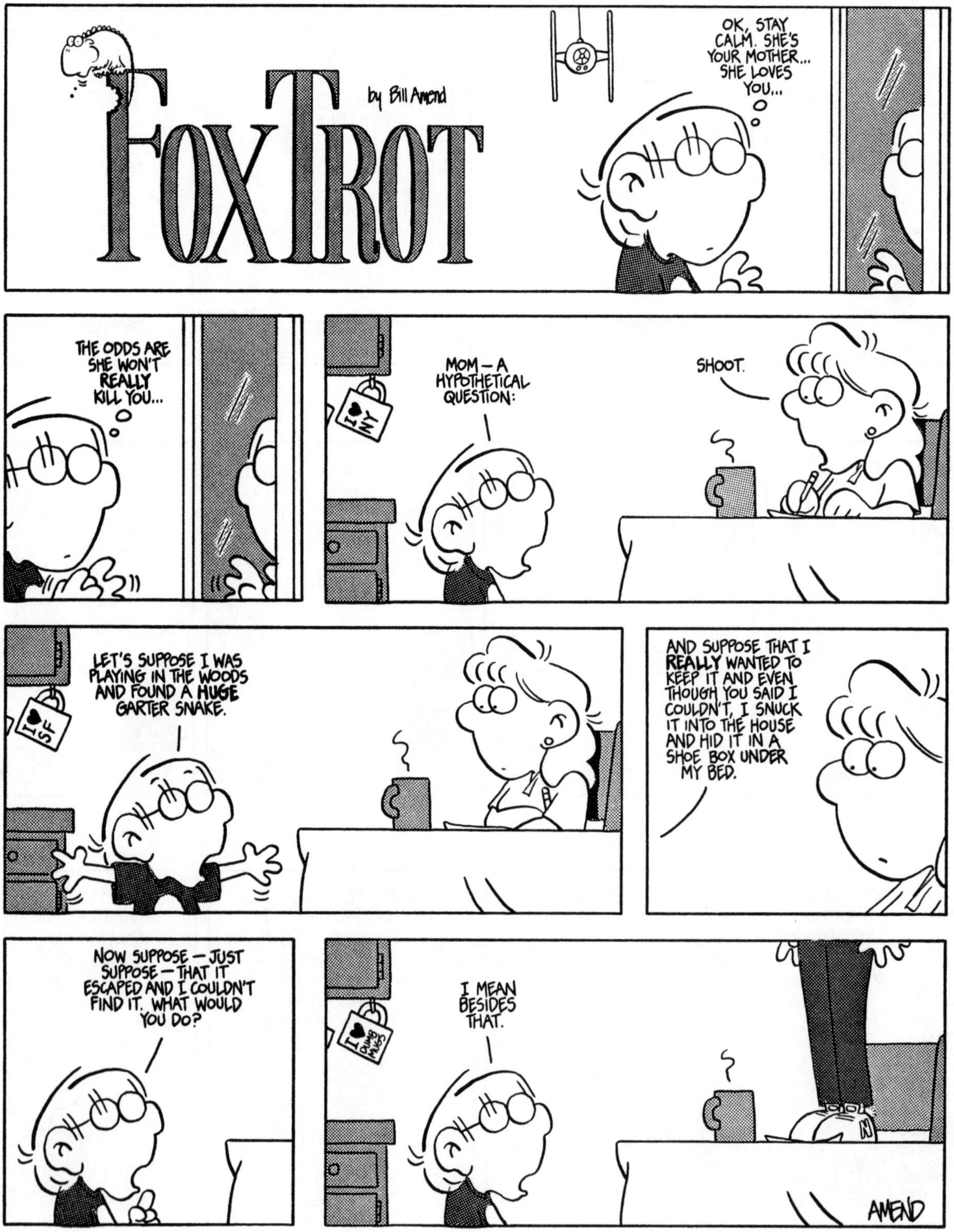
FoxTrot
by Bill Amend
OK, STAY CALM. SHE'S YOUR MOTHER... SHE LOVES YOU...
THE ODDS ARE SHE WON'T REALLY KILL YOU...
MOM — A HYPOTHETICAL QUESTION:
I ♥ NY
SHOOT.
LET'S SUPPOSE I WAS PLAYING IN THE WOODS AND FOUND A HUGE GARTER SNAKE.
I ♥ SF
AND SUPPOSE THAT I REALLY WANTED TO KEEP IT AND EVEN THOUGH YOU SAID I COULDN'T, I SNUCK IT INTO THE HOUSE AND HID IT IN A SHOE BOX UNDER MY BED.
NOW SUPPOSE — JUST SUPPOSE — THAT IT ESCAPED AND I COULDN'T FIND IT. WHAT WOULD YOU DO?
I MEAN BESIDES THAT.
I ♥ DUMB MUGS
AMEND

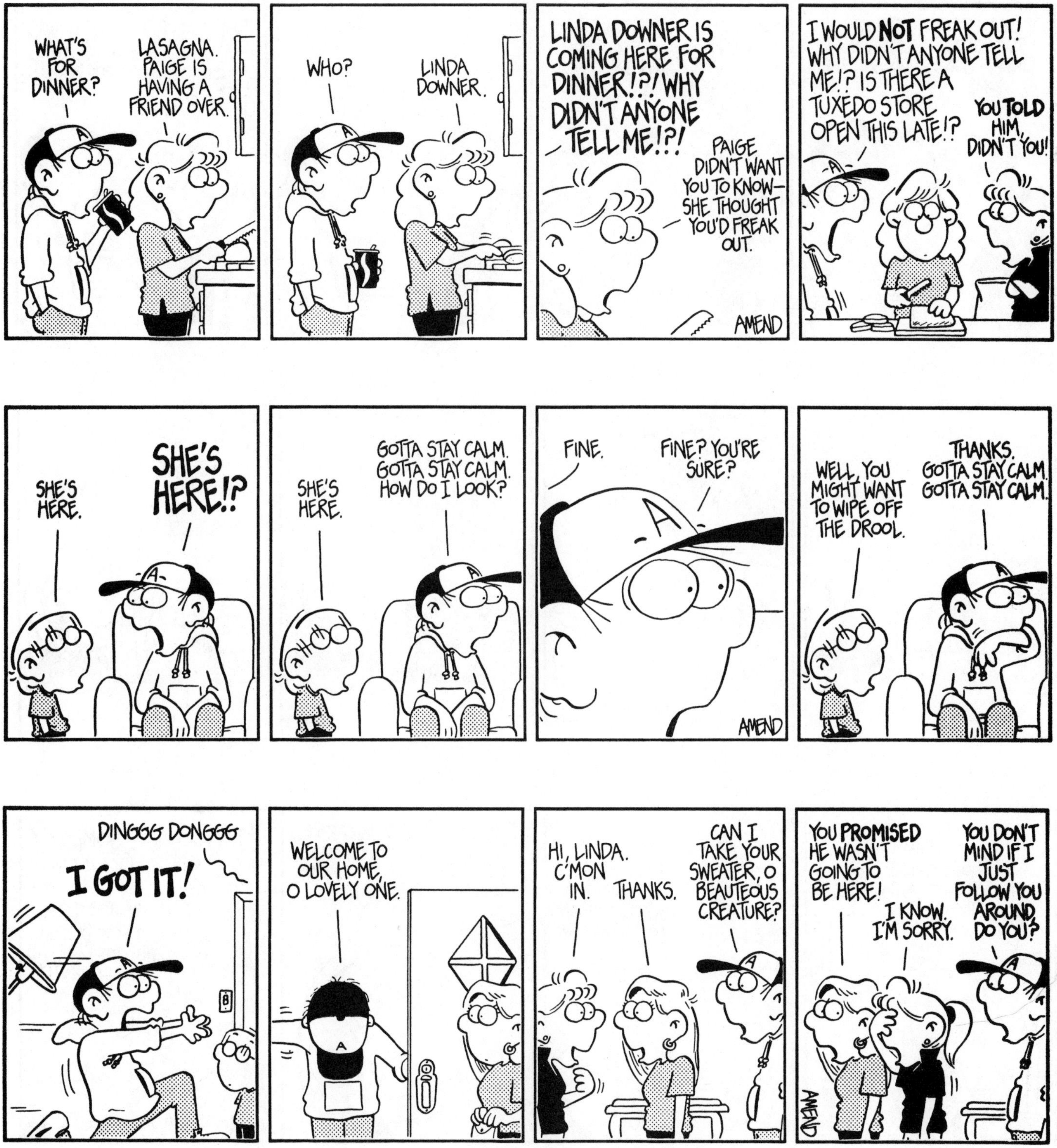
WHAT'S FOR DINNER?
LASAGNA. PAIGE IS HAVING A FRIEND OVER.
WHO?
LINDA DOWNER.
LINDA DOWNER IS COMING HERE FOR DINNER!?! WHY DIDN'T ANYONE TELL ME!?!
PAIGE DIDN'T WANT YOU TO KNOW— SHE THOUGHT YOU'D FREAK OUT.
AMEND
I WOULD NOT FREAK OUT! WHY DIDN'T ANYONE TELL ME!? IS THERE A TUXEDO STORE OPEN THIS LATE!?
YOU TOLD HIM, DIDN'T YOU!
SHE'S HERE.
SHE'S HERE!?
SHE'S HERE.
GOTTA STAY CALM. GOTTA STAY CALM. HOW DO I LOOK?
FINE.
FINE? YOU'RE SURE?
AMEND
WELL, YOU MIGHT WANT TO WIPE OFF THE DROOL.
THANKS. GOTTA STAY CALM. GOTTA STAY CALM.
DINGGG DONGGG
I GOT IT!
WELCOME TO OUR HOME, O LOVELY ONE.
HI, LINDA. C'MON IN.
THANKS.
CAN I TAKE YOUR SWEATER, O BEAUTEOUS CREATURE?
AMEND
YOU PROMISED HE WASN'T GOING TO BE HERE!
I KNOW. I'M SORRY.
YOU DON'T MIND IF I JUST FOLLOW YOU AROUND, DO YOU?

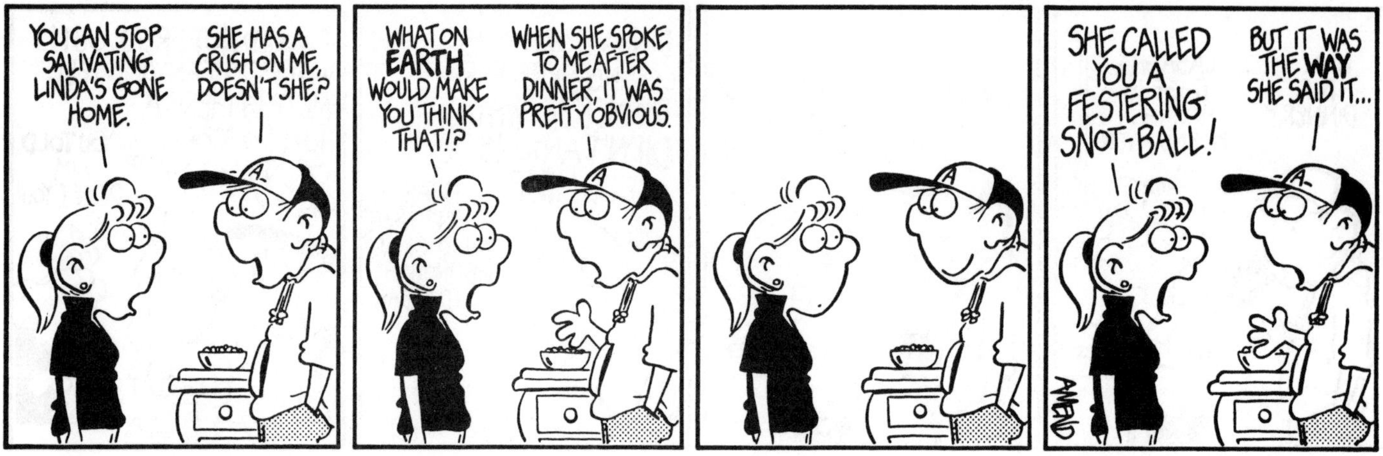
YOU CAN STOP SALIVATING. LINDA'S GONE HOME.
SHE HAS A CRUSH ON ME, DOESN'T SHE?
WHAT ON **EARTH** WOULD MAKE YOU THINK THAT!?
WHEN SHE SPOKE TO ME AFTER DINNER, IT WAS PRETTY OBVIOUS.
SHE CALLED YOU A FESTERING SNOT-BALL!
BUT IT WAS THE **WAY** SHE SAID IT...
AMEND

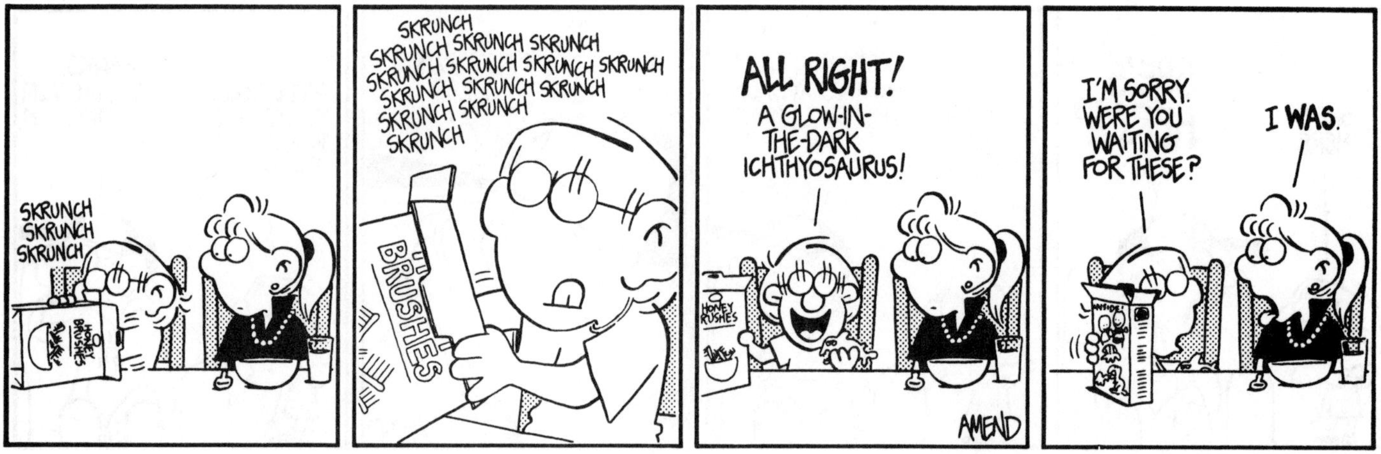
SKRUNCH SKRUNCH SKRUNCH
SKRUNCH SKRUNCH SKRUNCH SKRUNCH SKRUNCH SKRUNCH SKRUNCH SKRUNCH SKRUNCH SKRUNCH SKRUNCH SKRUNCH SKRUNCH SKRUNCH
ALL RIGHT!
A GLOW-IN-THE-DARK ICHTHYOSAURUS!
AMEND
I'M SORRY. WERE YOU WAITING FOR THESE?
I **WAS**.

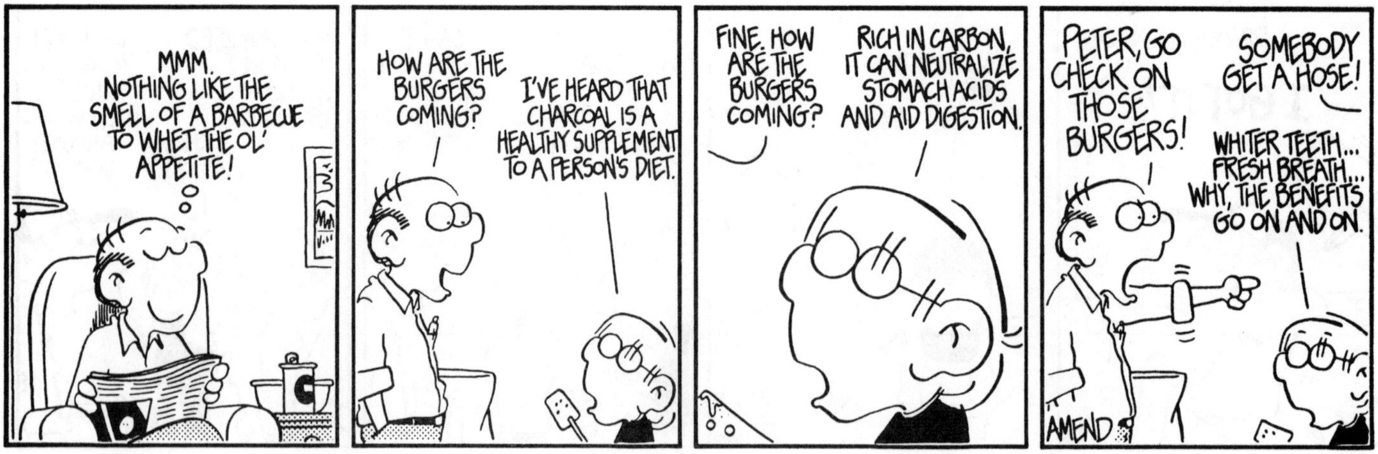
MMM. NOTHING LIKE THE SMELL OF A BARBECUE TO WHET THE OL' APPETITE!
HOW ARE THE BURGERS COMING?
I'VE HEARD THAT CHARCOAL IS A HEALTHY SUPPLEMENT TO A PERSON'S DIET.
FINE. HOW ARE THE BURGERS COMING?
RICH IN CARBON, IT CAN NEUTRALIZE STOMACH ACIDS AND AID DIGESTION.
PETER, GO CHECK ON THOSE BURGERS!
SOMEBODY GET A HOSE!
WHITER TEETH... FRESH BREATH... WHY, THE BENEFITS GO ON AND ON.
AMEND

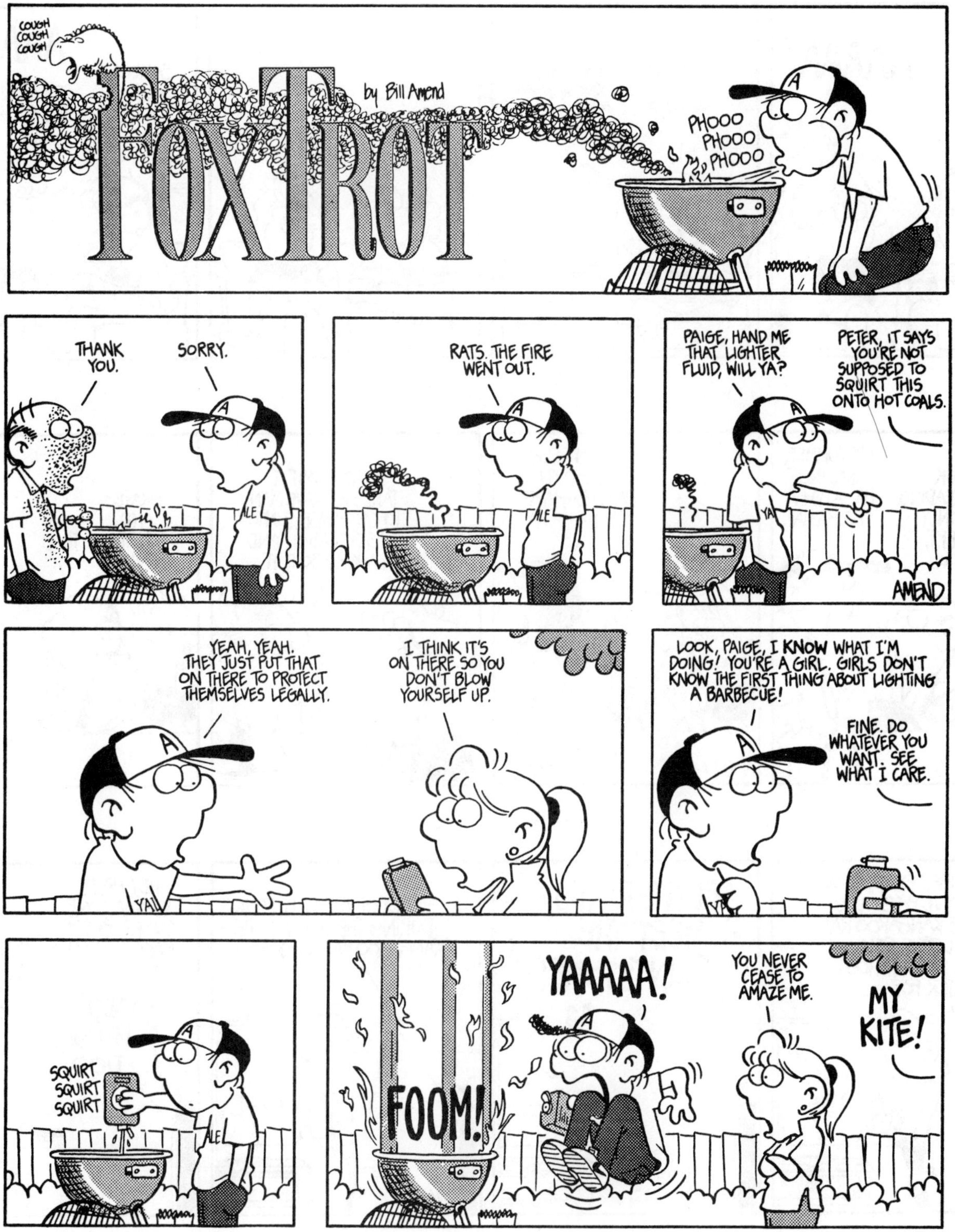
COUGH
COUGH
COUGH
FOXTROT
by Bill Amend
PHOOO
PHOOO
PHOOO
THANK YOU.
SORRY.
RATS. THE FIRE WENT OUT.
PAIGE, HAND ME THAT LIGHTER FLUID, WILL YA?
PETER, IT SAYS YOU'RE NOT SUPPOSED TO SQUIRT THIS ONTO HOT COALS.
AMEND
YEAH, YEAH. THEY JUST PUT THAT ON THERE TO PROTECT THEMSELVES LEGALLY.
I THINK IT'S ON THERE SO YOU DON'T BLOW YOURSELF UP.
LOOK, PAIGE, I KNOW WHAT I'M DOING! YOU'RE A GIRL. GIRLS DON'T KNOW THE FIRST THING ABOUT LIGHTING A BARBECUE!
FINE. DO WHATEVER YOU WANT. SEE WHAT I CARE.
SQUIRT
SQUIRT
SQUIRT
FOOM!
YAAAAA!
YOU NEVER CEASE TO AMAZE ME.
MY KITE!

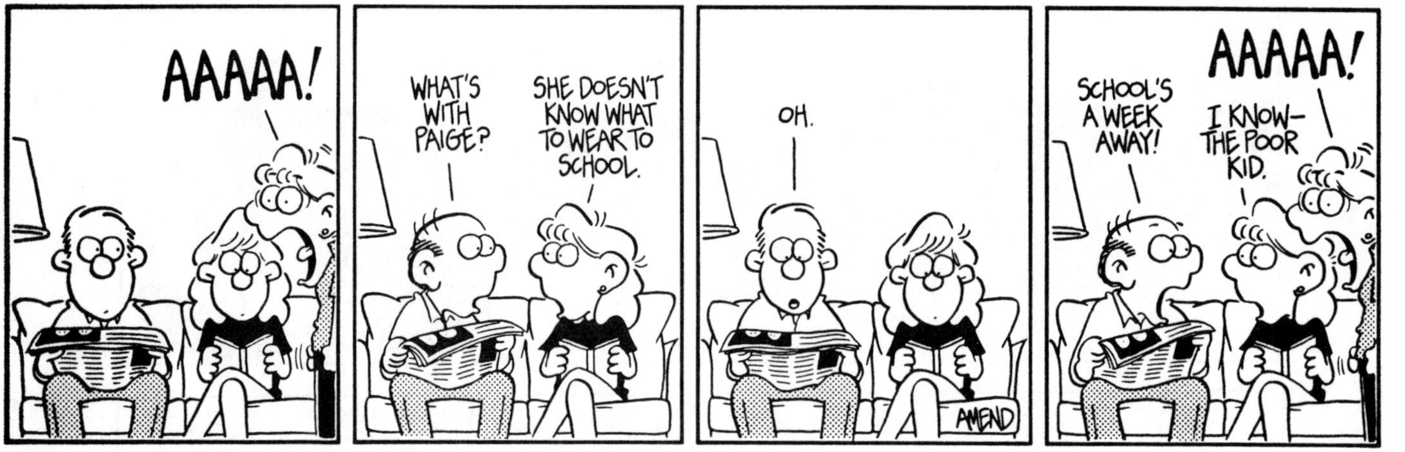
AAAAA!
WHAT'S WITH PAIGE?
SHE DOESN'T KNOW WHAT TO WEAR TO SCHOOL.
OH.
AMEND
SCHOOL'S A WEEK AWAY!
I KNOW— THE POOR KID.
AAAAA!

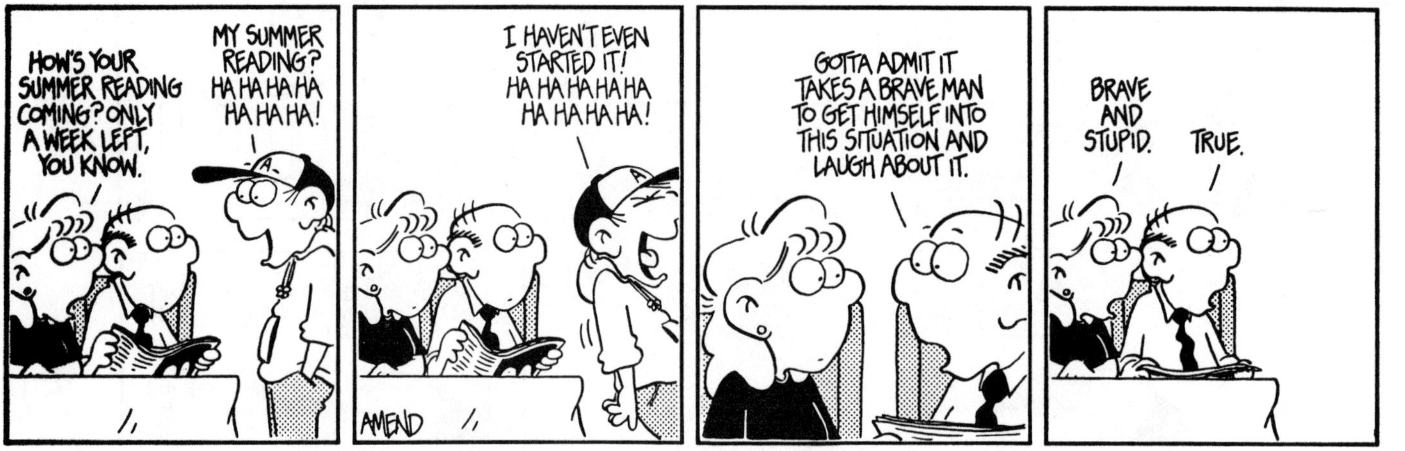
HOW'S YOUR SUMMER READING COMING? ONLY A WEEK LEFT, YOU KNOW.
MY SUMMER READING? HA HA HA HA HA HA HA!
I HAVEN'T EVEN STARTED IT! HA HA HA HA HA HA HA HA HA!
AMEND
GOTTA ADMIT IT TAKES A BRAVE MAN TO GET HIMSELF INTO THIS SITUATION AND LAUGH ABOUT IT.
BRAVE AND STUPID.
TRUE.

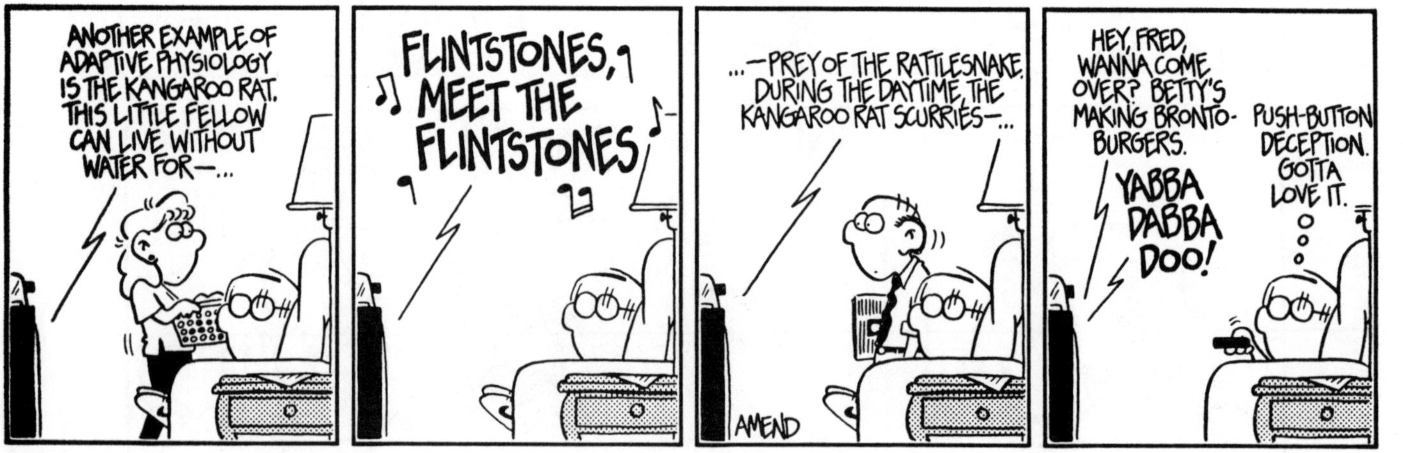
ANOTHER EXAMPLE OF ADAPTIVE PHYSIOLOGY IS THE KANGAROO RAT. THIS LITTLE FELLOW CAN LIVE WITHOUT WATER FOR—...
FLINTSTONES, MEET THE FLINTSTONES
...—PREY OF THE RATTLESNAKE. DURING THE DAYTIME, THE KANGAROO RAT SCURRIES—...
AMEND
HEY, FRED, WANNA COME OVER? BETTY'S MAKING BRONTO-BURGERS.
YABBA DABBA DOO!
PUSH-BUTTON DECEPTION. GOTTA LOVE IT.

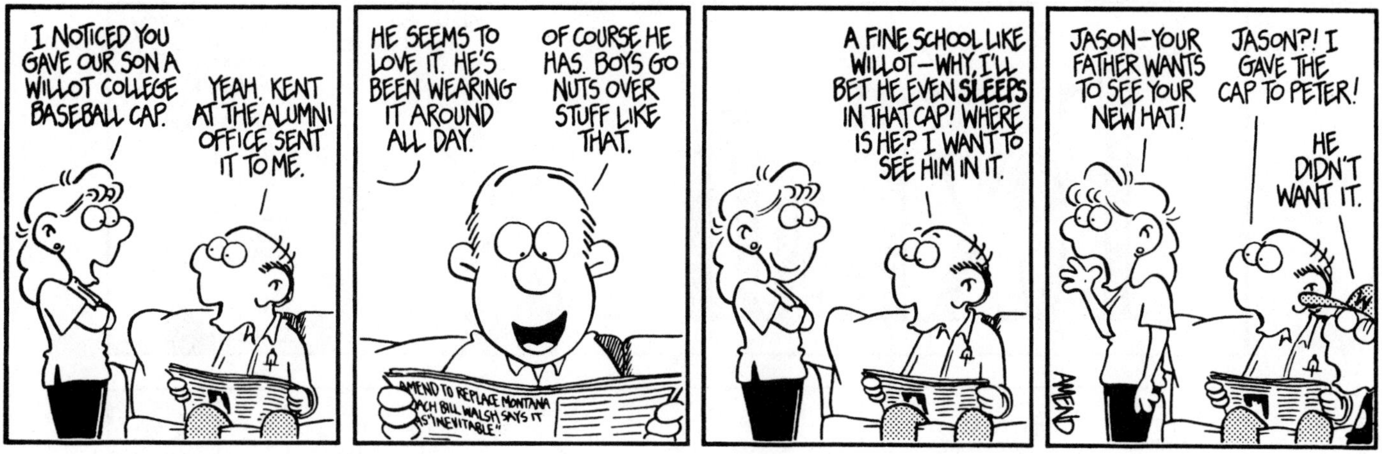

I NOTICED YOU GAVE OUR SON A WILLOT COLLEGE BASEBALL CAP.
YEAH. KENT AT THE ALUMNI OFFICE SENT IT TO ME.
HE SEEMS TO LOVE IT. HE'S BEEN WEARING IT AROUND ALL DAY.
OF COURSE HE HAS. BOYS GO NUTS OVER STUFF LIKE THAT.
AMEND TO REPLACE MONTANA
ACH BILL WALSH SAYS IT
IS "INEVITABLE".
A FINE SCHOOL LIKE WILLOT—WHY, I'LL BET HE EVEN **SLEEPS** IN THAT CAP! WHERE IS HE? I WANT TO SEE HIM IN IT.
JASON—YOUR FATHER WANTS TO SEE YOUR NEW HAT!
JASON?! I GAVE THE CAP TO PETER!
HE DIDN'T WANT IT.
AMEND

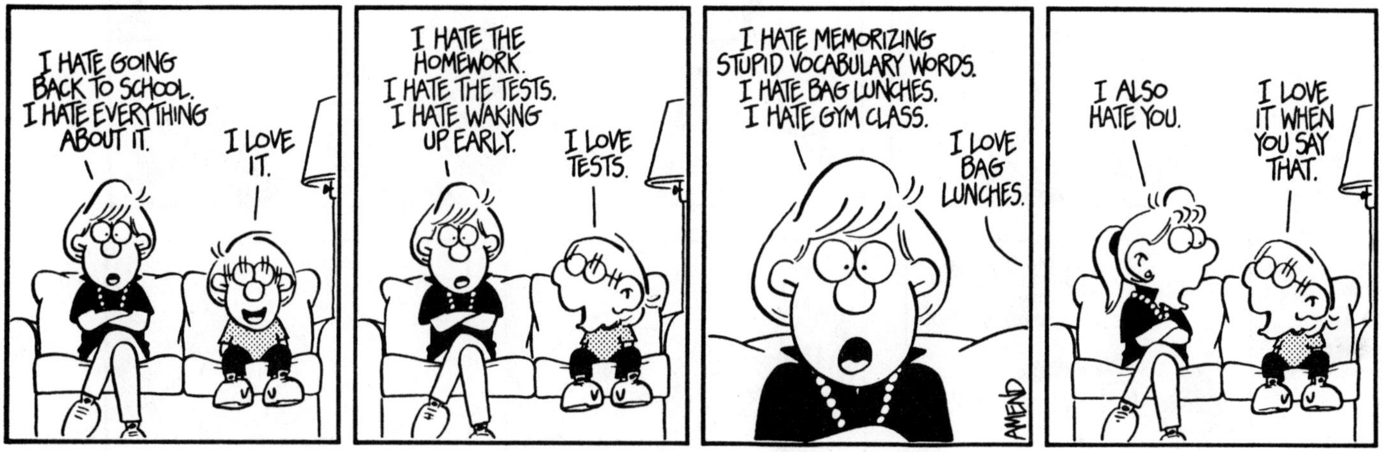

I HATE GOING BACK TO SCHOOL. I HATE EVERYTHING ABOUT IT.
I LOVE IT.
I HATE THE HOMEWORK. I HATE THE TESTS. I HATE WAKING UP EARLY.
I LOVE TESTS.
I HATE MEMORIZING STUPID VOCABULARY WORDS. I HATE BAG LUNCHES. I HATE GYM CLASS.
I LOVE BAG LUNCHES.
AMEND
I ALSO HATE YOU.
I LOVE IT WHEN YOU SAY THAT.

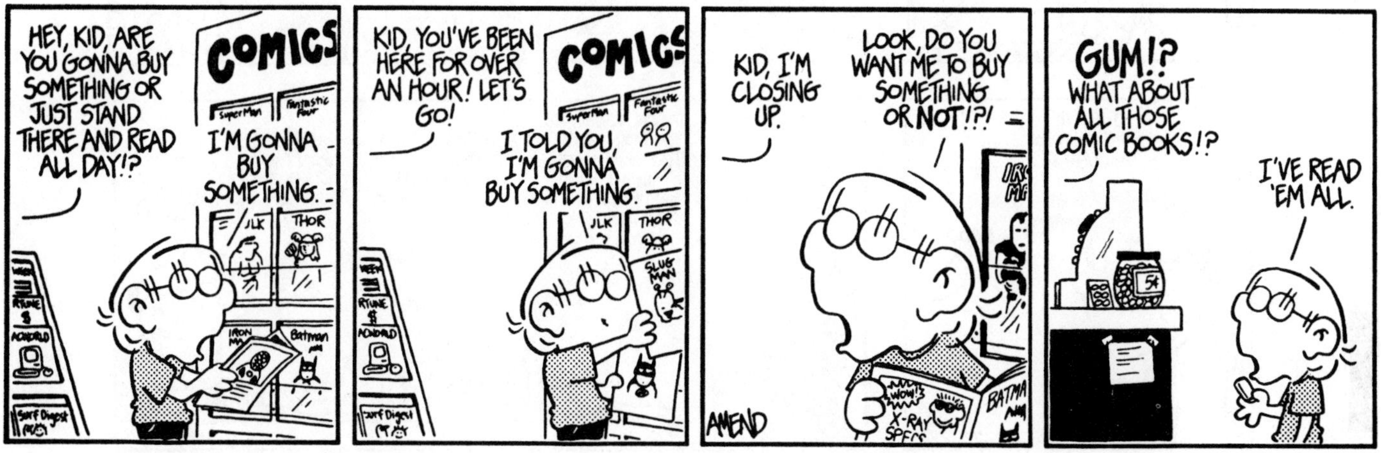

HEY, KID, ARE YOU GONNA BUY SOMETHING OR JUST STAND THERE AND READ ALL DAY!?
COMICS
I'M GONNA BUY SOMETHING.
KID, YOU'VE BEEN HERE FOR OVER AN HOUR! LET'S GO!
COMICS
I TOLD YOU, I'M GONNA BUY SOMETHING.
KID, I'M CLOSING UP.
LOOK, DO YOU WANT ME TO BUY SOMETHING OR **NOT**!?!
X-RAY SPECS
AMEND
GUM!? WHAT ABOUT ALL THOSE COMIC BOOKS!?
I'VE READ 'EM ALL.

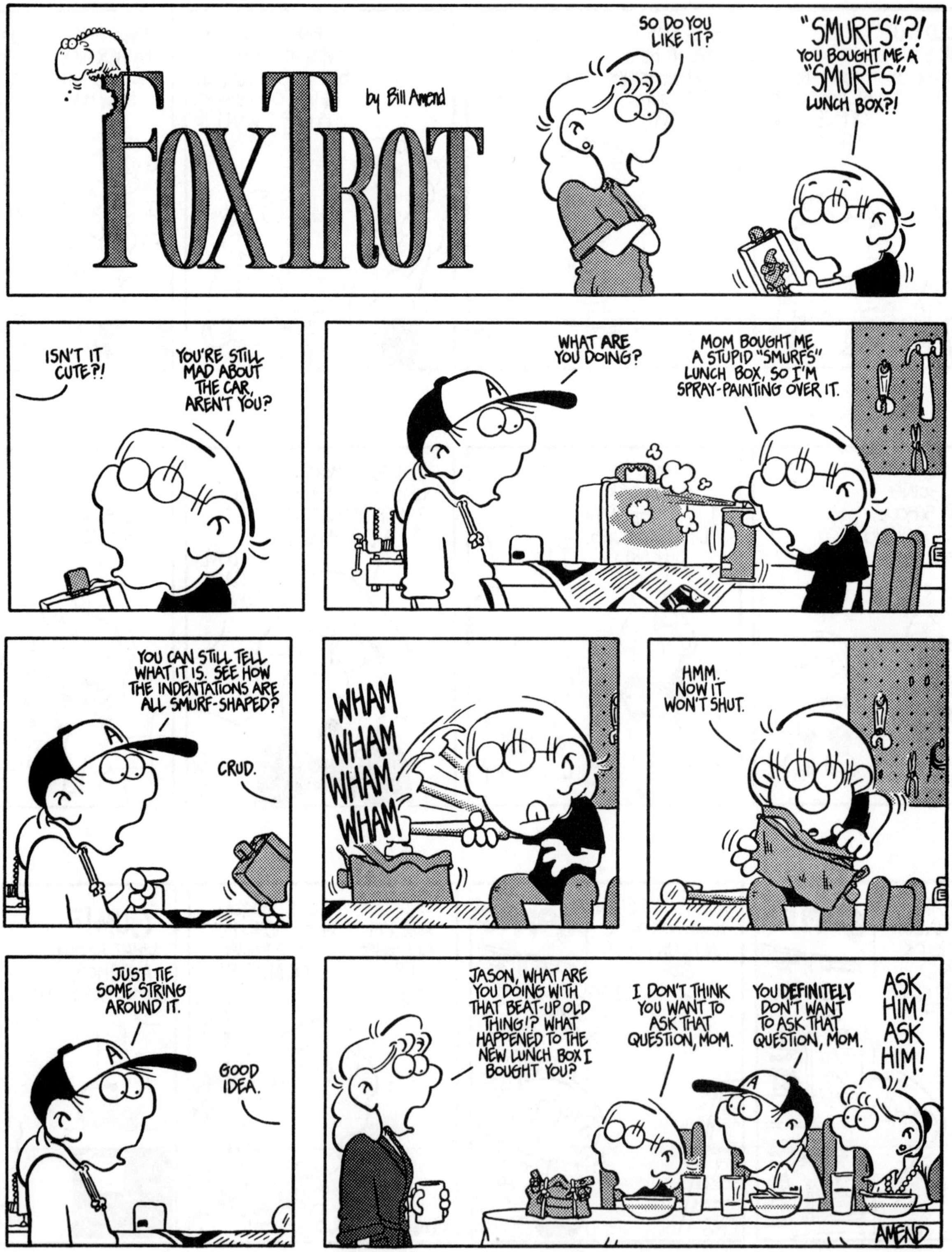
FoxTrot
by Bill Amend
SO DO YOU LIKE IT?
"SMURFS"?! YOU BOUGHT ME A "SMURFS" LUNCH BOX?!
ISN'T IT CUTE?!
YOU'RE STILL MAD ABOUT THE CAR, AREN'T YOU?
WHAT ARE YOU DOING?
MOM BOUGHT ME A STUPID "SMURFS" LUNCH BOX, SO I'M SPRAY-PAINTING OVER IT.
YOU CAN STILL TELL WHAT IT IS. SEE HOW THE INDENTATIONS ARE ALL SMURF-SHAPED?
CRUD.
WHAM WHAM WHAM WHAM
HMM. NOW IT WON'T SHUT.
JUST TIE SOME STRING AROUND IT.
GOOD IDEA.
JASON, WHAT ARE YOU DOING WITH THAT BEAT-UP OLD THING!? WHAT HAPPENED TO THE NEW LUNCH BOX I BOUGHT YOU?
I DON'T THINK YOU WANT TO ASK THAT QUESTION, MOM.
YOU DEFINITELY DON'T WANT TO ASK THAT QUESTION, MOM.
ASK HIM! ASK HIM!
AMEND

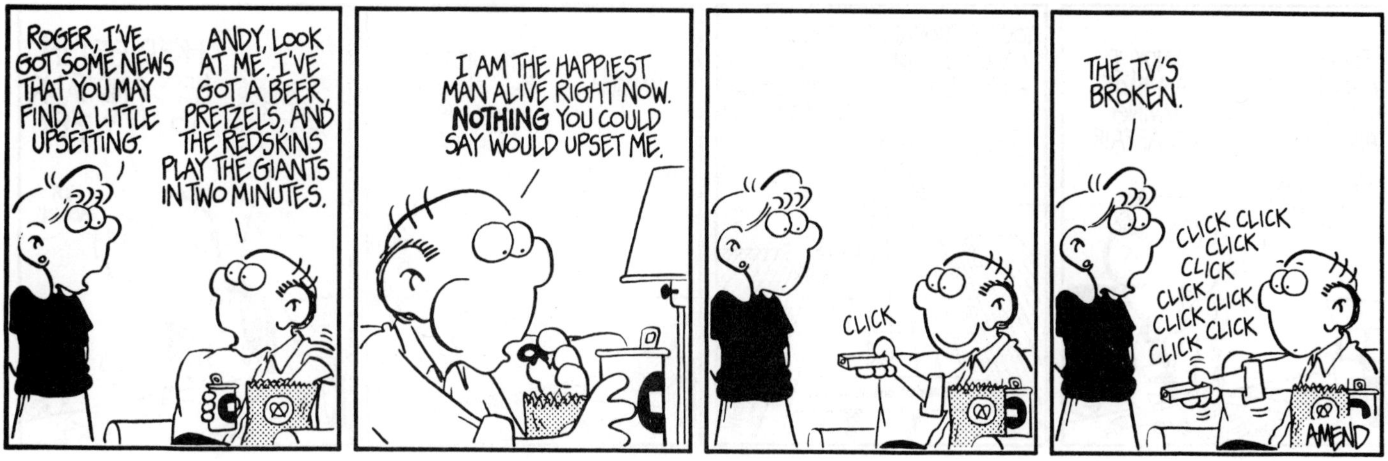
ROGER, I'VE GOT SOME NEWS THAT YOU MAY FIND A LITTLE UPSETTING.
ANDY, LOOK AT ME. I'VE GOT A BEER, PRETZELS, AND THE REDSKINS PLAY THE GIANTS IN TWO MINUTES.
I AM THE HAPPIEST MAN ALIVE RIGHT NOW. **NOTHING** YOU COULD SAY WOULD UPSET ME.
CLICK
THE TV'S BROKEN.
CLICK CLICK CLICK CLICK CLICK CLICK CLICK CLICK CLICK CLICK
AMEND

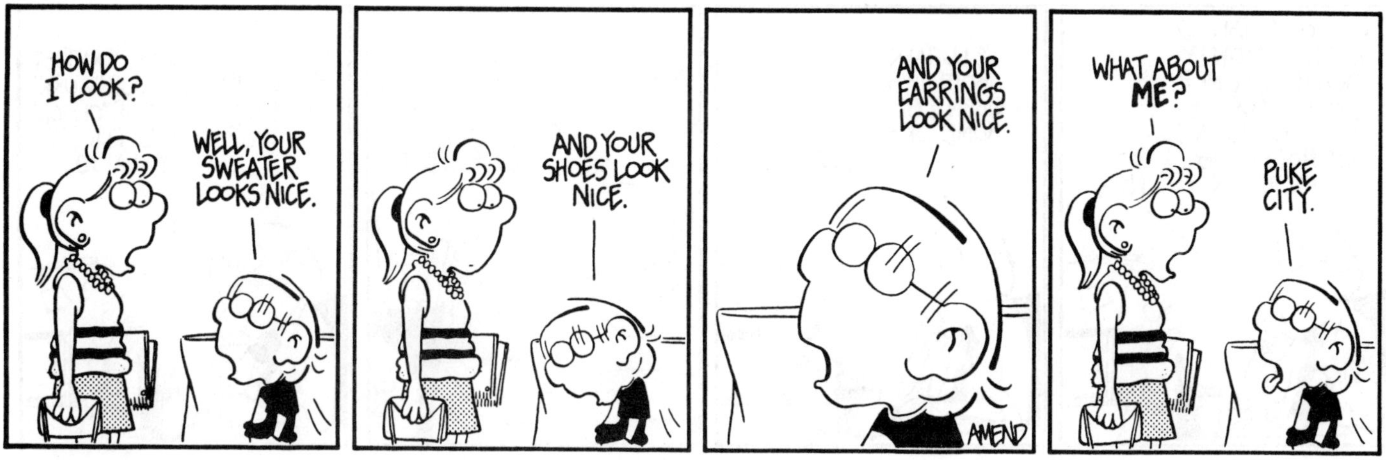
HOW DO I LOOK?
WELL, YOUR SWEATER LOOKS NICE.
AND YOUR SHOES LOOK NICE.
AND YOUR EARRINGS LOOK NICE.
AMEND
WHAT ABOUT **ME**?
PUKE CITY.

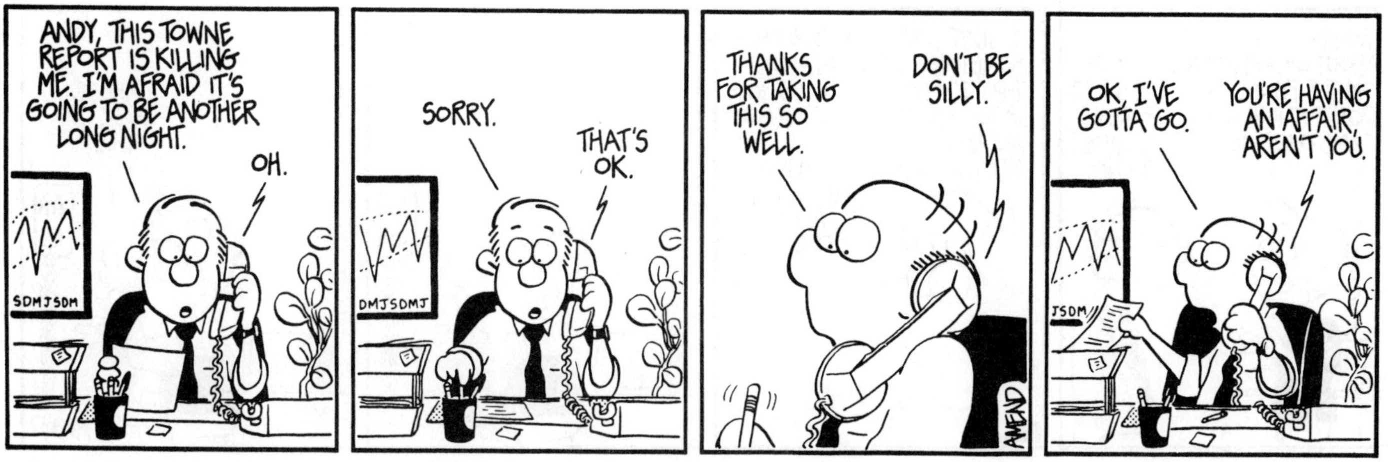
ANDY, THIS TOWNE REPORT IS KILLING ME. I'M AFRAID IT'S GOING TO BE ANOTHER LONG NIGHT.
OH.
SDMJSDM
SORRY.
THAT'S OK.
DMJSDMJ
THANKS FOR TAKING THIS SO WELL.
DON'T BE SILLY.
AMEND
OK, I'VE GOTTA GO.
YOU'RE HAVING AN AFFAIR, AREN'T YOU.
JSDM

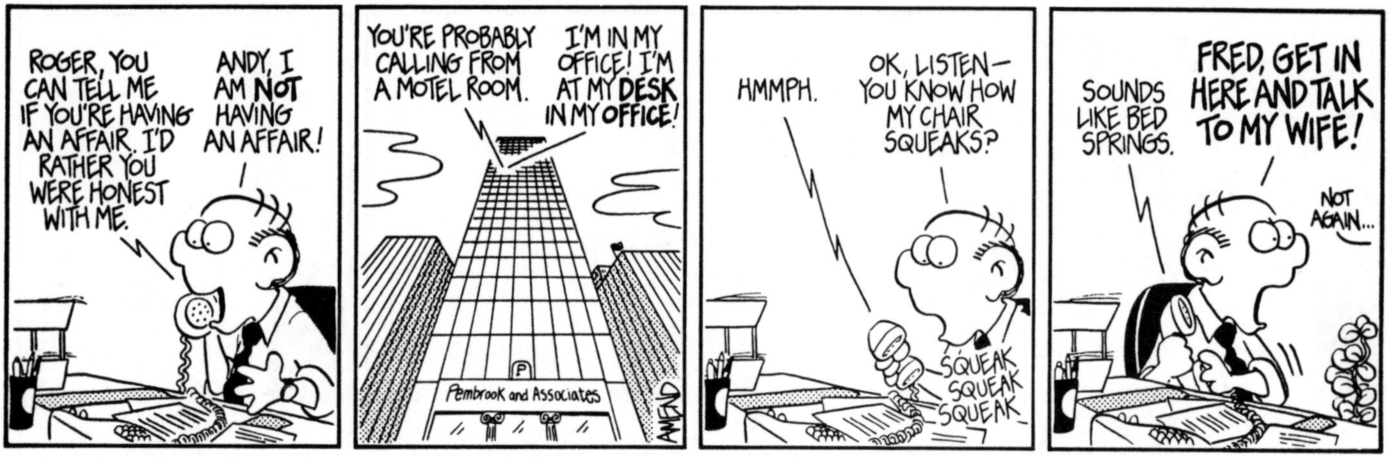
ROGER, YOU CAN TELL ME IF YOU'RE HAVING AN AFFAIR. I'D RATHER YOU WERE HONEST WITH ME.
ANDY, I AM **NOT** HAVING AN AFFAIR!
YOU'RE PROBABLY CALLING FROM A MOTEL ROOM.
I'M IN MY OFFICE! I'M AT MY **DESK** IN MY **OFFICE**!
Pembrook and Associates
AMEND
HMMPH.
OK, LISTEN— YOU KNOW HOW MY CHAIR SQUEAKS?
SQUEAK SQUEAK SQUEAK
SOUNDS LIKE BED SPRINGS.
FRED, GET IN HERE AND TALK TO MY WIFE!
NOT AGAIN...

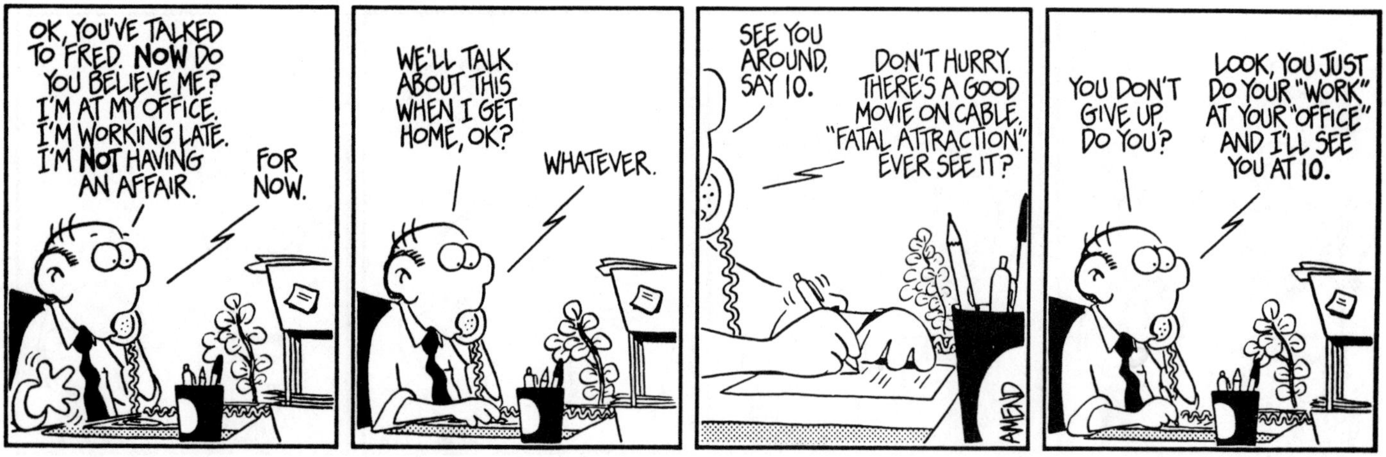
OK, YOU'VE TALKED TO FRED. **NOW** DO YOU BELIEVE ME? I'M AT MY OFFICE. I'M WORKING LATE. I'M **NOT** HAVING AN AFFAIR.
FOR NOW.
WE'LL TALK ABOUT THIS WHEN I GET HOME, OK?
WHATEVER.
SEE YOU AROUND, SAY 10.
DON'T HURRY. THERE'S A GOOD MOVIE ON CABLE. "FATAL ATTRACTION." EVER SEE IT?
AMEND
YOU DON'T GIVE UP, DO YOU?
LOOK, YOU JUST DO YOUR "WORK" AT YOUR "OFFICE" AND I'LL SEE YOU AT **10**.

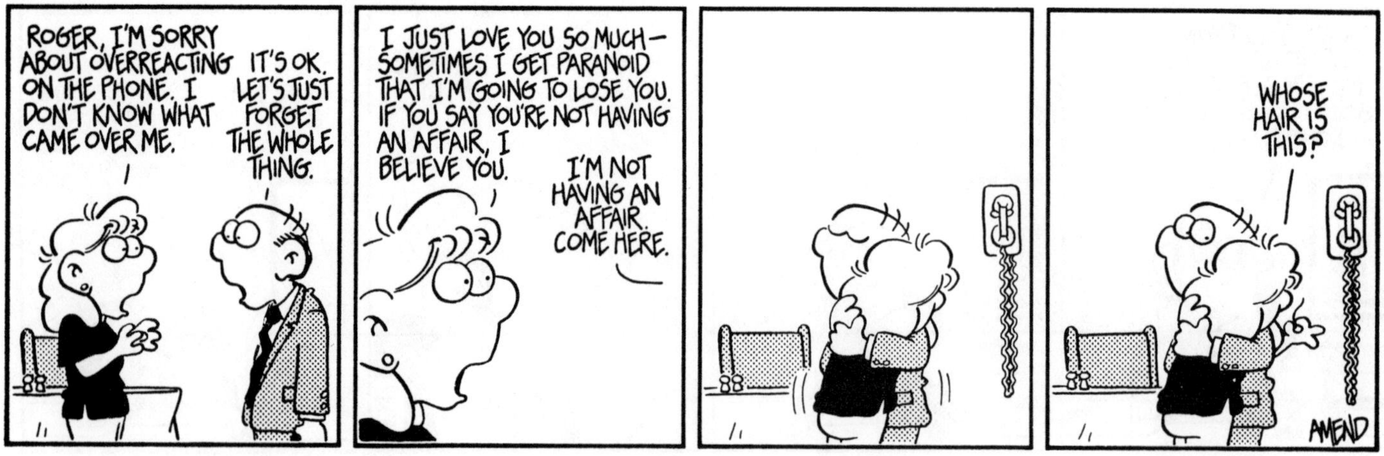
ROGER, I'M SORRY ABOUT OVERREACTING ON THE PHONE. I DON'T KNOW WHAT CAME OVER ME.
IT'S OK. LET'S JUST FORGET THE WHOLE THING.
I JUST LOVE YOU SO MUCH— SOMETIMES I GET PARANOID THAT I'M GOING TO LOSE YOU. IF YOU SAY YOU'RE NOT HAVING AN AFFAIR, I BELIEVE YOU.
I'M NOT HAVING AN AFFAIR. COME HERE.
WHOSE HAIR IS THIS?
AMEND

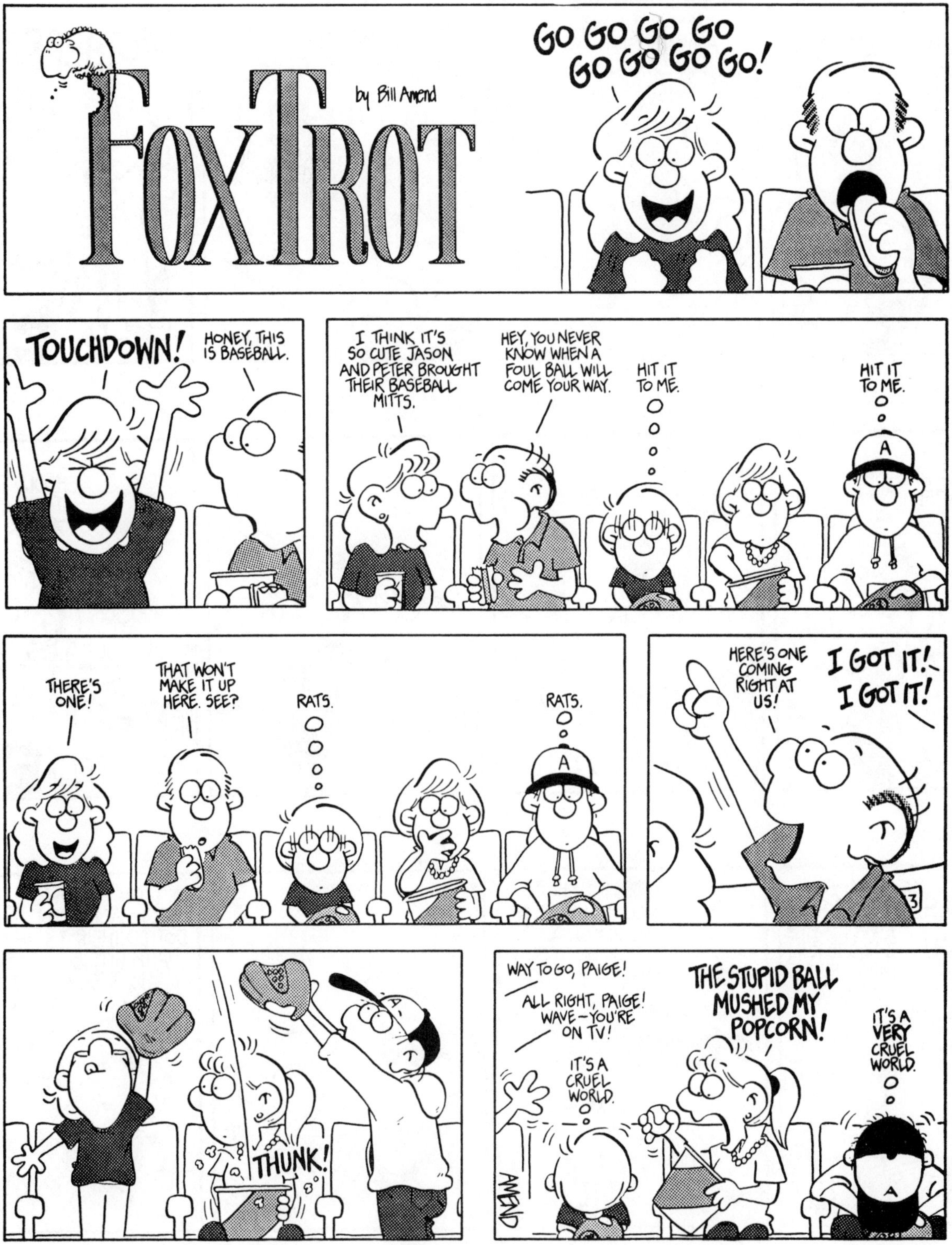
FoxTrot
by Bill Amend
GO GO GO GO
GO GO GO GO!
TOUCHDOWN!
HONEY, THIS IS BASEBALL.
I THINK IT'S SO CUTE JASON AND PETER BROUGHT THEIR BASEBALL MITTS.
HEY, YOU NEVER KNOW WHEN A FOUL BALL WILL COME YOUR WAY.
HIT IT TO ME.
HIT IT TO ME.
THERE'S ONE!
THAT WON'T MAKE IT UP HERE. SEE?
RATS.
RATS.
HERE'S ONE COMING RIGHT AT US!
I GOT IT! I GOT IT!
THUNK!
WAY TO GO, PAIGE!
ALL RIGHT, PAIGE! WAVE—YOU'RE ON TV!
THE STUPID BALL MUSHED MY POPCORN!
IT'S A CRUEL WORLD.
IT'S A VERY CRUEL WORLD.
AMEND

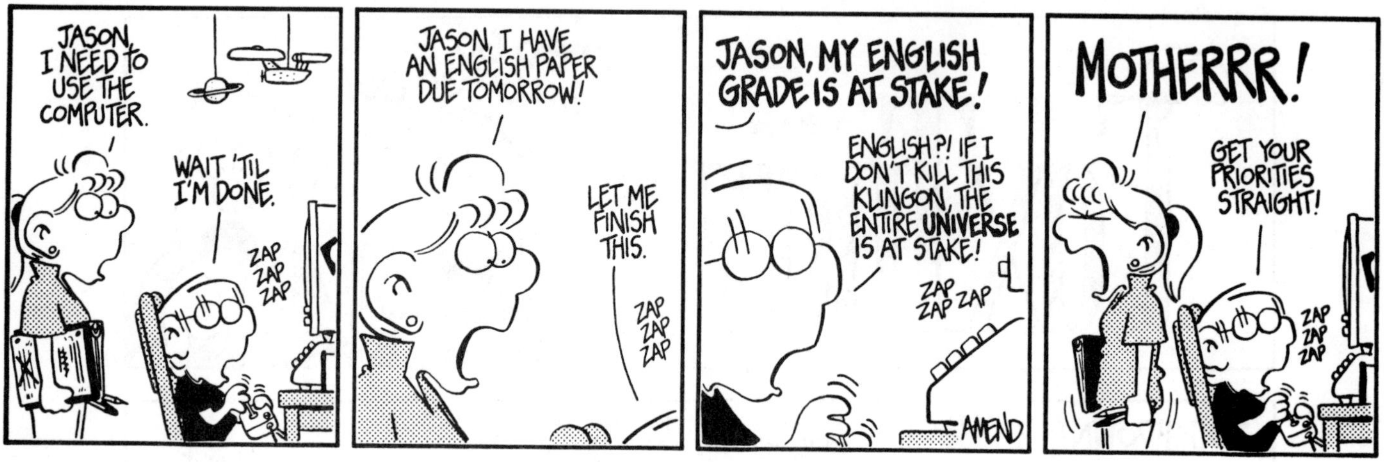
JASON, I NEED TO USE THE COMPUTER.
WAIT 'TIL I'M DONE.
ZAP ZAP ZAP
JASON, I HAVE AN ENGLISH PAPER DUE TOMORROW!
LET ME FINISH THIS.
ZAP ZAP ZAP
JASON, MY ENGLISH GRADE IS AT STAKE!
ENGLISH?! IF I DON'T KILL THIS KLINGON, THE ENTIRE **UNIVERSE** IS AT STAKE!
ZAP ZAP ZAP
AMEND
MOTHERRR!
GET YOUR PRIORITIES STRAIGHT!
ZAP ZAP ZAP

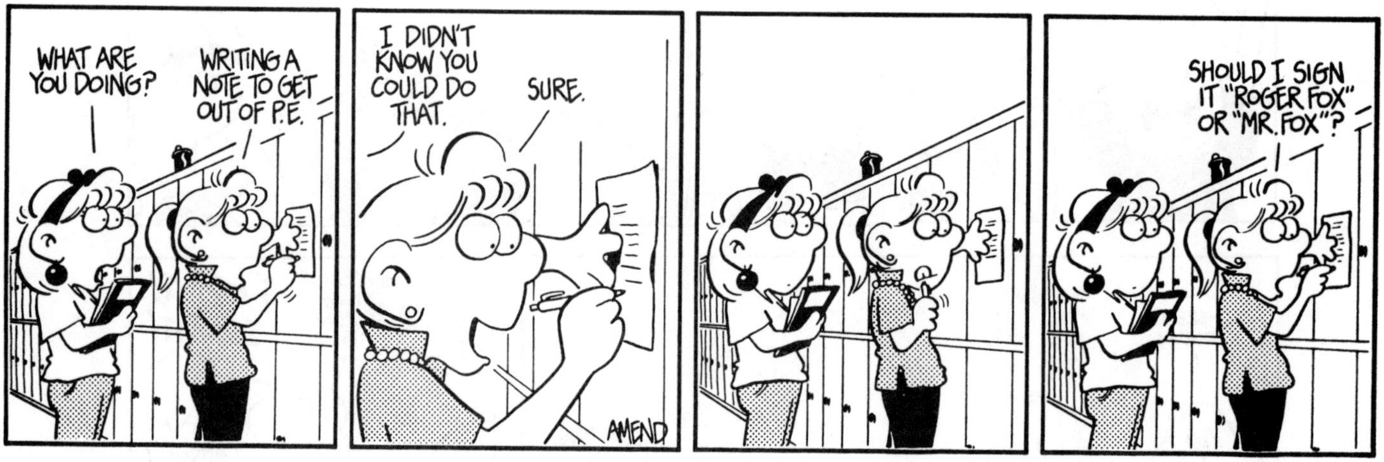
WHAT ARE YOU DOING?
WRITING A NOTE TO GET OUT OF P.E.
I DIDN'T KNOW YOU COULD DO THAT.
SURE.
AMEND
SHOULD I SIGN IT "ROGER FOX" OR "MR. FOX"?

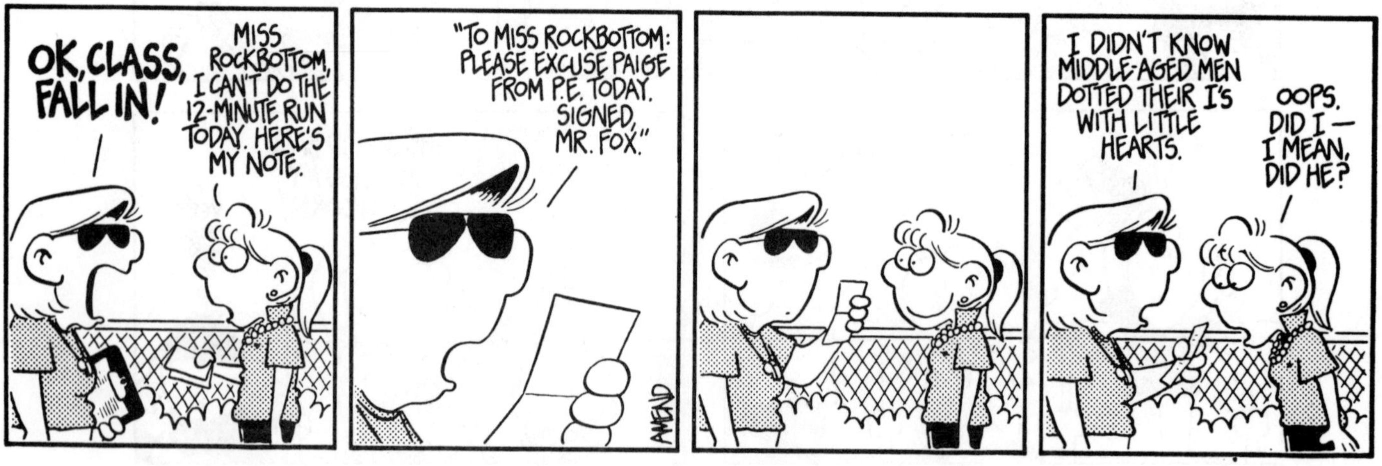
OK, CLASS, FALL IN!
MISS ROCKBOTTOM, I CAN'T DO THE 12-MINUTE RUN TODAY. HERE'S MY NOTE.
"TO MISS ROCKBOTTOM: PLEASE EXCUSE PAIGE FROM P.E. TODAY. SIGNED, MR. FOX."
AMEND
I DIDN'T KNOW MIDDLE-AGED MEN DOTTED THEIR I'S WITH LITTLE HEARTS.
OOPS. DID I — I MEAN, DID HE?

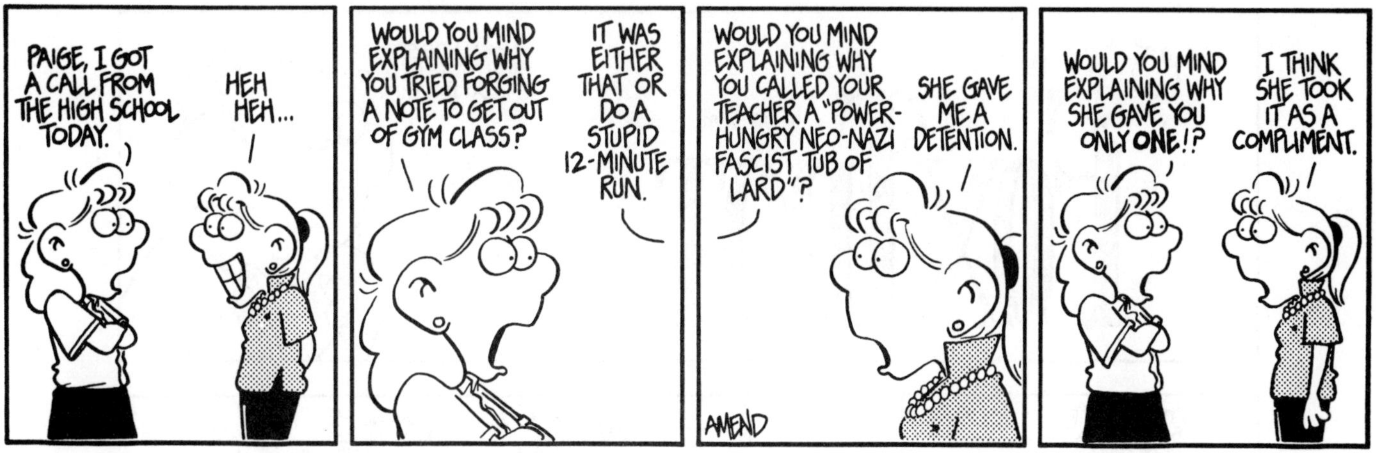
PAIGE, I GOT A CALL FROM THE HIGH SCHOOL TODAY.
HEH HEH...
WOULD YOU MIND EXPLAINING WHY YOU TRIED FORGING A NOTE TO GET OUT OF GYM CLASS?
IT WAS EITHER THAT OR DO A STUPID 12-MINUTE RUN.
WOULD YOU MIND EXPLAINING WHY YOU CALLED YOUR TEACHER A "POWER-HUNGRY NEO-NAZI FASCIST TUB OF LARD"?
SHE GAVE ME A DETENTION.
AMEND
WOULD YOU MIND EXPLAINING WHY SHE GAVE YOU ONLY **ONE**!?
I THINK SHE TOOK IT AS A **COMPLIMENT**.

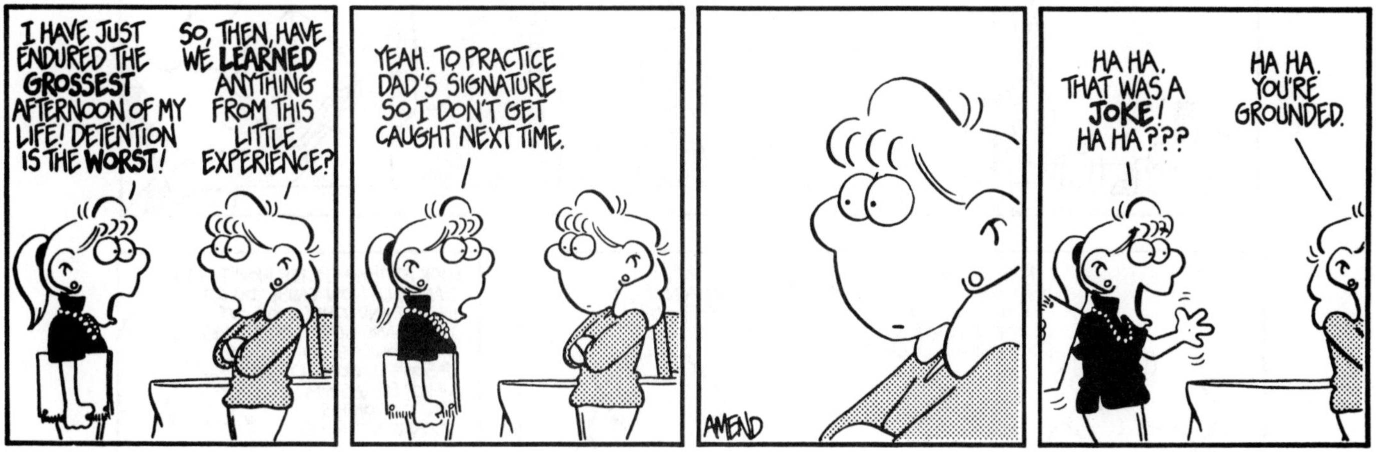
I HAVE JUST ENDURED THE **GROSSEST** AFTERNOON OF MY LIFE! DETENTION IS THE **WORST**!
SO, THEN, HAVE WE **LEARNED** ANYTHING FROM THIS LITTLE EXPERIENCE?
YEAH. TO PRACTICE DAD'S SIGNATURE SO I DON'T GET CAUGHT NEXT TIME.
AMEND
HA HA. THAT WAS A **JOKE**! HA HA???
HA HA. YOU'RE GROUNDED.

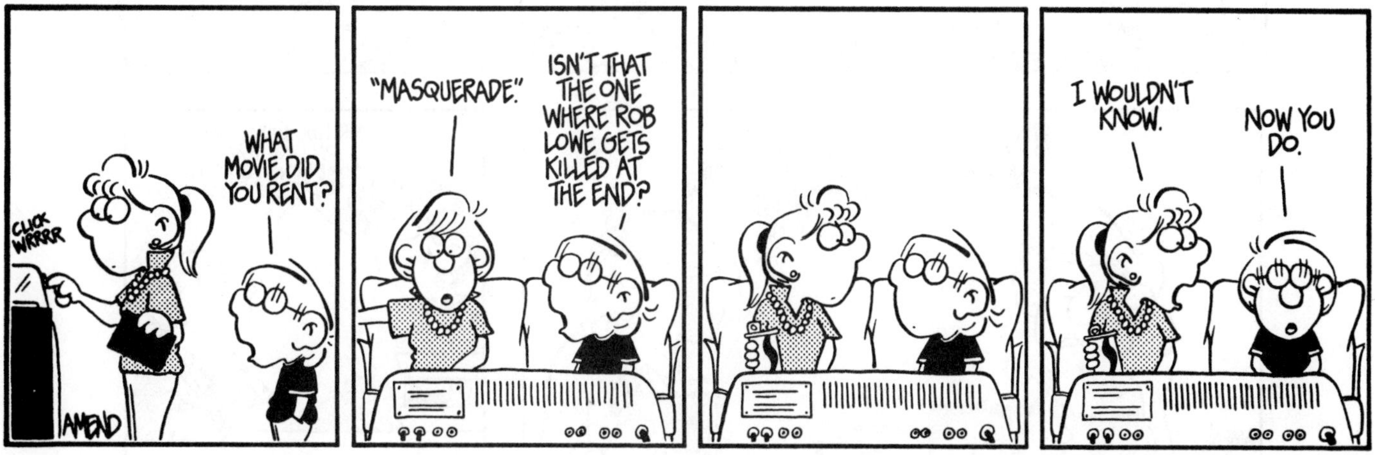
CLICK WRRRR
WHAT MOVIE DID YOU RENT?
AMEND
"MASQUERADE."
ISN'T THAT THE ONE WHERE ROB LOWE GETS KILLED AT THE END?
I WOULDN'T KNOW.
NOW YOU DO.

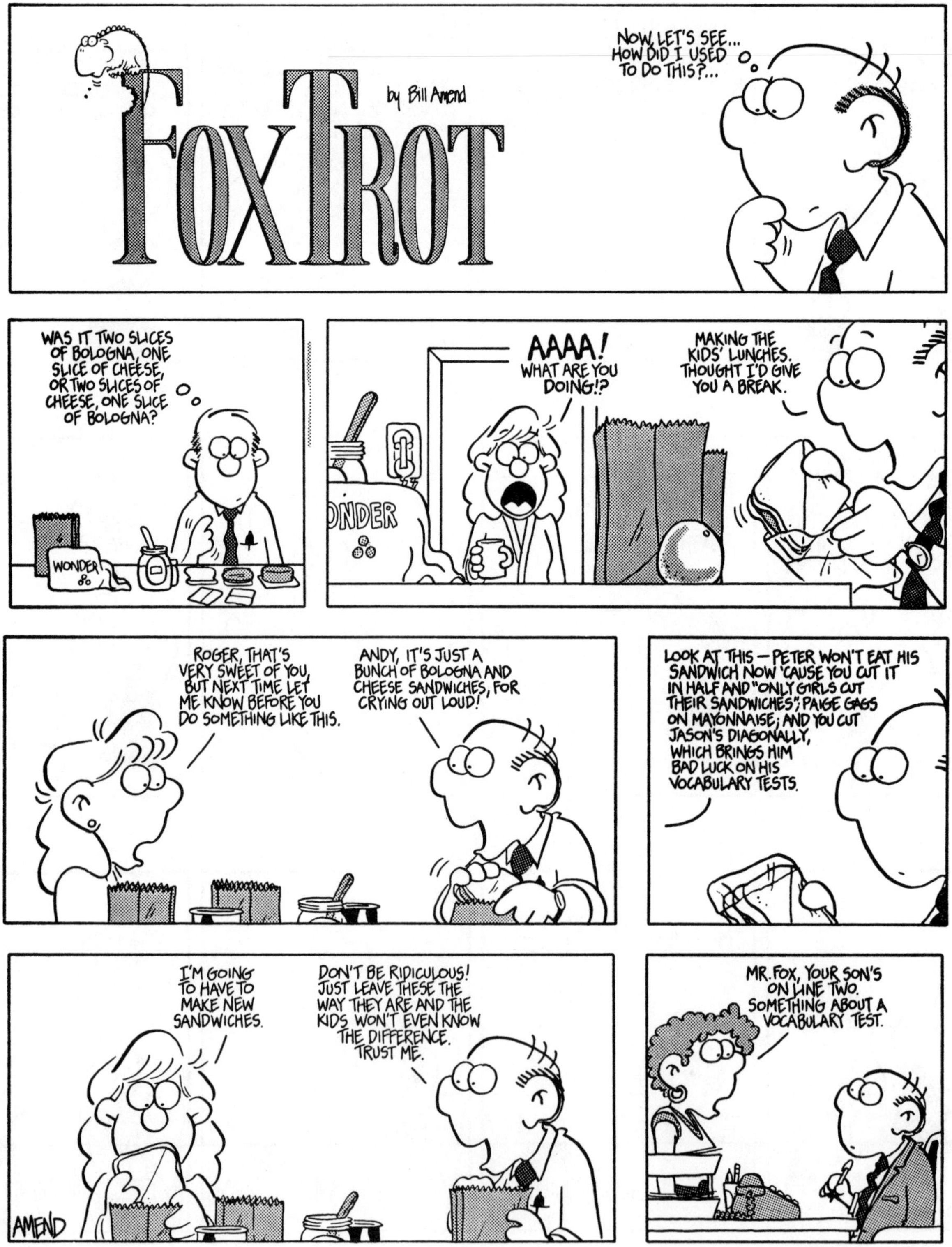
FoxTrot
by Bill Amend
NOW, LET'S SEE... HOW DID I USED TO DO THIS?...
WAS IT TWO SLICES OF BOLOGNA, ONE SLICE OF CHEESE, OR TWO SLICES OF CHEESE, ONE SLICE OF BOLOGNA?
WONDER
AAAA! WHAT ARE YOU DOING!?
MAKING THE KIDS' LUNCHES. THOUGHT I'D GIVE YOU A BREAK.
ROGER, THAT'S VERY SWEET OF YOU, BUT NEXT TIME LET ME KNOW BEFORE YOU DO SOMETHING LIKE THIS.
ANDY, IT'S JUST A BUNCH OF BOLOGNA AND CHEESE SANDWICHES, FOR CRYING OUT LOUD!
LOOK AT THIS — PETER WON'T EAT HIS SANDWICH NOW 'CAUSE YOU CUT IT IN HALF AND "ONLY GIRLS CUT THEIR SANDWICHES"; PAIGE GAGS ON MAYONNAISE; AND YOU CUT JASON'S DIAGONALLY, WHICH BRINGS HIM BAD LUCK ON HIS VOCABULARY TESTS.
I'M GOING TO HAVE TO MAKE NEW SANDWICHES.
DON'T BE RIDICULOUS! JUST LEAVE THESE THE WAY THEY ARE AND THE KIDS WON'T EVEN KNOW THE DIFFERENCE. TRUST ME.
AMEND
MR. FOX, YOUR SON'S ON LINE TWO. SOMETHING ABOUT A VOCABULARY TEST.

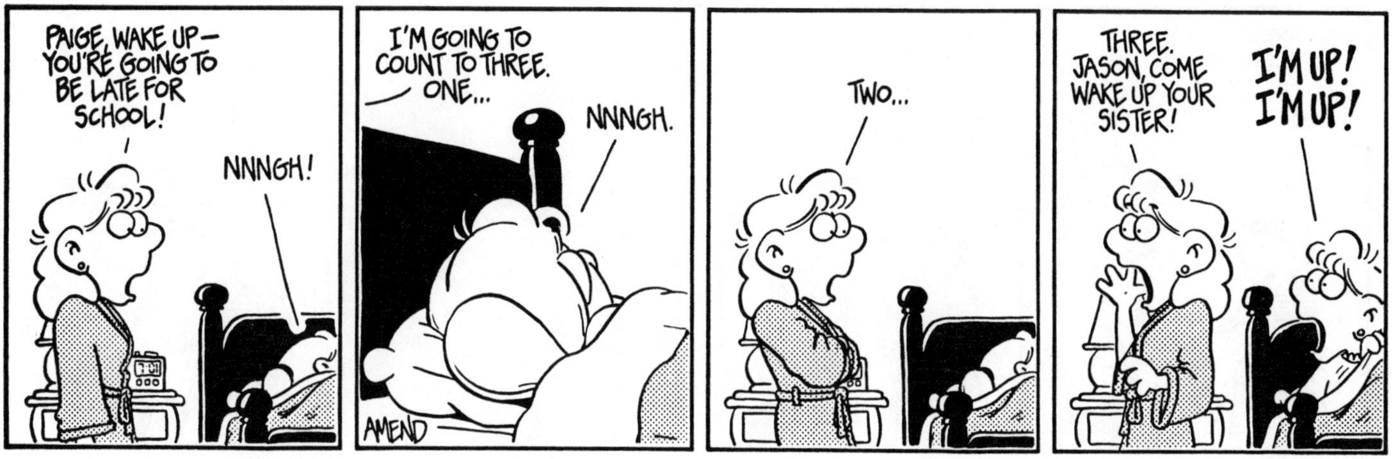
PAIGE, WAKE UP— YOU'RE GOING TO BE LATE FOR SCHOOL!
NNNGH!
I'M GOING TO COUNT TO THREE. ONE...
NNNGH.
AMEND
TWO...
THREE. JASON, COME WAKE UP YOUR SISTER!
I'M UP! I'M UP!

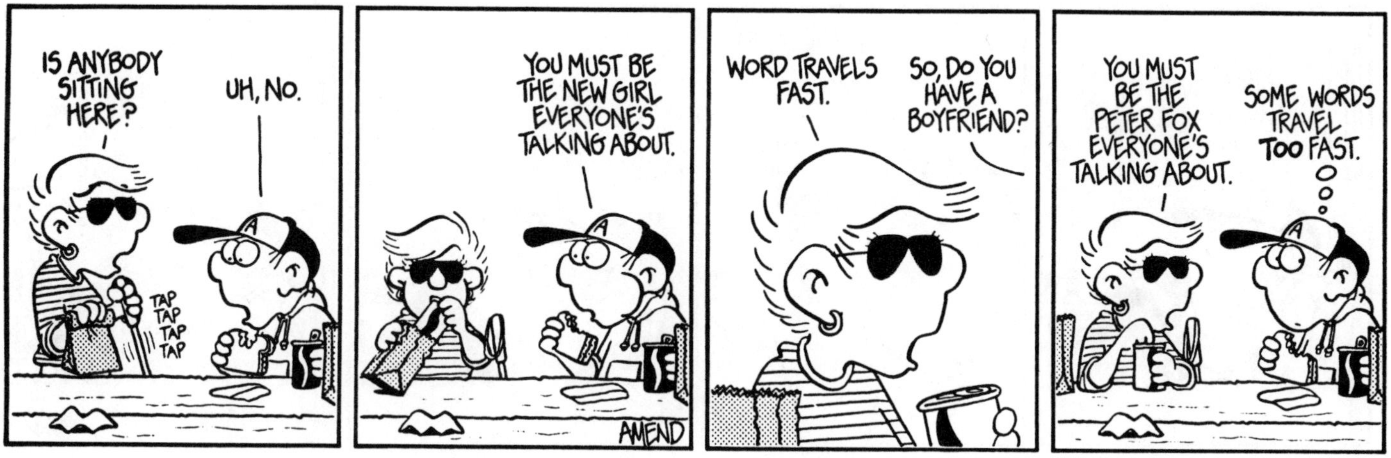
IS ANYBODY SITTING HERE?
UH, NO.
TAP TAP TAP TAP
YOU MUST BE THE NEW GIRL EVERYONE'S TALKING ABOUT.
AMEND
WORD TRAVELS FAST.
SO, DO YOU HAVE A BOYFRIEND?
YOU MUST BE THE PETER FOX EVERYONE'S TALKING ABOUT.
SOME WORDS TRAVEL TOO FAST.

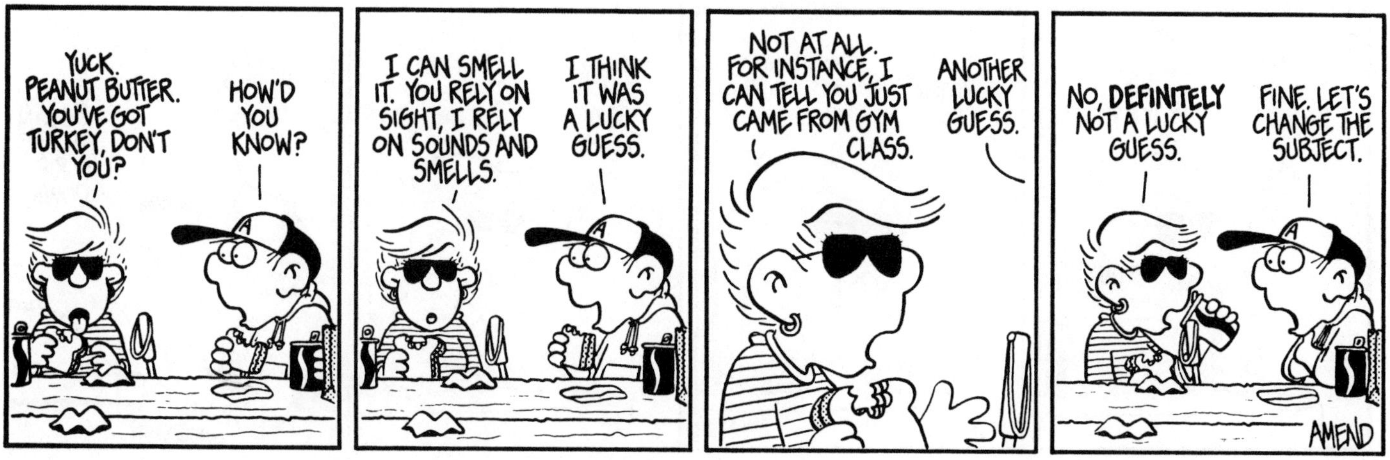
YUCK. PEANUT BUTTER. YOU'VE GOT TURKEY, DON'T YOU?
HOW'D YOU KNOW?
I CAN SMELL IT. YOU RELY ON SIGHT, I RELY ON SOUNDS AND SMELLS.
I THINK IT WAS A LUCKY GUESS.
NOT AT ALL. FOR INSTANCE, I CAN TELL YOU JUST CAME FROM GYM CLASS.
ANOTHER LUCKY GUESS.
NO, DEFINITELY NOT A LUCKY GUESS.
FINE. LET'S CHANGE THE SUBJECT.
AMEND

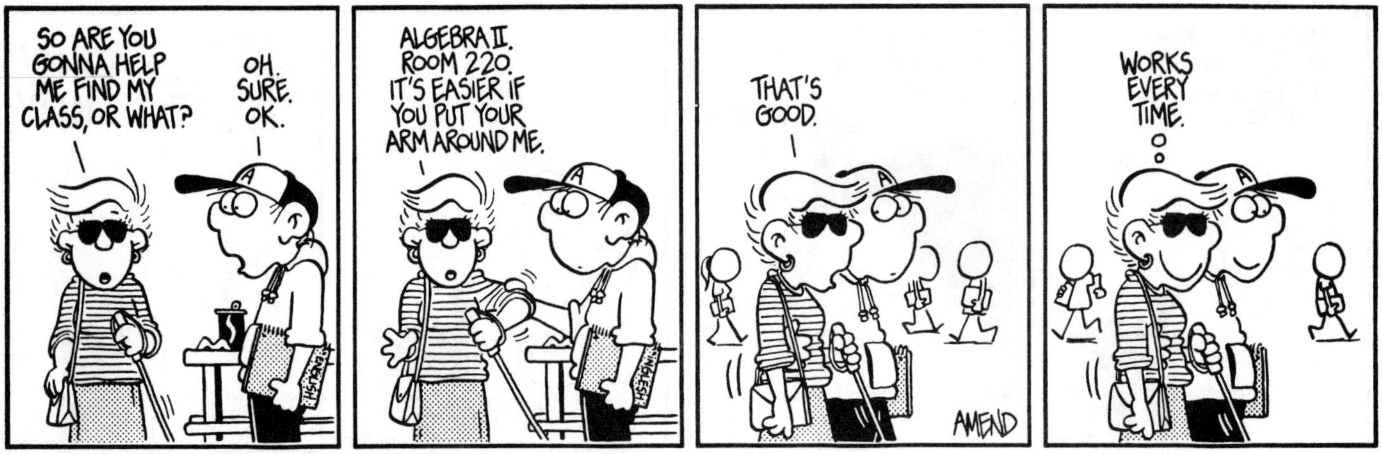
SO ARE YOU GONNA HELP ME FIND MY CLASS, OR WHAT?
OH. SURE. OK.
ALGEBRA II. ROOM 220. IT'S EASIER IF YOU PUT YOUR ARM AROUND ME.
THAT'S GOOD.
WORKS EVERY TIME.
AMEND

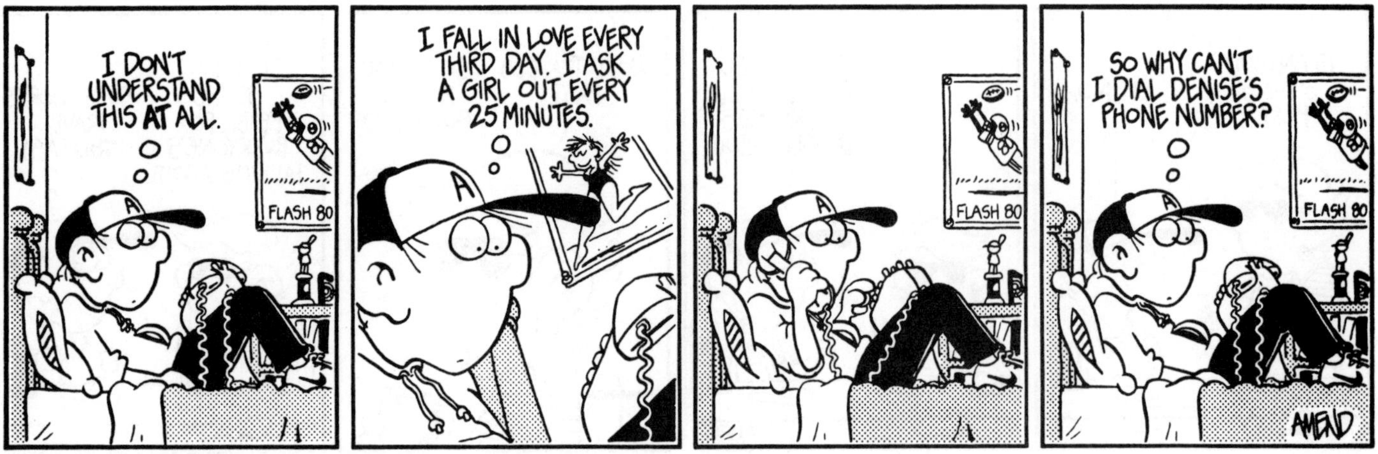
I DON'T UNDERSTAND THIS AT ALL.
FLASH 80
I FALL IN LOVE EVERY THIRD DAY. I ASK A GIRL OUT EVERY 25 MINUTES.
FLASH 80
SO WHY CAN'T I DIAL DENISE'S PHONE NUMBER?
FLASH 80
AMEND

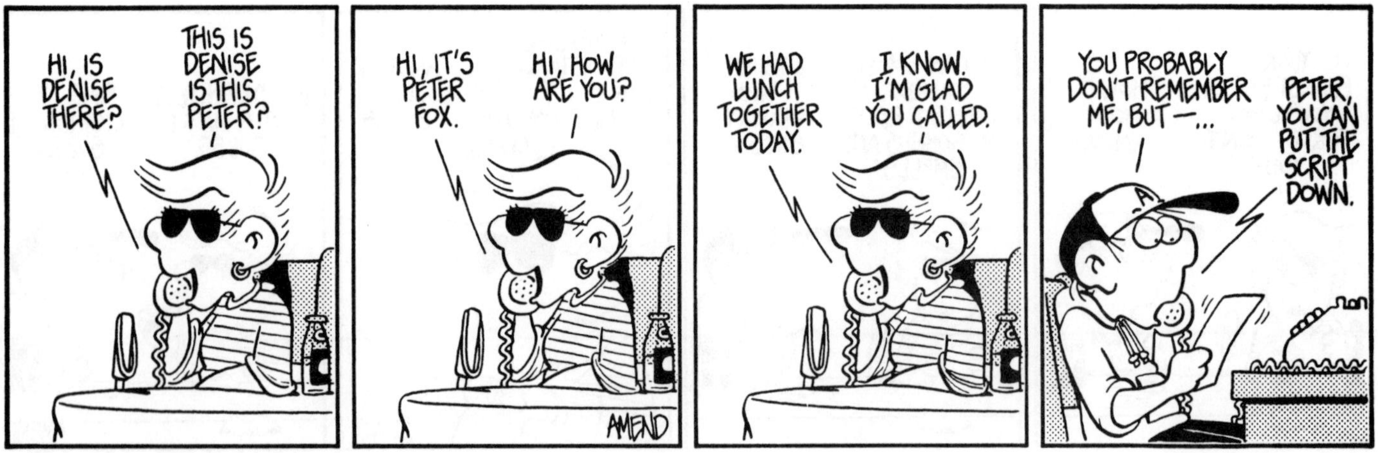
HI, IS DENISE THERE?
THIS IS DENISE IS THIS PETER?
HI, IT'S PETER FOX.
HI, HOW ARE YOU?
AMEND
WE HAD LUNCH TOGETHER TODAY.
I KNOW. I'M GLAD YOU CALLED.
YOU PROBABLY DON'T REMEMBER ME, BUT—...
PETER, YOU CAN PUT THE SCRIPT DOWN.

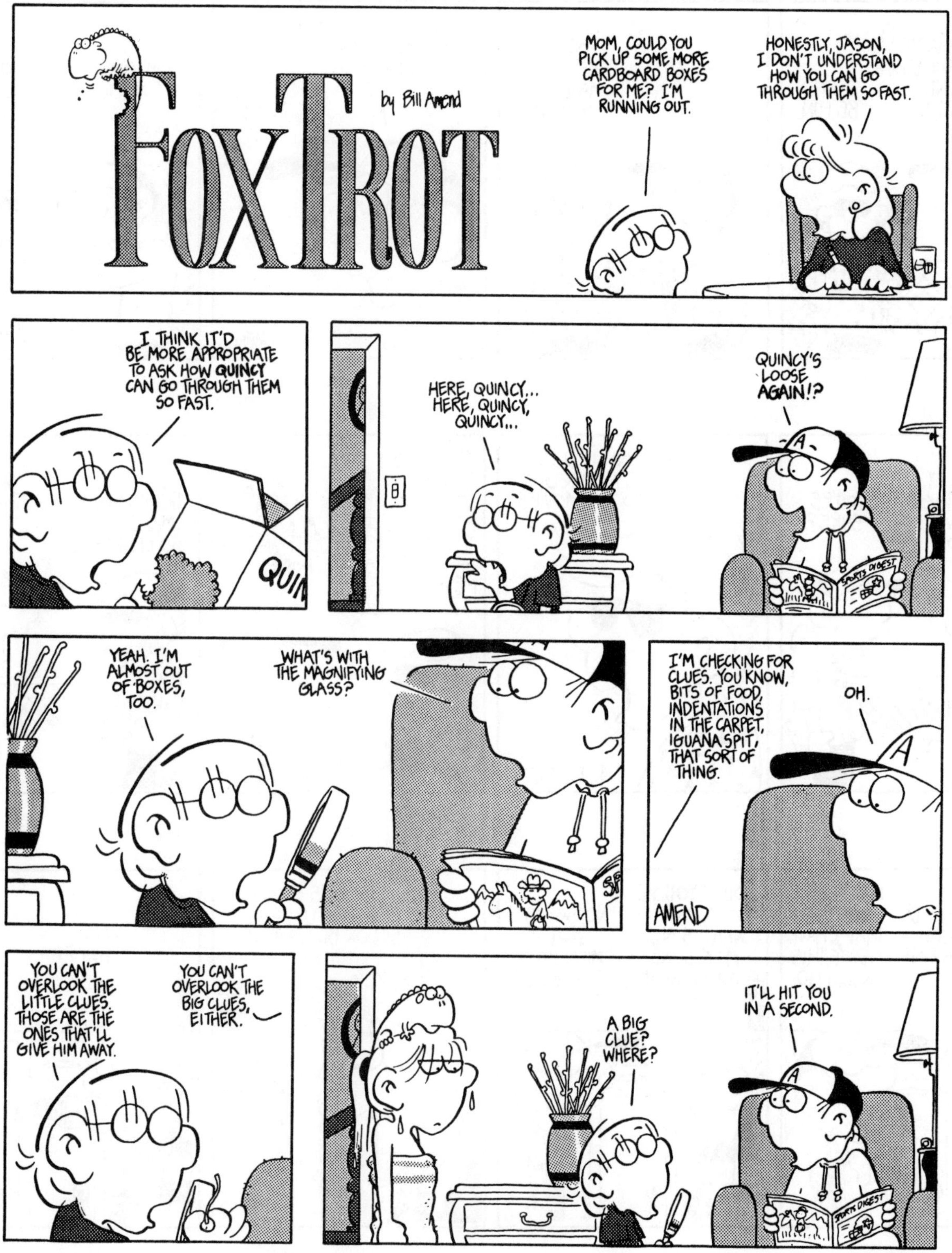
FoxTrot
by Bill Amend
MOM, COULD YOU PICK UP SOME MORE CARDBOARD BOXES FOR ME? I'M RUNNING OUT.
HONESTLY, JASON, I DON'T UNDERSTAND HOW YOU CAN GO THROUGH THEM SO FAST.
I THINK IT'D BE MORE APPROPRIATE TO ASK HOW QUINCY CAN GO THROUGH THEM SO FAST.
QUIN
HERE, QUINCY... HERE, QUINCY, QUINCY...
QUINCY'S LOOSE AGAIN!?
YEAH. I'M ALMOST OUT OF BOXES, TOO.
WHAT'S WITH THE MAGNIFYING GLASS?
I'M CHECKING FOR CLUES. YOU KNOW, BITS OF FOOD, INDENTATIONS IN THE CARPET, IGUANA SPIT, THAT SORT OF THING.
OH.
AMEND
YOU CAN'T OVERLOOK THE LITTLE CLUES. THOSE ARE THE ONES THAT'LL GIVE HIM AWAY.
YOU CAN'T OVERLOOK THE BIG CLUES, EITHER.
A BIG CLUE? WHERE?
IT'LL HIT YOU IN A SECOND.

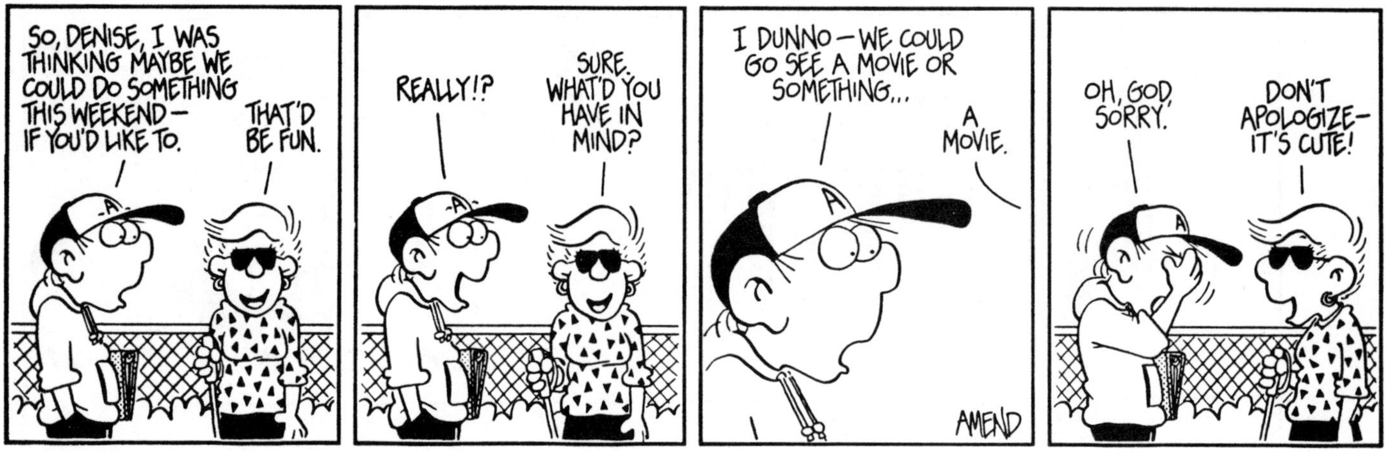
SO, DENISE, I WAS THINKING MAYBE WE COULD DO SOMETHING THIS WEEKEND— IF YOU'D LIKE TO.
THAT'D BE FUN.
REALLY!?
SURE. WHAT'D YOU HAVE IN MIND?
I DUNNO—WE COULD GO SEE A MOVIE OR SOMETHING...
A MOVIE.
AMEND
OH, GOD, SORRY.
DON'T APOLOGIZE— IT'S CUTE!

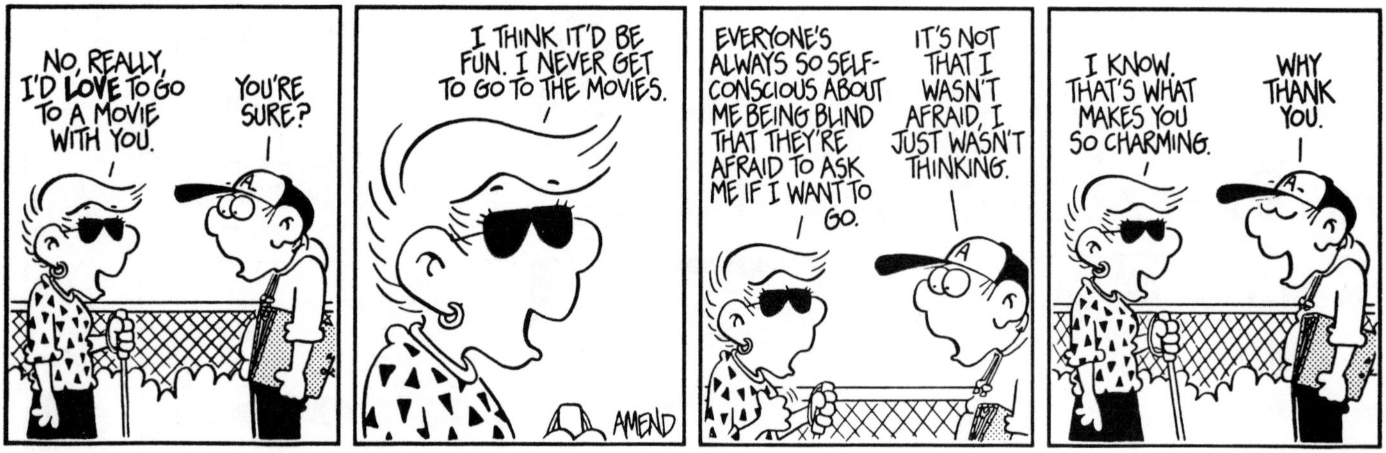
NO, REALLY, I'D LOVE TO GO TO A MOVIE WITH YOU.
YOU'RE SURE?
I THINK IT'D BE FUN. I NEVER GET TO GO TO THE MOVIES.
AMEND
EVERYONE'S ALWAYS SO SELF-CONSCIOUS ABOUT ME BEING BLIND THAT THEY'RE AFRAID TO ASK ME IF I WANT TO GO.
IT'S NOT THAT I WASN'T AFRAID, I JUST WASN'T THINKING.
I KNOW. THAT'S WHAT MAKES YOU SO CHARMING.
WHY THANK YOU.

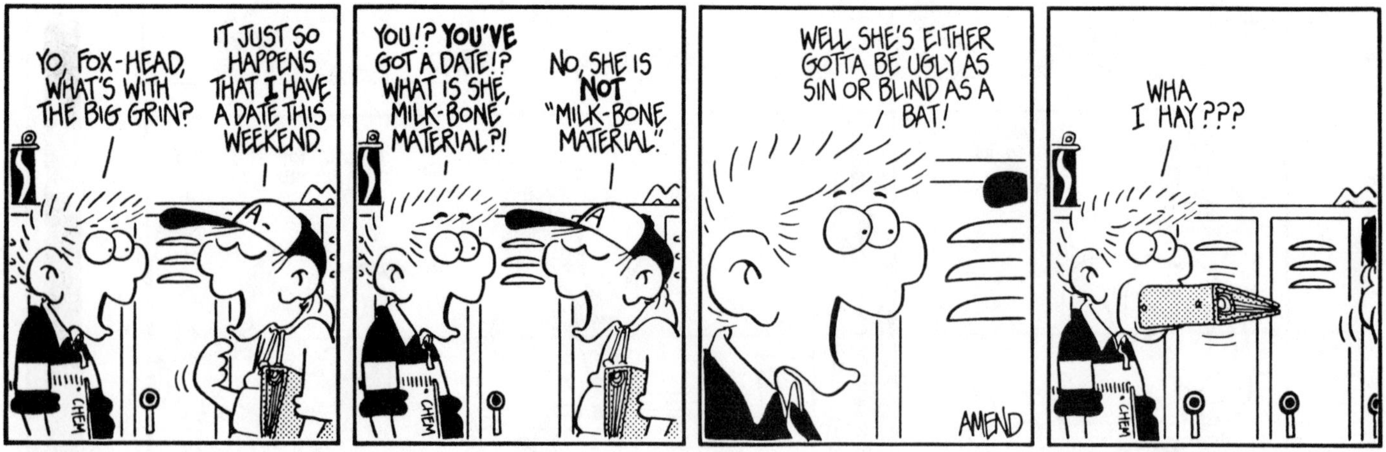
YO, FOX-HEAD, WHAT'S WITH THE BIG GRIN?
IT JUST SO HAPPENS THAT I HAVE A DATE THIS WEEKEND.
CHEM
YOU!? YOU'VE GOT A DATE!? WHAT IS SHE, MILK-BONE MATERIAL?!
NO, SHE IS NOT "MILK-BONE MATERIAL."
CHEM
WELL SHE'S EITHER GOTTA BE UGLY AS SIN OR BLIND AS A BAT!
AMEND
WHA I HAY???
CHEM

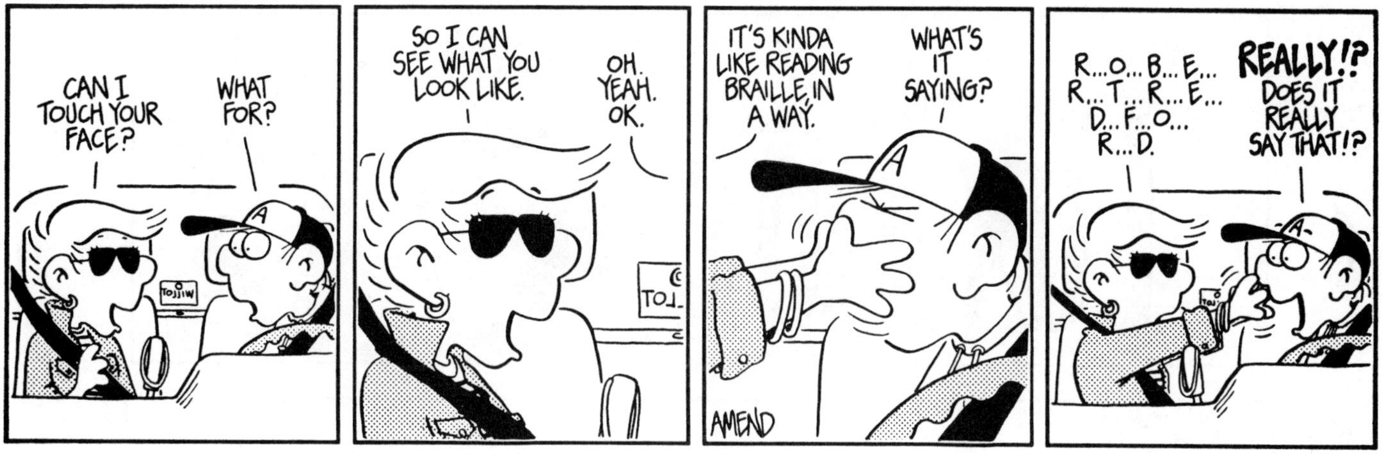
CAN I TOUCH YOUR FACE?
WHAT FOR?
SO I CAN SEE WHAT YOU LOOK LIKE.
OH. YEAH. OK.
IT'S KINDA LIKE READING BRAILLE, IN A WAY.
WHAT'S IT SAYING?
R...O... B... E... R... T... R... E... D... F... O... R... D.
REALLY!? DOES IT REALLY SAY THAT!?
AMEND

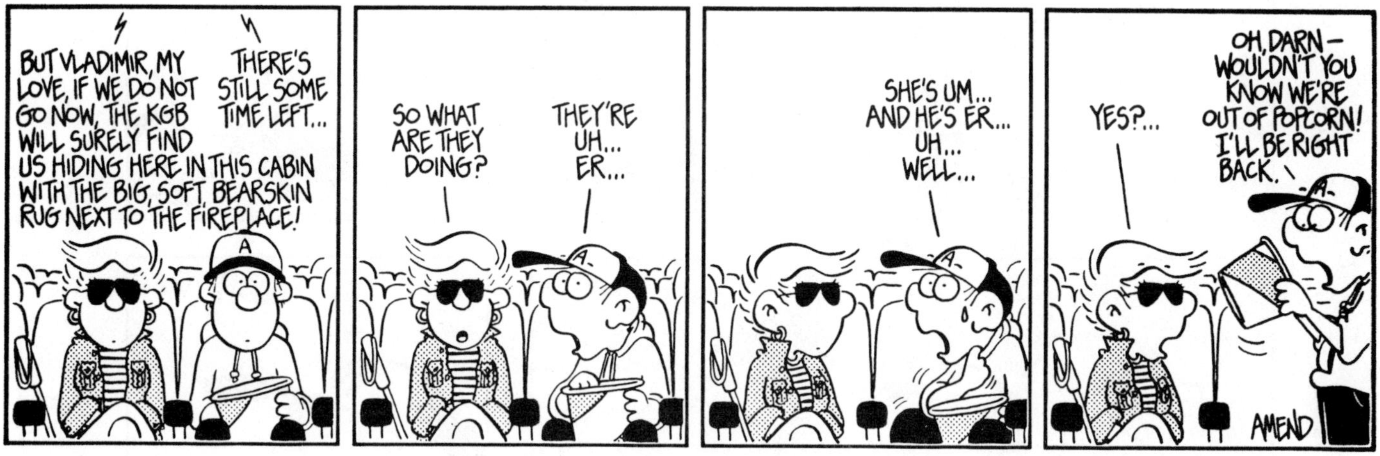
BUT VLADIMIR, MY LOVE, IF WE DO NOT GO NOW, THE KGB WILL SURELY FIND US HIDING HERE IN THIS CABIN WITH THE BIG, SOFT, BEARSKIN RUG NEXT TO THE FIREPLACE!
THERE'S STILL SOME TIME LEFT...
SO WHAT ARE THEY DOING?
THEY'RE UH... ER...
SHE'S UM... AND HE'S ER... UH... WELL...
YES?...
OH, DARN – WOULDN'T YOU KNOW WE'RE OUT OF POPCORN! I'LL BE RIGHT BACK.
AMEND

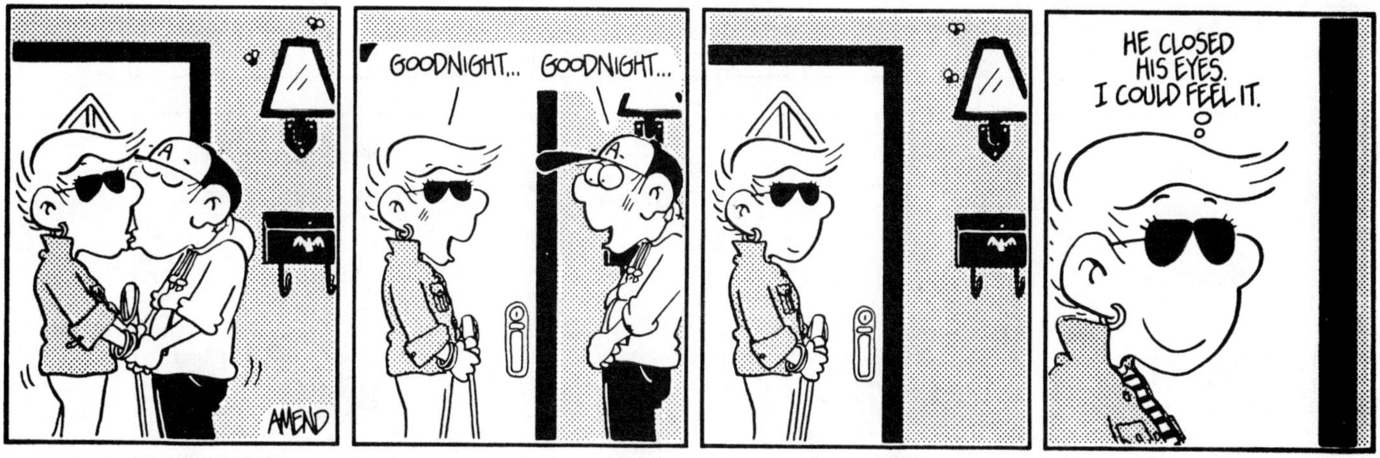
AMEND
GOODNIGHT...
GOODNIGHT...
HE CLOSED HIS EYES. I COULD FEEL IT.

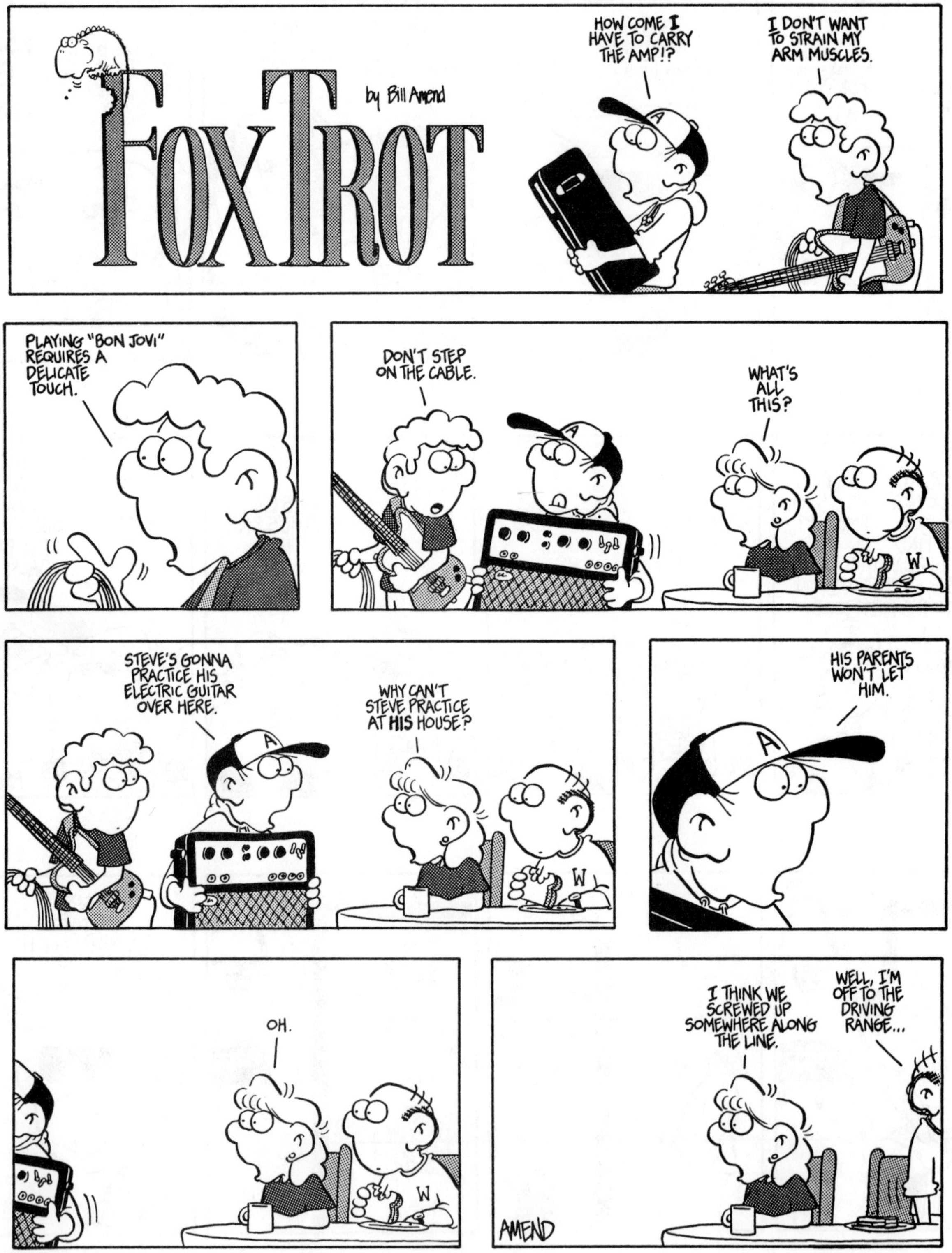
FoxTrot
by Bill Amend
HOW COME I HAVE TO CARRY THE AMP!?
I DON'T WANT TO STRAIN MY ARM MUSCLES.
PLAYING "BON JOVI" REQUIRES A DELICATE TOUCH.
DON'T STEP ON THE CABLE.
WHAT'S ALL THIS?
STEVE'S GONNA PRACTICE HIS ELECTRIC GUITAR OVER HERE.
WHY CAN'T STEVE PRACTICE AT HIS HOUSE?
HIS PARENTS WON'T LET HIM.
OH.
I THINK WE SCREWED UP SOMEWHERE ALONG THE LINE.
WELL, I'M OFF TO THE DRIVING RANGE...
AMEND

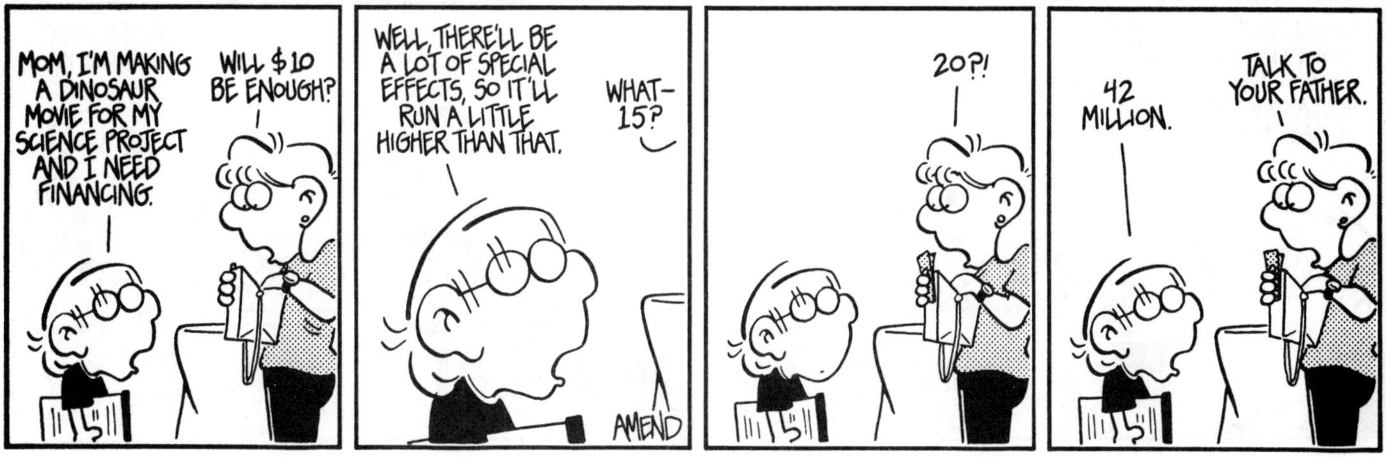
MOM, I'M MAKING A DINOSAUR MOVIE FOR MY SCIENCE PROJECT AND I NEED FINANCING.
WILL $10 BE ENOUGH?
WELL, THERE'LL BE A LOT OF SPECIAL EFFECTS, SO IT'LL RUN A LITTLE HIGHER THAN THAT.
WHAT-15?
AMEND
20?!
42 MILLION.
TALK TO YOUR FATHER.

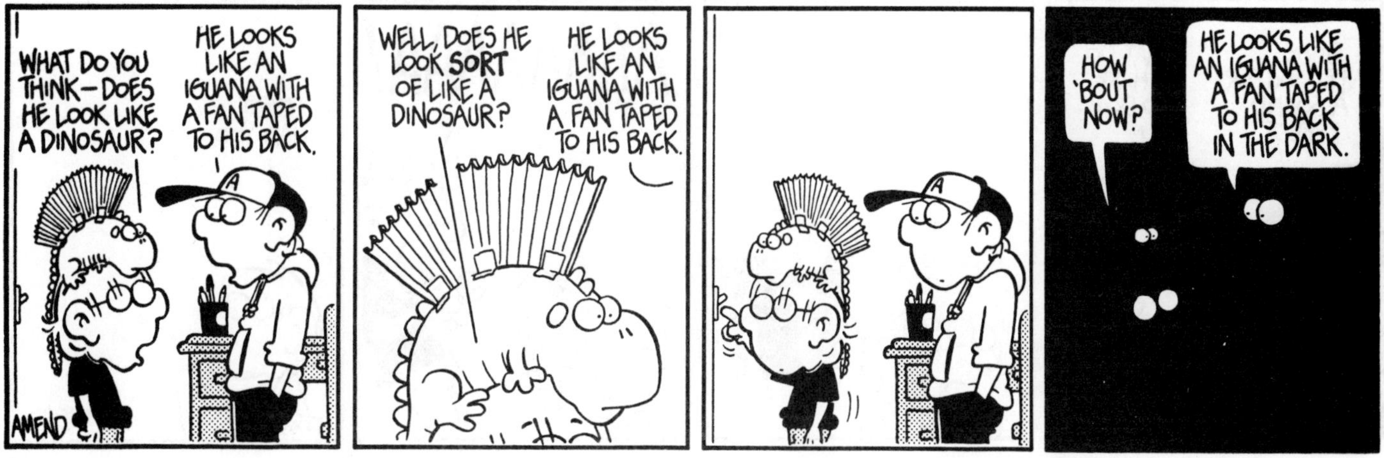
WHAT DO YOU THINK—DOES HE LOOK LIKE A DINOSAUR?
HE LOOKS LIKE AN IGUANA WITH A FAN TAPED TO HIS BACK.
AMEND
WELL, DOES HE LOOK SORT OF LIKE A DINOSAUR?
HE LOOKS LIKE AN IGUANA WITH A FAN TAPED TO HIS BACK.
HOW 'BOUT NOW?
HE LOOKS LIKE AN IGUANA WITH A FAN TAPED TO HIS BACK IN THE DARK.

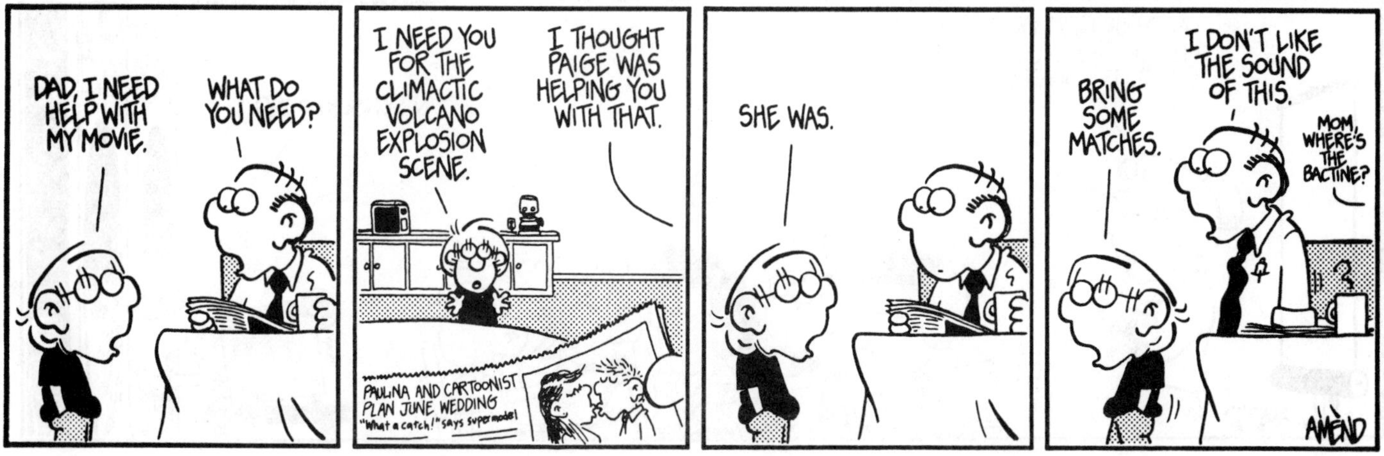
DAD, I NEED HELP WITH MY MOVIE.
WHAT DO YOU NEED?
I NEED YOU FOR THE CLIMACTIC VOLCANO EXPLOSION SCENE.
I THOUGHT PAIGE WAS HELPING YOU WITH THAT.
PAULINA AND CARTOONIST PLAN JUNE WEDDING
"What a catch!" says supermodel
SHE WAS.
BRING SOME MATCHES.
I DON'T LIKE THE SOUND OF THIS.
MOM, WHERE'S THE BACTINE?
AMEND

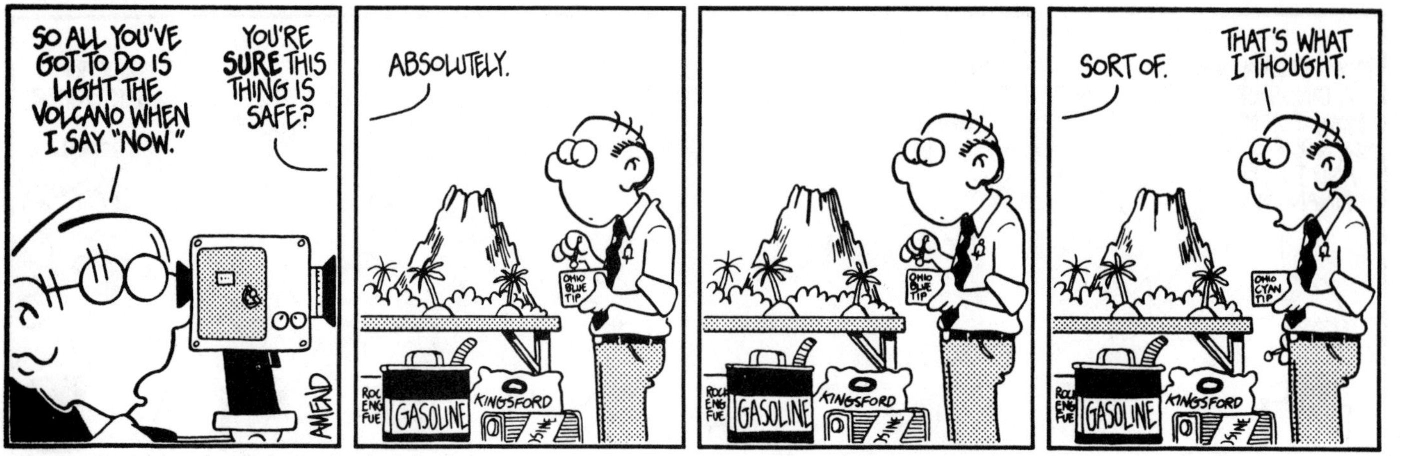
SO ALL YOU'VE GOT TO DO IS LIGHT THE VOLCANO WHEN I SAY "NOW."
YOU'RE SURE THIS THING IS SAFE?
AMEND
ABSOLUTELY.
SORT OF.
THAT'S WHAT I THOUGHT.

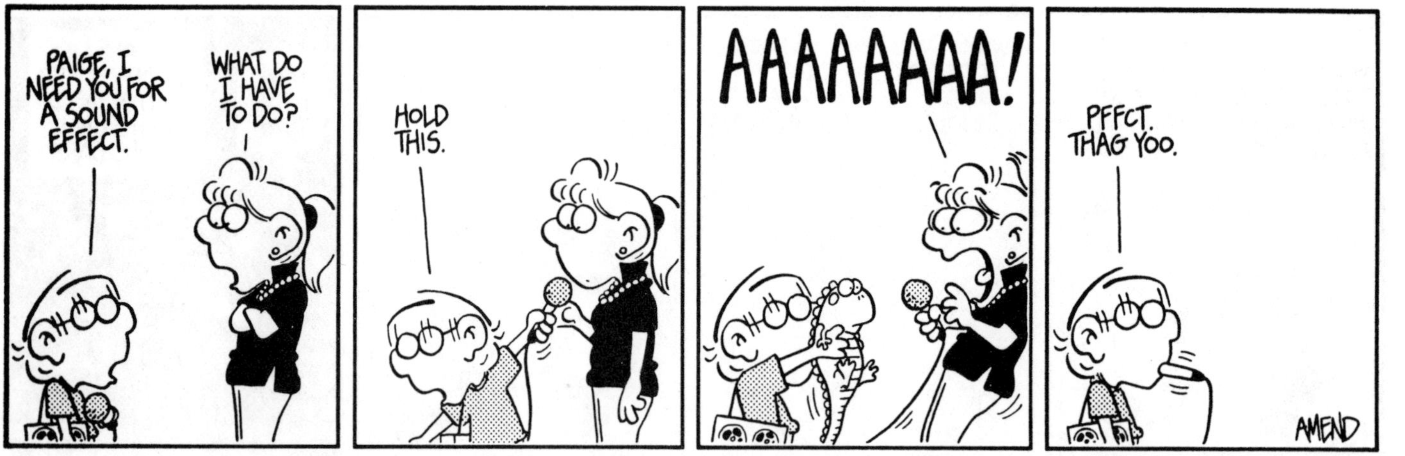
PAIGE, I NEED YOU FOR A SOUND EFFECT.
WHAT DO I HAVE TO DO?
HOLD THIS.
AAAAAAAA!
PFFCT. THAG YOO.
AMEND

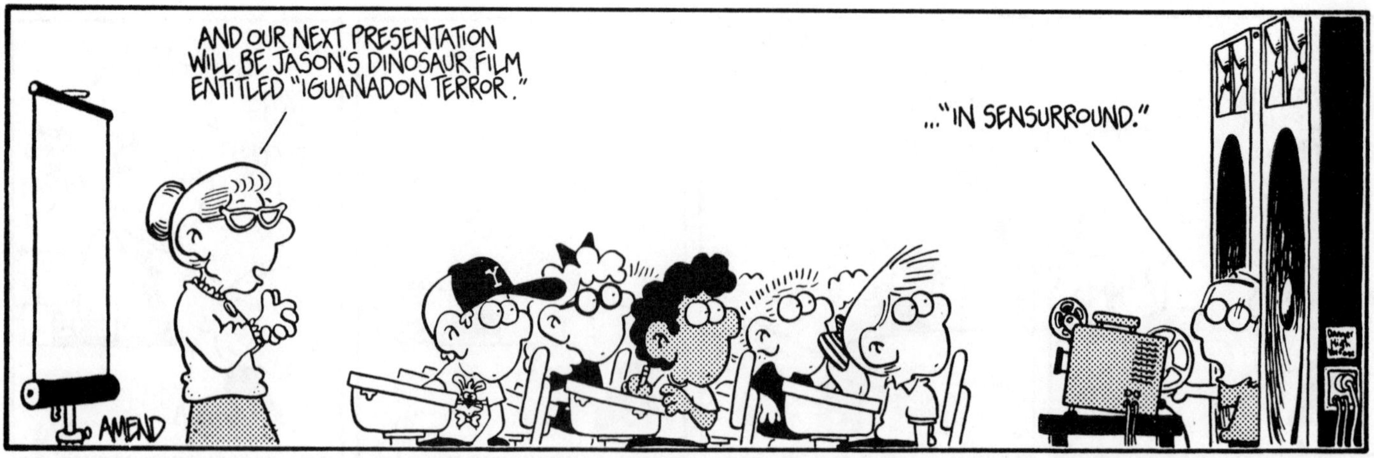
AND OUR NEXT PRESENTATION WILL BE JASON'S DINOSAUR FILM ENTITLED "IGUANADON TERROR."
..."IN SENSURROUND."
AMEND

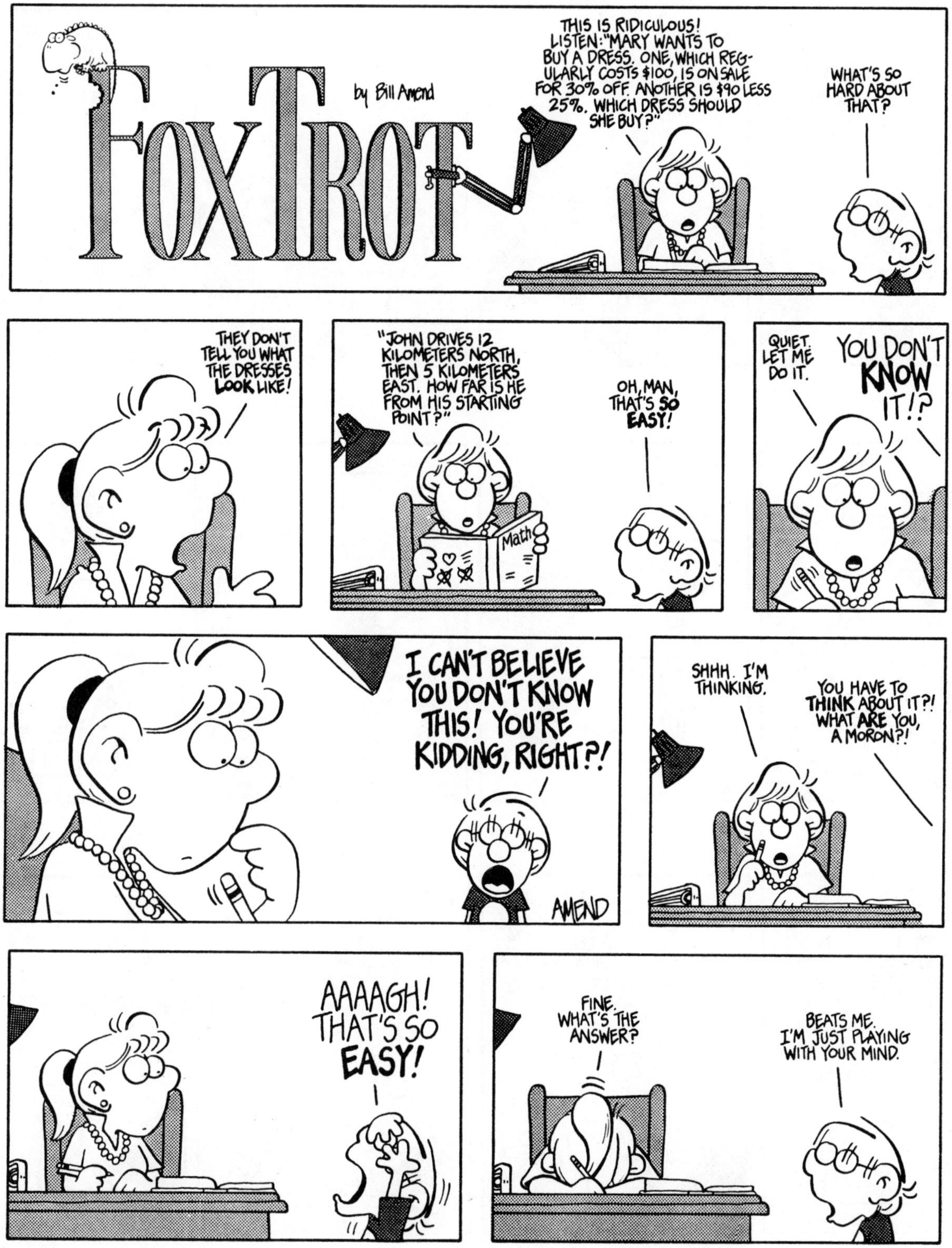

FoxTrot
by Bill Amend
THIS IS RIDICULOUS! LISTEN: "MARY WANTS TO BUY A DRESS. ONE, WHICH REGULARLY COSTS $100, IS ON SALE FOR 30% OFF. ANOTHER IS $90 LESS 25%. WHICH DRESS SHOULD SHE BUY?"
WHAT'S SO HARD ABOUT THAT?
THEY DON'T TELL YOU WHAT THE DRESSES **LOOK** LIKE!
"JOHN DRIVES 12 KILOMETERS NORTH, THEN 5 KILOMETERS EAST. HOW FAR IS HE FROM HIS STARTING POINT?"
Math
OH, MAN, THAT'S **SO EASY**!
QUIET. LET ME DO IT.
YOU DON'T **KNOW** IT!?
I CAN'T BELIEVE YOU DON'T KNOW THIS! YOU'RE KIDDING, RIGHT?!
AMEND
SHHH. I'M THINKING.
YOU HAVE TO **THINK** ABOUT IT?! WHAT **ARE** YOU, A MORON?!
AAAAGH! THAT'S SO **EASY**!
FINE. WHAT'S THE ANSWER?
BEATS ME. I'M JUST PLAYING WITH YOUR MIND.

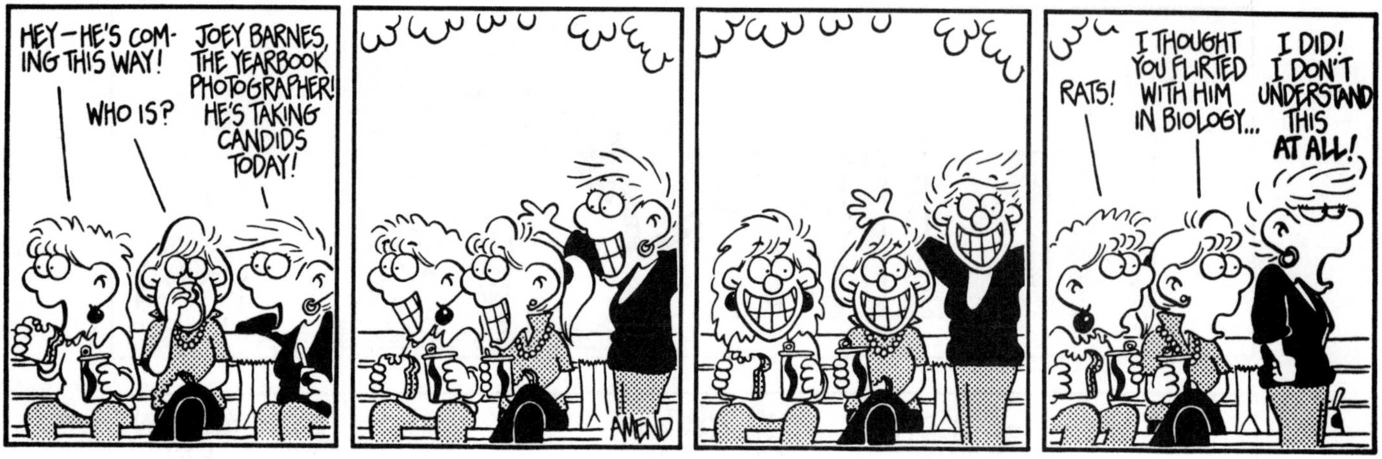
HEY—HE'S COMING THIS WAY!
WHO IS?
JOEY BARNES, THE YEARBOOK PHOTOGRAPHER! HE'S TAKING CANDIDS TODAY!
AMEND
RATS!
I THOUGHT YOU FLIRTED WITH HIM IN BIOLOGY...
I DID! I DON'T UNDERSTAND THIS AT ALL!

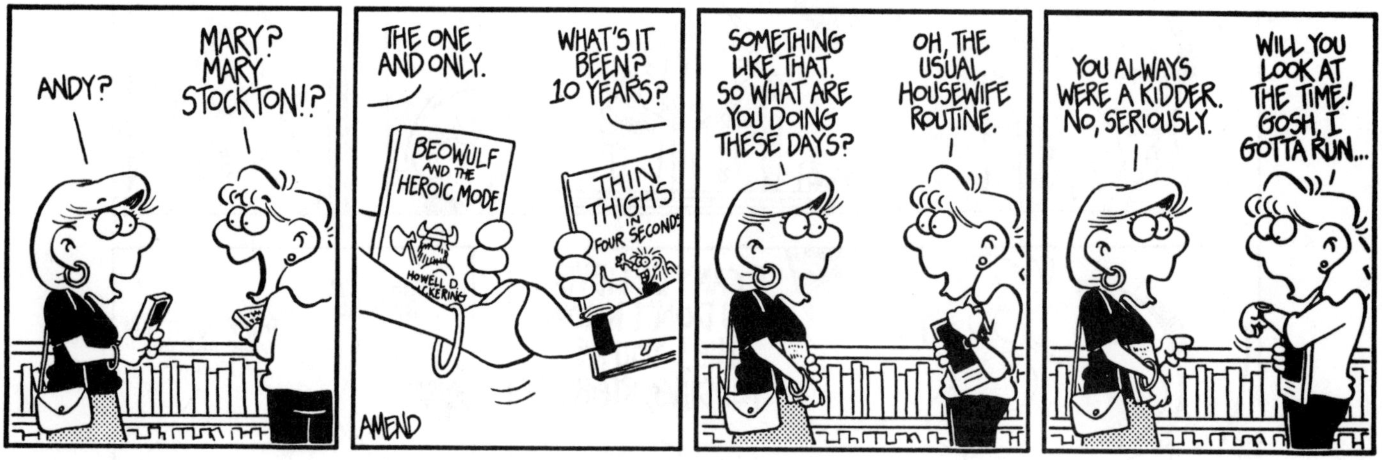
ANDY?
MARY? MARY STOCKTON!?
THE ONE AND ONLY.
WHAT'S IT BEEN? 10 YEARS?
BEOWULF AND THE HEROIC MODE
THIN THIGHS IN FOUR SECONDS
AMEND
SOMETHING LIKE THAT. SO WHAT ARE YOU DOING THESE DAYS?
OH, THE USUAL HOUSEWIFE ROUTINE.
YOU ALWAYS WERE A KIDDER. NO, SERIOUSLY.
WILL YOU LOOK AT THE TIME! GOSH, I GOTTA RUN...

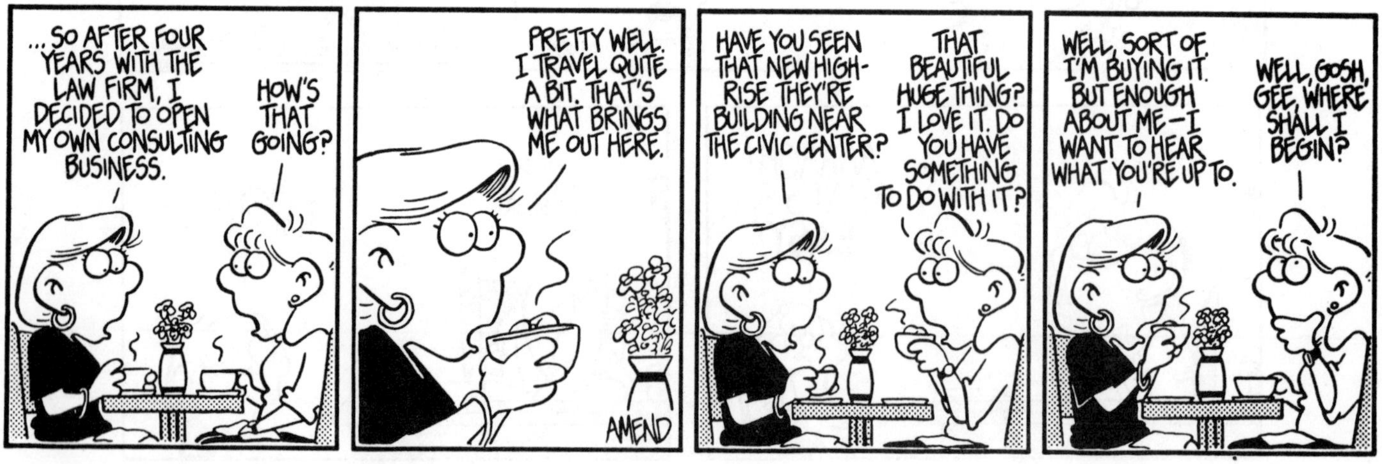
...SO AFTER FOUR YEARS WITH THE LAW FIRM, I DECIDED TO OPEN MY OWN CONSULTING BUSINESS.
HOW'S THAT GOING?
PRETTY WELL. I TRAVEL QUITE A BIT. THAT'S WHAT BRINGS ME OUT HERE.
AMEND
HAVE YOU SEEN THAT NEW HIGH-RISE THEY'RE BUILDING NEAR THE CIVIC CENTER?
THAT BEAUTIFUL HUGE THING? I LOVE IT. DO YOU HAVE SOMETHING TO DO WITH IT?
WELL, SORT OF. I'M BUYING IT. BUT ENOUGH ABOUT ME—I WANT TO HEAR WHAT YOU'RE UP TO.
WELL, GOSH, GEE, WHERE SHALL I BEGIN?

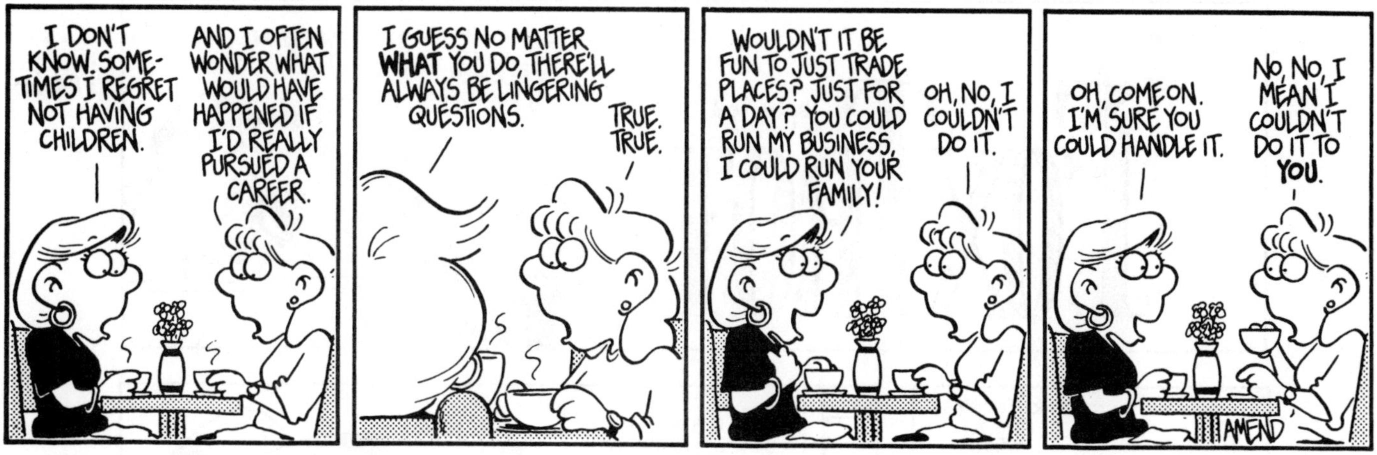
I DON'T KNOW. SOMETIMES I REGRET NOT HAVING CHILDREN.
AND I OFTEN WONDER WHAT WOULD HAVE HAPPENED IF I'D REALLY PURSUED A CAREER.
I GUESS NO MATTER WHAT YOU DO, THERE'LL ALWAYS BE LINGERING QUESTIONS.
TRUE. TRUE.
WOULDN'T IT BE FUN TO JUST TRADE PLACES? JUST FOR A DAY? YOU COULD RUN MY BUSINESS, I COULD RUN YOUR FAMILY!
OH, NO, I COULDN'T DO IT.
OH, COME ON. I'M SURE YOU COULD HANDLE IT.
NO, NO, I MEAN I COULDN'T DO IT TO YOU.
AMEND

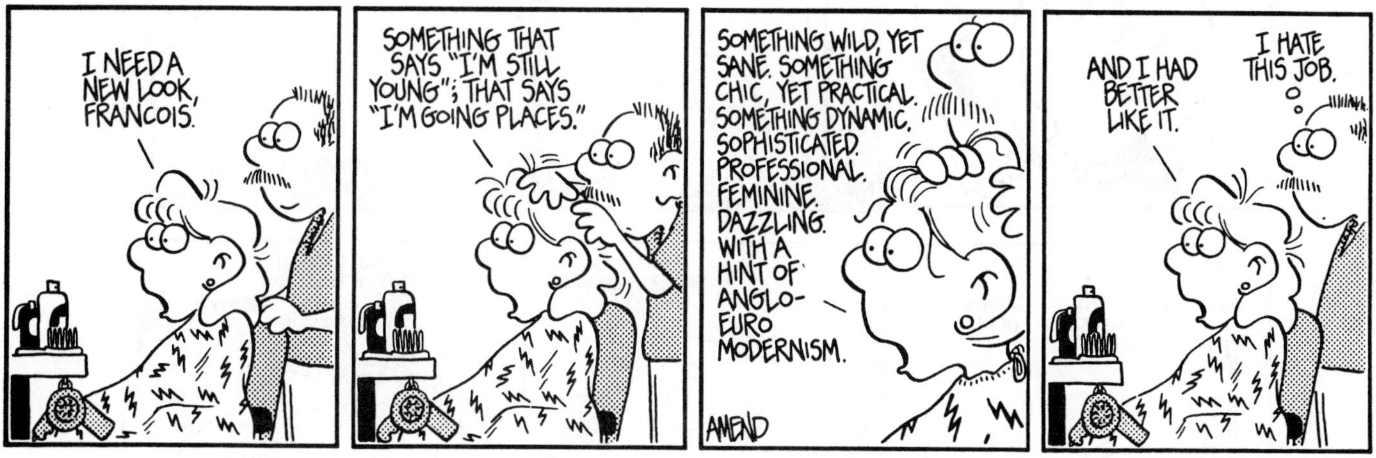
I NEED A NEW LOOK, FRANCOIS.
SOMETHING THAT SAYS "I'M STILL YOUNG"; THAT SAYS "I'M GOING PLACES."
SOMETHING WILD, YET SANE. SOMETHING CHIC, YET PRACTICAL. SOMETHING DYNAMIC, SOPHISTICATED. PROFESSIONAL. FEMININE. DAZZLING. WITH A HINT OF ANGLO-EURO MODERNISM.
AMEND
AND I HAD BETTER LIKE IT.
I HATE THIS JOB.

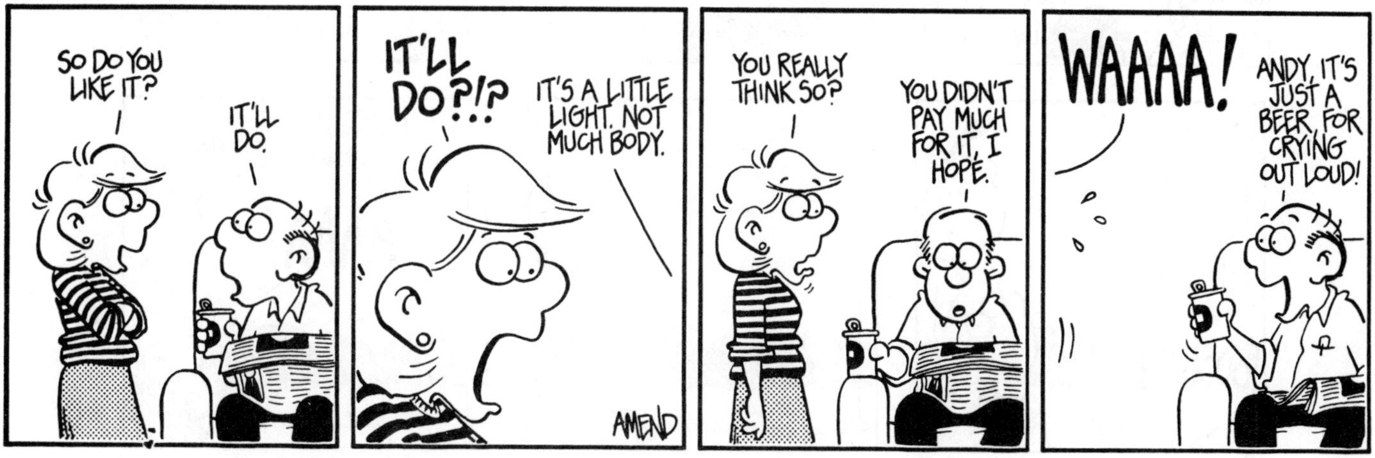
SO DO YOU LIKE IT?
IT'LL DO.
IT'LL DO?!? ...
IT'S A LITTLE LIGHT. NOT MUCH BODY.
AMEND
YOU REALLY THINK SO?
YOU DIDN'T PAY MUCH FOR IT, I HOPE.
WAAAA!
ANDY, IT'S JUST A BEER, FOR CRYING OUT LOUD!

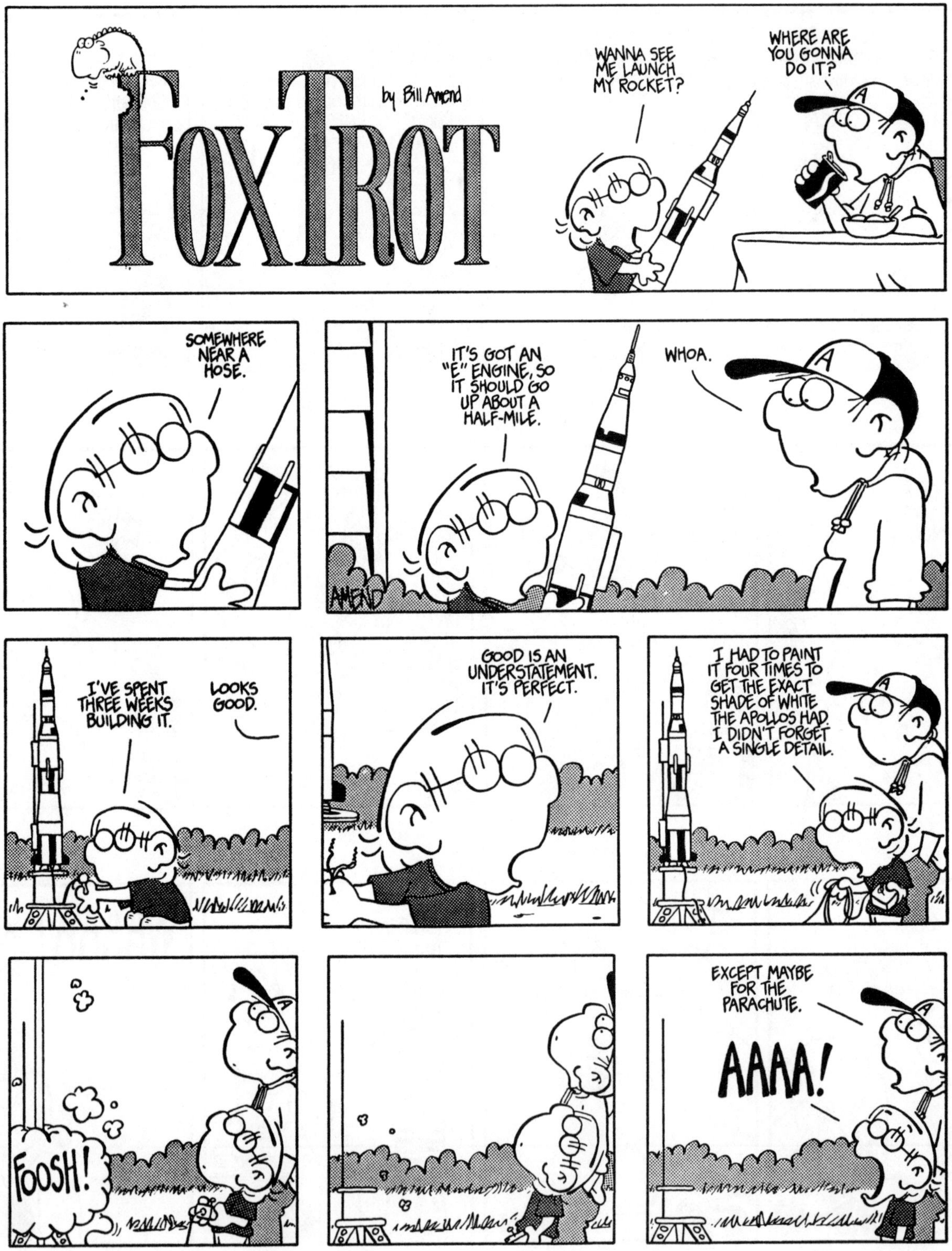
FoxTrot
by Bill Amend
WANNA SEE ME LAUNCH MY ROCKET?
WHERE ARE YOU GONNA DO IT?
SOMEWHERE NEAR A HOSE.
IT'S GOT AN "E" ENGINE, SO IT SHOULD GO UP ABOUT A HALF-MILE.
WHOA.
AMEND
I'VE SPENT THREE WEEKS BUILDING IT.
LOOKS GOOD.
GOOD IS AN UNDERSTATEMENT. IT'S PERFECT.
I HAD TO PAINT IT FOUR TIMES TO GET THE EXACT SHADE OF WHITE THE APOLLOS HAD. I DIDN'T FORGET A SINGLE DETAIL.
FOOSH!
EXCEPT MAYBE FOR THE PARACHUTE.
AAAA!

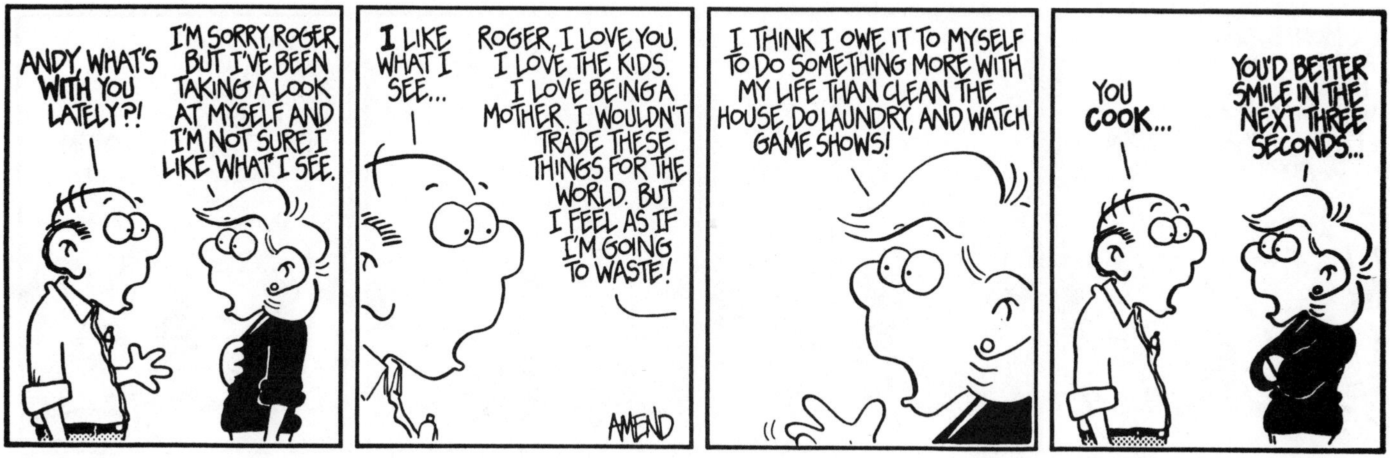
ANDY, WHAT'S **WITH** YOU LATELY?!
I'M SORRY, ROGER, BUT I'VE BEEN TAKING A LOOK AT MYSELF AND I'M NOT SURE I LIKE WHAT I SEE.
I LIKE WHAT I SEE...
ROGER, I LOVE YOU. I LOVE THE KIDS. I LOVE BEING A MOTHER. I WOULDN'T TRADE THESE THINGS FOR THE WORLD. BUT I FEEL AS IF I'M GOING TO WASTE!
AMEND
I THINK I OWE IT TO MYSELF TO DO SOMETHING MORE WITH MY LIFE THAN CLEAN THE HOUSE, DO LAUNDRY, AND WATCH GAME SHOWS!
YOU **COOK**...
YOU'D BETTER SMILE IN THE NEXT THREE SECONDS...

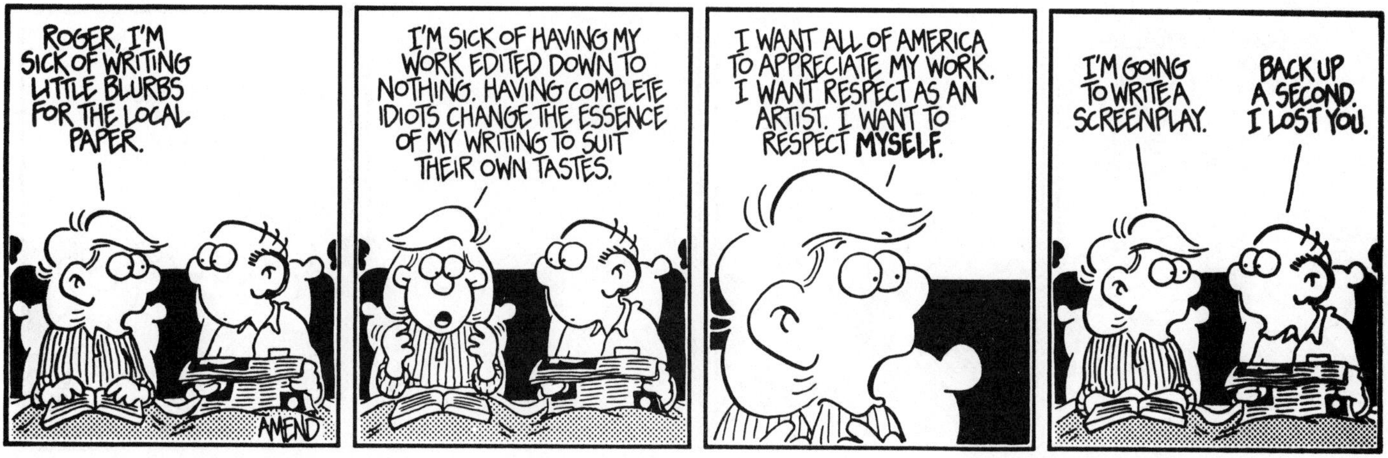
ROGER, I'M SICK OF WRITING LITTLE BLURBS FOR THE LOCAL PAPER.
AMEND
I'M SICK OF HAVING MY WORK EDITED DOWN TO NOTHING. HAVING COMPLETE IDIOTS CHANGE THE ESSENCE OF MY WRITING TO SUIT THEIR OWN TASTES.
I WANT ALL OF AMERICA TO APPRECIATE MY WORK. I WANT RESPECT AS AN ARTIST. I WANT TO RESPECT **MYSELF**.
I'M GOING TO WRITE A SCREENPLAY.
BACK UP A SECOND. I LOST YOU.

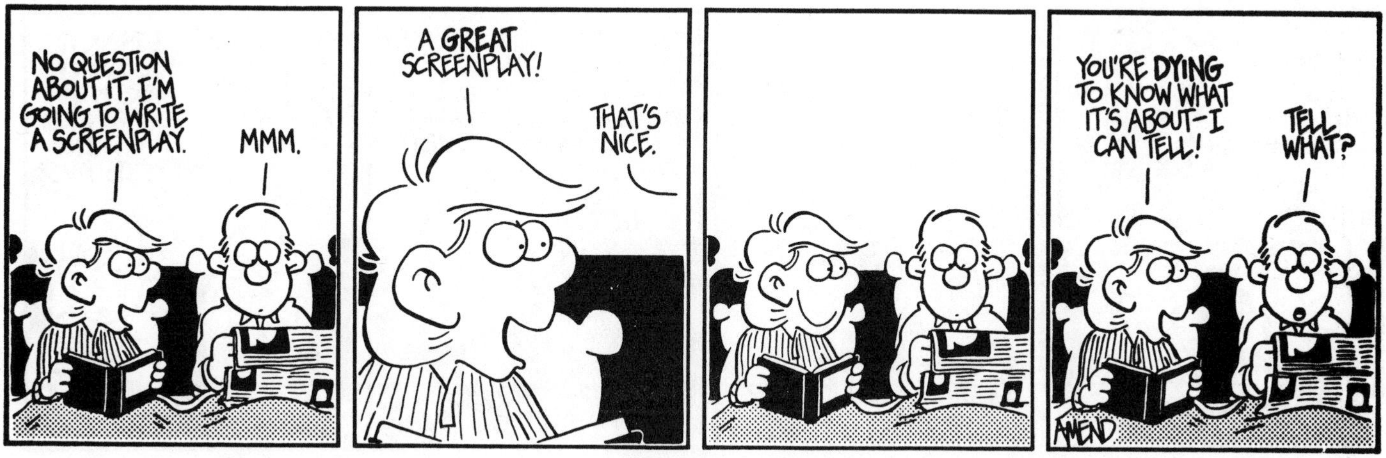
NO QUESTION ABOUT IT. I'M GOING TO WRITE A SCREENPLAY.
MMM.
A **GREAT** SCREENPLAY!
THAT'S NICE.
YOU'RE **DYING** TO KNOW WHAT IT'S ABOUT—I CAN TELL!
TELL WHAT?
AMEND

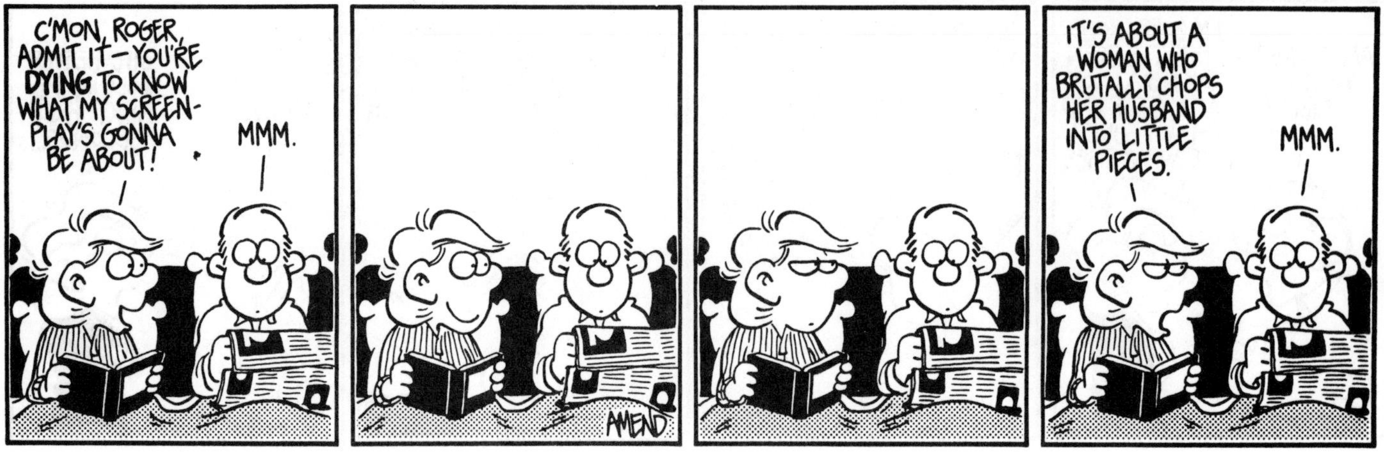
C'MON, ROGER, ADMIT IT—YOU'RE DYING TO KNOW WHAT MY SCREEN-PLAY'S GONNA BE ABOUT!
MMM.
AMEND
IT'S ABOUT A WOMAN WHO BRUTALLY CHOPS HER HUSBAND INTO LITTLE PIECES.
MMM.

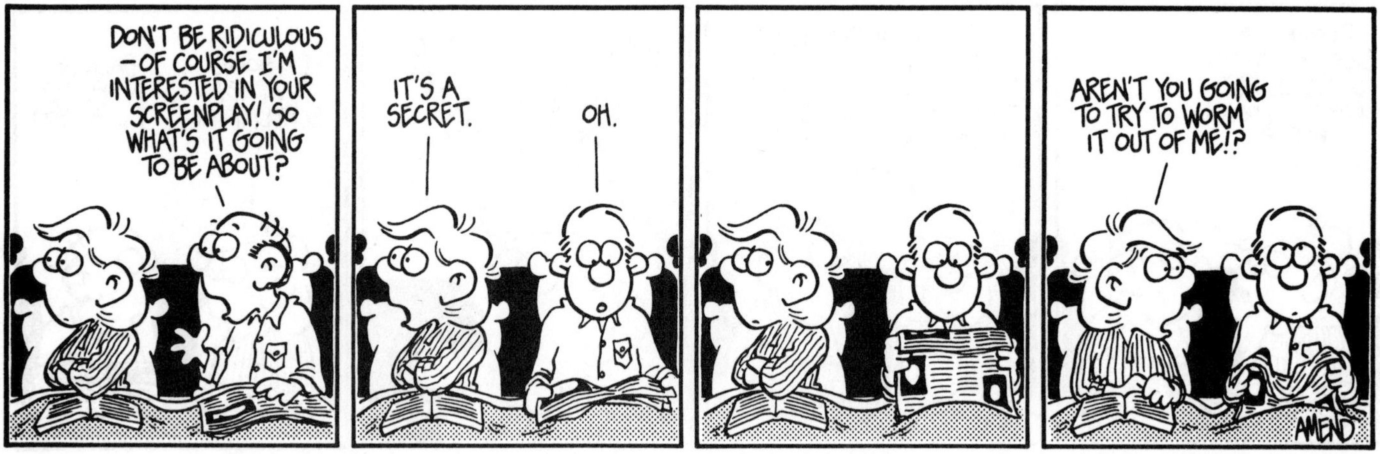
DON'T BE RIDICULOUS—OF COURSE I'M INTERESTED IN YOUR SCREENPLAY! SO WHAT'S IT GOING TO BE ABOUT?
IT'S A SECRET.
OH.
AREN'T YOU GOING TO TRY TO WORM IT OUT OF ME!?
AMEND

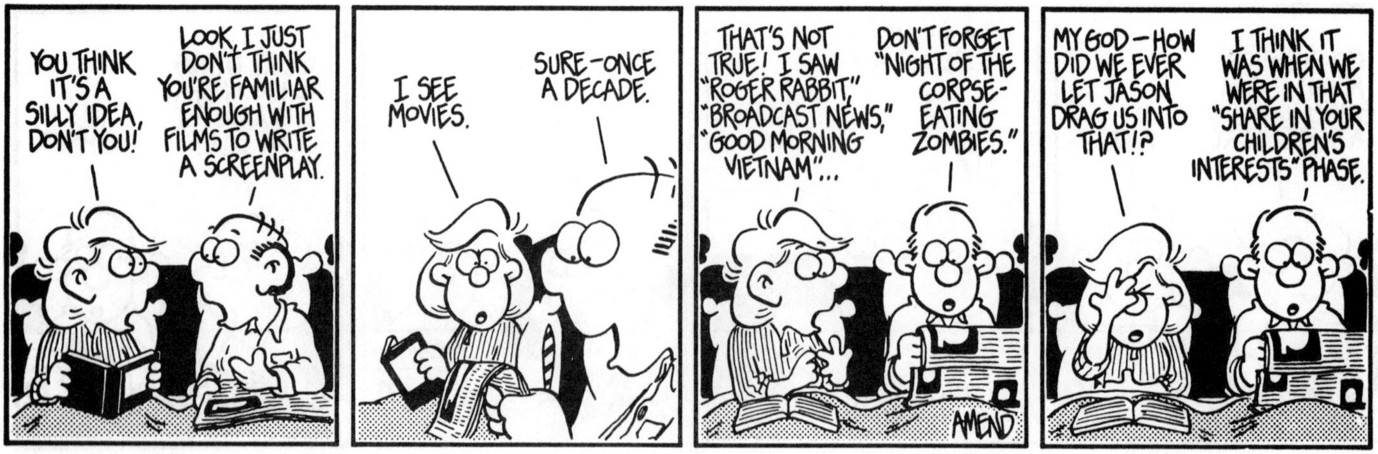
YOU THINK IT'S A SILLY IDEA, DON'T YOU!
LOOK, I JUST DON'T THINK YOU'RE FAMILIAR ENOUGH WITH FILMS TO WRITE A SCREENPLAY.
I SEE MOVIES.
SURE—ONCE A DECADE.
THAT'S NOT TRUE! I SAW "ROGER RABBIT," "BROADCAST NEWS," "GOOD MORNING VIETNAM"...
DON'T FORGET "NIGHT OF THE CORPSE-EATING ZOMBIES."
AMEND
MY GOD—HOW DID WE EVER LET JASON DRAG US INTO THAT!?
I THINK IT WAS WHEN WE WERE IN THAT "SHARE IN YOUR CHILDREN'S INTERESTS" PHASE.

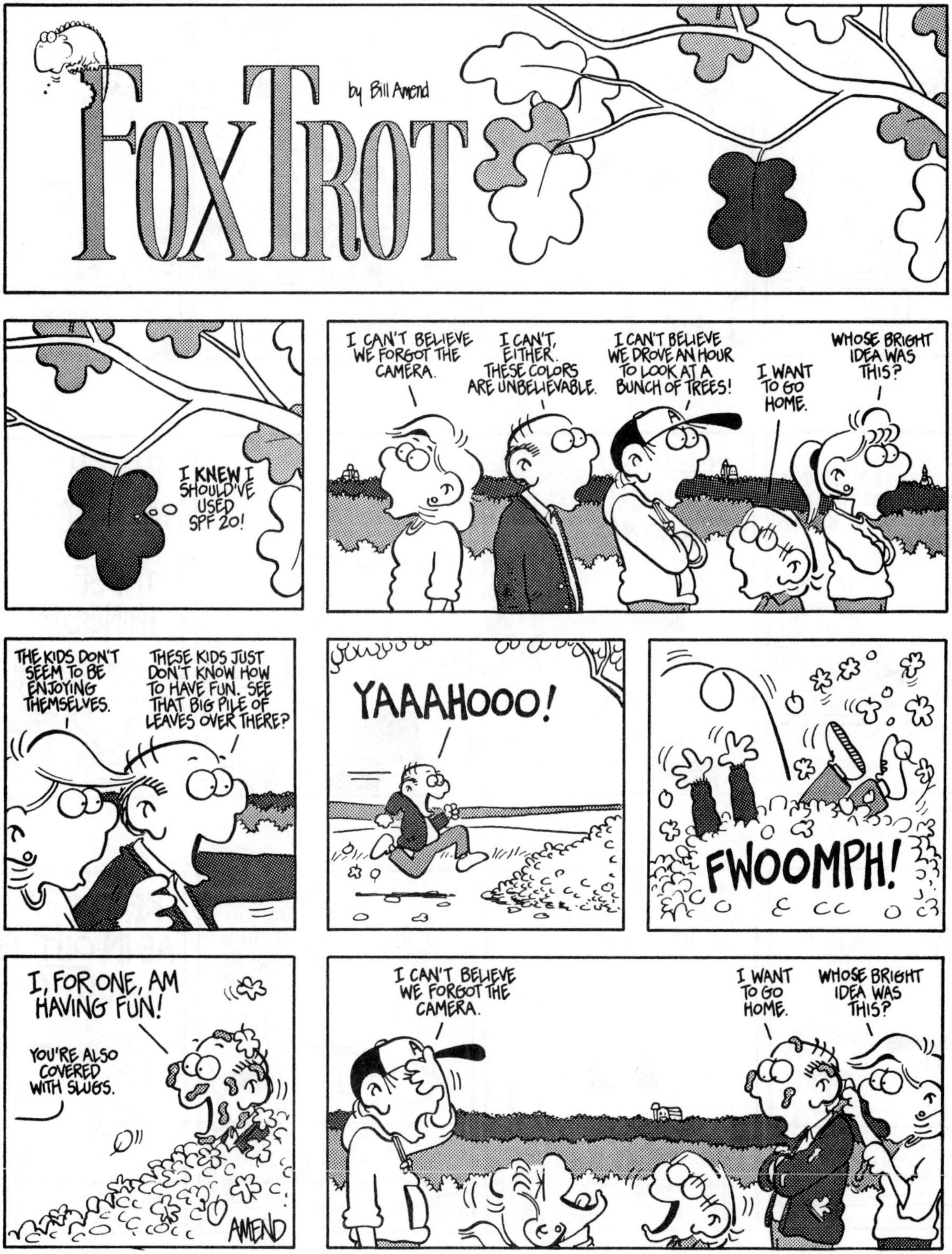
FoxTrot
by Bill Amend
I KNEW I SHOULD'VE USED SPF 20!
I CAN'T BELIEVE WE FORGOT THE CAMERA.
I CAN'T, EITHER. THESE COLORS ARE UNBELIEVABLE.
I CAN'T BELIEVE WE DROVE AN HOUR TO LOOK AT A BUNCH OF TREES!
I WANT TO GO HOME.
WHOSE BRIGHT IDEA WAS THIS?
THE KIDS DON'T SEEM TO BE ENJOYING THEMSELVES.
THESE KIDS JUST DON'T KNOW HOW TO HAVE FUN. SEE THAT BIG PILE OF LEAVES OVER THERE?
YAAAHOOO!
FWOOMPH!
I, FOR ONE, AM HAVING FUN!
YOU'RE ALSO COVERED WITH SLUGS.
AMEND
I CAN'T BELIEVE WE FORGOT THE CAMERA.
I WANT TO GO HOME.
WHOSE BRIGHT IDEA WAS THIS?

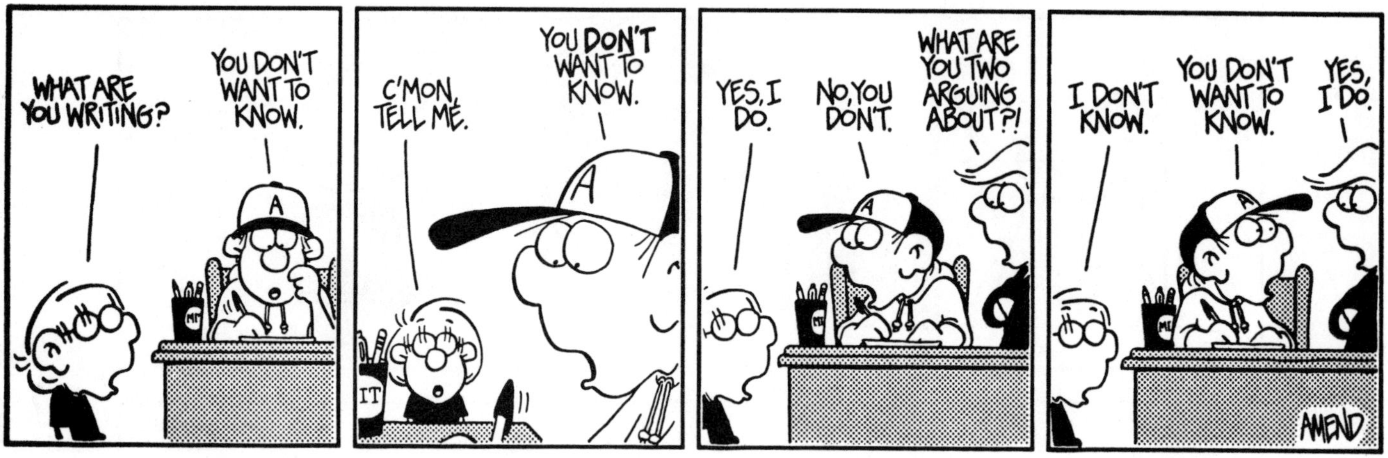
WHAT ARE YOU WRITING?
YOU DON'T WANT TO KNOW.
C'MON, TELL ME.
YOU DON'T WANT TO KNOW.
YES, I DO.
NO, YOU DON'T.
WHAT ARE YOU TWO ARGUING ABOUT?!
I DON'T KNOW.
YOU DON'T WANT TO KNOW.
YES, I DO.
AMEND

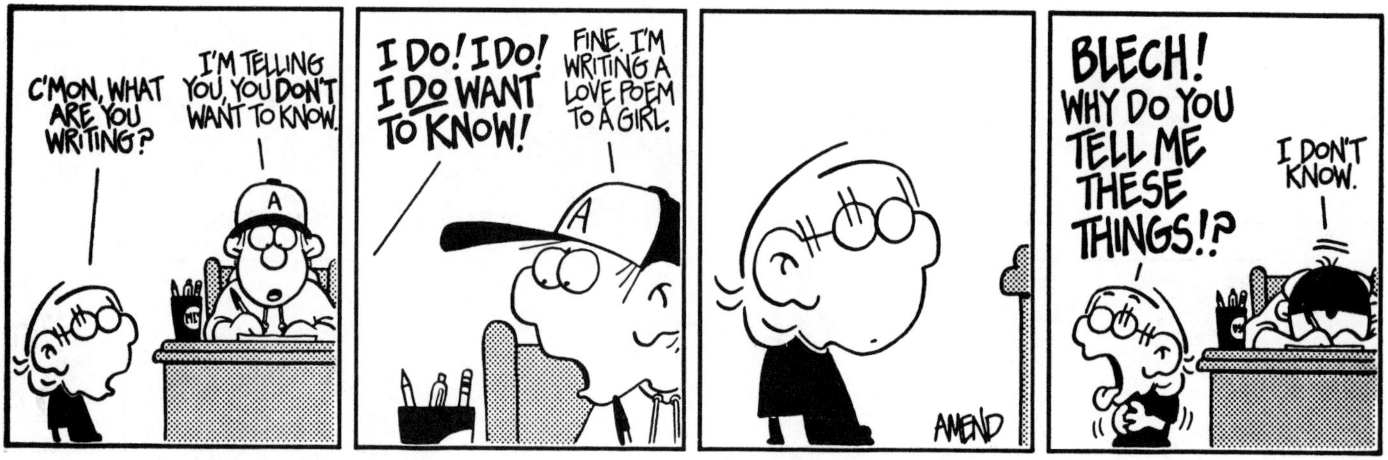
C'MON, WHAT ARE YOU WRITING?
I'M TELLING YOU, YOU DON'T WANT TO KNOW.
I DO! I DO! I DO WANT TO KNOW!
FINE. I'M WRITING A LOVE POEM TO A GIRL.
AMEND
BLECH! WHY DO YOU TELL ME THESE THINGS!?
I DON'T KNOW.

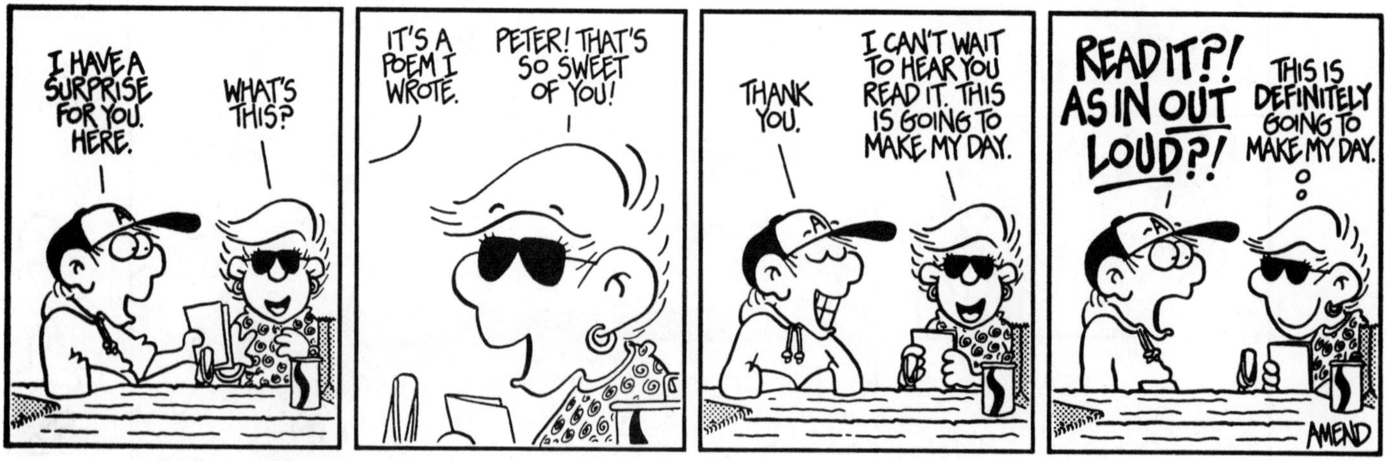
I HAVE A SURPRISE FOR YOU. HERE.
WHAT'S THIS?
IT'S A POEM I WROTE.
PETER! THAT'S SO SWEET OF YOU!
THANK YOU.
I CAN'T WAIT TO HEAR YOU READ IT. THIS IS GOING TO MAKE MY DAY.
READ IT?! AS IN OUT LOUD?!
THIS IS DEFINITELY GOING TO MAKE MY DAY.
AMEND

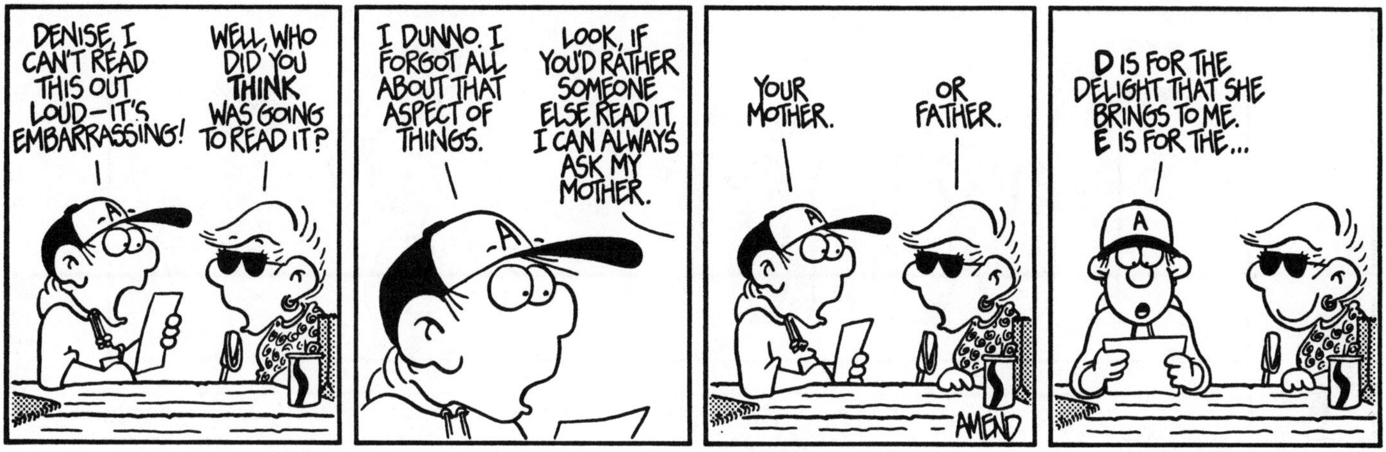
DENISE, I CAN'T READ THIS OUT LOUD—IT'S EMBARRASSING!
WELL, WHO DID YOU THINK WAS GOING TO READ IT?
I DUNNO. I FORGOT ALL ABOUT THAT ASPECT OF THINGS.
LOOK, IF YOU'D RATHER SOMEONE ELSE READ IT, I CAN ALWAYS ASK MY MOTHER.
YOUR MOTHER.
OR FATHER.
D IS FOR THE DELIGHT THAT SHE BRINGS TO ME. E IS FOR THE...
AMEND

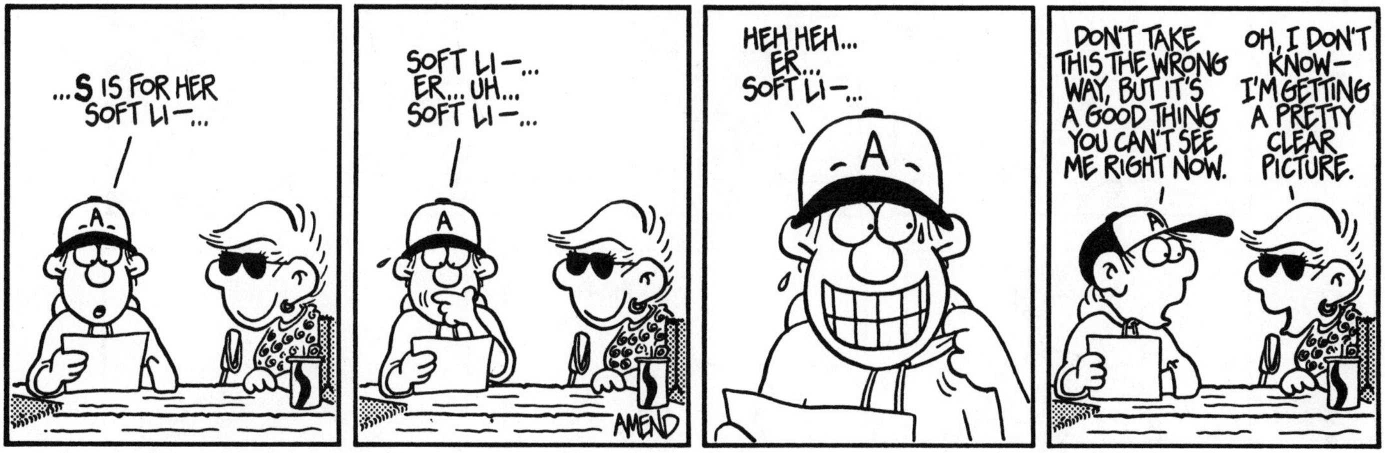
...S IS FOR HER SOFT LI—...
SOFT LI—... ER... UH... SOFT LI—...
AMEND
HEH HEH... ER... SOFT LI—...
DON'T TAKE THIS THE WRONG WAY, BUT IT'S A GOOD THING YOU CAN'T SEE ME RIGHT NOW.
OH, I DON'T KNOW—I'M GETTING A PRETTY CLEAR PICTURE.

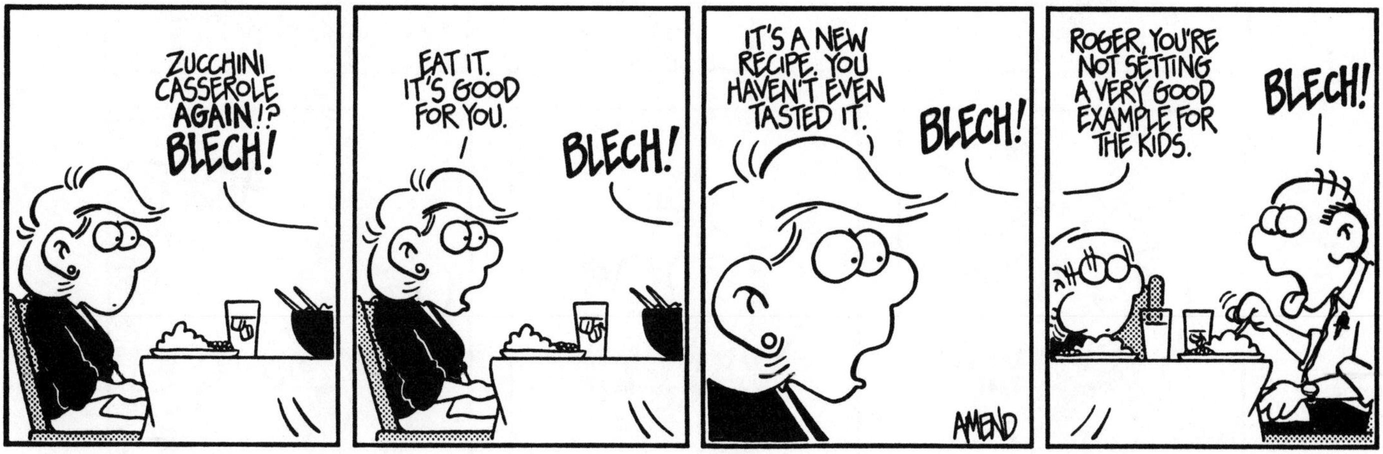
ZUCCHINI CASSEROLE AGAIN!? BLECH!
EAT IT. IT'S GOOD FOR YOU.
BLECH!
IT'S A NEW RECIPE. YOU HAVEN'T EVEN TASTED IT.
BLECH!
AMEND
ROGER, YOU'RE NOT SETTING A VERY GOOD EXAMPLE FOR THE KIDS.
BLECH!

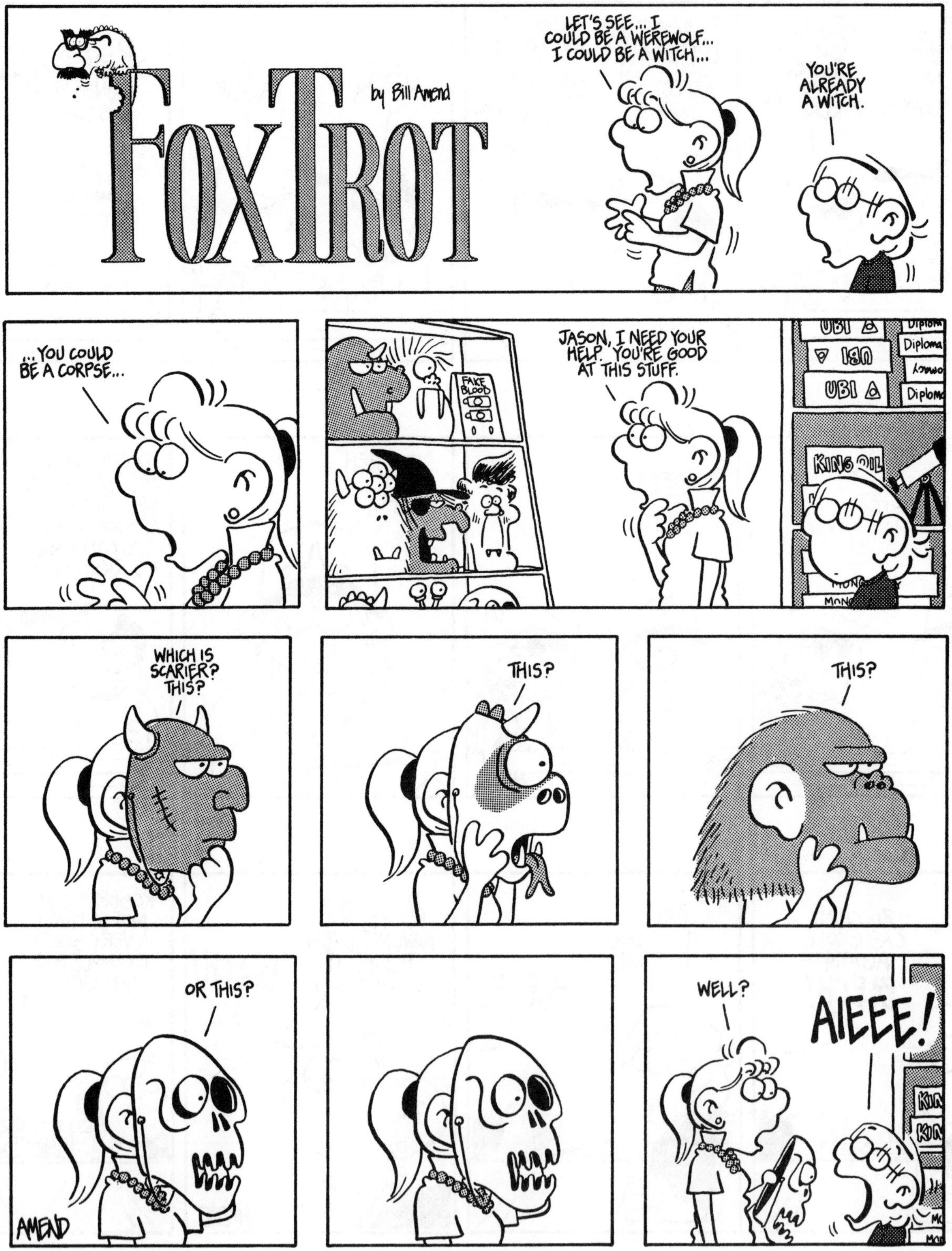
FoxTrot
by Bill Amend
LET'S SEE... I COULD BE A WEREWOLF... I COULD BE A WITCH...
YOU'RE ALREADY A WITCH.
...YOU COULD BE A CORPSE...
FAKE BLOOD
JASON, I NEED YOUR HELP. YOU'RE GOOD AT THIS STUFF.
Diploma
KING OIL
WHICH IS SCARIER? THIS?
THIS?
THIS?
OR THIS?
AMEND
WELL?
AIEEE!

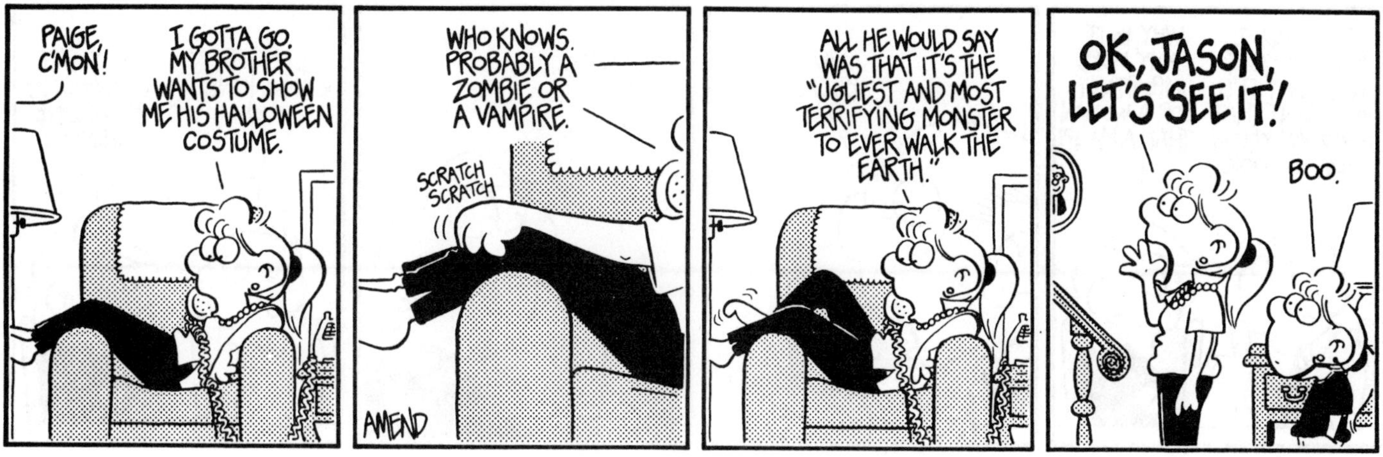
PAIGE, C'MON!
I GOTTA GO. MY BROTHER WANTS TO SHOW ME HIS HALLOWEEN COSTUME.
WHO KNOWS. PROBABLY A ZOMBIE OR A VAMPIRE.
SCRATCH SCRATCH
AMEND
ALL HE WOULD SAY WAS THAT IT'S THE "UGLIEST AND MOST TERRIFYING MONSTER TO EVER WALK THE EARTH."
OK, JASON, LET'S SEE IT!
BOO.

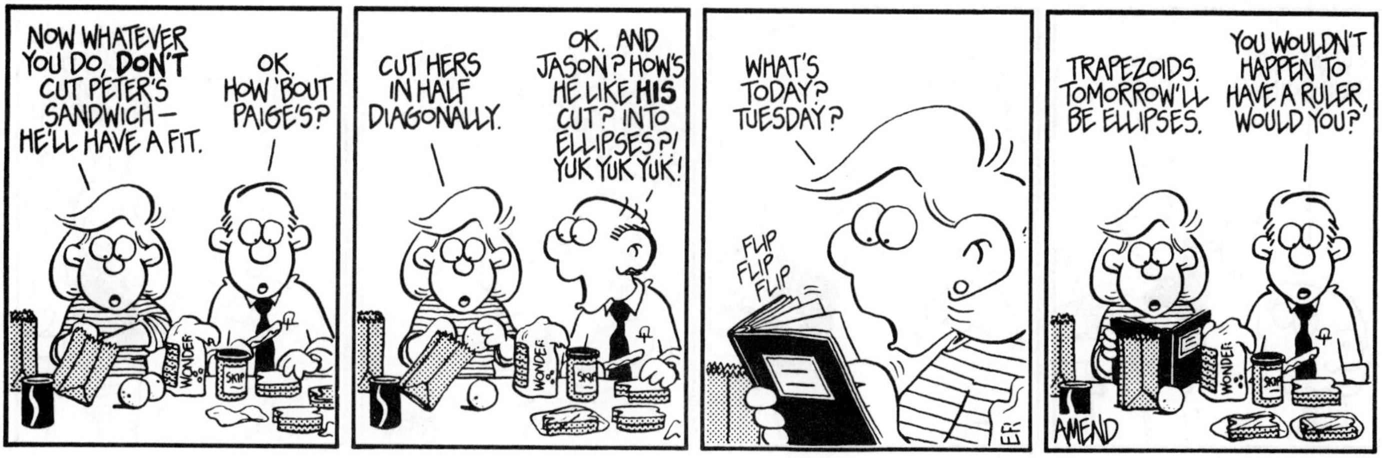
NOW WHATEVER YOU DO, **DON'T** CUT PETER'S SANDWICH— HE'LL HAVE A FIT.
OK. HOW 'BOUT PAIGE'S?
CUT HERS IN HALF DIAGONALLY.
OK. AND JASON? HOW'S HE LIKE **HIS** CUT? INTO ELLIPSES?! YUK YUK YUK!
WHAT'S TODAY? TUESDAY?
FLIP FLIP FLIP
TRAPEZOIDS. TOMORROW'LL BE ELLIPSES.
YOU WOULDN'T HAPPEN TO HAVE A RULER, WOULD YOU?
AMEND

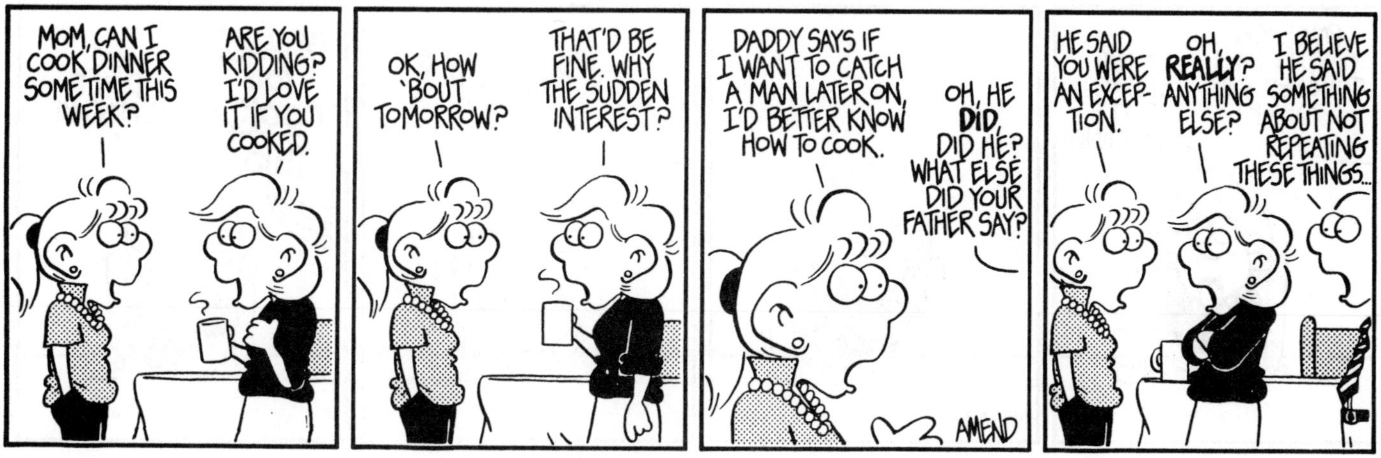
MOM, CAN I COOK DINNER SOMETIME THIS WEEK?
ARE YOU KIDDING? I'D LOVE IT IF YOU COOKED.
OK, HOW 'BOUT TOMORROW?
THAT'D BE FINE. WHY THE SUDDEN INTEREST?
DADDY SAYS IF I WANT TO CATCH A MAN LATER ON, I'D BETTER KNOW HOW TO COOK.
OH, HE **DID**, DID HE? WHAT ELSE DID YOUR FATHER SAY?
AMEND
HE SAID YOU WERE AN EXCEP-TION.
OH, **REALLY**? ANYTHING ELSE?
I BELIEVE HE SAID SOMETHING ABOUT NOT REPEATING THESE THINGS...

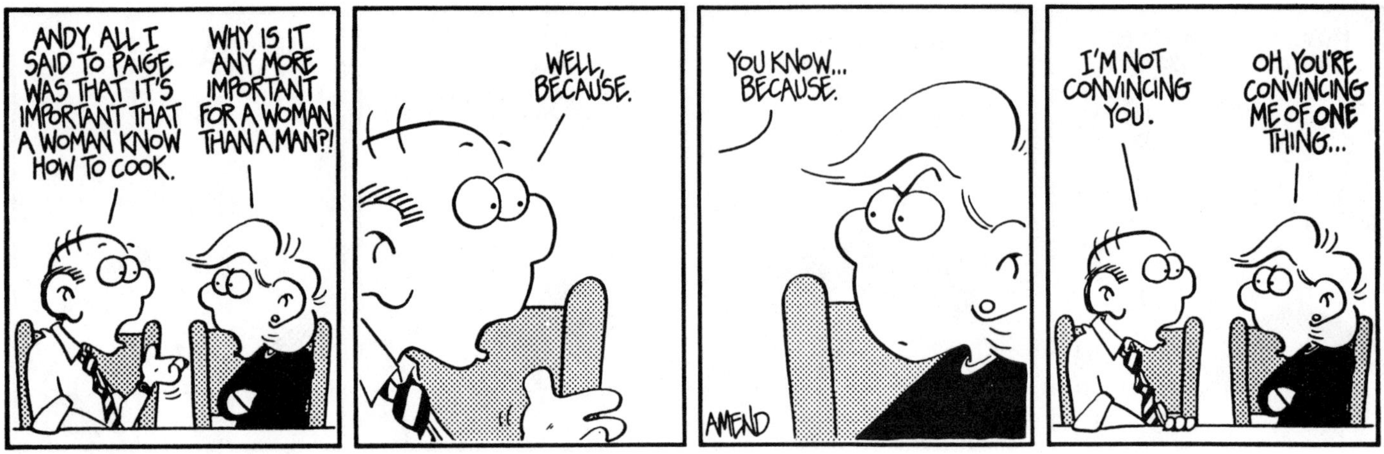
ANDY, ALL I SAID TO PAIGE WAS THAT IT'S IMPORTANT THAT A WOMAN KNOW HOW TO COOK.
WHY IS IT ANY MORE IMPORTANT FOR A WOMAN THAN A MAN?!
WELL, BECAUSE.
YOU KNOW... BECAUSE.
AMEND
I'M NOT CONVINCING YOU.
OH, YOU'RE CONVINCING ME OF **ONE** THING...

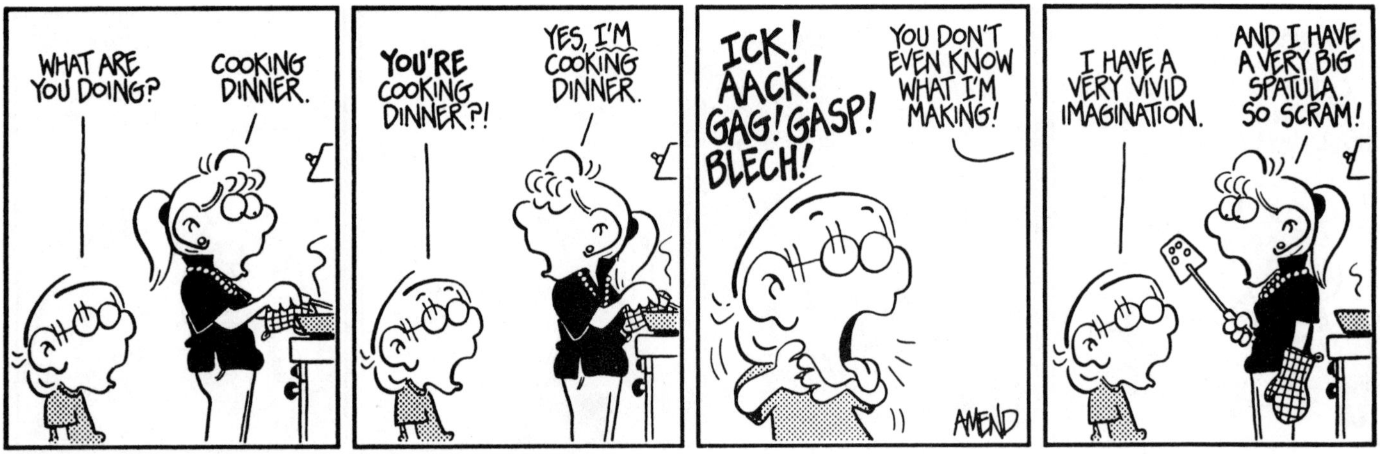
WHAT ARE YOU DOING?
COOKING DINNER.
YOU'RE COOKING DINNER?!
YES, I'M COOKING DINNER.
ICK! AACK! GAG! GASP! BLECH!
YOU DON'T EVEN KNOW WHAT I'M MAKING!
AMEND
I HAVE A VERY VIVID IMAGINATION.
AND I HAVE A VERY BIG SPATULA. SO SCRAM!

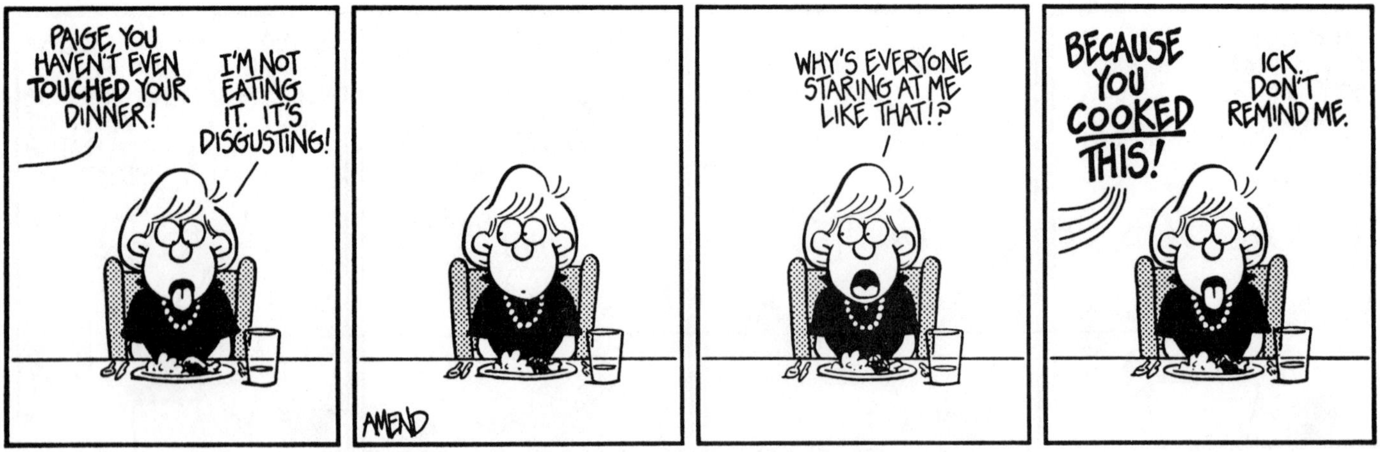
PAIGE, YOU HAVEN'T EVEN **TOUCHED** YOUR DINNER!
I'M NOT EATING IT. IT'S DISGUSTING!
AMEND
WHY'S EVERYONE STARING AT ME LIKE THAT!?
BECAUSE YOU COOKED THIS!
ICK. DON'T REMIND ME.

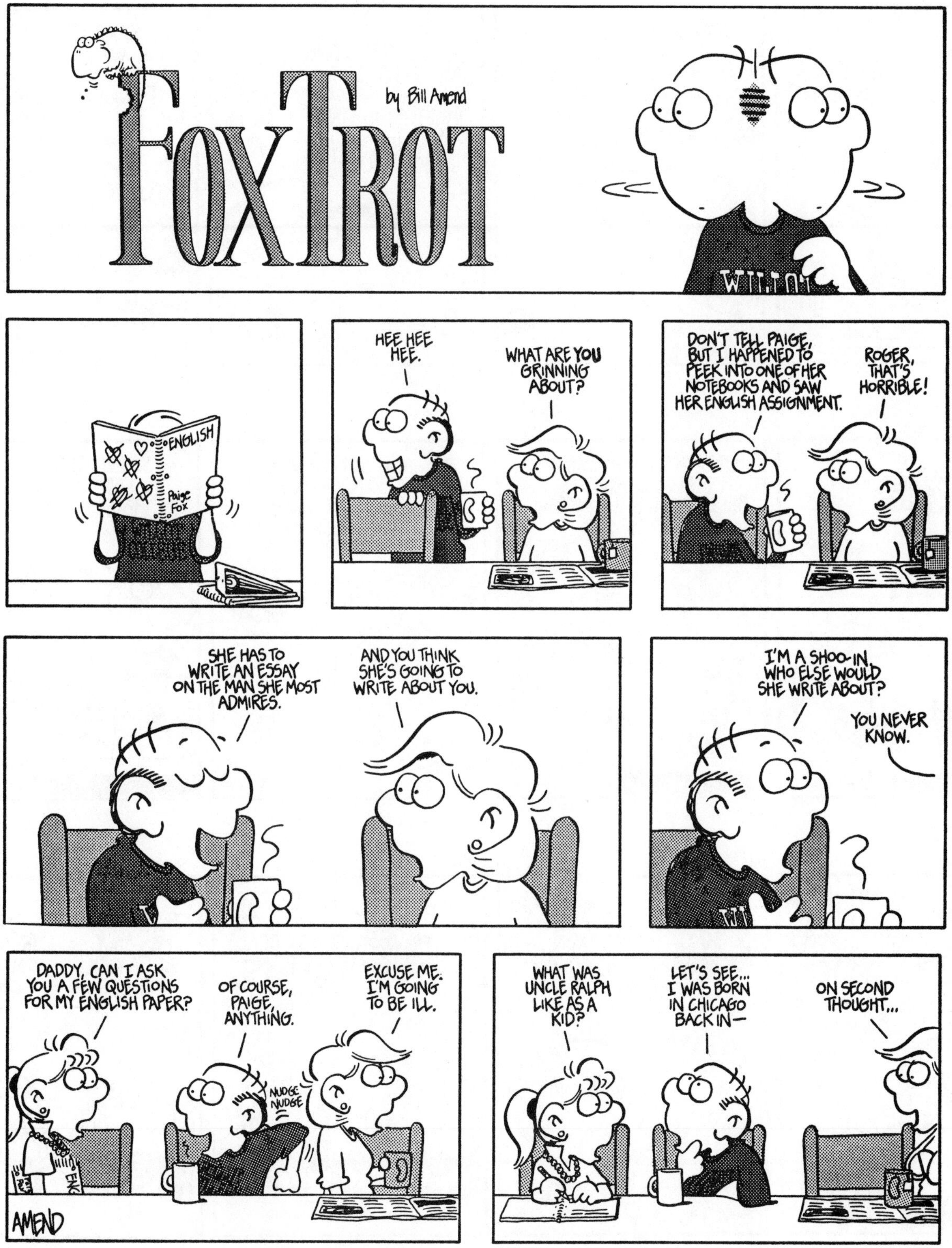

FoxTrot
by Bill Amend
ENGLISH
Paige Fox
HEE HEE HEE.
WHAT ARE YOU GRINNING ABOUT?
DON'T TELL PAIGE, BUT I HAPPENED TO PEEK INTO ONE OF HER NOTEBOOKS AND SAW HER ENGLISH ASSIGNMENT.
ROGER, THAT'S HORRIBLE!
SHE HAS TO WRITE AN ESSAY ON THE MAN SHE MOST ADMIRES.
AND YOU THINK SHE'S GOING TO WRITE ABOUT YOU.
I'M A SHOO-IN. WHO ELSE WOULD SHE WRITE ABOUT?
YOU NEVER KNOW.
DADDY, CAN I ASK YOU A FEW QUESTIONS FOR MY ENGLISH PAPER?
OF COURSE, PAIGE, ANYTHING.
NUDGE NUDGE
EXCUSE ME. I'M GOING TO BE ILL.
AMEND
WHAT WAS UNCLE RALPH LIKE AS A KID?
LET'S SEE... I WAS BORN IN CHICAGO BACK IN—
ON SECOND THOUGHT...

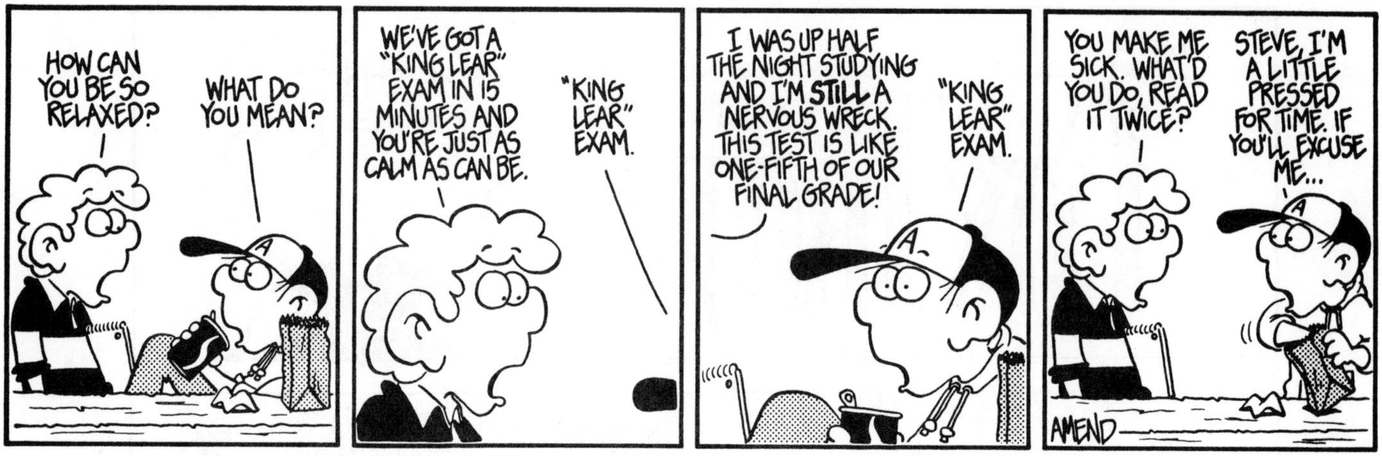
HOW CAN YOU BE SO RELAXED?
WHAT DO YOU MEAN?
WE'VE GOT A "KING LEAR" EXAM IN 15 MINUTES AND YOU'RE JUST AS CALM AS CAN BE.
"KING LEAR" EXAM.
I WAS UP HALF THE NIGHT STUDYING AND I'M **STILL** A NERVOUS WRECK. THIS TEST IS LIKE ONE-FIFTH OF OUR FINAL GRADE!
"KING LEAR" EXAM.
YOU MAKE ME SICK. WHAT'D YOU DO, READ IT TWICE?
STEVE, I'M A LITTLE PRESSED FOR TIME. IF YOU'LL EXCUSE ME...
AMEND

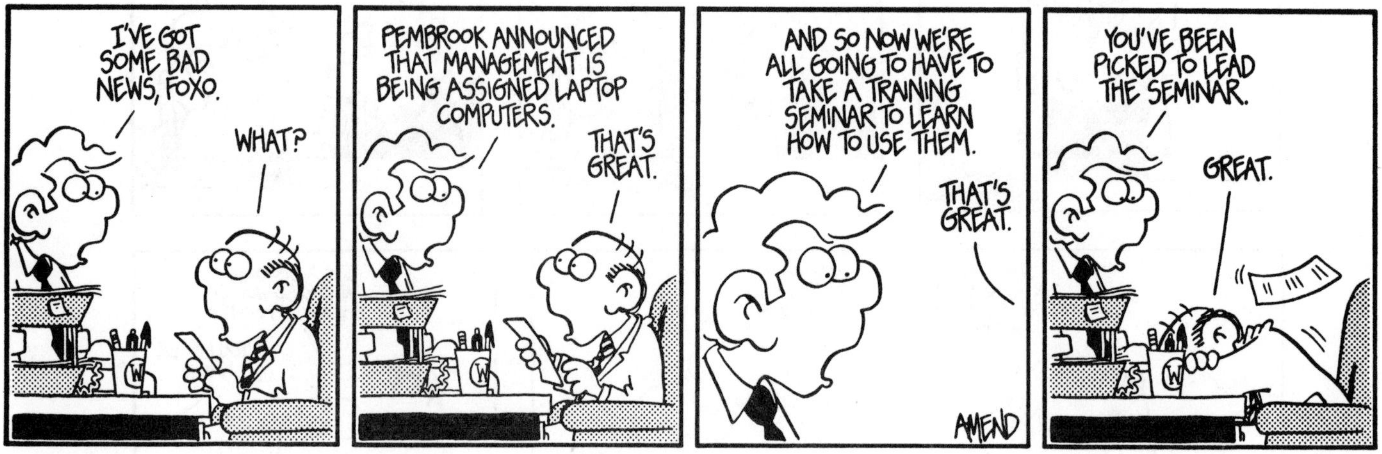
I'VE GOT SOME BAD NEWS, FOXO.
WHAT?
PEMBROOK ANNOUNCED THAT MANAGEMENT IS BEING ASSIGNED LAPTOP COMPUTERS.
THAT'S GREAT.
AND SO NOW WE'RE ALL GOING TO HAVE TO TAKE A TRAINING SEMINAR TO LEARN HOW TO USE THEM.
THAT'S GREAT.
AMEND
YOU'VE BEEN PICKED TO LEAD THE SEMINAR.
GREAT.

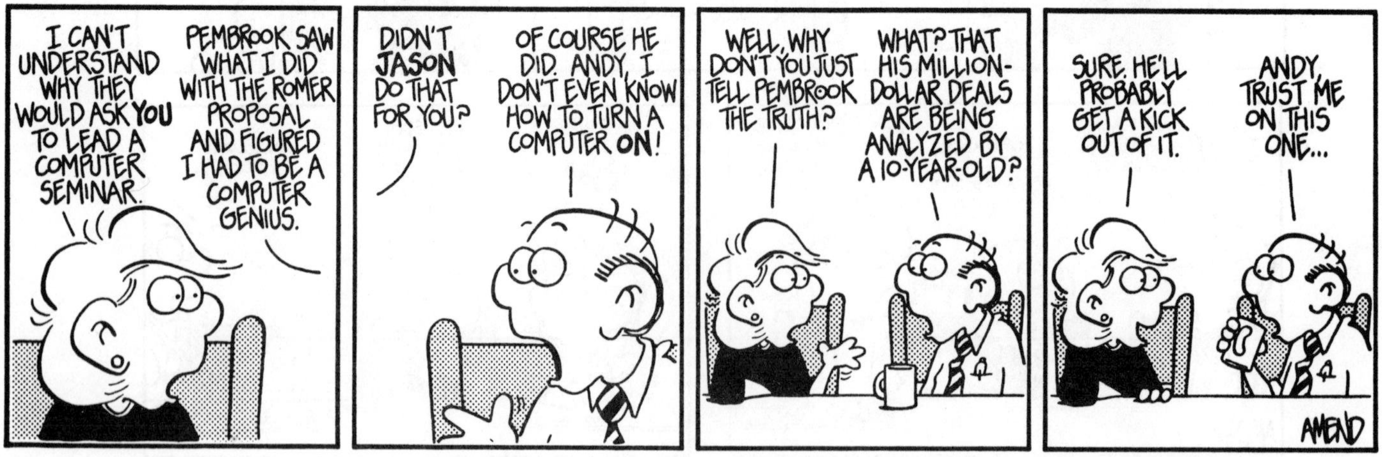
I CAN'T UNDERSTAND WHY THEY WOULD ASK **YOU** TO LEAD A COMPUTER SEMINAR.
PEMBROOK SAW WHAT I DID WITH THE ROMER PROPOSAL AND FIGURED I HAD TO BE A COMPUTER GENIUS.
DIDN'T **JASON** DO THAT FOR YOU?
OF COURSE HE DID. ANDY, I DON'T EVEN KNOW HOW TO TURN A COMPUTER **ON**!
WELL, WHY DON'T YOU JUST TELL PEMBROOK THE TRUTH?
WHAT? THAT HIS MILLION-DOLLAR DEALS ARE BEING ANALYZED BY A 10-YEAR-OLD?
SURE. HE'LL PROBABLY GET A KICK OUT OF IT.
ANDY, TRUST ME ON THIS ONE...
AMEND

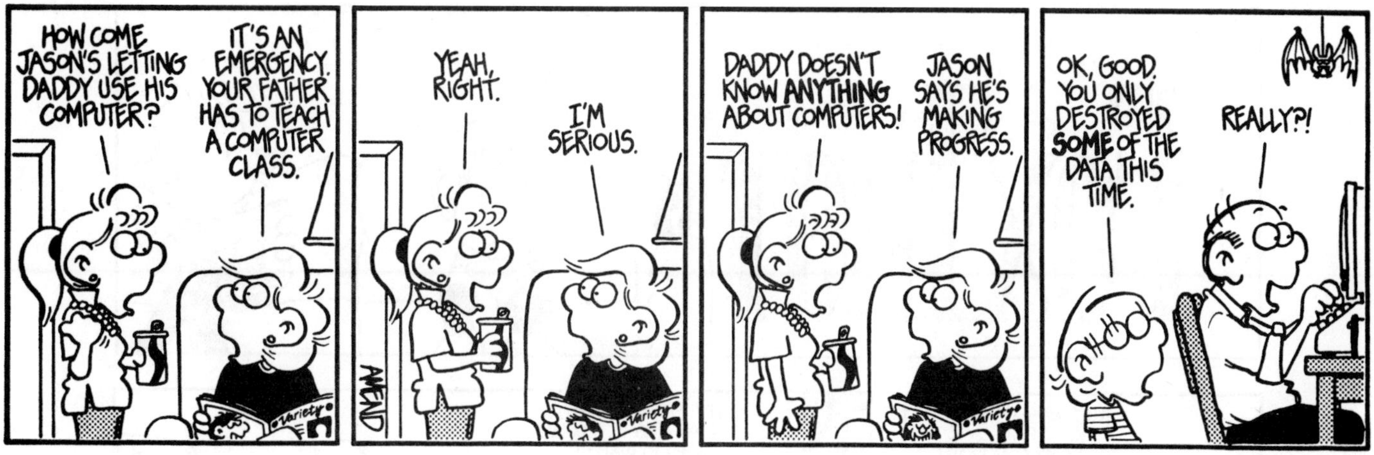
HOW COME JASON'S LETTING DADDY USE HIS COMPUTER?
IT'S AN EMERGENCY. YOUR FATHER HAS TO TEACH A COMPUTER CLASS.
YEAH, RIGHT.
I'M SERIOUS.
AMEND
DADDY DOESN'T KNOW **ANYTHING** ABOUT COMPUTERS!
JASON SAYS HE'S MAKING PROGRESS.
OK, GOOD. YOU ONLY DESTROYED **SOME** OF THE DATA THIS TIME.
REALLY?!

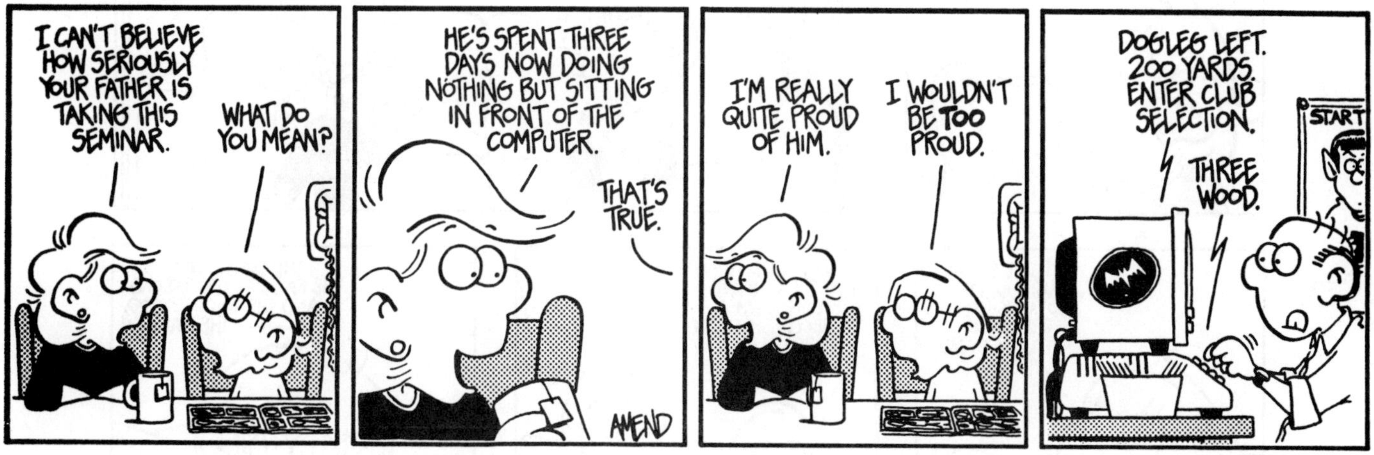
I CAN'T BELIEVE HOW SERIOUSLY YOUR FATHER IS TAKING THIS SEMINAR.
WHAT DO YOU MEAN?
HE'S SPENT THREE DAYS NOW DOING NOTHING BUT SITTING IN FRONT OF THE COMPUTER.
THAT'S TRUE.
AMEND
I'M REALLY QUITE PROUD OF HIM.
I WOULDN'T BE **TOO** PROUD.
DOGLEG LEFT. 200 YARDS. ENTER CLUB SELECTION.
START
THREE WOOD.

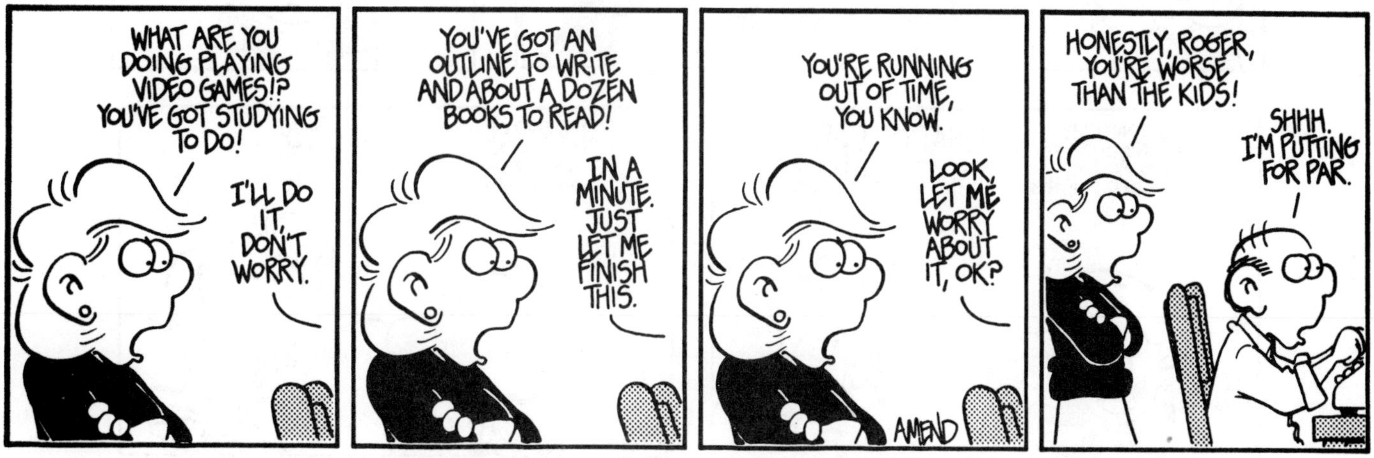
WHAT ARE YOU DOING PLAYING VIDEO GAMES!? YOU'VE GOT STUDYING TO DO!
I'LL DO IT, DON'T WORRY.
YOU'VE GOT AN OUTLINE TO WRITE AND ABOUT A DOZEN BOOKS TO READ!
IN A MINUTE. JUST LET ME FINISH THIS.
YOU'RE RUNNING OUT OF TIME, YOU KNOW.
LOOK, LET **ME** WORRY ABOUT IT, OK?
AMEND
HONESTLY, ROGER, YOU'RE WORSE THAN THE KIDS!
SHHH. I'M PUTTING FOR PAR.

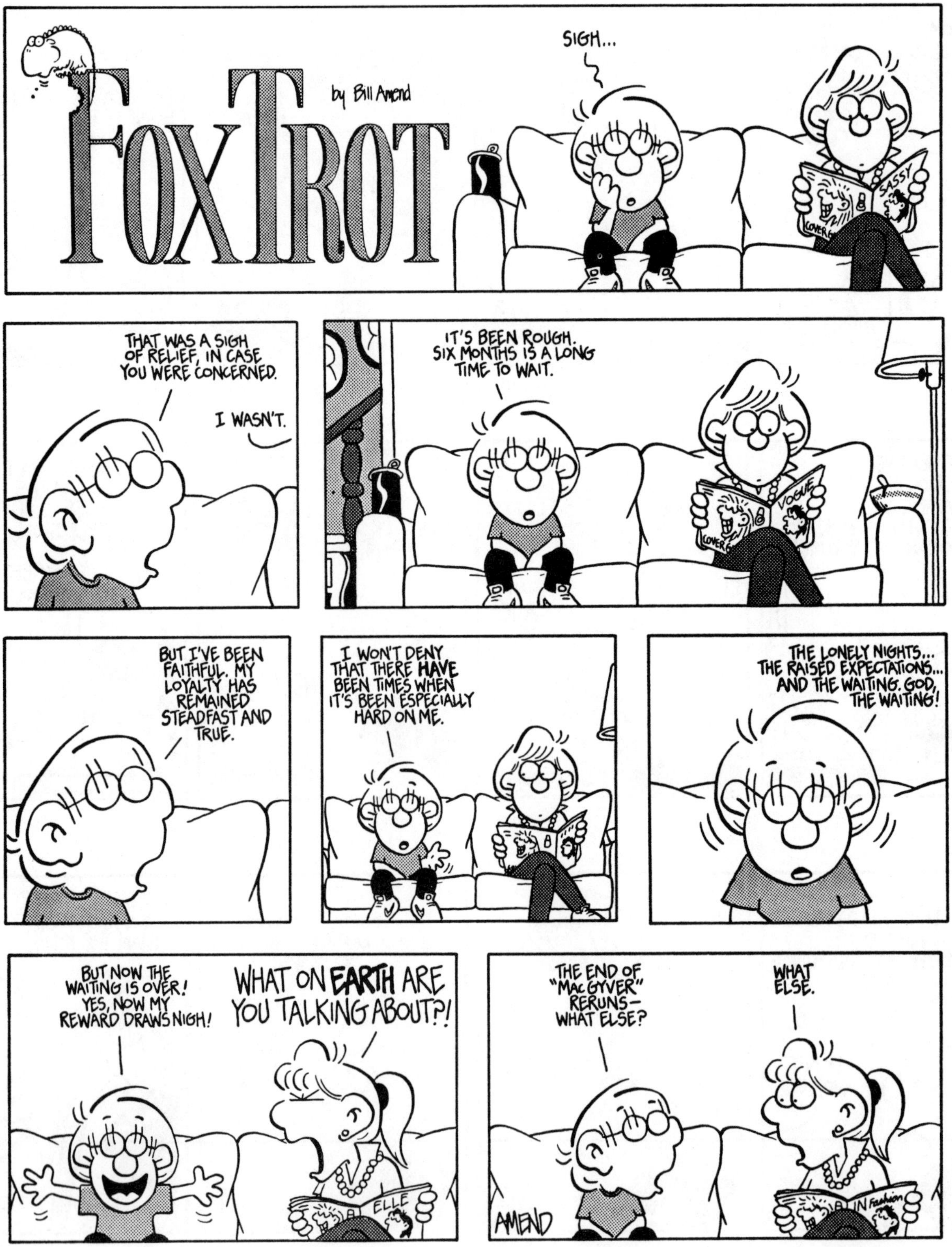
FoxTrot
by Bill Amend
SIGH...
SASSY
COVER
THAT WAS A SIGH OF RELIEF, IN CASE YOU WERE CONCERNED.
I WASN'T.
IT'S BEEN ROUGH. SIX MONTHS IS A LONG TIME TO WAIT.
VOGUE
BUT I'VE BEEN FAITHFUL. MY LOYALTY HAS REMAINED STEADFAST AND TRUE.
I WON'T DENY THAT THERE HAVE BEEN TIMES WHEN IT'S BEEN ESPECIALLY HARD ON ME.
THE LONELY NIGHTS... THE RAISED EXPECTATIONS... AND THE WAITING. GOD, THE WAITING!
BUT NOW THE WAITING IS OVER! YES, NOW MY REWARD DRAWS NIGH!
WHAT ON EARTH ARE YOU TALKING ABOUT?!
ELLE
THE END OF "MACGYVER" RERUNS— WHAT ELSE?
WHAT ELSE.
AMEND

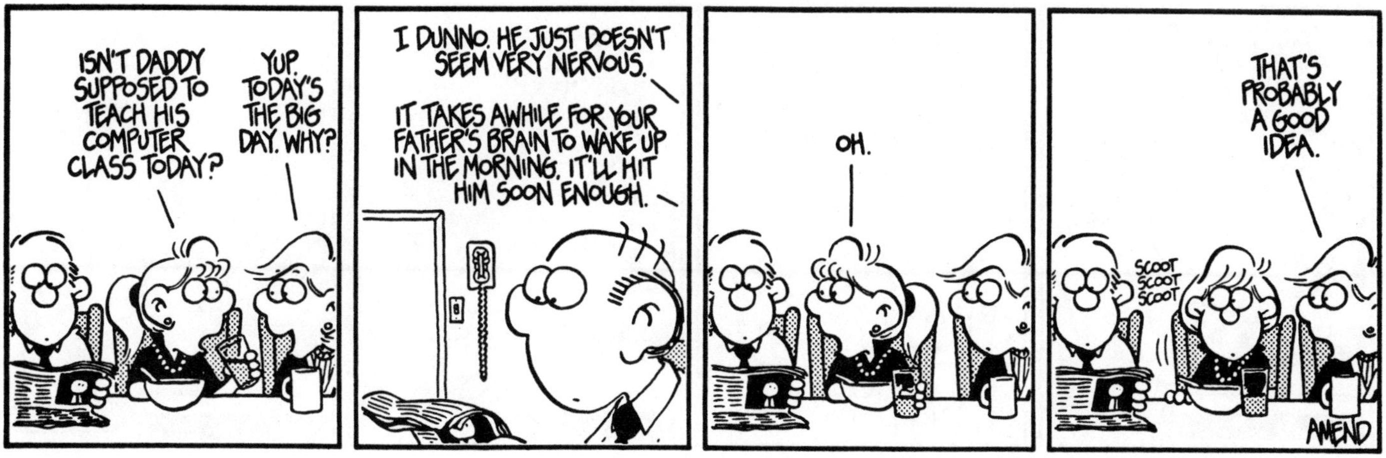
ISN'T DADDY SUPPOSED TO TEACH HIS COMPUTER CLASS TODAY?
YUP. TODAY'S THE BIG DAY. WHY?
I DUNNO. HE JUST DOESN'T SEEM VERY NERVOUS.
IT TAKES AWHILE FOR YOUR FATHER'S BRAIN TO WAKE UP IN THE MORNING. IT'LL HIT HIM SOON ENOUGH.
OH.
SCOOT SCOOT SCOOT
THAT'S PROBABLY A GOOD IDEA.
AMEND

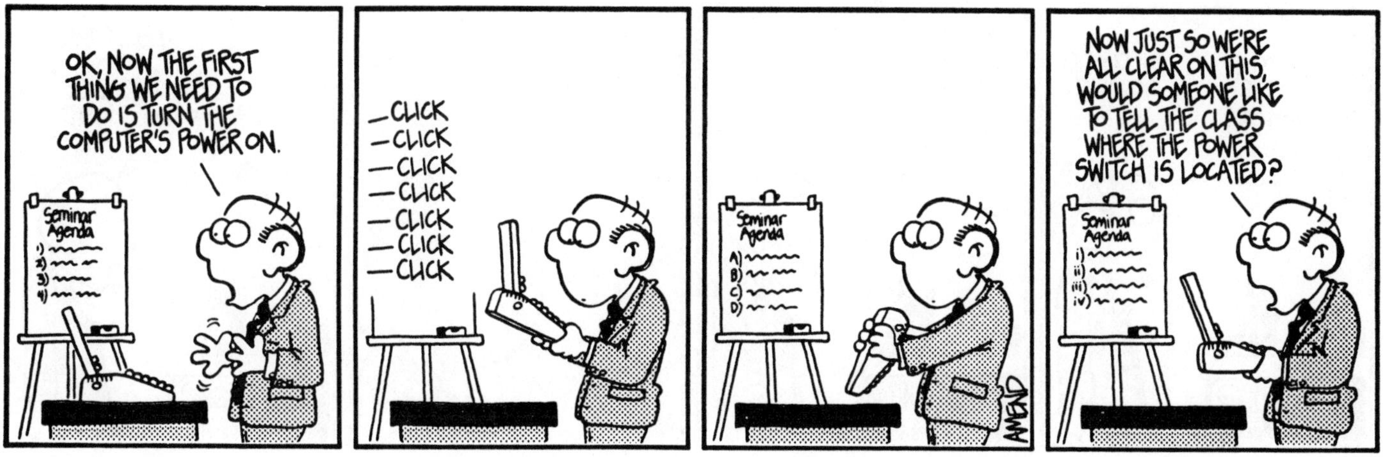
OK, NOW THE FIRST THING WE NEED TO DO IS TURN THE COMPUTER'S POWER ON.
Seminar Agenda
CLICK
CLICK
CLICK
CLICK
CLICK
CLICK
CLICK
AMEND
NOW JUST SO WE'RE ALL CLEAR ON THIS, WOULD SOMEONE LIKE TO TELL THE CLASS WHERE THE POWER SWITCH IS LOCATED?

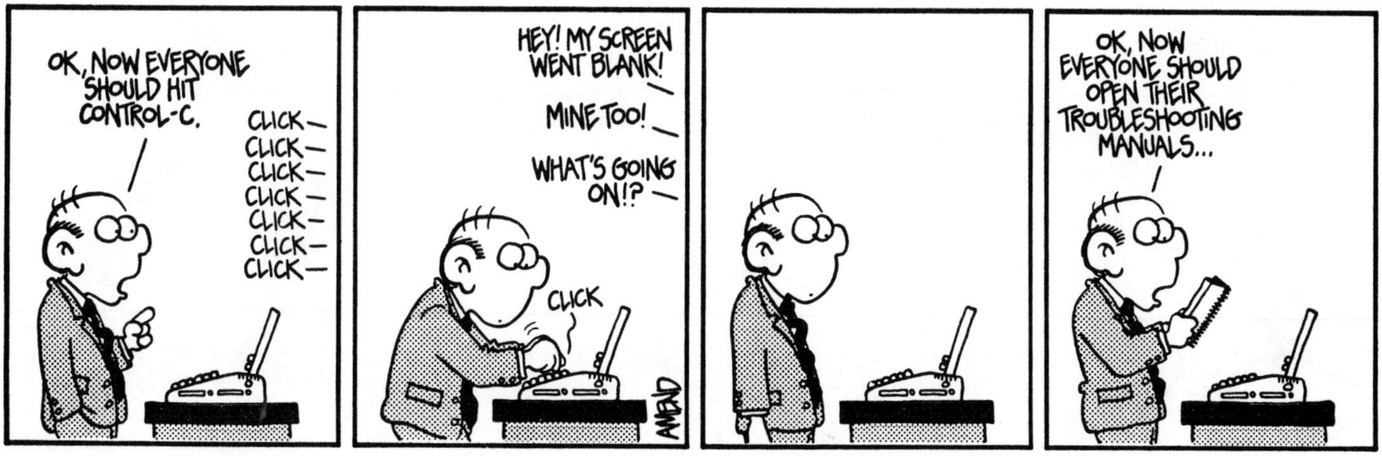
OK, NOW EVERYONE SHOULD HIT CONTROL-C.
CLICK
CLICK
CLICK
CLICK
CLICK
CLICK
CLICK
HEY! MY SCREEN WENT BLANK!
MINE TOO!
WHAT'S GOING ON!?
CLICK
AMEND
OK, NOW EVERYONE SHOULD OPEN THEIR TROUBLESHOOTING MANUALS...

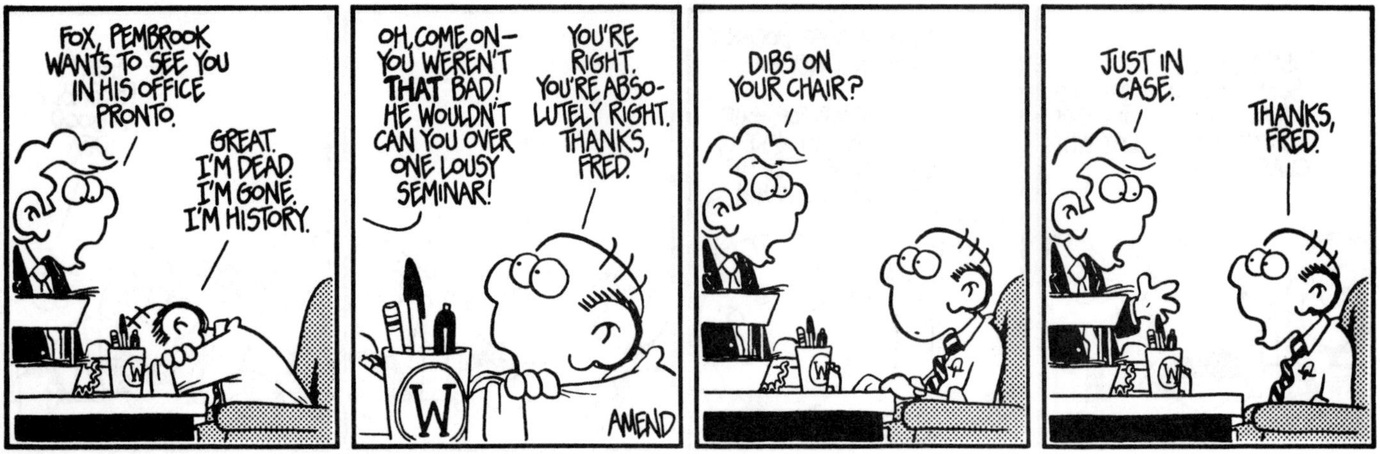
FOX, PEMBROOK WANTS TO SEE YOU IN HIS OFFICE PRONTO.
GREAT. I'M DEAD. I'M GONE. I'M HISTORY.
OH, COME ON— YOU WEREN'T THAT BAD! HE WOULDN'T CAN YOU OVER ONE LOUSY SEMINAR!
YOU'RE RIGHT. YOU'RE ABSOLUTELY RIGHT. THANKS, FRED.
AMEND
DIBS ON YOUR CHAIR?
JUST IN CASE.
THANKS, FRED.

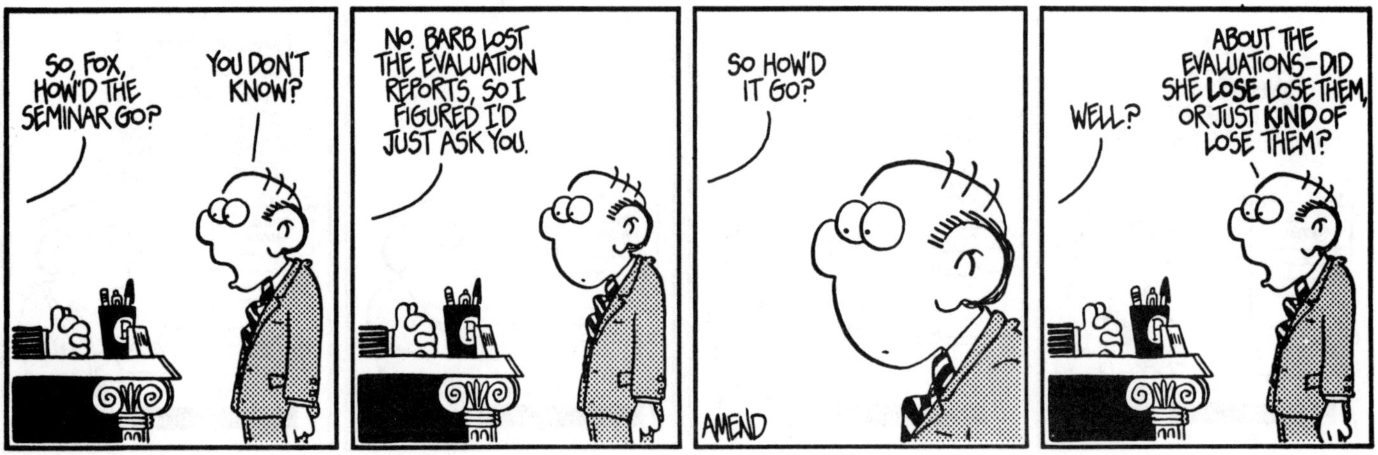
SO, FOX, HOW'D THE SEMINAR GO?
YOU DON'T KNOW?
NO. BARB LOST THE EVALUATION REPORTS, SO I FIGURED I'D JUST ASK YOU.
SO HOW'D IT GO?
AMEND
WELL?
ABOUT THE EVALUATIONS—DID SHE LOSE LOSE THEM, OR JUST KIND OF LOSE THEM?

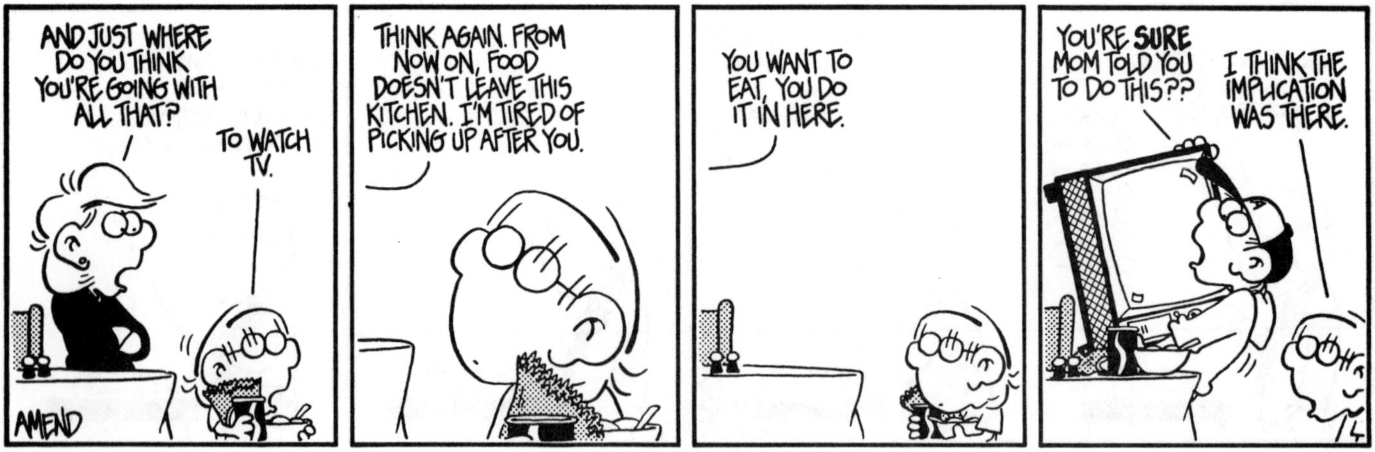
AND JUST WHERE DO YOU THINK YOU'RE GOING WITH ALL THAT?
TO WATCH TV.
AMEND
THINK AGAIN. FROM NOW ON, FOOD DOESN'T LEAVE THIS KITCHEN. I'M TIRED OF PICKING UP AFTER YOU.
YOU WANT TO EAT, YOU DO IT IN HERE.
YOU'RE SURE MOM TOLD YOU TO DO THIS??
I THINK THE IMPLICATION WAS THERE.

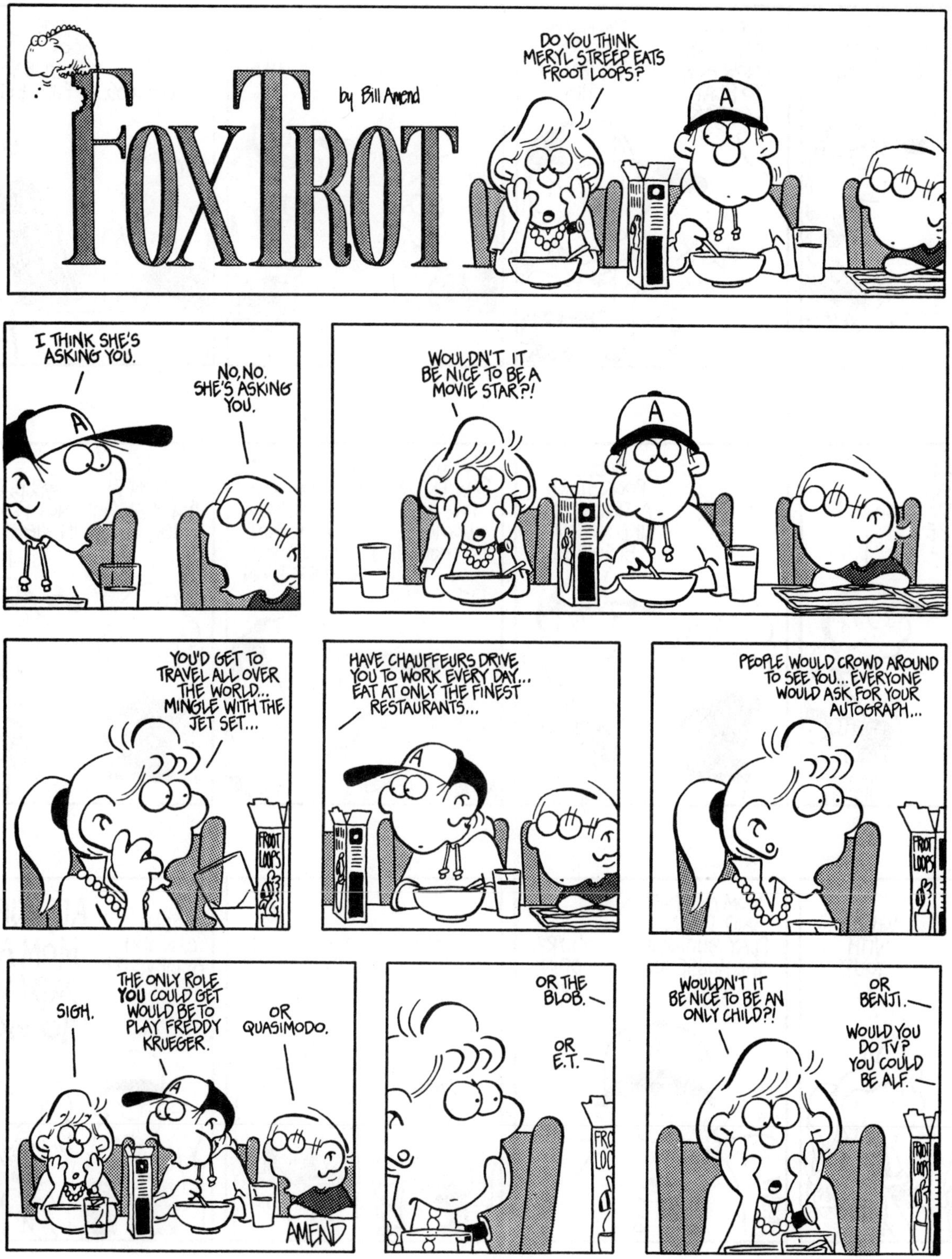
FOXTROT
by Bill Amend
DO YOU THINK MERYL STREEP EATS FROOT LOOPS?
I THINK SHE'S ASKING YOU.
NO, NO. SHE'S ASKING YOU.
WOULDN'T IT BE NICE TO BE A MOVIE STAR?!
YOU'D GET TO TRAVEL ALL OVER THE WORLD... MINGLE WITH THE JET SET...
FROOT LOOPS
HAVE CHAUFFEURS DRIVE YOU TO WORK EVERY DAY... EAT AT ONLY THE FINEST RESTAURANTS...
PEOPLE WOULD CROWD AROUND TO SEE YOU... EVERYONE WOULD ASK FOR YOUR AUTOGRAPH...
SIGH.
THE ONLY ROLE YOU COULD GET WOULD BE TO PLAY FREDDY KRUEGER.
OR QUASIMODO.
AMEND
OR THE BLOB.
OR E.T.
WOULDN'T IT BE NICE TO BE AN ONLY CHILD?!
OR BENJI.
WOULD YOU DO TV? YOU COULD BE ALF.

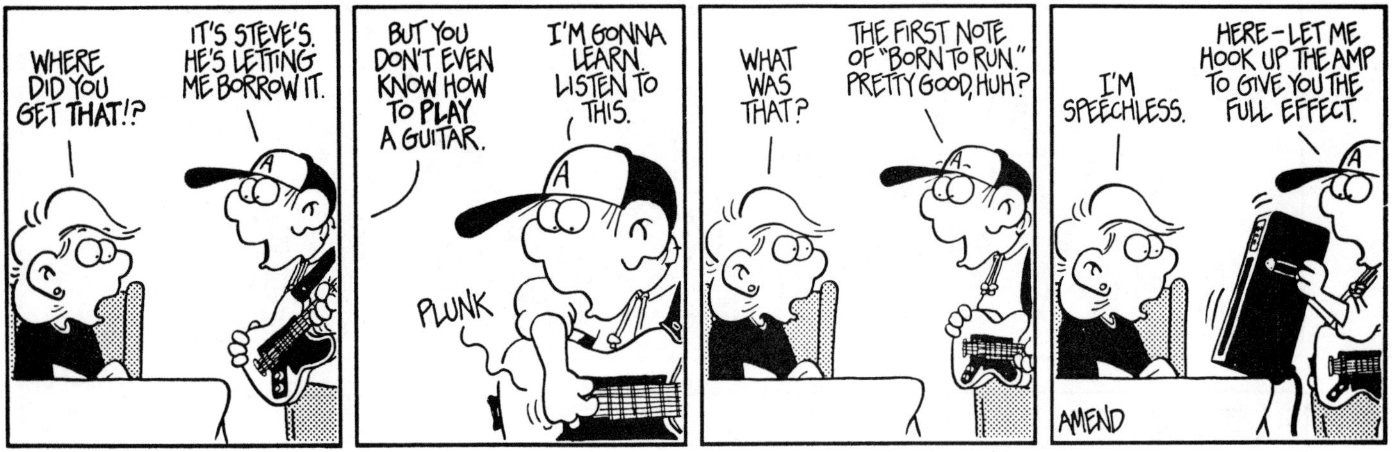
WHERE DID YOU GET THAT!?
IT'S STEVE'S. HE'S LETTING ME BORROW IT.
BUT YOU DON'T EVEN KNOW HOW TO PLAY A GUITAR.
I'M GONNA LEARN. LISTEN TO THIS.
PLUNK
WHAT WAS THAT?
THE FIRST NOTE OF "BORN TO RUN." PRETTY GOOD, HUH?
I'M SPEECHLESS.
HERE–LET ME HOOK UP THE AMP TO GIVE YOU THE FULL EFFECT.
AMEND

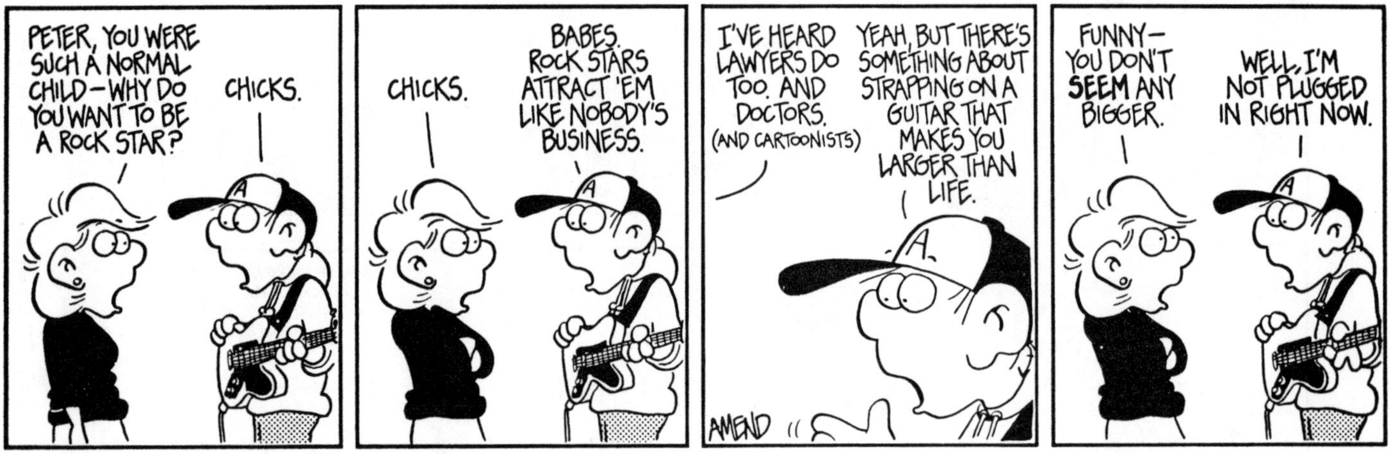
PETER, YOU WERE SUCH A NORMAL CHILD–WHY DO YOU WANT TO BE A ROCK STAR?
CHICKS.
CHICKS.
BABES. ROCK STARS ATTRACT 'EM LIKE NOBODY'S BUSINESS.
I'VE HEARD LAWYERS DO TOO. AND DOCTORS.
(AND CARTOONISTS)
YEAH, BUT THERE'S SOMETHING ABOUT STRAPPING ON A GUITAR THAT MAKES YOU LARGER THAN LIFE.
AMEND
FUNNY–YOU DON'T SEEM ANY BIGGER.
WELL, I'M NOT PLUGGED IN RIGHT NOW.

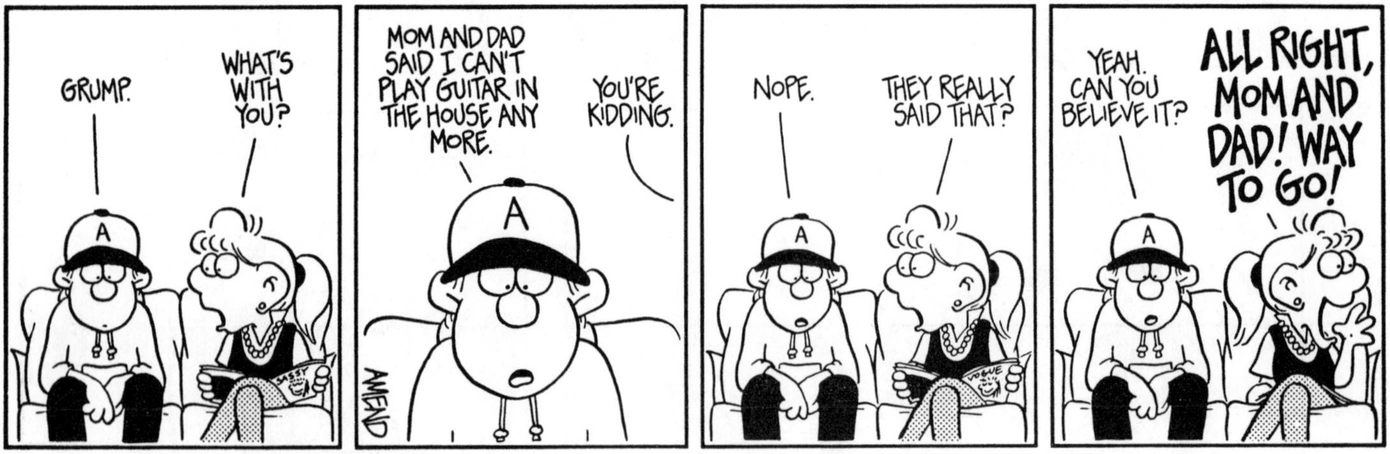
GRUMP.
WHAT'S WITH YOU?
MOM AND DAD SAID I CAN'T PLAY GUITAR IN THE HOUSE ANY MORE.
YOU'RE KIDDING.
AMEND
NOPE.
THEY REALLY SAID THAT?
YEAH. CAN YOU BELIEVE IT?
ALL RIGHT, MOM AND DAD! WAY TO GO!

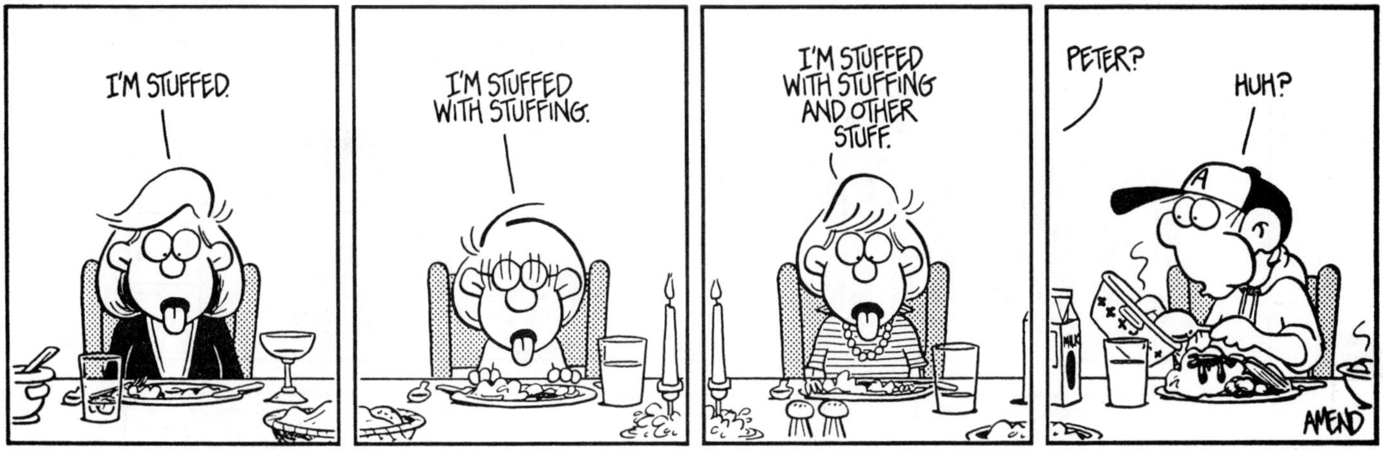
I'M STUFFED.
I'M STUFFED WITH STUFFING.
I'M STUFFED WITH STUFFING AND OTHER STUFF.
PETER?
HUH?
MILK
AMEND

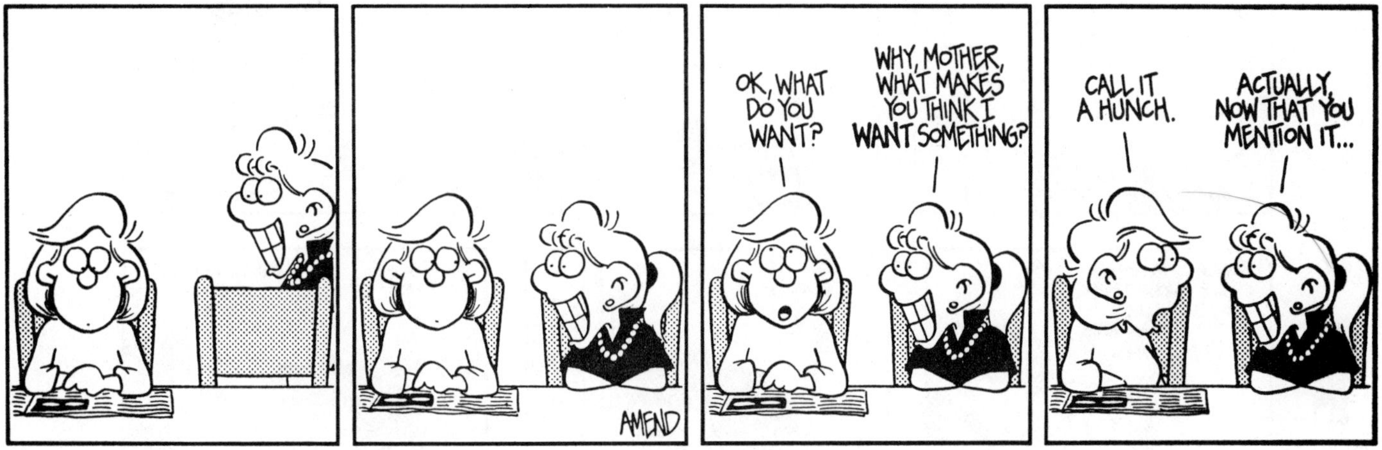
AMEND
OK, WHAT DO YOU WANT?
WHY, MOTHER, WHAT MAKES YOU THINK I **WANT** SOMETHING?
CALL IT A HUNCH.
ACTUALLY, NOW THAT YOU MENTION IT...

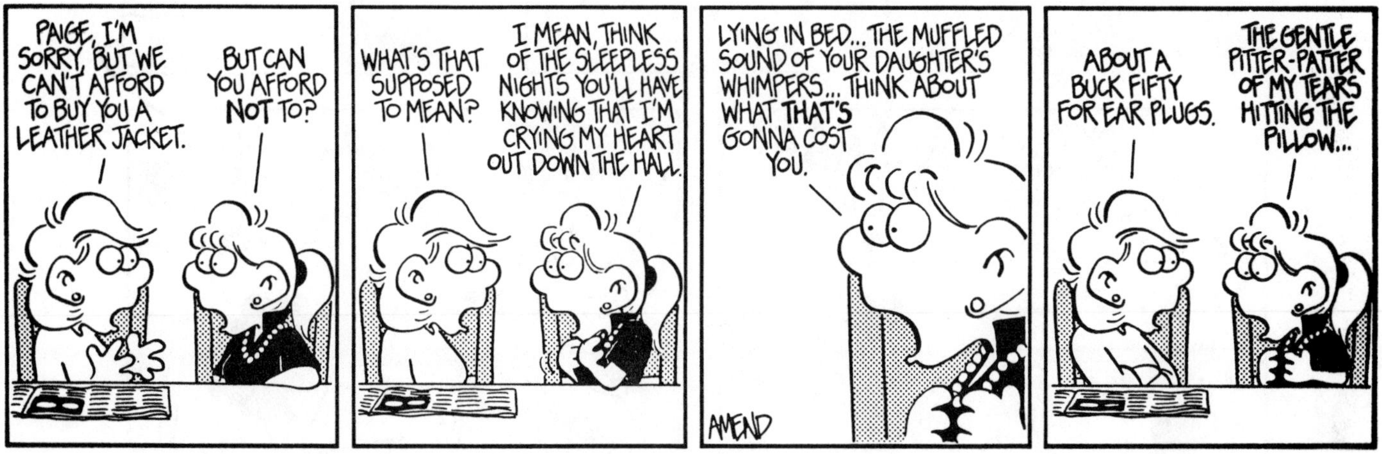
PAIGE, I'M SORRY, BUT WE CAN'T AFFORD TO BUY YOU A LEATHER JACKET.
BUT CAN YOU AFFORD **NOT** TO?
WHAT'S THAT SUPPOSED TO MEAN?
I MEAN, THINK OF THE SLEEPLESS NIGHTS YOU'LL HAVE KNOWING THAT I'M CRYING MY HEART OUT DOWN THE HALL.
LYING IN BED... THE MUFFLED SOUND OF YOUR DAUGHTER'S WHIMPERS... THINK ABOUT WHAT **THAT'S** GONNA COST YOU.
AMEND
ABOUT A BUCK FIFTY FOR EAR PLUGS.
THE GENTLE PITTER-PATTER OF MY TEARS HITTING THE PILLOW...

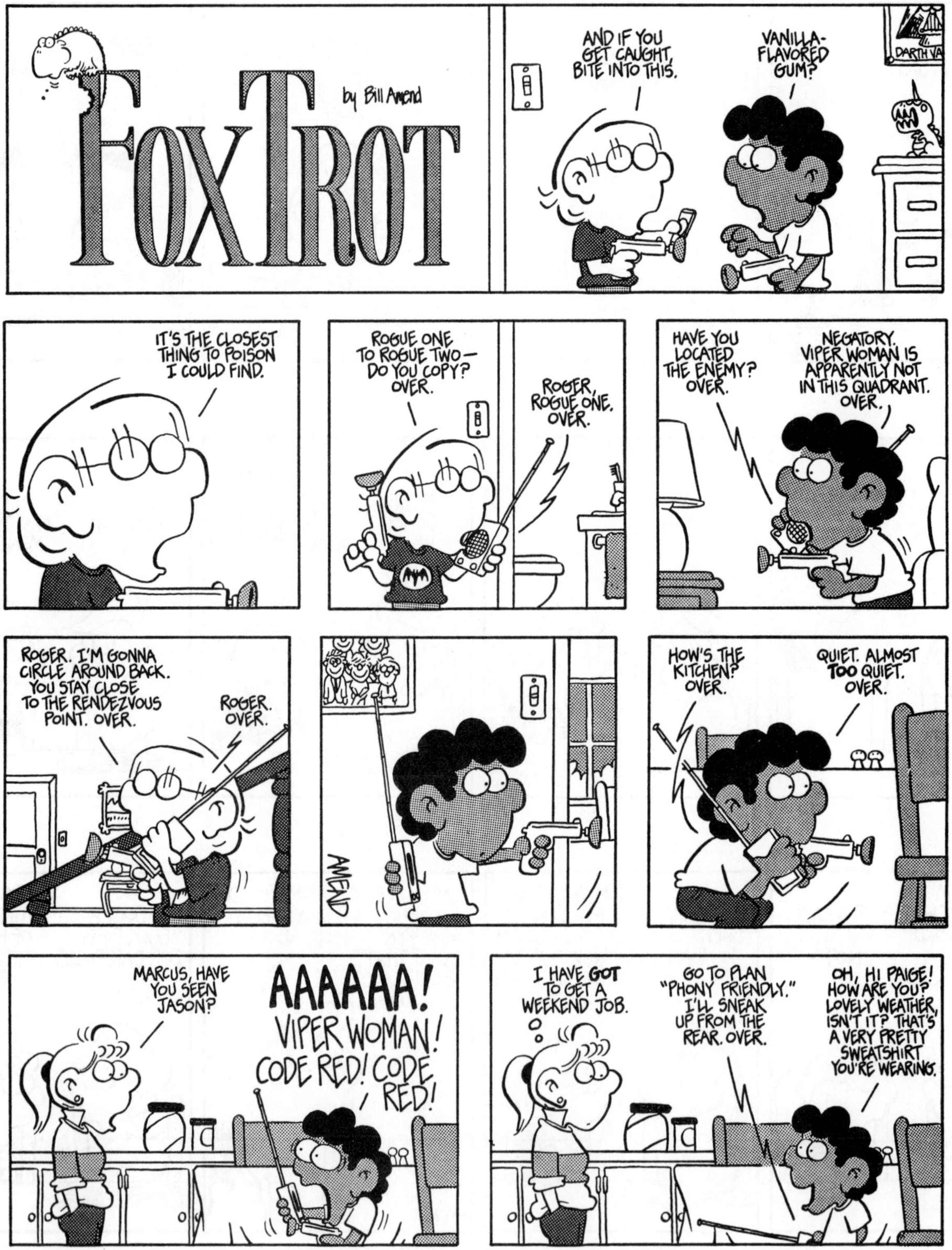
FOXTROT
by Bill Amend
AND IF YOU GET CAUGHT, BITE INTO THIS.
VANILLA-FLAVORED GUM?
IT'S THE CLOSEST THING TO POISON I COULD FIND.
ROGUE ONE TO ROGUE TWO— DO YOU COPY? OVER.
ROGER, ROGUE ONE. OVER.
HAVE YOU LOCATED THE ENEMY? OVER.
NEGATORY. VIPER WOMAN IS APPARENTLY NOT IN THIS QUADRANT. OVER.
ROGER. I'M GONNA CIRCLE AROUND BACK. YOU STAY CLOSE TO THE RENDEZVOUS POINT. OVER.
ROGER. OVER.
AMEND
HOW'S THE KITCHEN? OVER.
QUIET. ALMOST TOO QUIET. OVER.
MARCUS, HAVE YOU SEEN JASON?
AAAAAA!
VIPER WOMAN! CODE RED! CODE RED!
I HAVE GOT TO GET A WEEKEND JOB.
GO TO PLAN "PHONY FRIENDLY." I'LL SNEAK UP FROM THE REAR. OVER.
OH, HI PAIGE! HOW ARE YOU? LOVELY WEATHER, ISN'T IT? THAT'S A VERY PRETTY SWEATSHIRT YOU'RE WEARING.

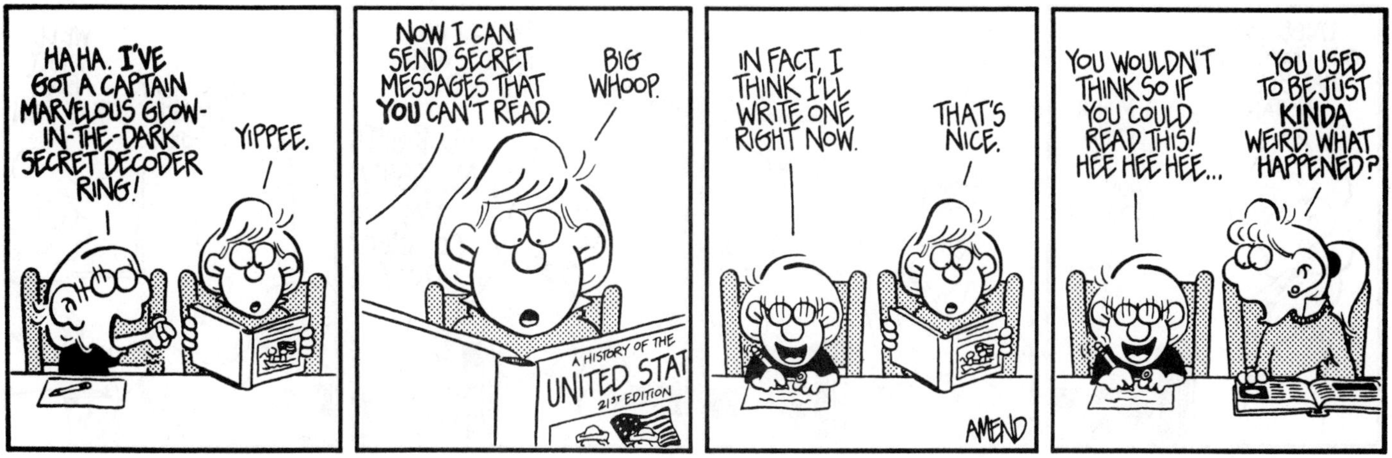
HA HA. I'VE GOT A CAPTAIN MARVELOUS GLOW-IN-THE-DARK SECRET DECODER RING!
YIPPEE.
NOW I CAN SEND SECRET MESSAGES THAT YOU CAN'T READ.
BIG WHOOP.
A HISTORY OF THE UNITED STAT 21ST EDITION
IN FACT, I THINK I'LL WRITE ONE RIGHT NOW.
THAT'S NICE.
AMEND
YOU WOULDN'T THINK SO IF YOU COULD READ THIS! HEE HEE HEE...
YOU USED TO BE JUST KINDA WEIRD. WHAT HAPPENED?

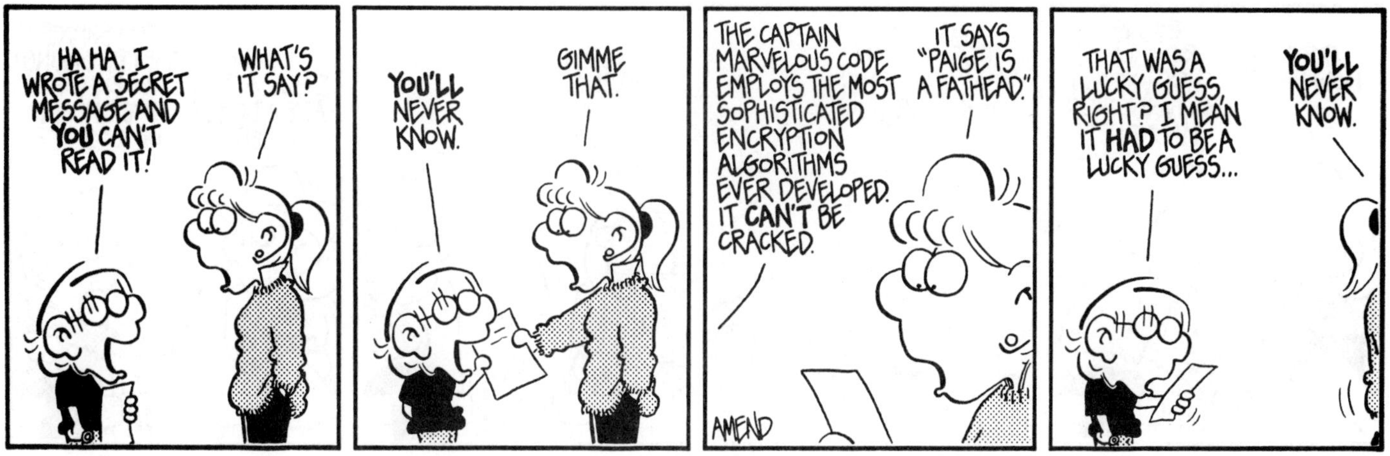
HA HA. I WROTE A SECRET MESSAGE AND YOU CAN'T READ IT!
WHAT'S IT SAY?
YOU'LL NEVER KNOW.
GIMME THAT.
THE CAPTAIN MARVELOUS CODE EMPLOYS THE MOST SOPHISTICATED ENCRYPTION ALGORITHMS EVER DEVELOPED. IT CAN'T BE CRACKED.
IT SAYS "PAIGE IS A FATHEAD."
AMEND
THAT WAS A LUCKY GUESS, RIGHT? I MEAN IT HAD TO BE A LUCKY GUESS...
YOU'LL NEVER KNOW.

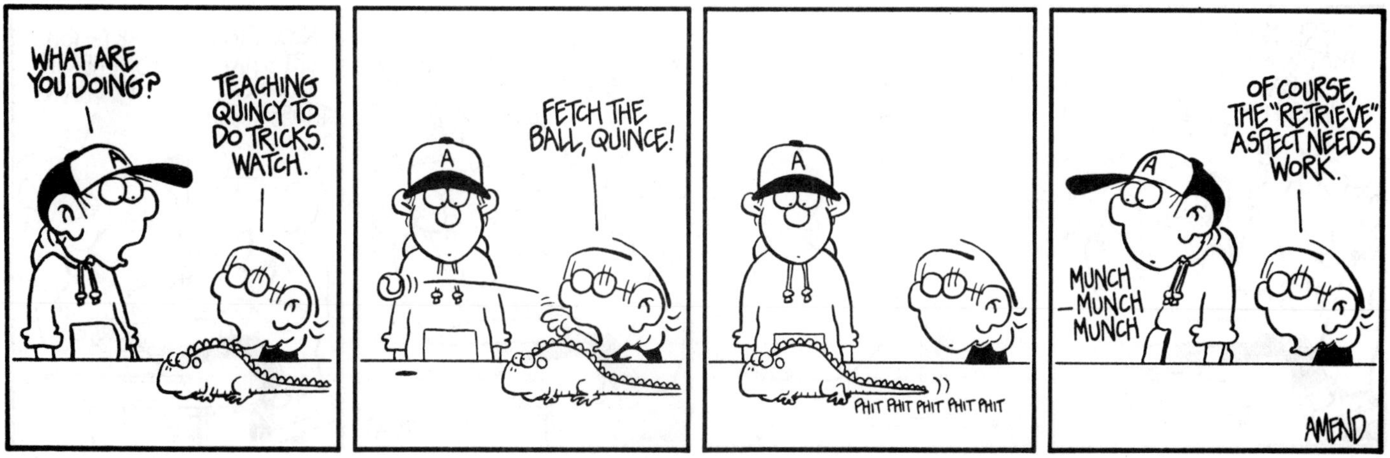
WHAT ARE YOU DOING?
TEACHING QUINCY TO DO TRICKS. WATCH.
FETCH THE BALL, QUINCE!
PHIT PHIT PHIT PHIT PHIT
MUNCH -MUNCH MUNCH
OF COURSE, THE "RETRIEVE" ASPECT NEEDS WORK.
AMEND

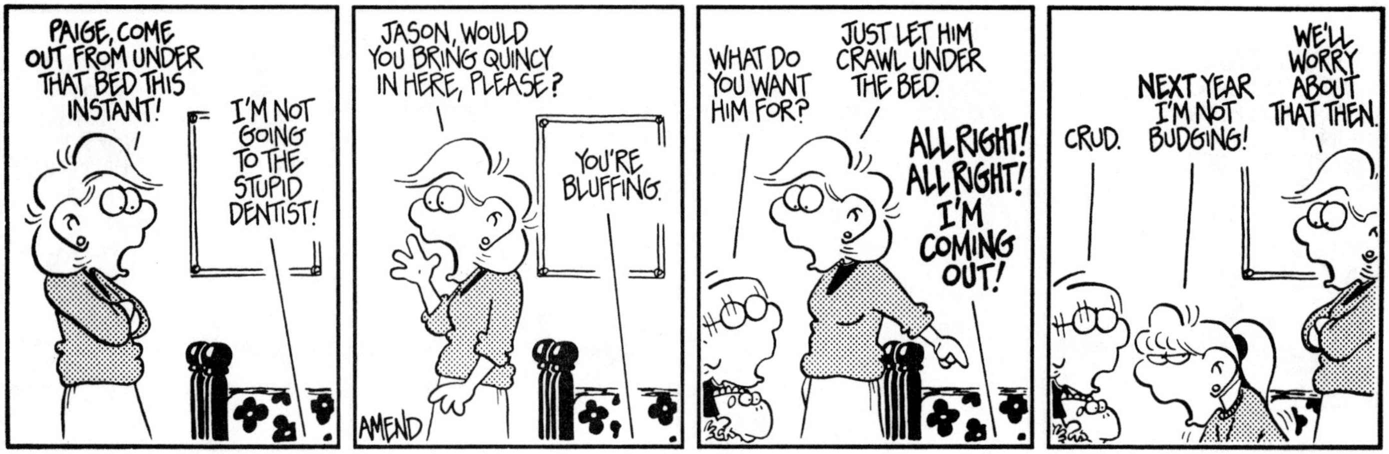
PAIGE, COME OUT FROM UNDER THAT BED THIS INSTANT!
I'M NOT GOING TO THE STUPID DENTIST!
JASON, WOULD YOU BRING QUINCY IN HERE, PLEASE?
YOU'RE BLUFFING.
AMEND
WHAT DO YOU WANT HIM FOR?
JUST LET HIM CRAWL UNDER THE BED.
ALL RIGHT! ALL RIGHT! I'M COMING OUT!
CRUD.
NEXT YEAR I'M NOT BUDGING!
WE'LL WORRY ABOUT THAT THEN.

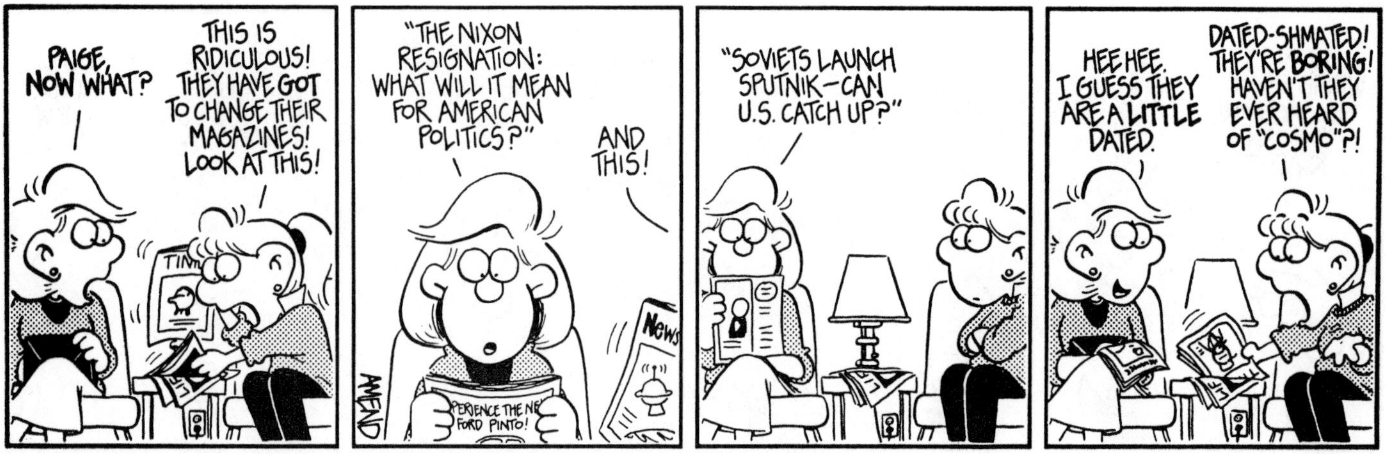
PAIGE, NOW WHAT?
THIS IS RIDICULOUS! THEY HAVE GOT TO CHANGE THEIR MAGAZINES! LOOK AT THIS!
"THE NIXON RESIGNATION: WHAT WILL IT MEAN FOR AMERICAN POLITICS?"
AND THIS!
AMEND
"SOVIETS LAUNCH SPUTNIK—CAN U.S. CATCH UP?"
HEE HEE. I GUESS THEY ARE A LITTLE DATED.
DATED-SHMATED! THEY'RE BORING! HAVEN'T THEY EVER HEARD OF "COSMO"?!

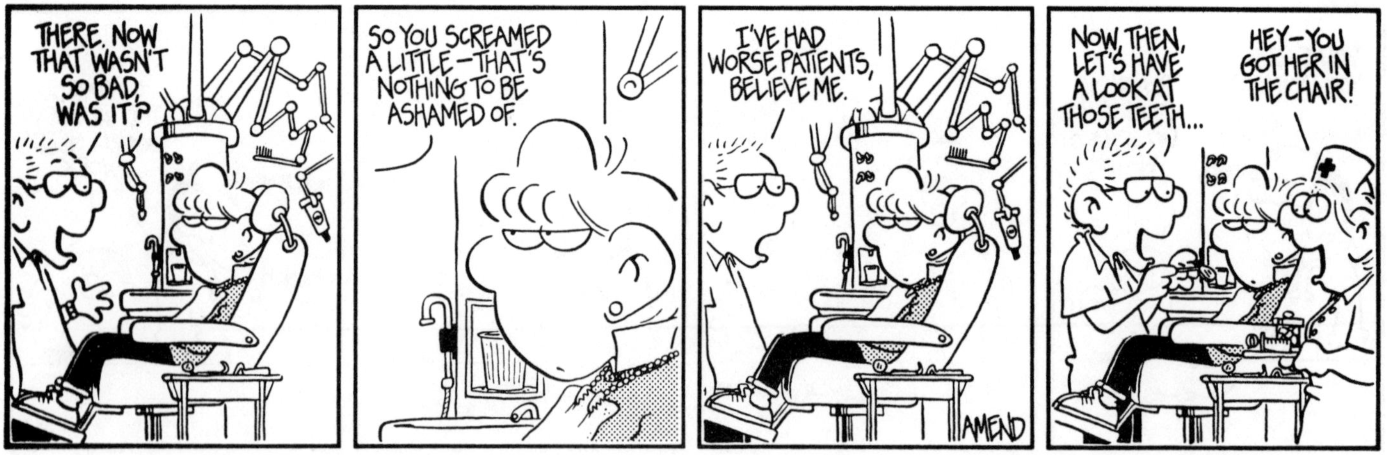
THERE. NOW THAT WASN'T SO BAD, WAS IT?
SO YOU SCREAMED A LITTLE—THAT'S NOTHING TO BE ASHAMED OF.
I'VE HAD WORSE PATIENTS, BELIEVE ME.
AMEND
NOW, THEN, LET'S HAVE A LOOK AT THOSE TEETH...
HEY—YOU GOT HER IN THE CHAIR!

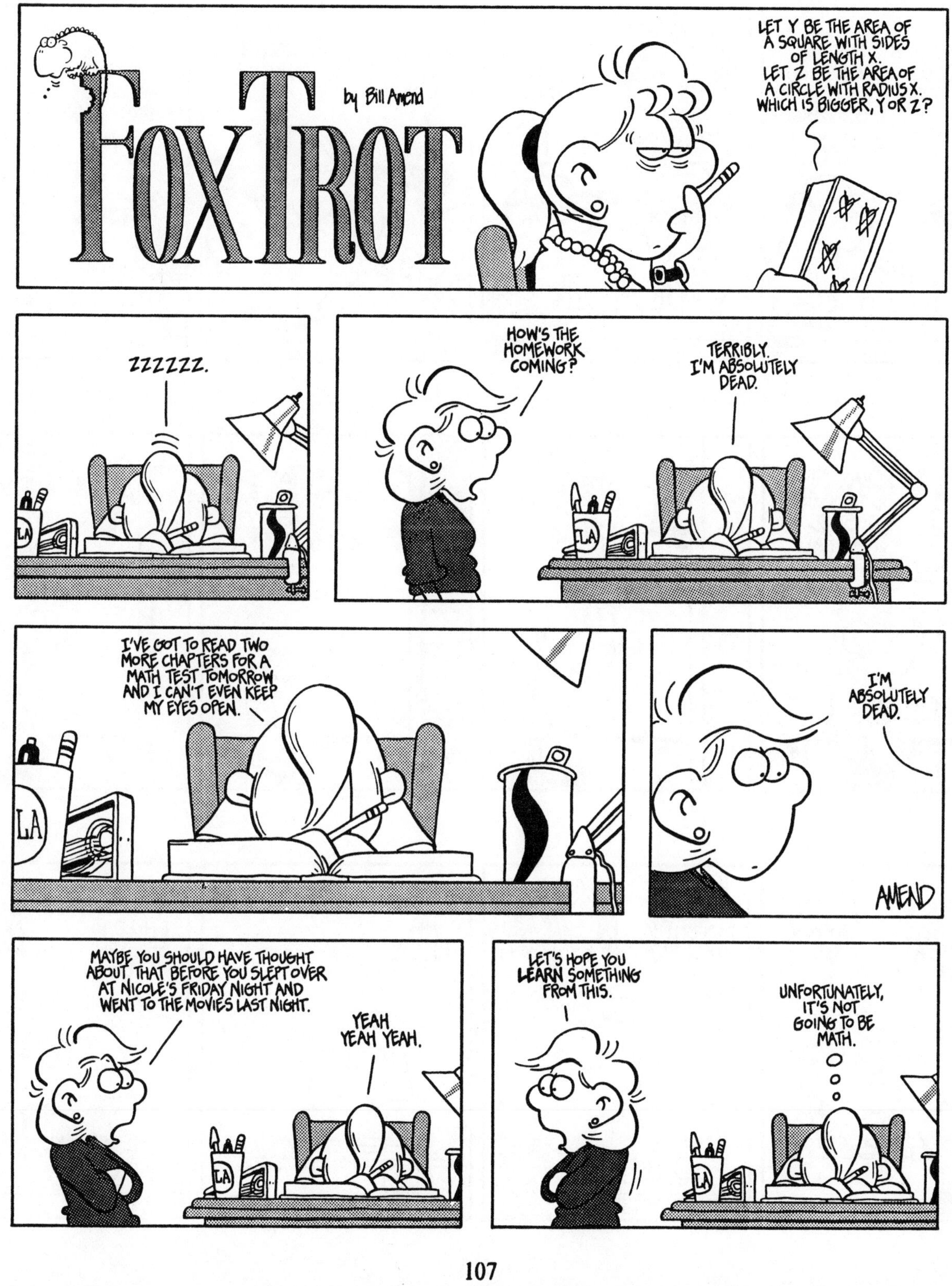

FoxTrot
by Bill Amend
LET Y BE THE AREA OF A SQUARE WITH SIDES OF LENGTH X. LET Z BE THE AREA OF A CIRCLE WITH RADIUS X. WHICH IS BIGGER, Y OR Z?
ZZZZZZ.
HOW'S THE HOMEWORK COMING?
TERRIBLY. I'M ABSOLUTELY DEAD.
I'VE GOT TO READ TWO MORE CHAPTERS FOR A MATH TEST TOMORROW AND I CAN'T EVEN KEEP MY EYES OPEN.
I'M ABSOLUTELY DEAD.
AMEND
MAYBE YOU SHOULD HAVE THOUGHT ABOUT THAT BEFORE YOU SLEPT OVER AT NICOLE'S FRIDAY NIGHT AND WENT TO THE MOVIES LAST NIGHT.
YEAH YEAH YEAH.
LET'S HOPE YOU **LEARN** SOMETHING FROM THIS.
UNFORTUNATELY, IT'S NOT GOING TO BE MATH.

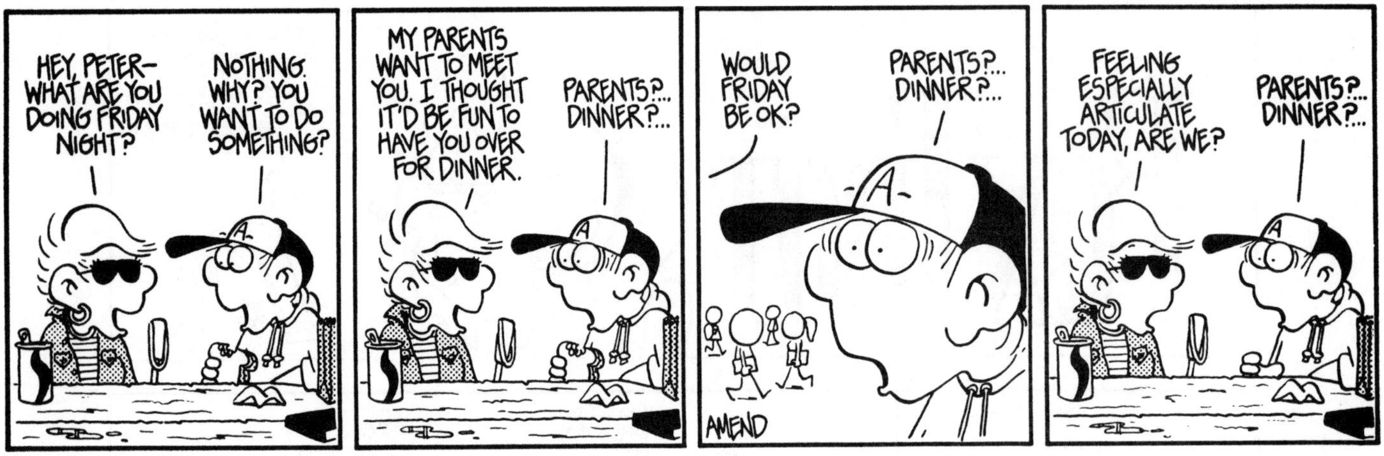
HEY, PETER–
WHAT ARE YOU
DOING FRIDAY
NIGHT?
NOTHING.
WHY? YOU
WANT TO DO
SOMETHING?
MY PARENTS
WANT TO MEET
YOU. I THOUGHT
IT'D BE FUN TO
HAVE YOU OVER
FOR DINNER.
PARENTS?...
DINNER?...
WOULD
FRIDAY
BE OK?
PARENTS?...
DINNER?...
AMEND
FEELING
ESPECIALLY
ARTICULATE
TODAY, ARE WE?
PARENTS?...
DINNER?...

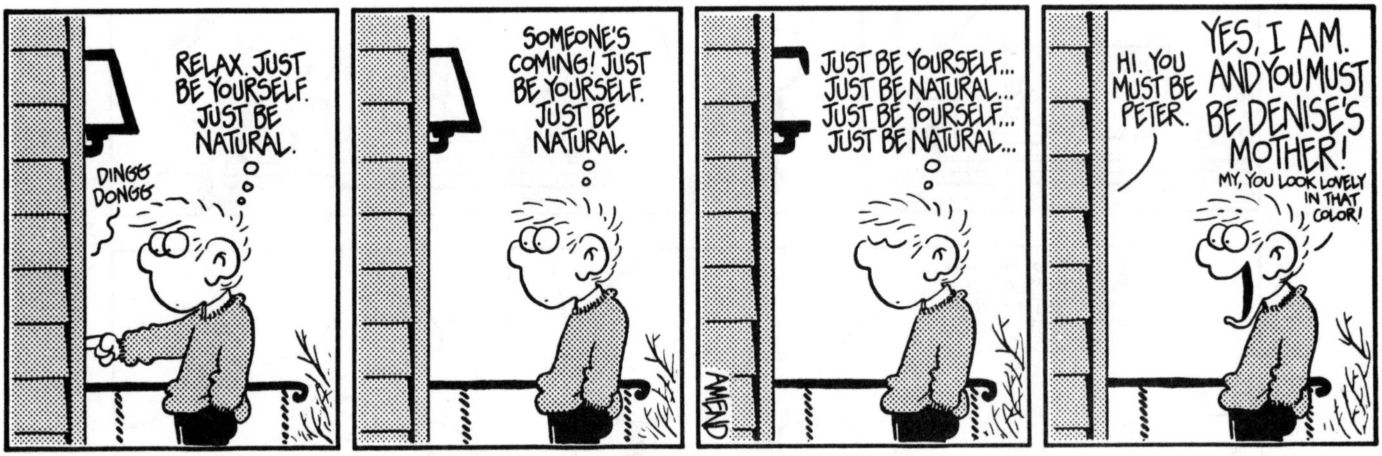
RELAX. JUST
BE YOURSELF.
JUST BE
NATURAL.
DINGG
DONGG
SOMEONE'S
COMING! JUST
BE YOURSELF.
JUST BE
NATURAL.
JUST BE YOURSELF...
JUST BE NATURAL...
JUST BE YOURSELF...
JUST BE NATURAL...
AMEND
HI. YOU
MUST BE
PETER.
YES, I AM.
AND YOU MUST
BE DENISE'S
MOTHER!
MY, YOU LOOK LOVELY
IN THAT
COLOR!

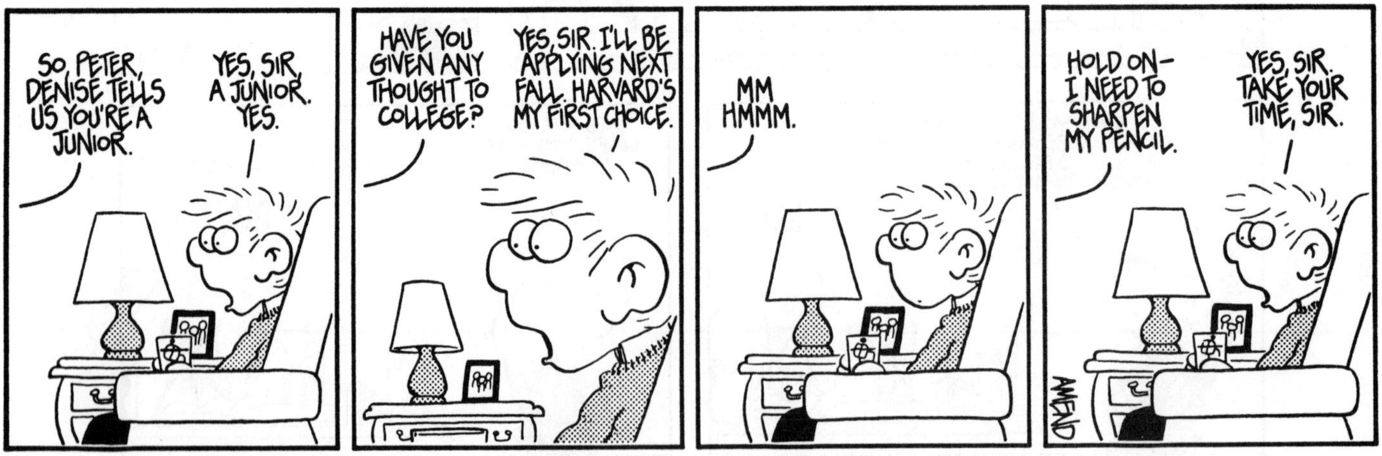
SO, PETER,
DENISE TELLS
US YOU'RE A
JUNIOR.
YES, SIR,
A JUNIOR.
YES.
HAVE YOU
GIVEN ANY
THOUGHT TO
COLLEGE?
YES, SIR. I'LL BE
APPLYING NEXT
FALL. HARVARD'S
MY FIRST CHOICE.
MM
HMMM.
HOLD ON–
I NEED TO
SHARPEN
MY PENCIL.
YES, SIR.
TAKE YOUR
TIME, SIR.
AMEND

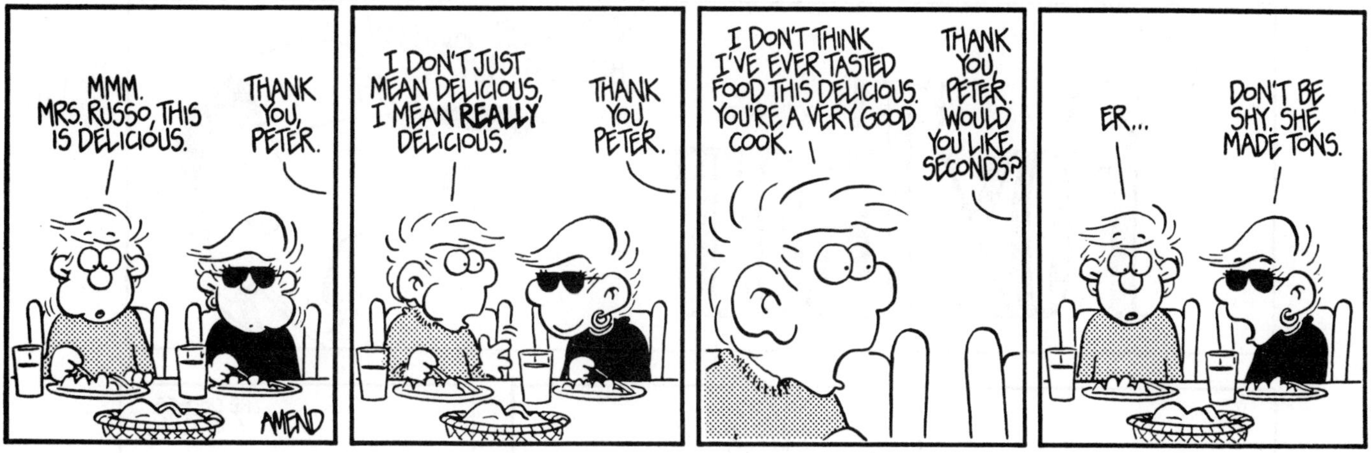
MMM. MRS. RUSSO, THIS IS DELICIOUS.
THANK YOU, PETER.
AMEND
I DON'T JUST MEAN DELICIOUS, I MEAN **REALLY** DELICIOUS.
THANK YOU, PETER.
I DON'T THINK I'VE EVER TASTED FOOD THIS DELICIOUS. YOU'RE A VERY GOOD COOK.
THANK YOU, PETER. WOULD YOU LIKE SECONDS?
ER...
DON'T BE SHY. SHE MADE TONS.

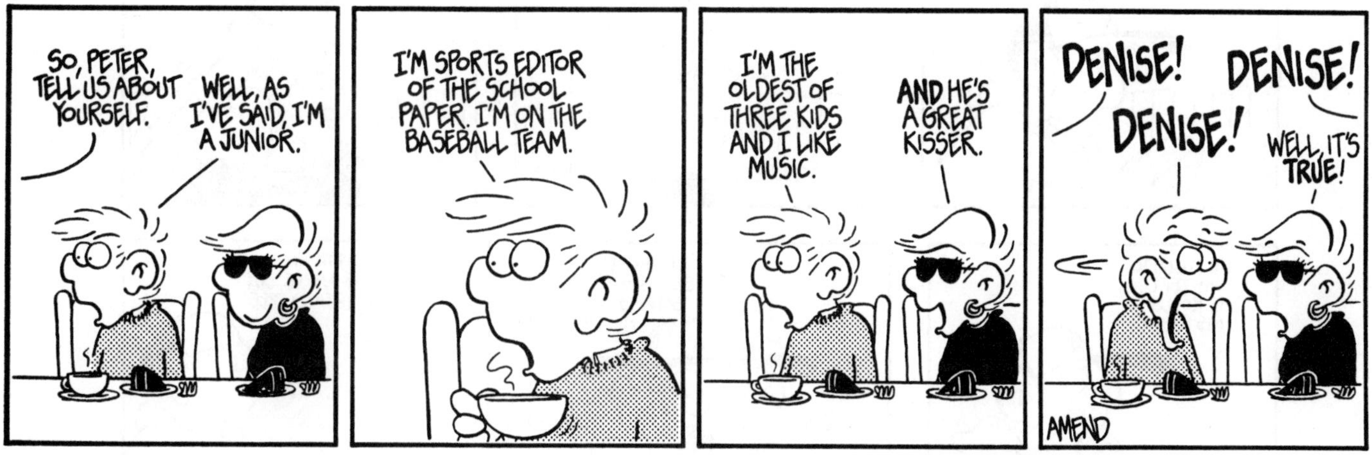
SO, PETER, TELL US ABOUT YOURSELF.
WELL, AS I'VE SAID, I'M A JUNIOR.
I'M SPORTS EDITOR OF THE SCHOOL PAPER. I'M ON THE BASEBALL TEAM.
I'M THE OLDEST OF THREE KIDS AND I LIKE MUSIC.
AND HE'S A GREAT KISSER.
DENISE!
DENISE!
DENISE!
WELL, IT'S **TRUE**!
AMEND

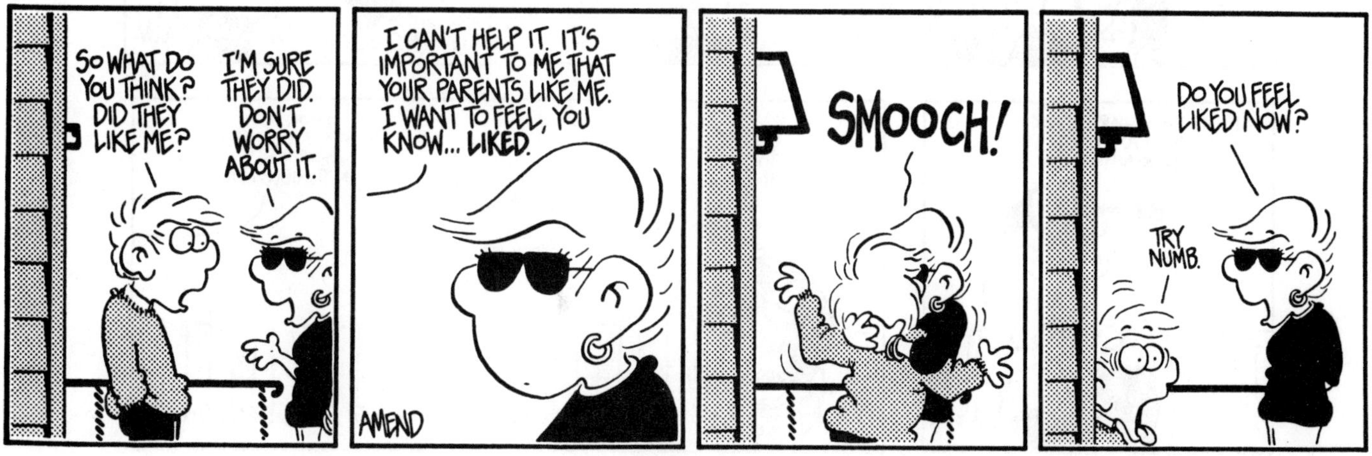
SO WHAT DO YOU THINK? DID THEY LIKE ME?
I'M SURE THEY DID. DON'T WORRY ABOUT IT.
I CAN'T HELP IT. IT'S IMPORTANT TO ME THAT YOUR PARENTS LIKE ME. I WANT TO FEEL, YOU KNOW... **LIKED**.
AMEND
SMOOCH!
DO YOU FEEL LIKED NOW?
TRY NUMB.

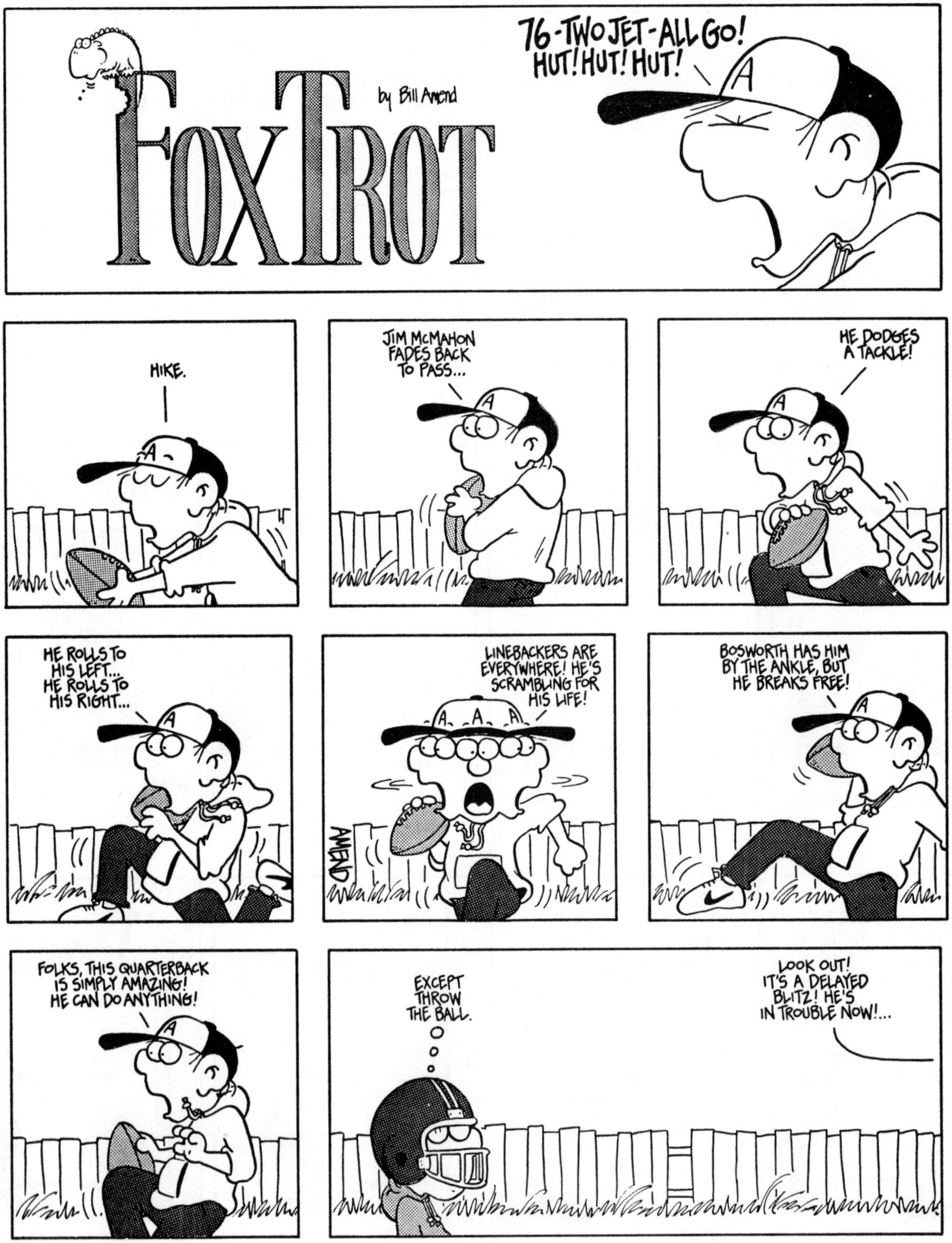
FoxTrot
by Bill Amend
76-TWO JET-ALL GO! HUT! HUT! HUT!
HIKE.
JIM McMAHON FADES BACK TO PASS...
HE DODGES A TACKLE!
HE ROLLS TO HIS LEFT... HE ROLLS TO HIS RIGHT...
LINEBACKERS ARE EVERYWHERE! HE'S SCRAMBLING FOR HIS LIFE!
AMEND
BOSWORTH HAS HIM BY THE ANKLE, BUT HE BREAKS FREE!
FOLKS, THIS QUARTERBACK IS SIMPLY AMAZING! HE CAN DO ANYTHING!
EXCEPT THROW THE BALL.
LOOK OUT! IT'S A DELAYED BLITZ! HE'S IN TROUBLE NOW!...

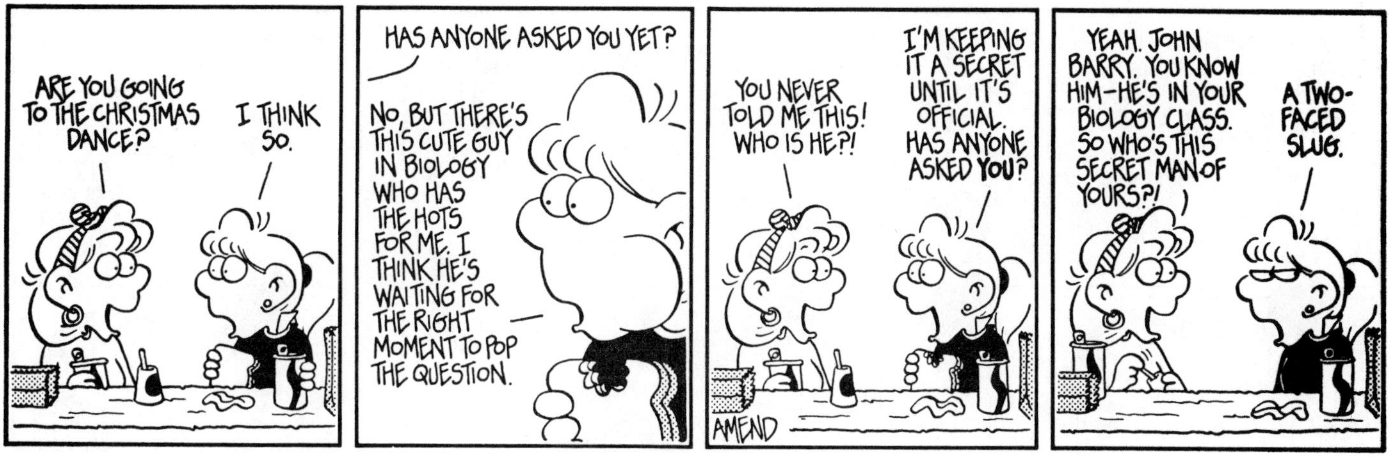
ARE YOU GOING TO THE CHRISTMAS DANCE?
I THINK SO.
HAS ANYONE ASKED YOU YET?
NO, BUT THERE'S THIS CUTE GUY IN BIOLOGY WHO HAS THE HOTS FOR ME. I THINK HE'S WAITING FOR THE RIGHT MOMENT TO POP THE QUESTION.
YOU NEVER TOLD ME THIS! WHO IS HE?!
I'M KEEPING IT A SECRET UNTIL IT'S OFFICIAL. HAS ANYONE ASKED YOU?
AMEND
YEAH. JOHN BARRY. YOU KNOW HIM—HE'S IN YOUR BIOLOGY CLASS. SO WHO'S THIS SECRET MAN OF YOURS?!
A TWO-FACED SLUG.

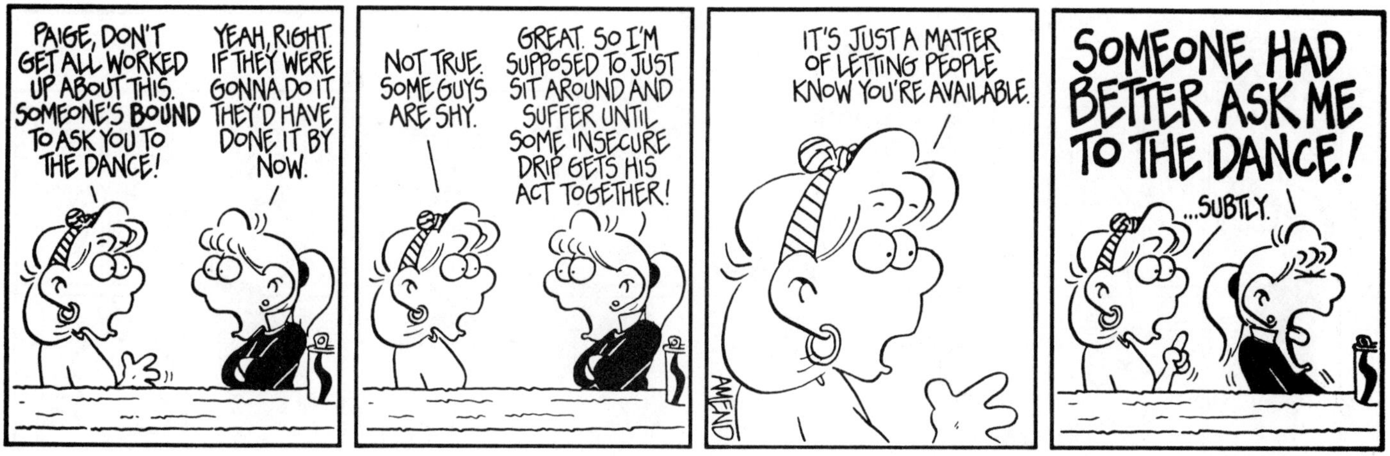
PAIGE, DON'T GET ALL WORKED UP ABOUT THIS. SOMEONE'S BOUND TO ASK YOU TO THE DANCE!
YEAH, RIGHT. IF THEY WERE GONNA DO IT, THEY'D HAVE DONE IT BY NOW.
NOT TRUE. SOME GUYS ARE SHY.
GREAT. SO I'M SUPPOSED TO JUST SIT AROUND AND SUFFER UNTIL SOME INSECURE DRIP GETS HIS ACT TOGETHER!
IT'S JUST A MATTER OF LETTING PEOPLE KNOW YOU'RE AVAILABLE.
AMEND
SOMEONE HAD BETTER ASK ME TO THE DANCE!
...SUBTLY.

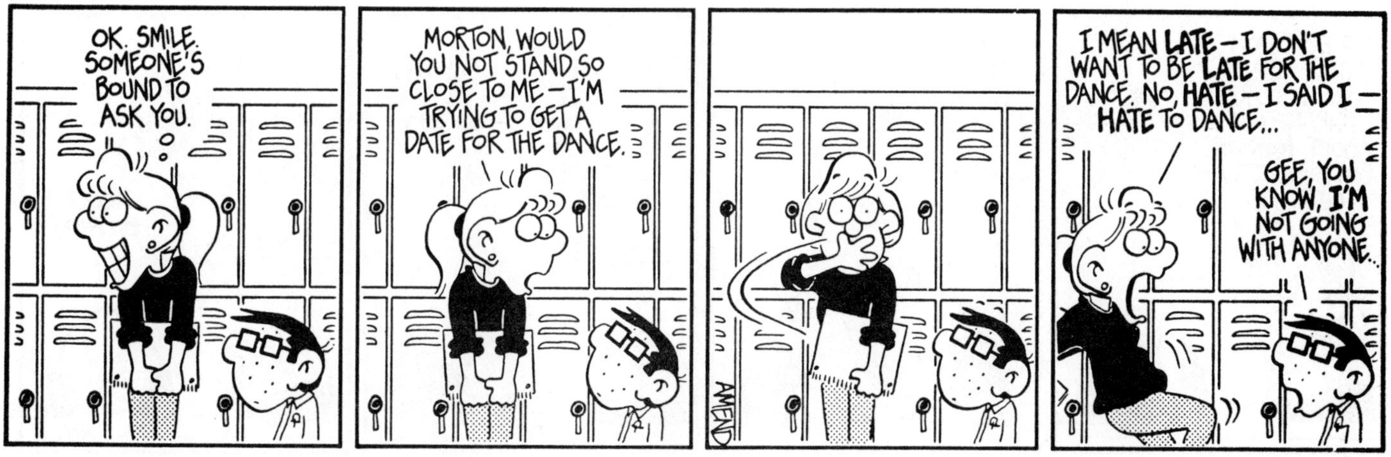
OK. SMILE. SOMEONE'S BOUND TO ASK YOU.
MORTON, WOULD YOU NOT STAND SO CLOSE TO ME—I'M TRYING TO GET A DATE FOR THE DANCE.
AMEND
I MEAN LATE—I DON'T WANT TO BE LATE FOR THE DANCE. NO, HATE—I SAID I HATE TO DANCE...
GEE, YOU KNOW, I'M NOT GOING WITH ANYONE...

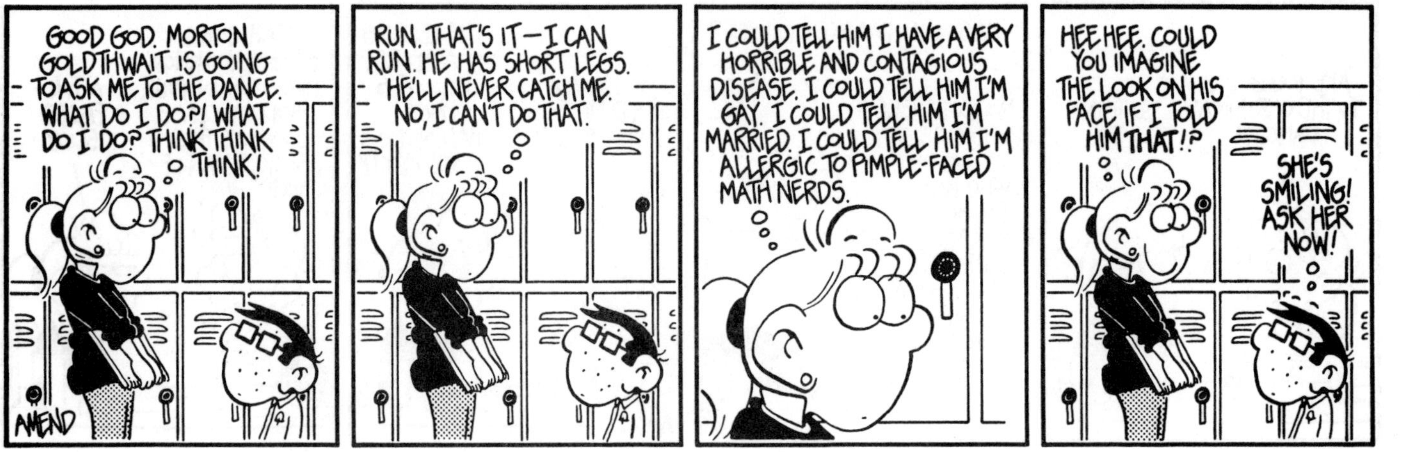
GOOD GOD. MORTON GOLDTHWAIT IS GOING TO ASK ME TO THE DANCE. WHAT DO I DO?! WHAT DO I DO? THINK THINK THINK!
AMEND
RUN. THAT'S IT—I CAN RUN. HE HAS SHORT LEGS. HE'LL NEVER CATCH ME. NO, I CAN'T DO THAT.
I COULD TELL HIM I HAVE A VERY HORRIBLE AND CONTAGIOUS DISEASE. I COULD TELL HIM I'M GAY. I COULD TELL HIM I'M MARRIED. I COULD TELL HIM I'M ALLERGIC TO PIMPLE-FACED MATH NERDS.
HEE HEE. COULD YOU IMAGINE THE LOOK ON HIS FACE IF I TOLD HIM THAT!?
SHE'S SMILING! ASK HER NOW!

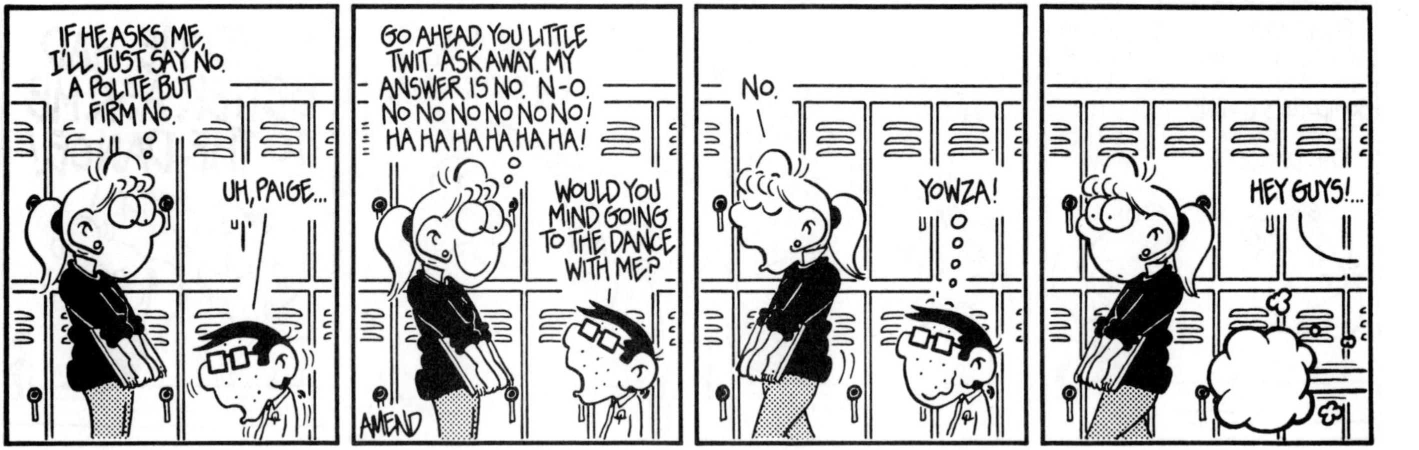
IF HE ASKS ME, I'LL JUST SAY NO. A POLITE BUT FIRM NO.
UH, PAIGE...
GO AHEAD, YOU LITTLE TWIT. ASK AWAY. MY ANSWER IS NO. N-O. NO NO NO NO NO NO! HA HA HA HA HA HA!
WOULD YOU MIND GOING TO THE DANCE WITH ME?
AMEND
NO.
YOWZA!
HEY GUYS!...

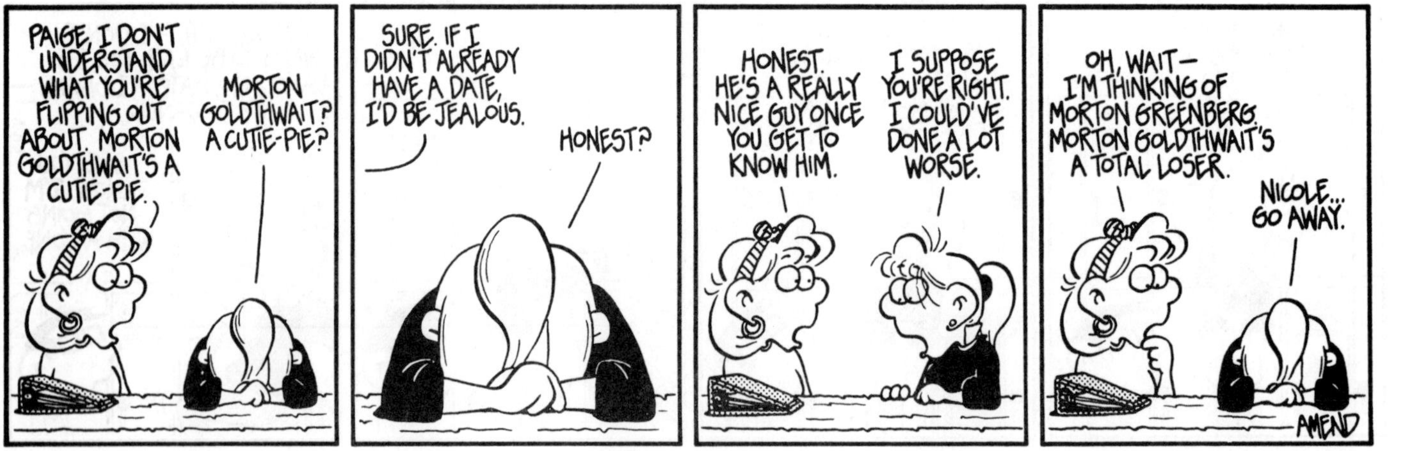
PAIGE, I DON'T UNDERSTAND WHAT YOU'RE FLIPPING OUT ABOUT. MORTON GOLDTHWAIT'S A CUTIE-PIE.
MORTON GOLDTHWAIT? A CUTIE-PIE?
SURE. IF I DIDN'T ALREADY HAVE A DATE, I'D BE JEALOUS.
HONEST?
HONEST. HE'S A REALLY NICE GUY ONCE YOU GET TO KNOW HIM.
I SUPPOSE YOU'RE RIGHT. I COULD'VE DONE A LOT WORSE.
OH, WAIT— I'M THINKING OF MORTON GREENBERG. MORTON GOLDTHWAIT'S A TOTAL LOSER.
NICOLE... GO AWAY.
AMEND

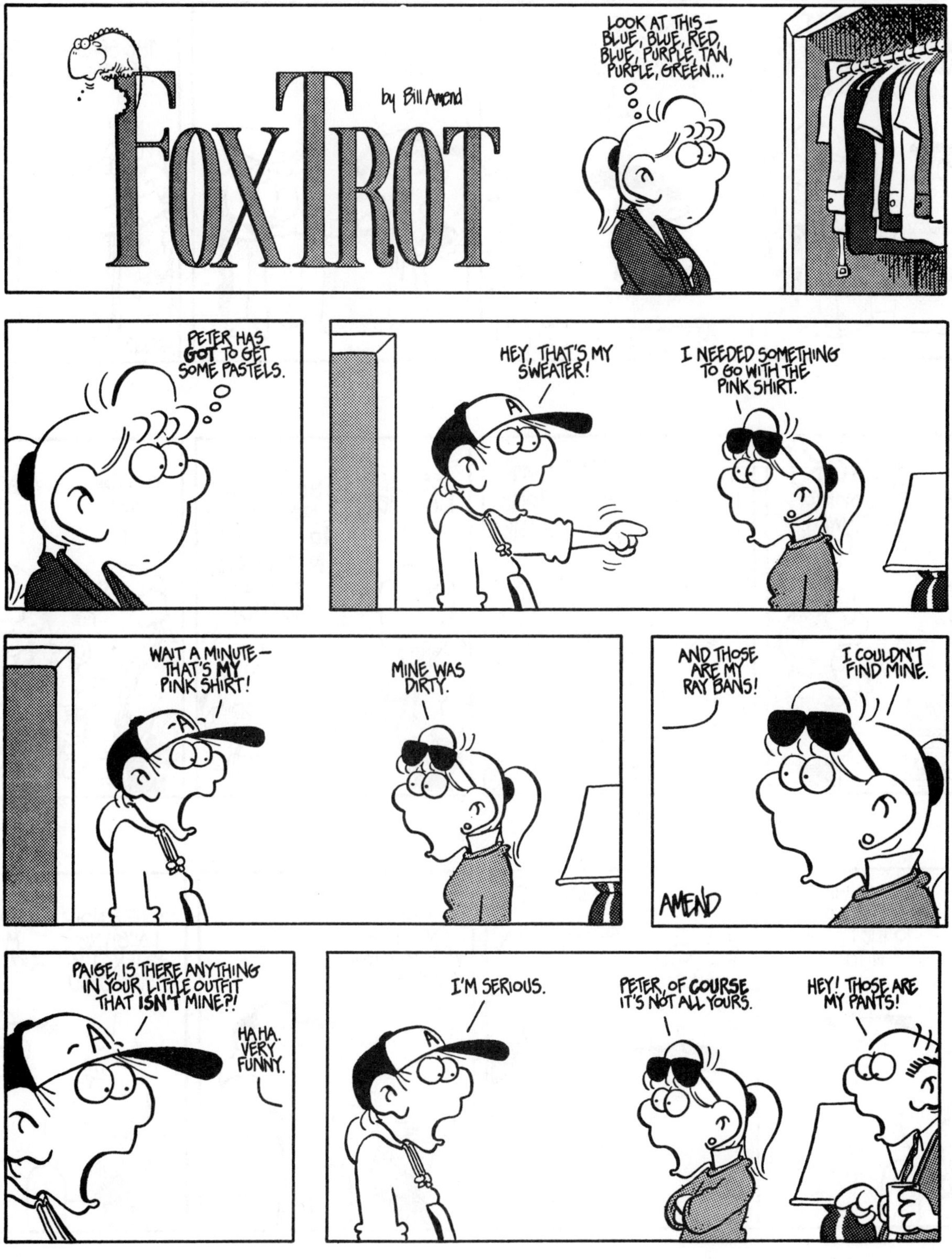
FoxTrot
by Bill Amend
LOOK AT THIS— BLUE, BLUE, RED, BLUE, PURPLE, TAN, PURPLE, GREEN...
PETER HAS GOT TO GET SOME PASTELS.
HEY, THAT'S MY SWEATER!
I NEEDED SOMETHING TO GO WITH THE PINK SHIRT.
WAIT A MINUTE— THAT'S MY PINK SHIRT!
MINE WAS DIRTY.
AND THOSE ARE MY RAY BANS!
I COULDN'T FIND MINE.
AMEND
PAIGE, IS THERE ANYTHING IN YOUR LITTLE OUTFIT THAT ISN'T MINE?!
HA HA. VERY FUNNY.
I'M SERIOUS.
PETER, OF COURSE IT'S NOT ALL YOURS.
HEY! THOSE ARE MY PANTS!

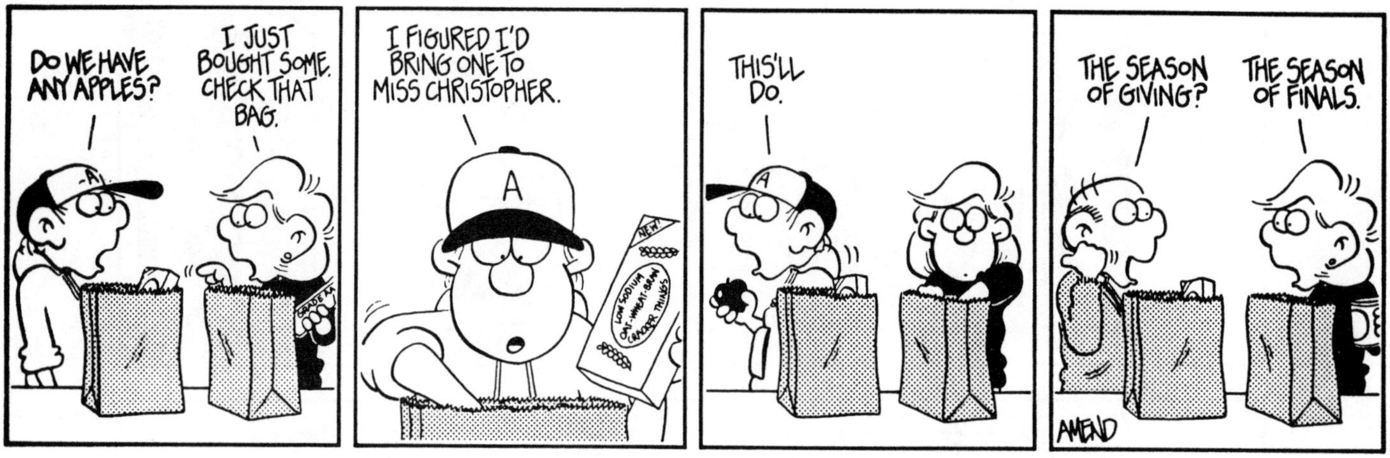
DO WE HAVE ANY APPLES?
I JUST BOUGHT SOME. CHECK THAT BAG.
I FIGURED I'D BRING ONE TO MISS CHRISTOPHER.
NEW!
THIS'LL DO.
THE SEASON OF GIVING?
THE SEASON OF FINALS.
AMEND

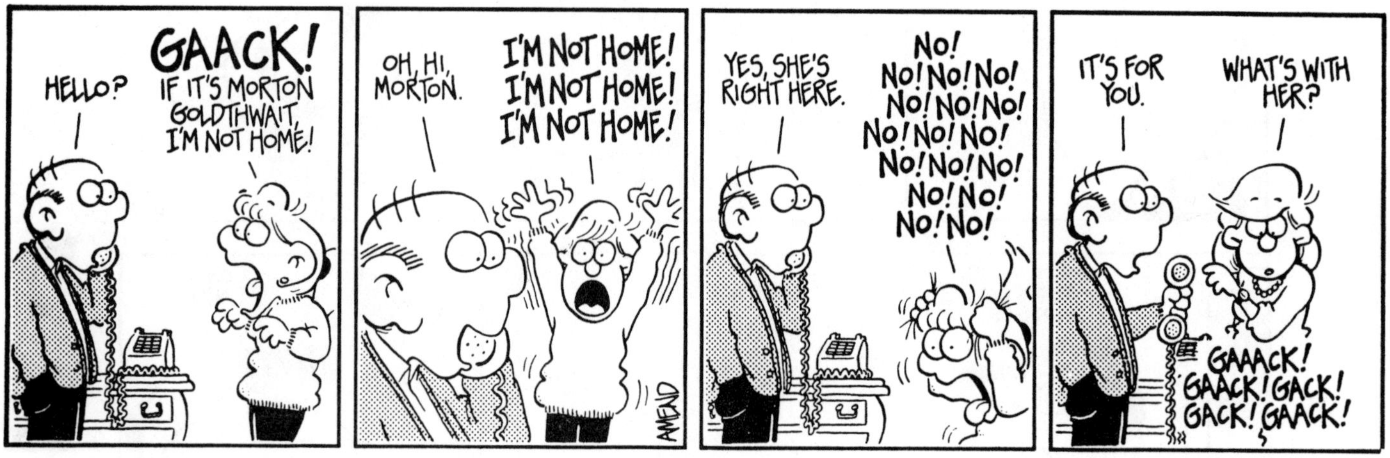
HELLO?
GAACK!
IF IT'S MORTON GOLDTHWAIT, I'M NOT HOME!
OH, HI, MORTON.
I'M NOT HOME! I'M NOT HOME! I'M NOT HOME!
AMEND
YES, SHE'S RIGHT HERE.
NO! NO! NO! NO! NO! NO! NO! NO! NO! NO! NO! NO! NO! NO! NO! NO!
IT'S FOR YOU.
WHAT'S WITH HER?
GAAACK! GAACK! GACK! GACK! GAACK!

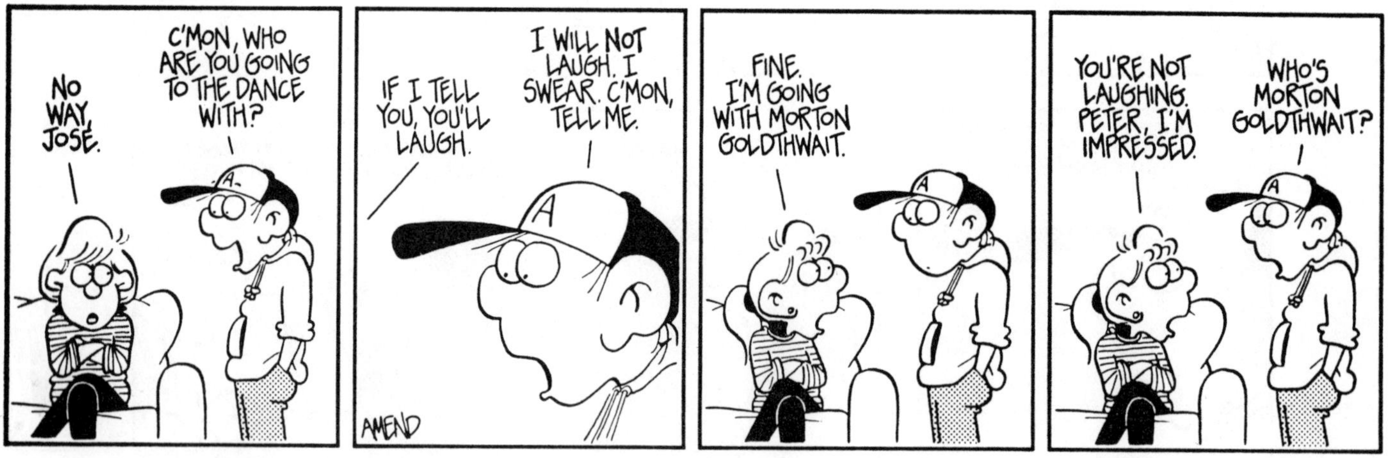
NO WAY, JOSÉ.
C'MON, WHO ARE YOU GOING TO THE DANCE WITH?
IF I TELL YOU, YOU'LL LAUGH.
I WILL NOT LAUGH. I SWEAR. C'MON, TELL ME.
AMEND
FINE. I'M GOING WITH MORTON GOLDTHWAIT.
YOU'RE NOT LAUGHING. PETER, I'M IMPRESSED.
WHO'S MORTON GOLDTHWAIT?

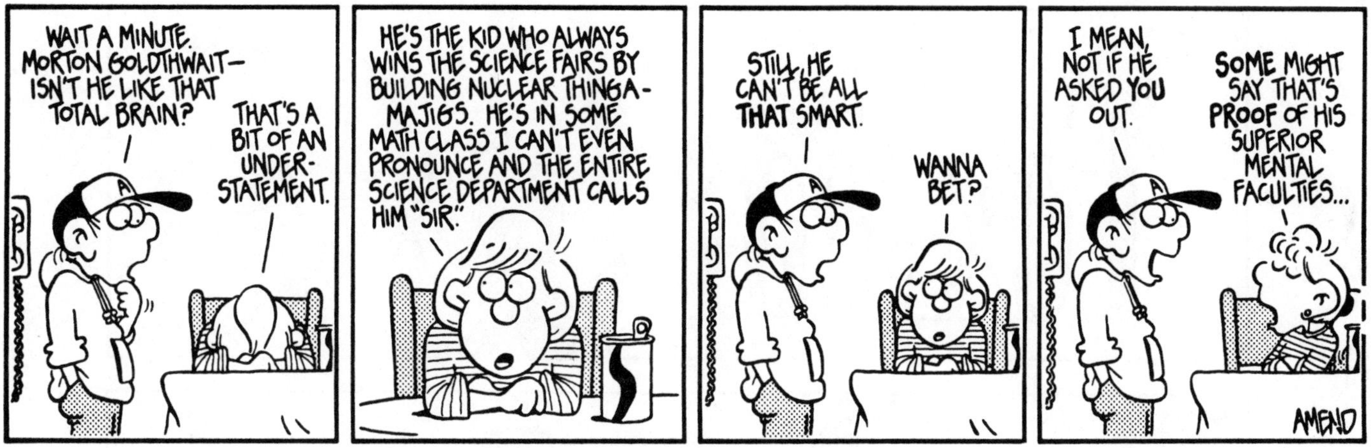
WAIT A MINUTE. MORTON GOLDTHWAIT— ISN'T HE LIKE THAT TOTAL BRAIN?
THAT'S A BIT OF AN UNDER-STATEMENT.
HE'S THE KID WHO ALWAYS WINS THE SCIENCE FAIRS BY BUILDING NUCLEAR THINGA-MAJIGS. HE'S IN SOME MATH CLASS I CAN'T EVEN PRONOUNCE AND THE ENTIRE SCIENCE DEPARTMENT CALLS HIM "SIR."
STILL, HE CAN'T BE ALL **THAT** SMART.
WANNA BET?
I MEAN, NOT IF HE ASKED **YOU** OUT.
SOME MIGHT SAY THAT'S **PROOF** OF HIS SUPERIOR MENTAL FACULTIES...
AMEND

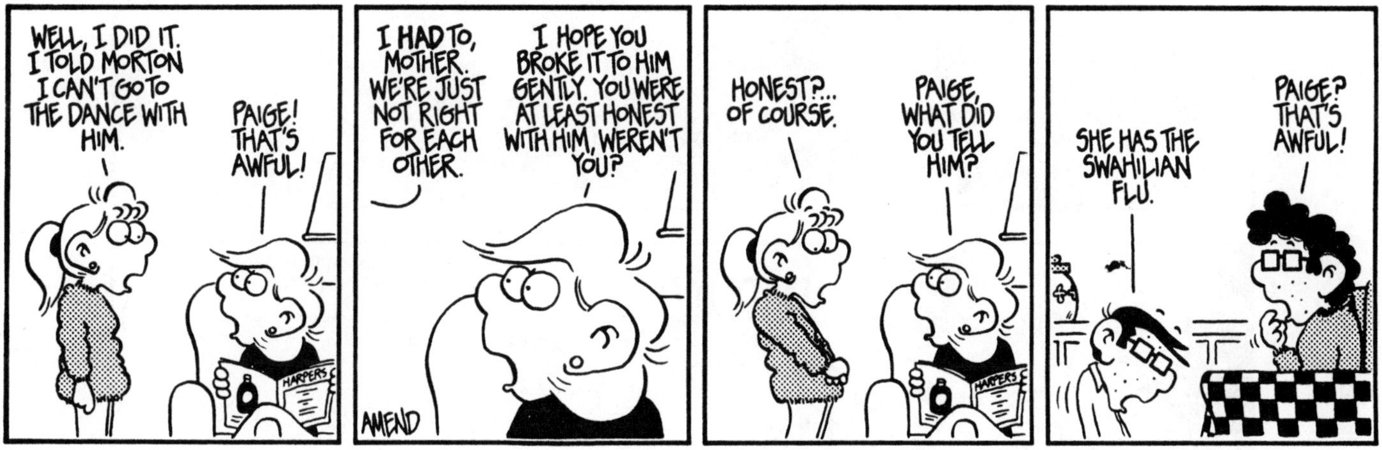
WELL, I DID IT. I TOLD MORTON I CAN'T GO TO THE DANCE WITH HIM.
PAIGE! THAT'S AWFUL!
HARPERS
I **HAD** TO, MOTHER. WE'RE JUST NOT RIGHT FOR EACH OTHER.
I HOPE YOU BROKE IT TO HIM GENTLY. YOU WERE AT LEAST HONEST WITH HIM, WEREN'T YOU?
AMEND
HONEST?... OF COURSE.
PAIGE, WHAT DID YOU TELL HIM?
HARPERS
SHE HAS THE SWAHILIAN FLU.
PAIGE? THAT'S AWFUL!

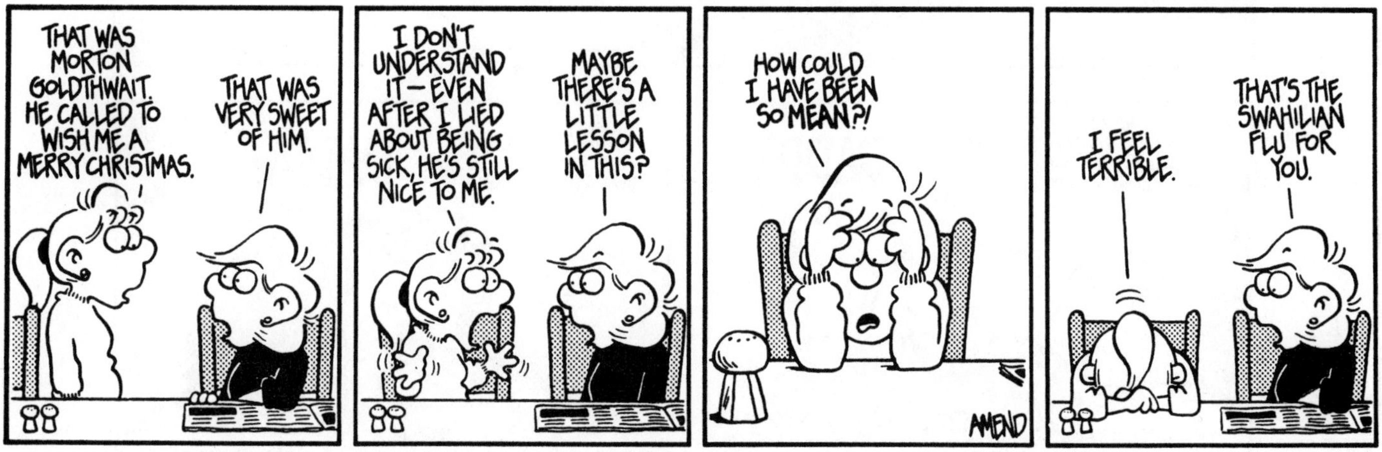
THAT WAS MORTON GOLDTHWAIT. HE CALLED TO WISH ME A MERRY CHRISTMAS.
THAT WAS VERY SWEET OF HIM.
I DON'T UNDERSTAND IT— EVEN AFTER I LIED ABOUT BEING SICK, HE'S STILL NICE TO ME.
MAYBE THERE'S A LITTLE LESSON IN THIS?
HOW COULD I HAVE BEEN SO **MEAN**?!
AMEND
I FEEL TERRIBLE.
THAT'S THE SWAHILIAN FLU FOR YOU.

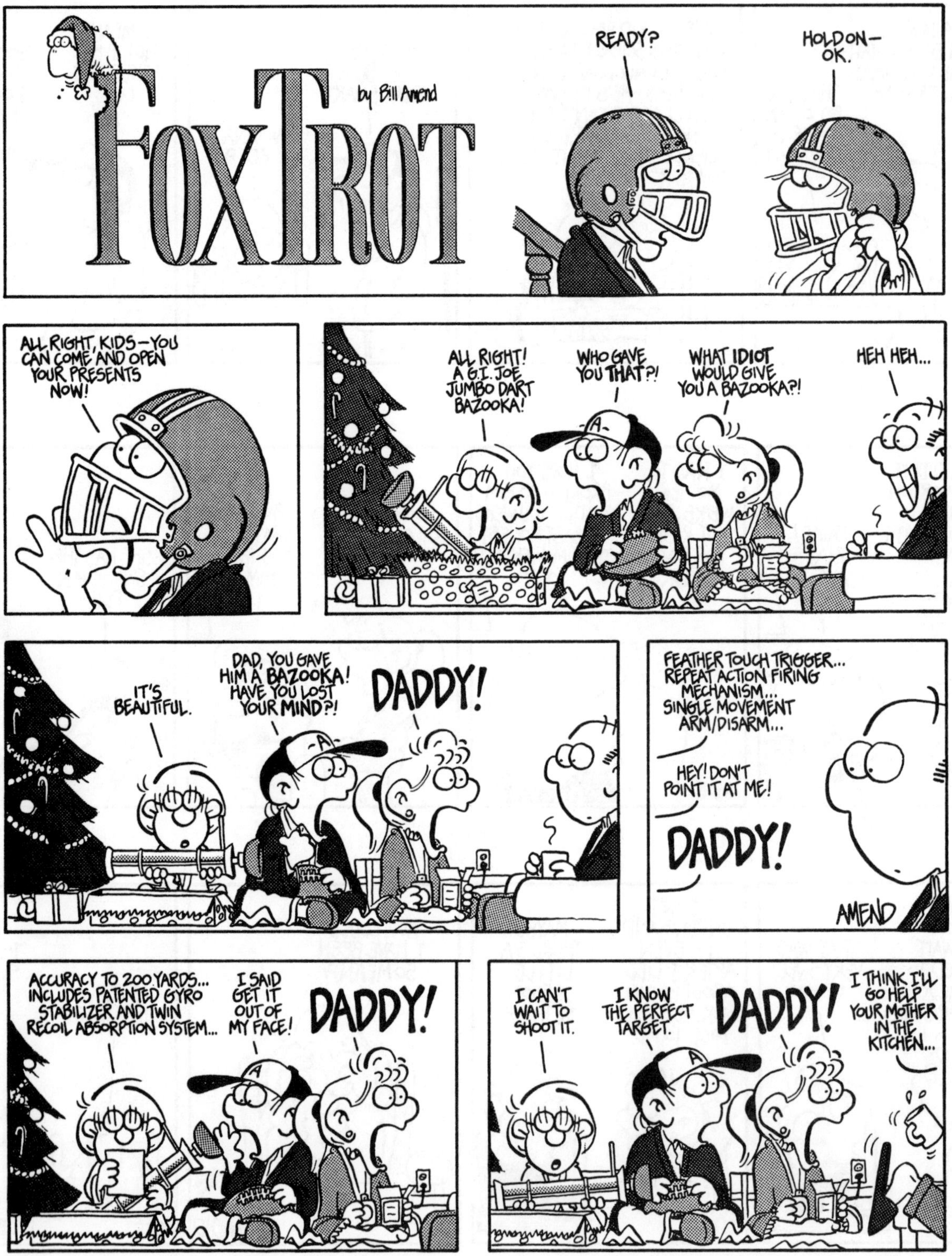
FoxTrot
by Bill Amend
READY?
HOLD ON— OK.
ALL RIGHT, KIDS—YOU CAN COME AND OPEN YOUR PRESENTS NOW!
ALL RIGHT! A G.I. JOE JUMBO DART BAZOOKA!
WHO GAVE YOU THAT?!
WHAT IDIOT WOULD GIVE YOU A BAZOOKA?!
HEH HEH...
IT'S BEAUTIFUL.
DAD, YOU GAVE HIM A BAZOOKA! HAVE YOU LOST YOUR MIND?!
DADDY!
FEATHER TOUCH TRIGGER... REPEAT ACTION FIRING MECHANISM... SINGLE MOVEMENT ARM/DISARM...
HEY! DON'T POINT IT AT ME!
DADDY!
AMEND
ACCURACY TO 200 YARDS... INCLUDES PATENTED GYRO STABILIZER AND TWIN RECOIL ABSORPTION SYSTEM...
I SAID GET IT OUT OF MY FACE!
DADDY!
I CAN'T WAIT TO SHOOT IT.
I KNOW THE PERFECT TARGET.
DADDY!
I THINK I'LL GO HELP YOUR MOTHER IN THE KITCHEN...

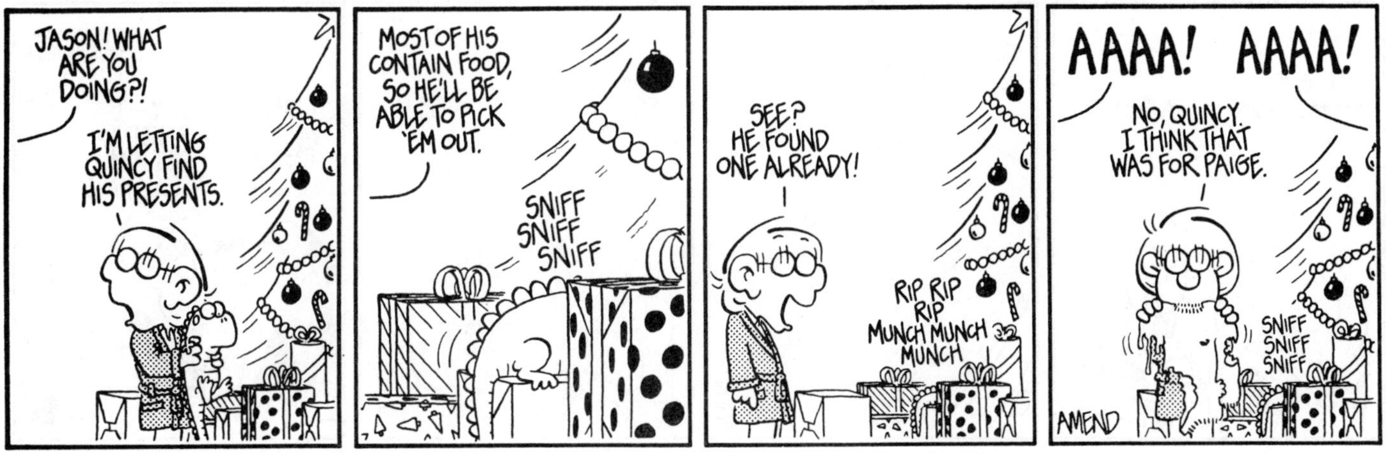
JASON! WHAT ARE YOU DOING?!
I'M LETTING QUINCY FIND HIS PRESENTS.
MOST OF HIS CONTAIN FOOD, SO HE'LL BE ABLE TO PICK 'EM OUT.
SNIFF SNIFF SNIFF
SEE? HE FOUND ONE ALREADY!
RIP RIP RIP MUNCH MUNCH MUNCH
AAAA! AAAA!
NO, QUINCY. I THINK THAT WAS FOR PAIGE.
SNIFF SNIFF SNIFF
AMEND

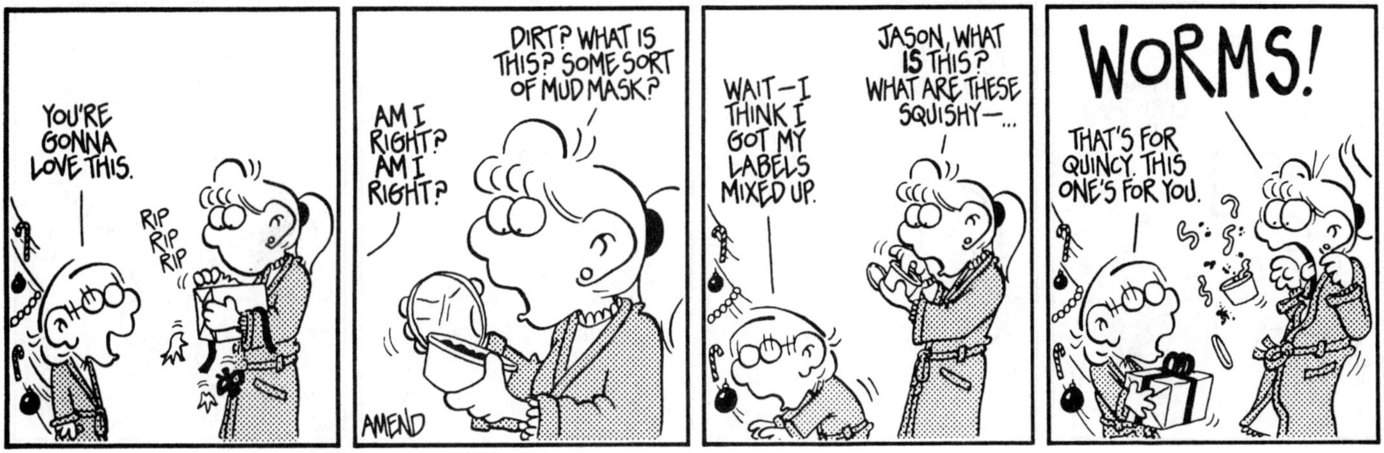
YOU'RE GONNA LOVE THIS.
RIP RIP RIP
AM I RIGHT? AM I RIGHT?
DIRT? WHAT IS THIS? SOME SORT OF MUD MASK?
AMEND
WAIT—I THINK I GOT MY LABELS MIXED UP.
JASON, WHAT IS THIS? WHAT ARE THESE SQUISHY—...
WORMS!
THAT'S FOR QUINCY. THIS ONE'S FOR YOU.

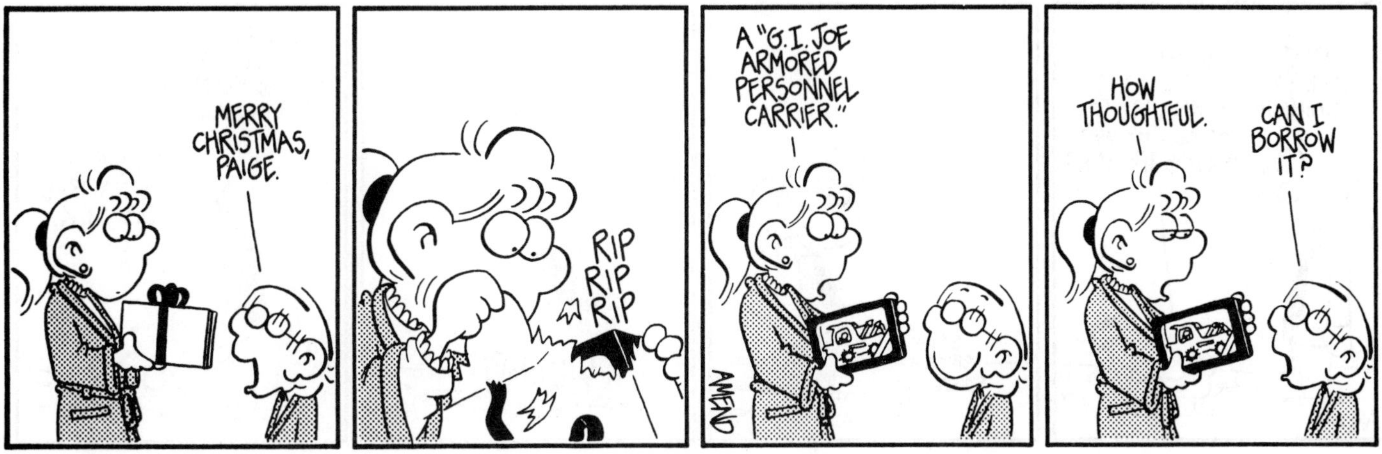
MERRY CHRISTMAS, PAIGE.
RIP RIP RIP
A "G.I. JOE ARMORED PERSONNEL CARRIER."
AMEND
HOW THOUGHTFUL.
CAN I BORROW IT?

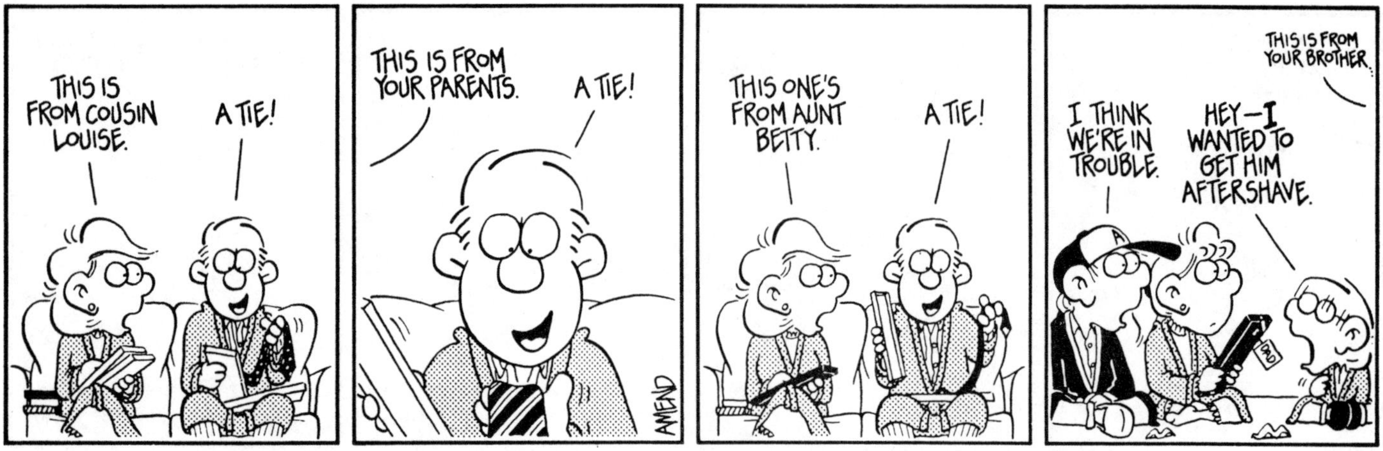
THIS IS FROM COUSIN LOUISE.
A TIE!
THIS IS FROM YOUR PARENTS.
A TIE!
AMEND
THIS ONE'S FROM AUNT BETTY.
A TIE!
THIS IS FROM YOUR BROTHER.
I THINK WE'RE IN TROUBLE.
HEY—I WANTED TO GET HIM AFTERSHAVE.

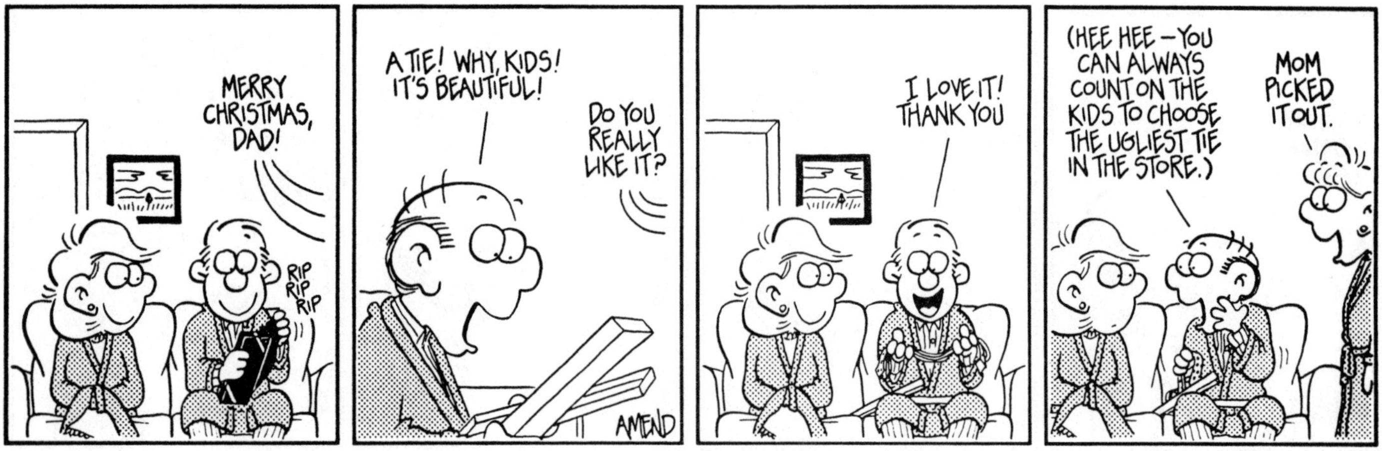
MERRY CHRISTMAS, DAD!
RIP RIP RIP
A TIE! WHY, KIDS! IT'S BEAUTIFUL!
DO YOU REALLY LIKE IT?
AMEND
I LOVE IT! THANK YOU
(HEE HEE—YOU CAN ALWAYS COUNT ON THE KIDS TO CHOOSE THE UGLIEST TIE IN THE STORE.)
MOM PICKED IT OUT.

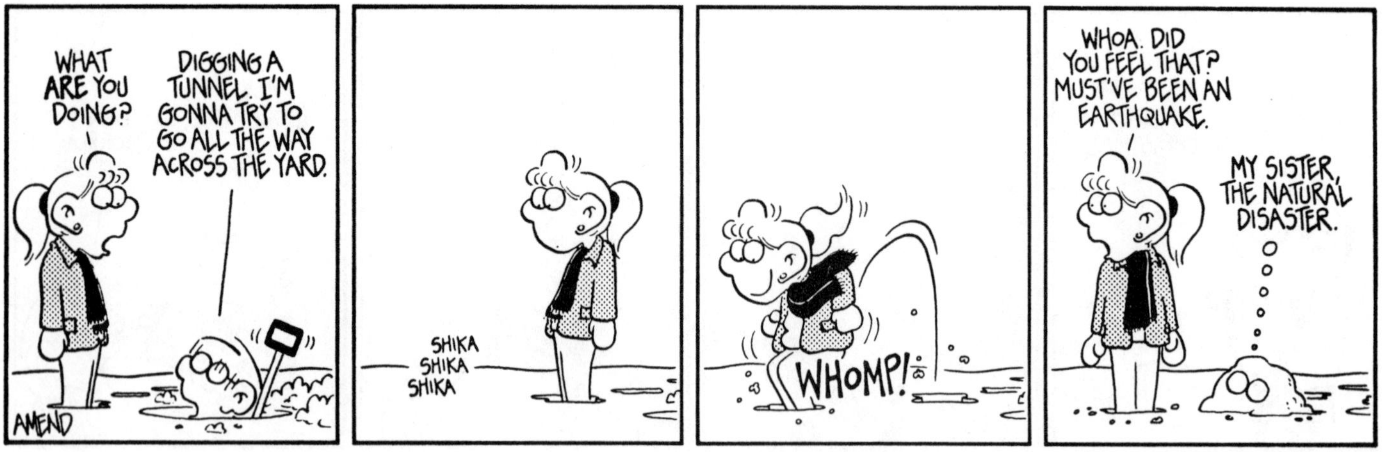
WHAT ARE YOU DOING?
DIGGING A TUNNEL. I'M GONNA TRY TO GO ALL THE WAY ACROSS THE YARD.
AMEND
SHIKA SHIKA SHIKA
WHOMP!
WHOA. DID YOU FEEL THAT? MUST'VE BEEN AN EARTHQUAKE.
MY SISTER, THE NATURAL DISASTER.

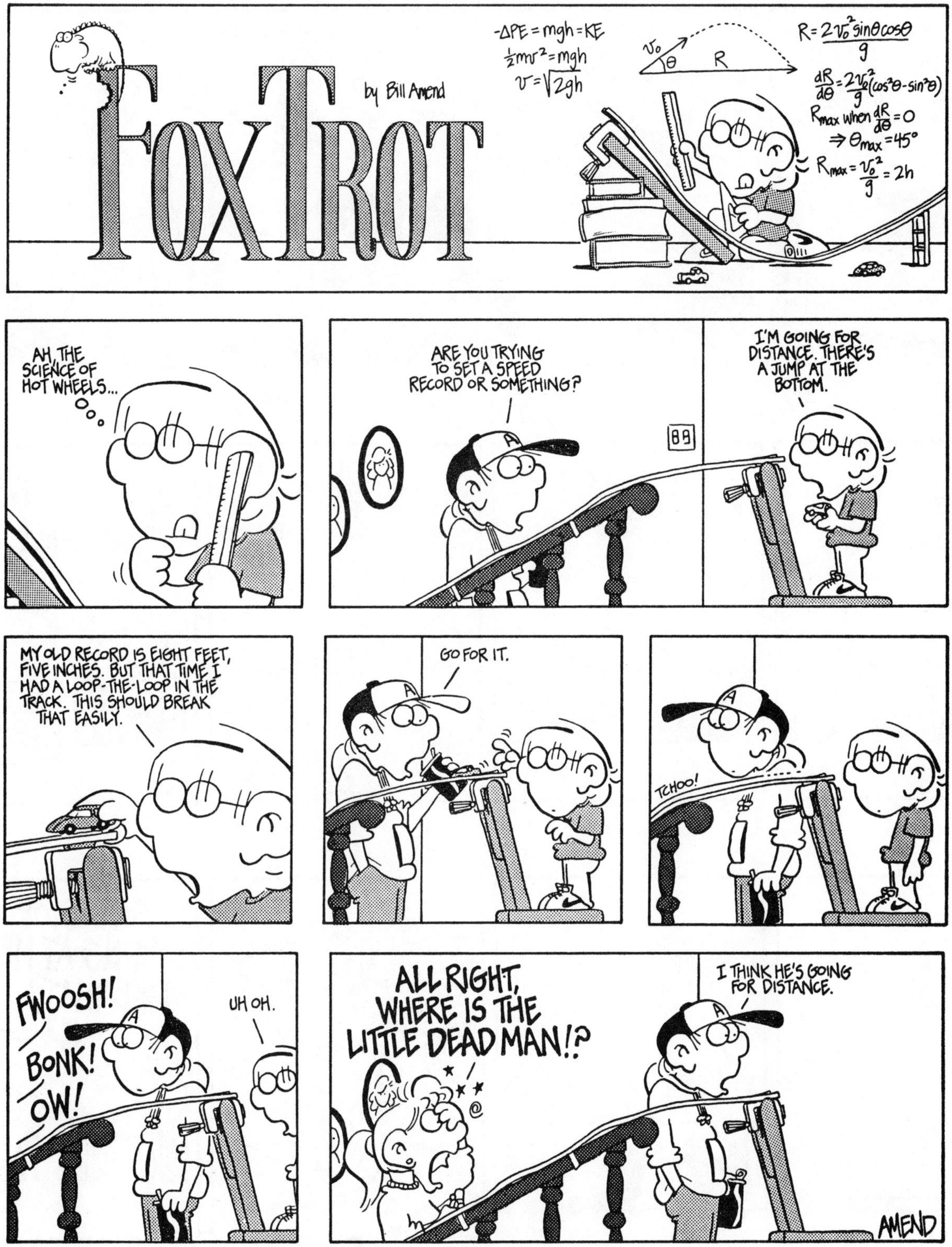
FOXTROT
by Bill Amend
-ΔPE = mgh = KE
½mv² = mgh
v = √2gh
v₀ θ R
R = 2v₀² sinθ cosθ / g
dR/dθ = 2v₀²/g (cos²θ - sin²θ)
R_max when dR/dθ = 0 ⇒ θ_max = 45°
R_max = v₀²/g = 2h
AH, THE SCIENCE OF HOT WHEELS...
ARE YOU TRYING TO SET A SPEED RECORD OR SOMETHING?
I'M GOING FOR DISTANCE. THERE'S A JUMP AT THE BOTTOM.
MY OLD RECORD IS EIGHT FEET, FIVE INCHES. BUT THAT TIME I HAD A LOOP-THE-LOOP IN THE TRACK. THIS SHOULD BREAK THAT EASILY.
GO FOR IT.
TCHOO!
FWOOSH!
BONK!
OW!
UH OH.
ALL RIGHT, WHERE IS THE LITTLE DEAD MAN!?
I THINK HE'S GOING FOR DISTANCE.
AMEND

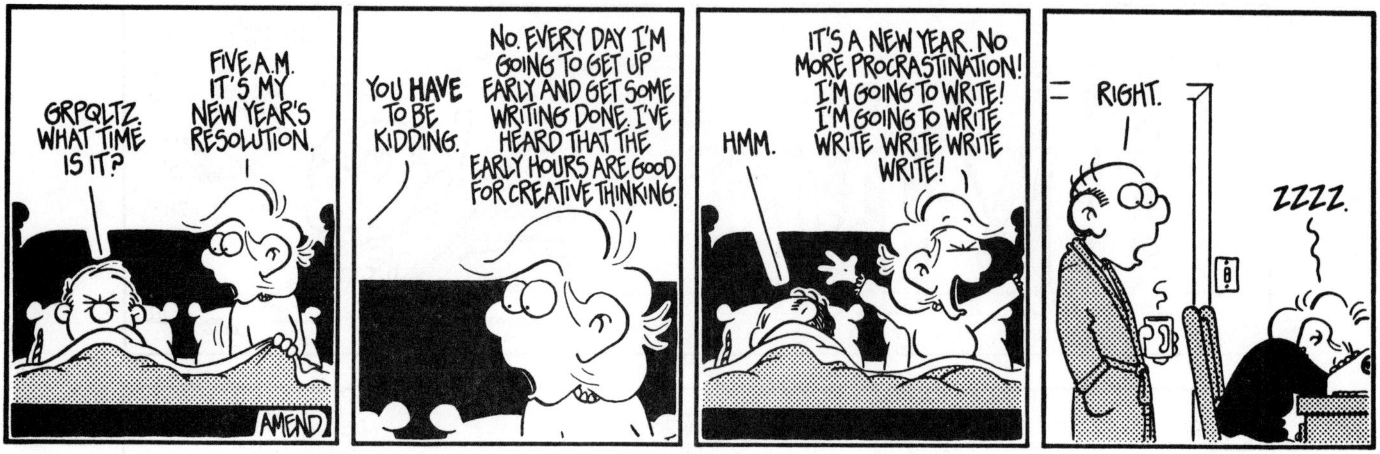
GRPQLTZ. WHAT TIME IS IT?
FIVE A.M. IT'S MY NEW YEAR'S RESOLUTION.
YOU HAVE TO BE KIDDING.
NO. EVERY DAY I'M GOING TO GET UP EARLY AND GET SOME WRITING DONE. I'VE HEARD THAT THE EARLY HOURS ARE GOOD FOR CREATIVE THINKING.
HMM.
IT'S A NEW YEAR. NO MORE PROCRASTINATION! I'M GOING TO WRITE! I'M GOING TO WRITE WRITE WRITE WRITE WRITE!
RIGHT.
ZZZZ.
AMEND

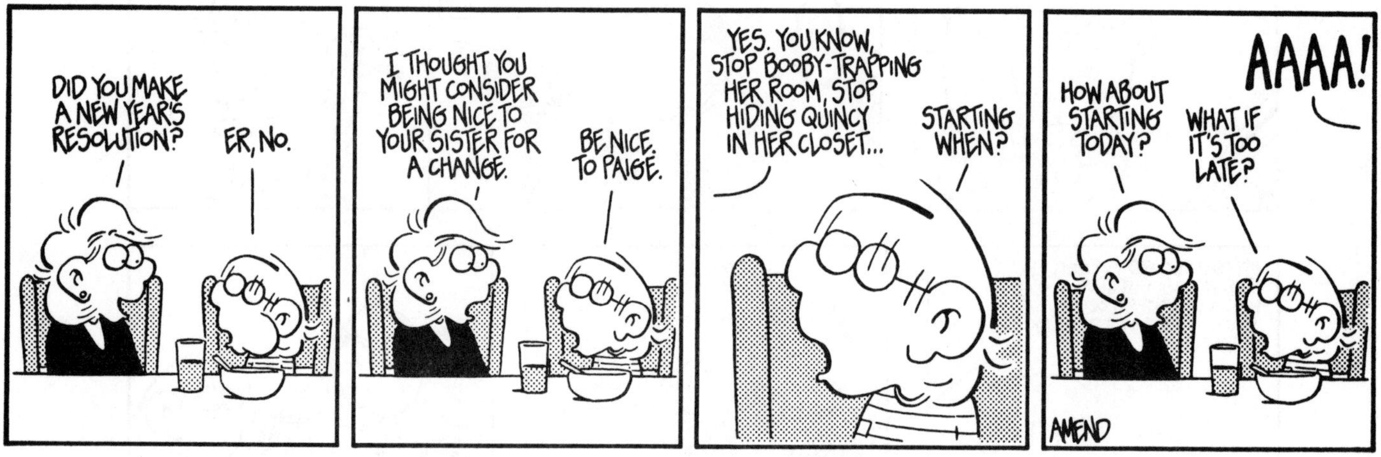
DID YOU MAKE A NEW YEAR'S RESOLUTION?
ER, NO.
I THOUGHT YOU MIGHT CONSIDER BEING NICE TO YOUR SISTER FOR A CHANGE.
BE NICE TO PAIGE.
YES. YOU KNOW, STOP BOOBY-TRAPPING HER ROOM, STOP HIDING QUINCY IN HER CLOSET...
STARTING WHEN?
HOW ABOUT STARTING TODAY?
WHAT IF IT'S TOO LATE?
AAAA!
AMEND

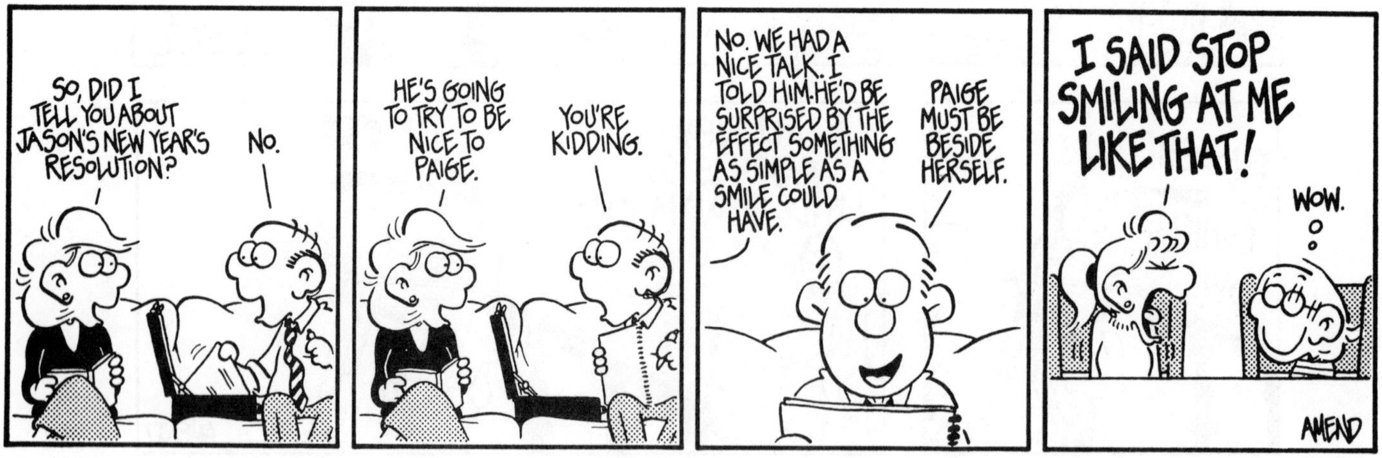
SO, DID I TELL YOU ABOUT JASON'S NEW YEAR'S RESOLUTION?
NO.
HE'S GOING TO TRY TO BE NICE TO PAIGE.
YOU'RE KIDDING.
NO. WE HAD A NICE TALK. I TOLD HIM HE'D BE SURPRISED BY THE EFFECT SOMETHING AS SIMPLE AS A SMILE COULD HAVE.
PAIGE MUST BE BESIDE HERSELF.
I SAID STOP SMILING AT ME LIKE THAT!
WOW.
AMEND

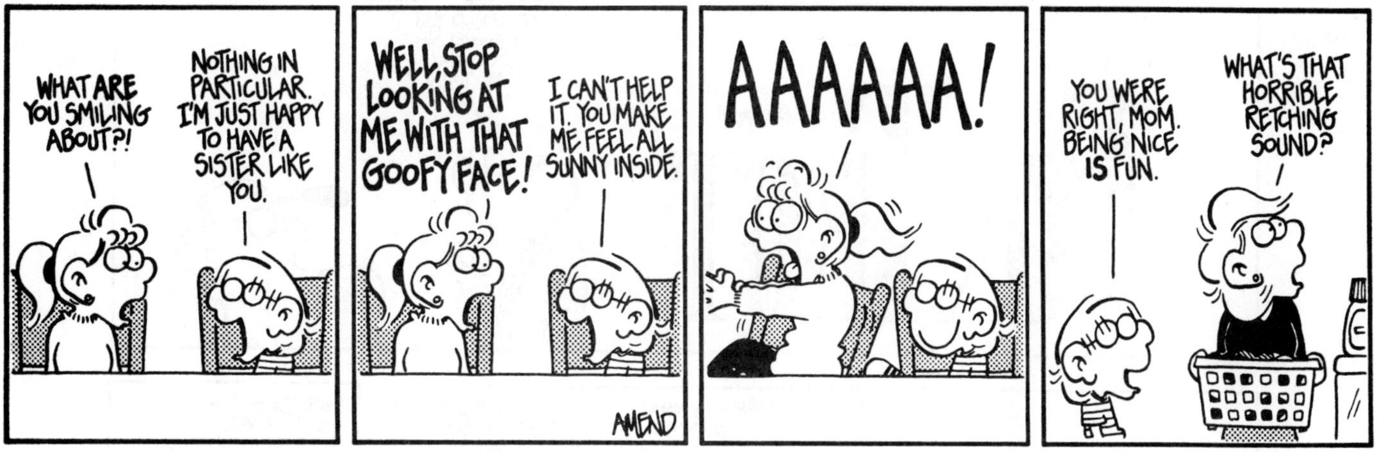
WHAT ARE YOU SMILING ABOUT?!
NOTHING IN PARTICULAR. I'M JUST HAPPY TO HAVE A SISTER LIKE YOU.
WELL, STOP LOOKING AT ME WITH THAT GOOFY FACE!
I CAN'T HELP IT. YOU MAKE ME FEEL ALL SUNNY INSIDE.
AMEND
AAAAAA!
YOU WERE RIGHT, MOM. BEING NICE IS FUN.
WHAT'S THAT HORRIBLE RETCHING SOUND?

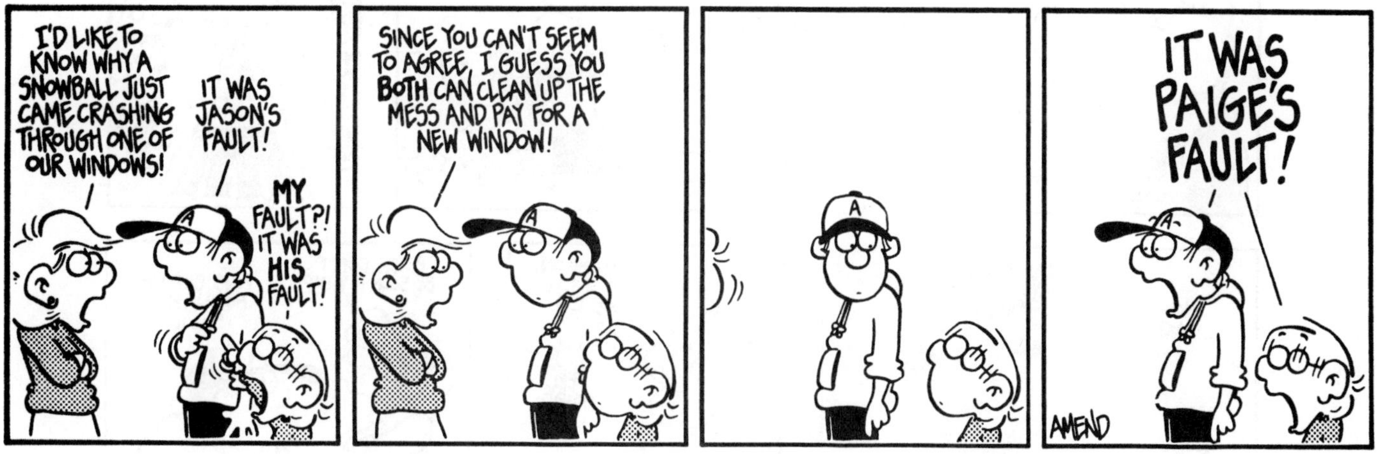
I'D LIKE TO KNOW WHY A SNOWBALL JUST CAME CRASHING THROUGH ONE OF OUR WINDOWS!
IT WAS JASON'S FAULT!
MY FAULT?! IT WAS HIS FAULT!
SINCE YOU CAN'T SEEM TO AGREE, I GUESS YOU BOTH CAN CLEAN UP THE MESS AND PAY FOR A NEW WINDOW!
IT WAS PAIGE'S FAULT!
AMEND

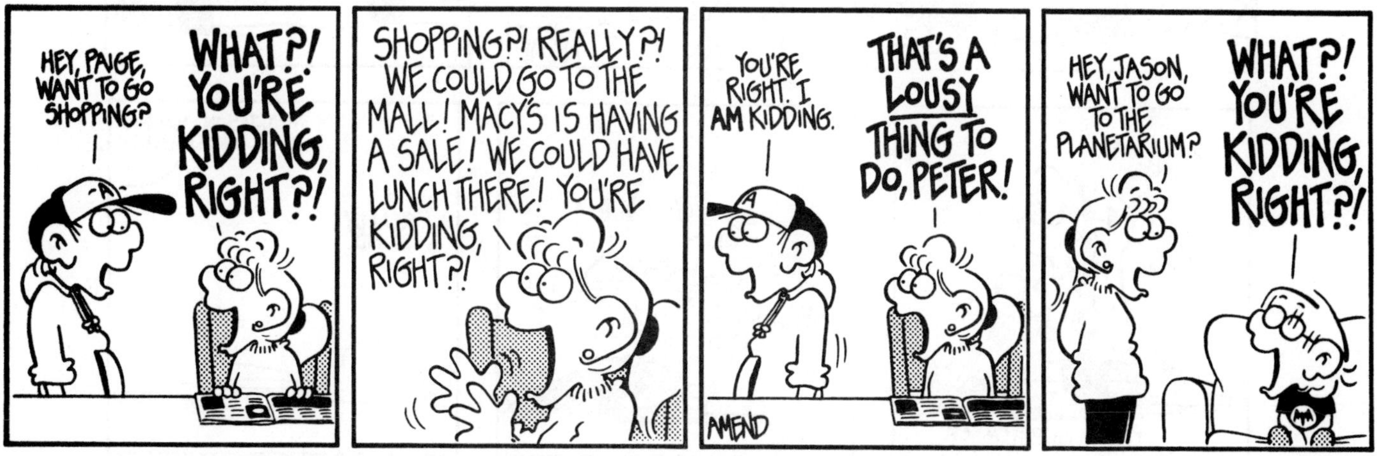
HEY, PAIGE, WANT TO GO SHOPPING?
WHAT?! YOU'RE KIDDING, RIGHT?!
SHOPPING?! REALLY?! WE COULD GO TO THE MALL! MACY'S IS HAVING A SALE! WE COULD HAVE LUNCH THERE! YOU'RE KIDDING, RIGHT?!
YOU'RE RIGHT. I AM KIDDING.
THAT'S A LOUSY THING TO DO, PETER!
AMEND
HEY, JASON, WANT TO GO TO THE PLANETARIUM?
WHAT?! YOU'RE KIDDING, RIGHT?!

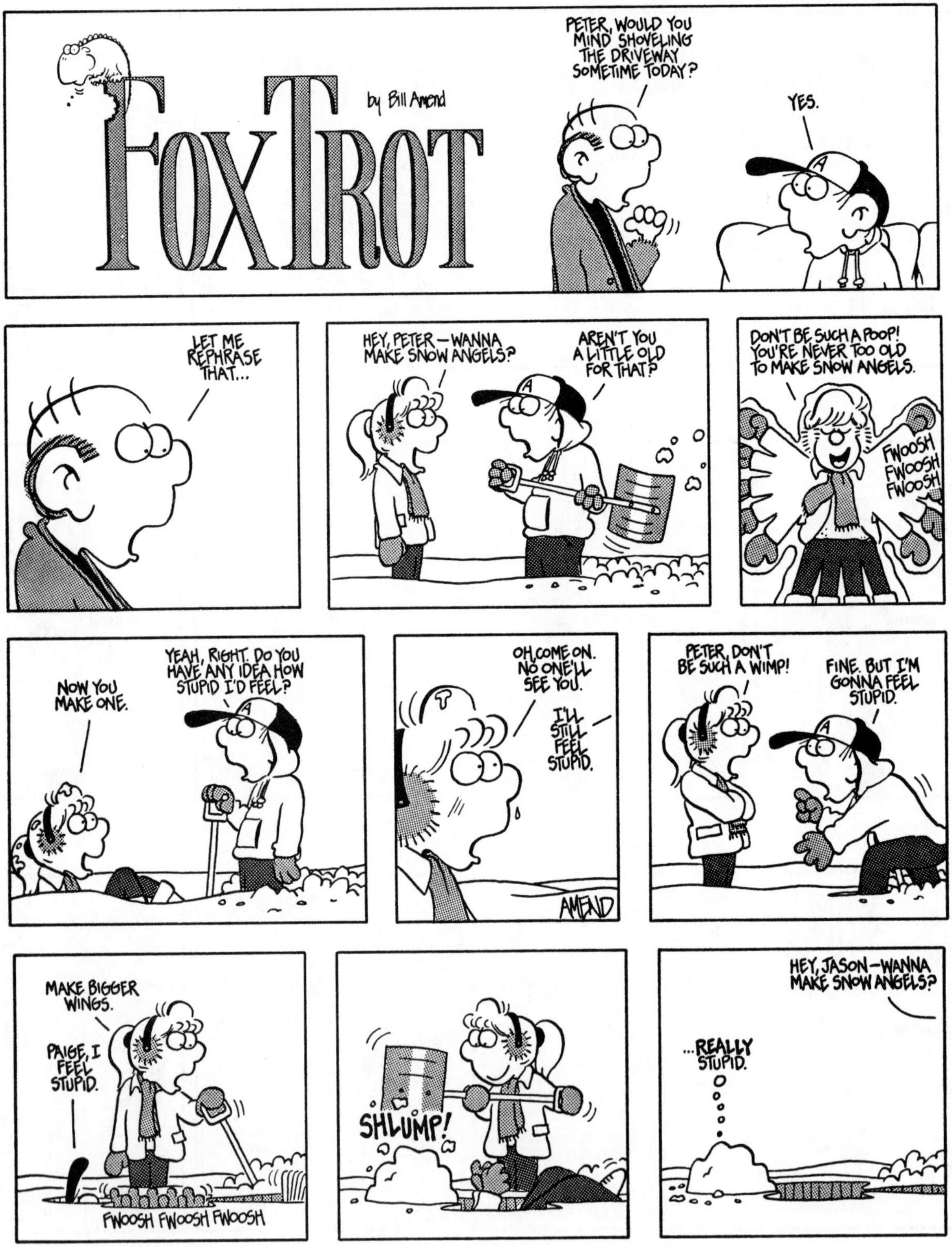
FoxTrot
by Bill Amend
PETER, WOULD YOU MIND SHOVELING THE DRIVEWAY SOMETIME TODAY?
YES.
LET ME REPHRASE THAT...
HEY, PETER—WANNA MAKE SNOW ANGELS?
AREN'T YOU A LITTLE OLD FOR THAT?
DON'T BE SUCH A POOP! YOU'RE NEVER TOO OLD TO MAKE SNOW ANGELS.
FWOOSH FWOOSH FWOOSH
NOW YOU MAKE ONE.
YEAH, RIGHT. DO YOU HAVE ANY IDEA HOW STUPID I'D FEEL?
OH, COME ON. NO ONE'LL SEE YOU.
I'LL STILL FEEL STUPID.
AMEND
PETER, DON'T BE SUCH A WIMP!
FINE. BUT I'M GONNA FEEL STUPID.
MAKE BIGGER WINGS.
PAIGE, I FEEL STUPID.
FWOOSH FWOOSH FWOOSH
SHLUMP!
HEY, JASON—WANNA MAKE SNOW ANGELS?
...REALLY STUPID.

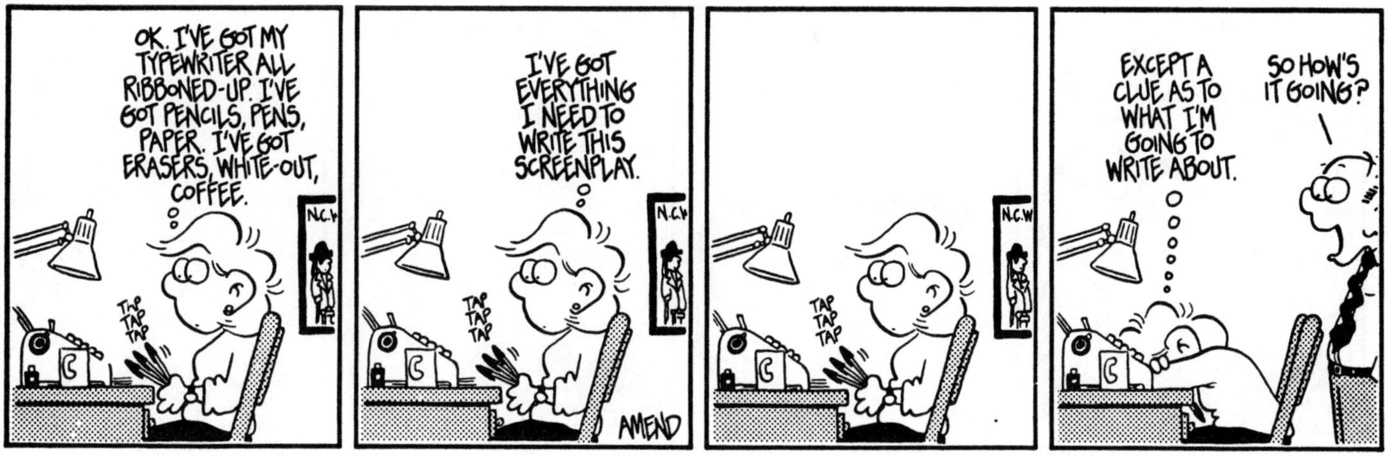
OK. I'VE GOT MY TYPEWRITER ALL RIBBONED-UP. I'VE GOT PENCILS, PENS, PAPER. I'VE GOT ERASERS, WHITE-OUT, COFFEE.
TAP TAP TAP
N.C.W
I'VE GOT EVERYTHING I NEED TO WRITE THIS SCREENPLAY.
TAP TAP TAP
AMEND
TAP TAP TAP
EXCEPT A CLUE AS TO WHAT I'M GOING TO WRITE ABOUT.
SO HOW'S IT GOING?

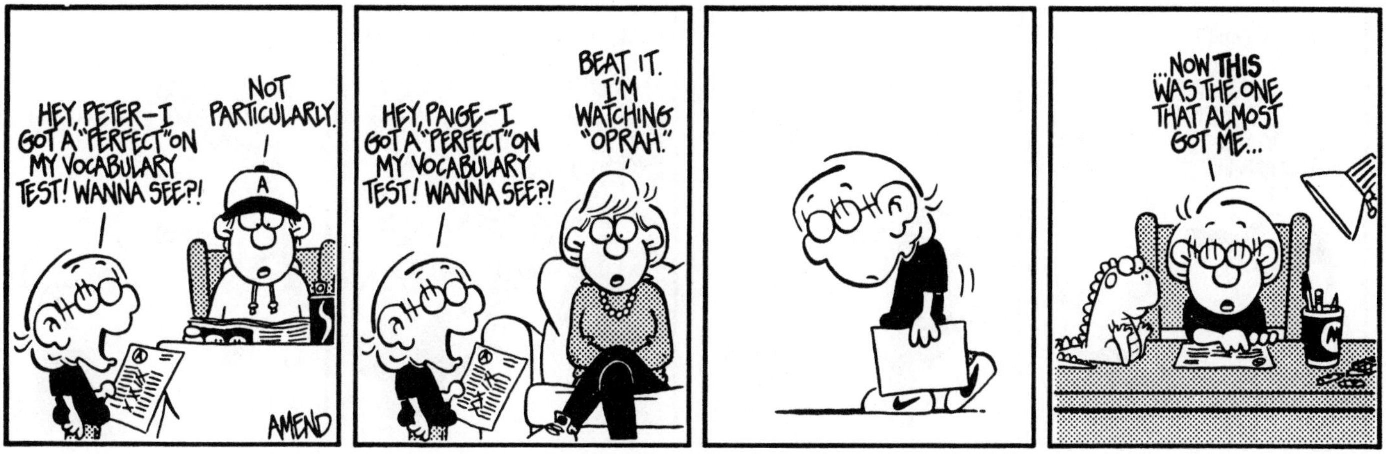
HEY, PETER—I GOT A "PERFECT" ON MY VOCABULARY TEST! WANNA SEE?!
NOT PARTICULARLY.
AMEND
HEY, PAIGE—I GOT A "PERFECT" ON MY VOCABULARY TEST! WANNA SEE?!
BEAT IT. I'M WATCHING "OPRAH."
...NOW THIS WAS THE ONE THAT ALMOST GOT ME...

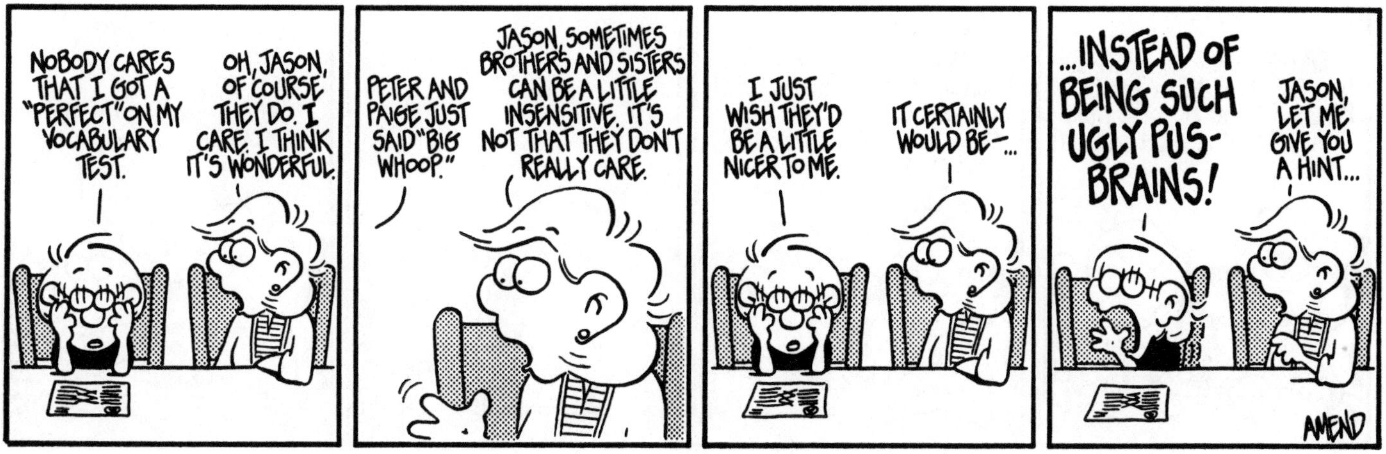
NOBODY CARES THAT I GOT A "PERFECT" ON MY VOCABULARY TEST.
OH, JASON, OF COURSE THEY DO. I CARE. I THINK IT'S WONDERFUL.
PETER AND PAIGE JUST SAID "BIG WHOOP."
JASON, SOMETIMES BROTHERS AND SISTERS CAN BE A LITTLE INSENSITIVE. IT'S NOT THAT THEY DON'T REALLY CARE.
I JUST WISH THEY'D BE A LITTLE NICER TO ME.
IT CERTAINLY WOULD BE—...
...INSTEAD OF BEING SUCH UGLY PUS-BRAINS!
JASON, LET ME GIVE YOU A HINT...
AMEND

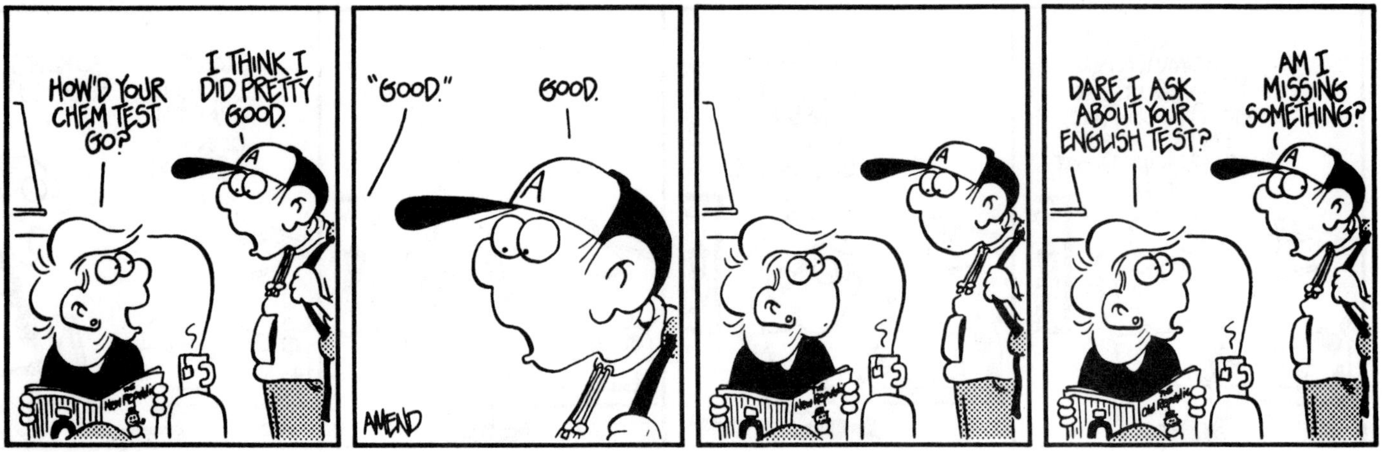
HOW'D YOUR CHEM TEST GO?
I THINK I DID PRETTY GOOD.
"GOOD."
GOOD.
AMEND
DARE I ASK ABOUT YOUR ENGLISH TEST?
AM I MISSING SOMETHING?

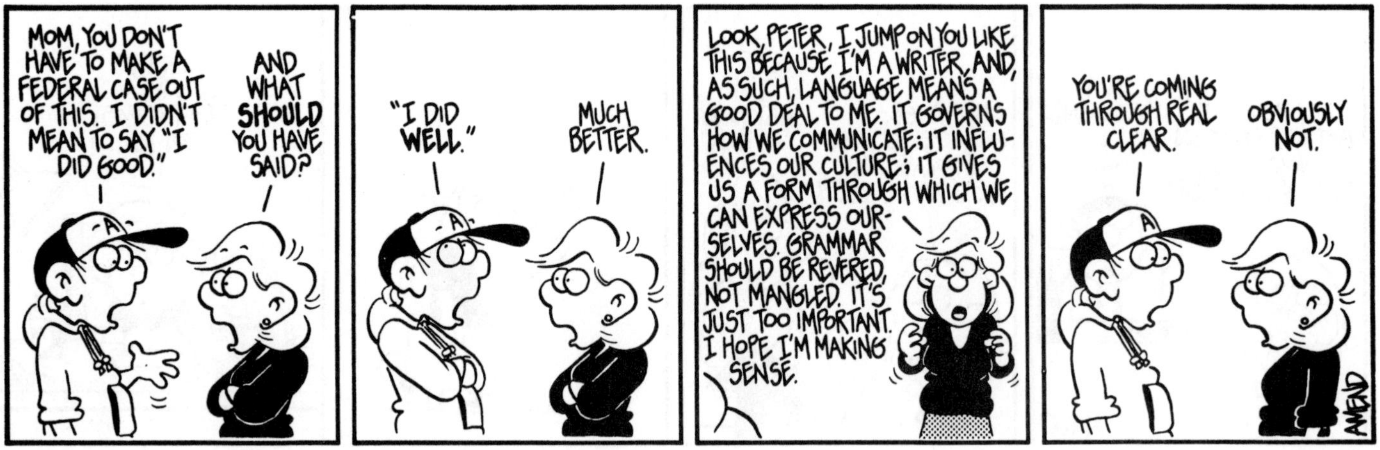
MOM, YOU DON'T HAVE TO MAKE A FEDERAL CASE OUT OF THIS. I DIDN'T MEAN TO SAY "I DID GOOD."
AND WHAT SHOULD YOU HAVE SAID?
"I DID WELL."
MUCH BETTER.
LOOK, PETER, I JUMP ON YOU LIKE THIS BECAUSE I'M A WRITER, AND, AS SUCH, LANGUAGE MEANS A GOOD DEAL TO ME. IT GOVERNS HOW WE COMMUNICATE; IT INFLUENCES OUR CULTURE; IT GIVES US A FORM THROUGH WHICH WE CAN EXPRESS OURSELVES. GRAMMAR SHOULD BE REVERED, NOT MANGLED. IT'S JUST TOO IMPORTANT. I HOPE I'M MAKING SENSE.
YOU'RE COMING THROUGH REAL CLEAR.
OBVIOUSLY NOT.
AMEND

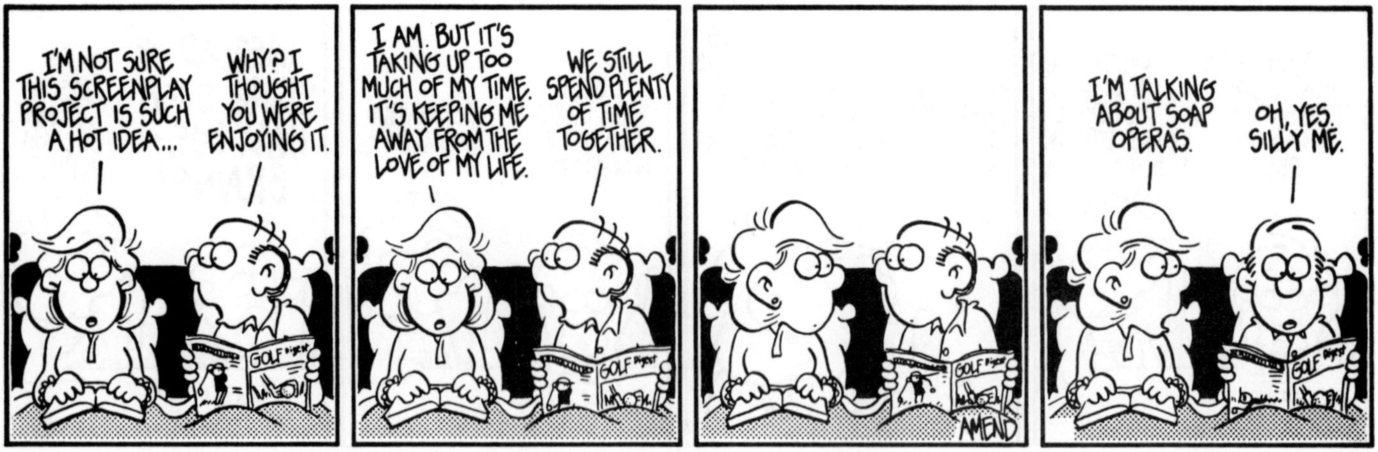
I'M NOT SURE THIS SCREENPLAY PROJECT IS SUCH A HOT IDEA...
WHY? I THOUGHT YOU WERE ENJOYING IT.
I AM. BUT IT'S TAKING UP TOO MUCH OF MY TIME. IT'S KEEPING ME AWAY FROM THE LOVE OF MY LIFE.
WE STILL SPEND PLENTY OF TIME TOGETHER.
AMEND
I'M TALKING ABOUT SOAP OPERAS.
OH, YES. SILLY ME.

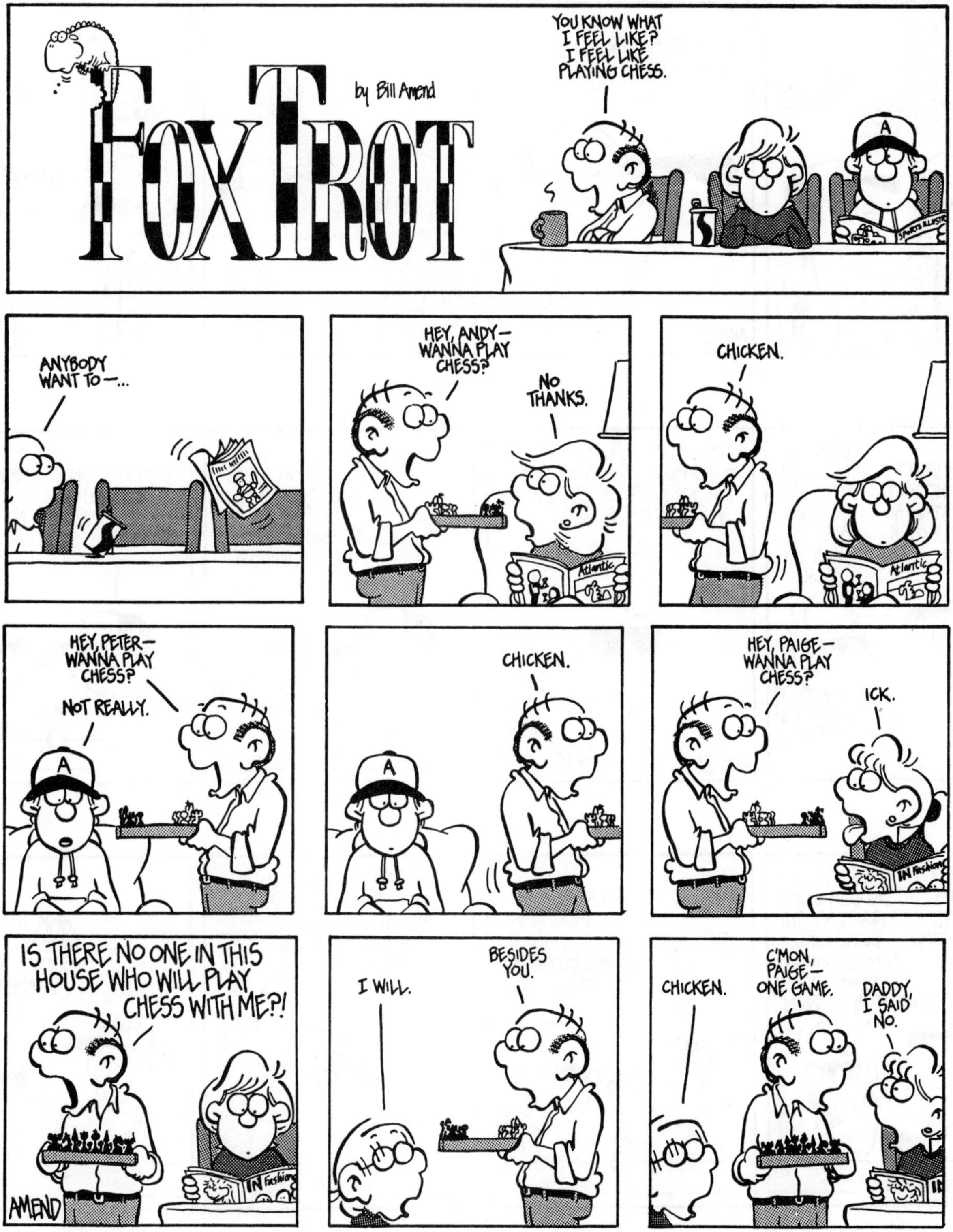
FoxTrot
by Bill Amend
YOU KNOW WHAT I FEEL LIKE? I FEEL LIKE PLAYING CHESS.
ANYBODY WANT TO—...
HEY, ANDY— WANNA PLAY CHESS?
NO THANKS.
CHICKEN.
HEY, PETER— WANNA PLAY CHESS?
NOT REALLY.
CHICKEN.
HEY, PAIGE— WANNA PLAY CHESS?
ICK.
IS THERE NO ONE IN THIS HOUSE WHO WILL PLAY CHESS WITH ME?!
AMEND
I WILL.
BESIDES YOU.
CHICKEN.
C'MON, PAIGE— ONE GAME.
DADDY, I SAID NO.

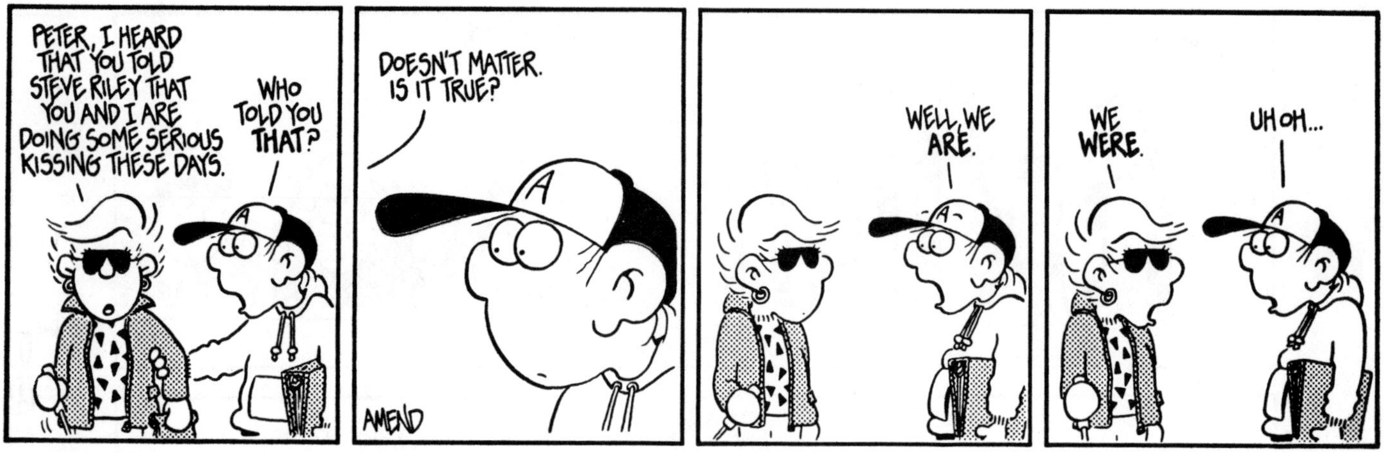
PETER, I HEARD THAT YOU TOLD STEVE RILEY THAT YOU AND I ARE DOING SOME SERIOUS KISSING THESE DAYS.
WHO TOLD YOU THAT?
DOESN'T MATTER. IS IT TRUE?
AMEND
WELL, WE ARE.
WE WERE.
UH OH...

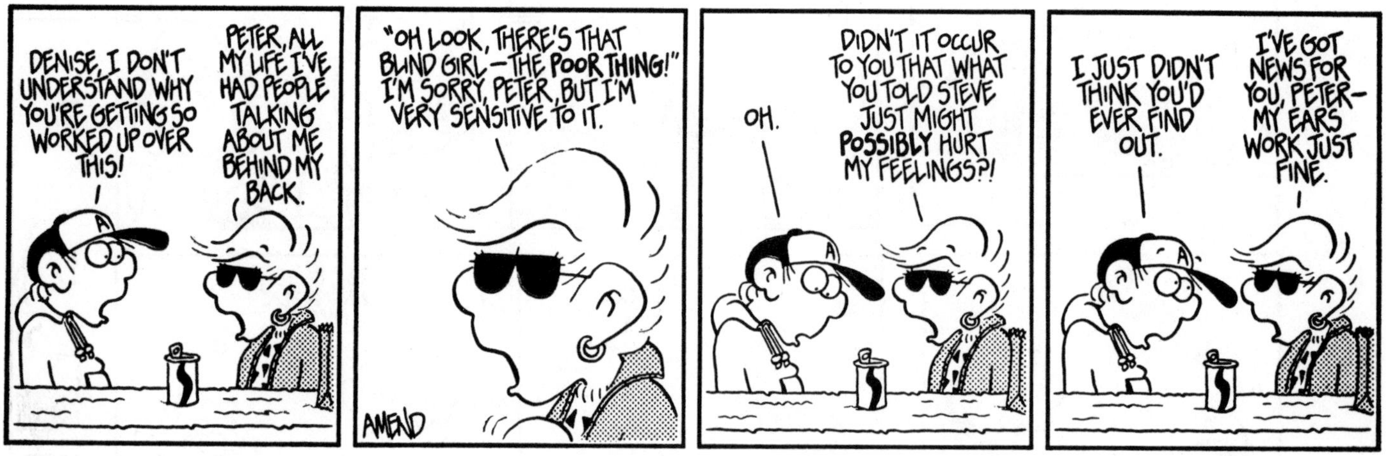
DENISE, I DON'T UNDERSTAND WHY YOU'RE GETTING SO WORKED UP OVER THIS!
PETER, ALL MY LIFE I'VE HAD PEOPLE TALKING ABOUT ME BEHIND MY BACK.
"OH LOOK, THERE'S THAT BLIND GIRL — THE POOR THING!" I'M SORRY, PETER, BUT I'M VERY SENSITIVE TO IT.
AMEND
OH.
DIDN'T IT OCCUR TO YOU THAT WHAT YOU TOLD STEVE JUST MIGHT POSSIBLY HURT MY FEELINGS?!
I JUST DIDN'T THINK YOU'D EVER FIND OUT.
I'VE GOT NEWS FOR YOU, PETER— MY EARS WORK JUST FINE.

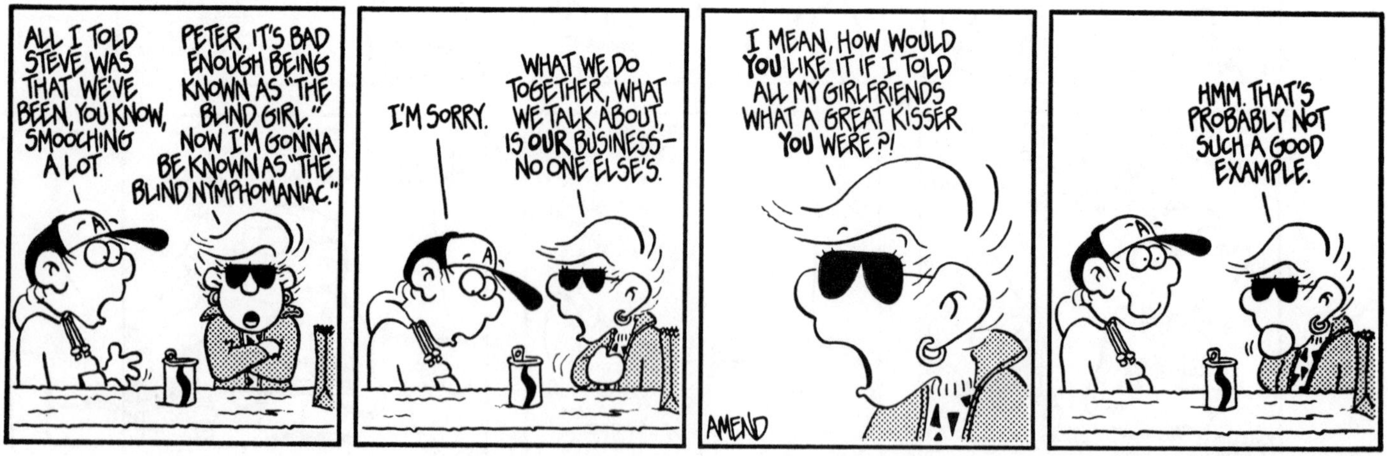
ALL I TOLD STEVE WAS THAT WE'VE BEEN, YOU KNOW, SMOOCHING A LOT.
PETER, IT'S BAD ENOUGH BEING KNOWN AS "THE BLIND GIRL." NOW I'M GONNA BE KNOWN AS "THE BLIND NYMPHOMANIAC."
I'M SORRY.
WHAT WE DO TOGETHER, WHAT WE TALK ABOUT, IS OUR BUSINESS— NO ONE ELSE'S.
I MEAN, HOW WOULD YOU LIKE IT IF I TOLD ALL MY GIRLFRIENDS WHAT A GREAT KISSER YOU WERE?!
AMEND
HMM. THAT'S PROBABLY NOT SUCH A GOOD EXAMPLE.

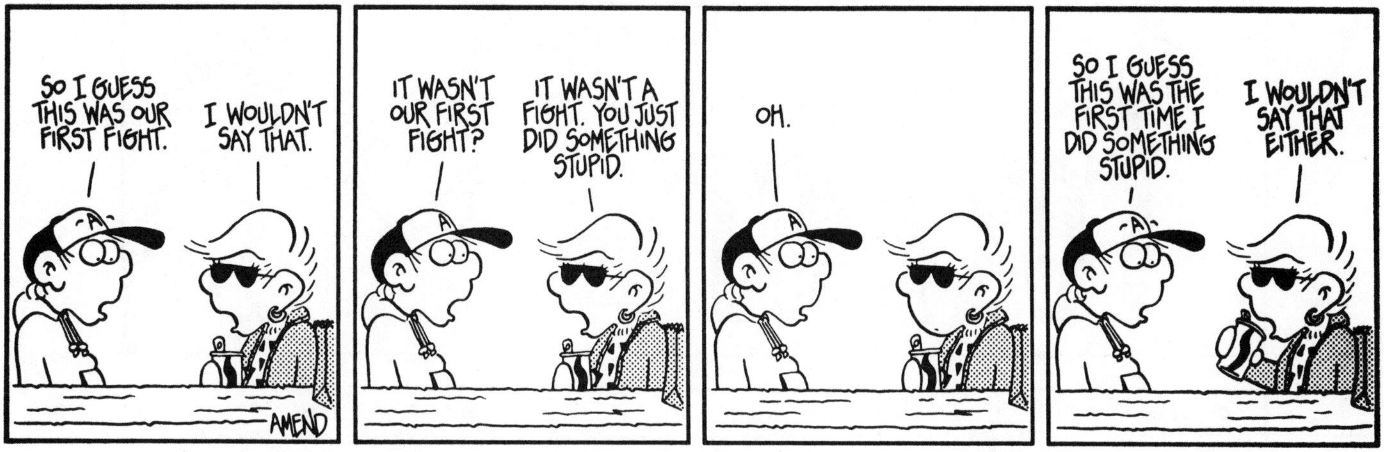
SO I GUESS THIS WAS OUR FIRST FIGHT.
I WOULDN'T SAY THAT.
IT WASN'T OUR FIRST FIGHT?
IT WASN'T A FIGHT. YOU JUST DID SOMETHING STUPID.
OH.
SO I GUESS THIS WAS THE FIRST TIME I DID SOMETHING STUPID.
I WOULDN'T SAY THAT EITHER.
AMEND

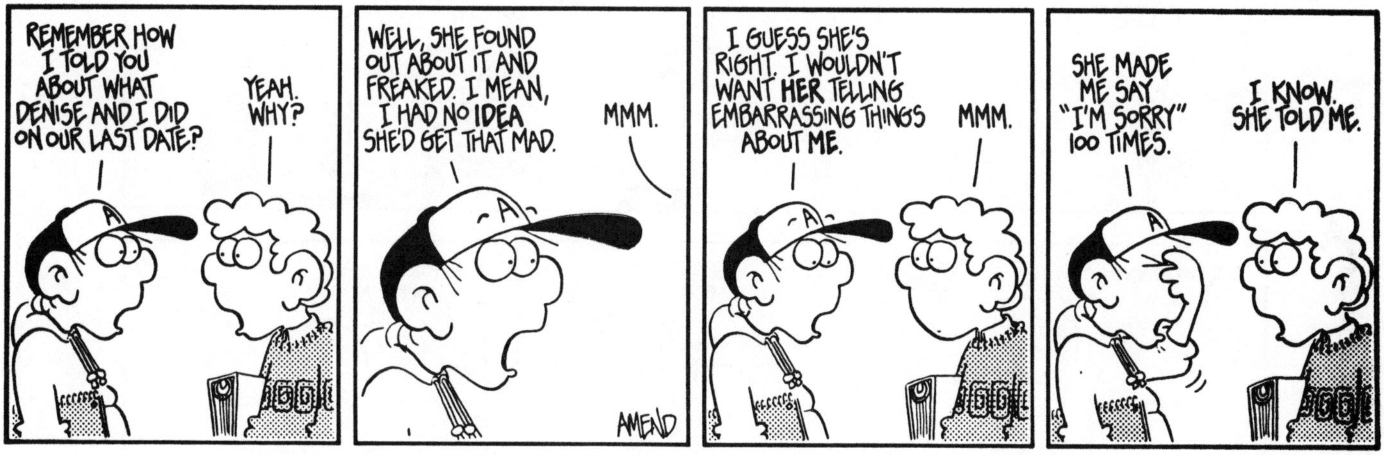
REMEMBER HOW I TOLD YOU ABOUT WHAT DENISE AND I DID ON OUR LAST DATE?
YEAH. WHY?
WELL, SHE FOUND OUT ABOUT IT AND FREAKED. I MEAN, I HAD NO IDEA SHE'D GET THAT MAD.
MMM.
I GUESS SHE'S RIGHT. I WOULDN'T WANT HER TELLING EMBARRASSING THINGS ABOUT ME.
MMM.
SHE MADE ME SAY "I'M SORRY" 100 TIMES.
I KNOW. SHE TOLD ME.
AMEND

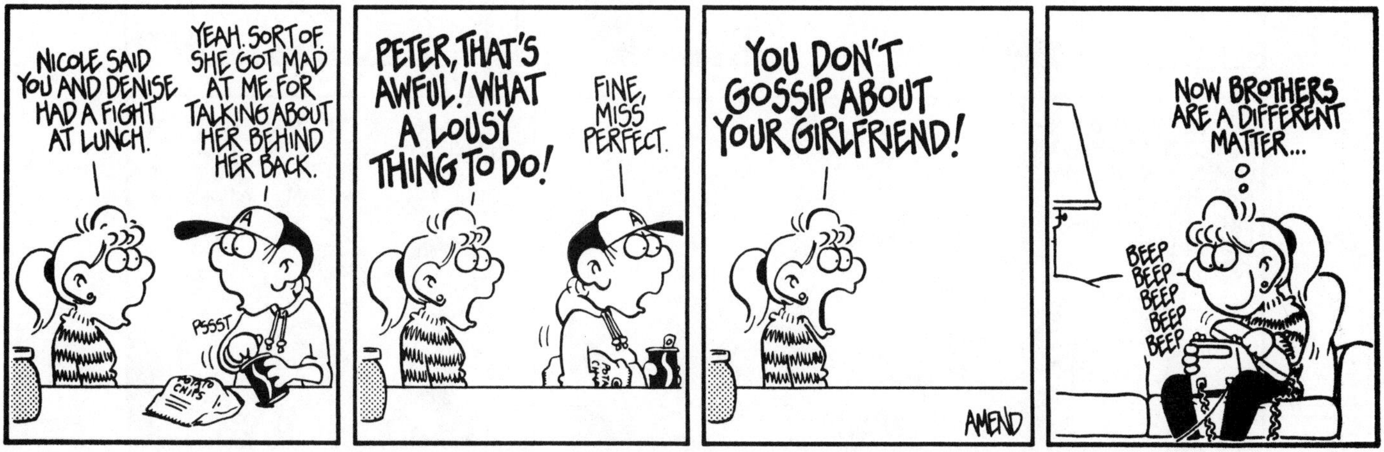
NICOLE SAID YOU AND DENISE HAD A FIGHT AT LUNCH.
YEAH. SORT OF. SHE GOT MAD AT ME FOR TALKING ABOUT HER BEHIND HER BACK.
PSSST
POTATO CHIPS
PETER, THAT'S AWFUL! WHAT A LOUSY THING TO DO!
FINE, MISS PERFECT.
YOU DON'T GOSSIP ABOUT YOUR GIRLFRIEND!
NOW BROTHERS ARE A DIFFERENT MATTER...
BEEP BEEP BEEP BEEP BEEP
AMEND

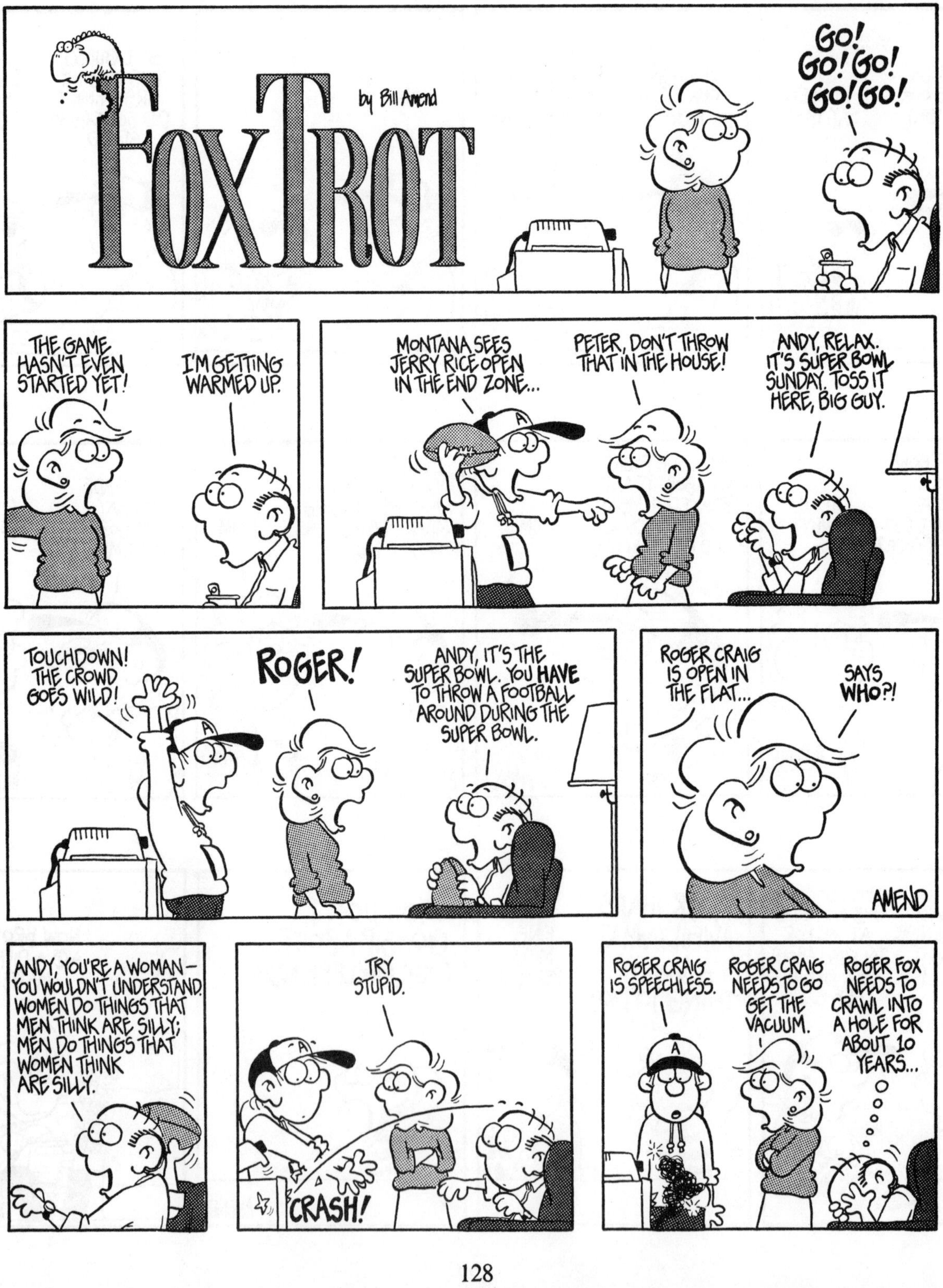
FoxTrot
by Bill Amend
GO! GO! GO! GO! GO!
THE GAME HASN'T EVEN STARTED YET!
I'M GETTING WARMED UP.
MONTANA SEES JERRY RICE OPEN IN THE END ZONE...
PETER, DON'T THROW THAT IN THE HOUSE!
ANDY, RELAX. IT'S SUPER BOWL SUNDAY. TOSS IT HERE, BIG GUY.
TOUCHDOWN! THE CROWD GOES WILD!
ROGER!
ANDY, IT'S THE SUPER BOWL. YOU HAVE TO THROW A FOOTBALL AROUND DURING THE SUPER BOWL.
ROGER CRAIG IS OPEN IN THE FLAT...
SAYS WHO?!
AMEND
ANDY, YOU'RE A WOMAN – YOU WOULDN'T UNDERSTAND. WOMEN DO THINGS THAT MEN THINK ARE SILLY; MEN DO THINGS THAT WOMEN THINK ARE SILLY.
TRY STUPID.
CRASH!
ROGER CRAIG IS SPEECHLESS.
ROGER CRAIG NEEDS TO GO GET THE VACUUM.
ROGER FOX NEEDS TO CRAWL INTO A HOLE FOR ABOUT 10 YEARS...